CARNAP AND TW
TH(

MW01113853

Rudolf Carnap (1891–1970) is widely regarded as one of the most
important philosophers of the twentieth century. Born in Germany
and later a US citizen, he was a founder of the philosophical movement known as Logical Empiricism. He was strongly influenced by a
number of different philosophical traditions (including the legacies of
both Kant and Husserl), and also by the German Youth Movement,
the First World War (in which he was wounded and decorated) and
radical socialism. This book places his central ideas in a broad cultural,
political and intellectual context showing how he synthesised many
different currents of thought to achieve a philosophical perspective
that remains strikingly relevant today. Its rich account of a philosopher's response to his times will appeal to all who are interested in the
development of philosophy in the twentieth century.

A. W. CARUS is an Affiliated Lecturer in the Department of Economics, University of Cambridge.

CARNAP AND TWENTIETH-CENTURY THOUGHT

THOUGHT

Explication as Enlightenment

A. W. CARUS

CAMBRIDGE UNIVERSITY PRESS
Cambridge, New York, Melbourne, Madrid, Cape Town, Singapore,
São Paulo, Delhi, Dubai, Tokyo

Cambridge University Press
The Edinburgh Building, Cambridge CB2 8RU, UK

Published in the United States of America by Cambridge University Press, New York

www.cambridge.org
Information on this title: www.cambridge.org/9780521130868

First published 2007
Third printing 2009
This digitally printed version 2010

A catalogue record for this publication is available from the British Library

ISBN 978-0-521-86227-1 Hardback
ISBN 978-0-521-13086-8 Paperback

For
Howard Stein

Let us be prepared to set aside the habits of our own day and to honour the past as a treasure of neglected and forgotten, but still living, possibilities. There is no other way to escape the indignity of the despotism inflicted by our provinciality in time, no other way to regain the freedom only history can afford. We had let ourselves be convinced that history is useless. Much too late it began to dawn on us how narrowly this confines our horizons, how our growth is stunted when we seek nothing in history but contradiction or reinforcement, instead of frolicking carelessly and selflessly in its meadows, led only by curiosity.

Emil Staiger (1949)

Contents

Preface

Mathematicians, unlike the rest of us, have retained something of the original Enlightenment spirit, thought the novelist Robert Musil; they provide examples of a spiritual daring that has otherwise fallen by the wayside. 'We others', Musil regretted, 'have let our courage drop since the time of the Enlightenment. Some small bungle was enough to get us off the track of reason, and we now let every soft-headed visionary denounce the projects of a d'Alembert or a Diderot as misguided rationalism.' We are apt to plead the cause of feeling against the intellect, forgetting that we inhabit an intellect-constructed world (Musil 1913a). By 'we' he meant Central Europeans of the early twentieth century, but his warnings are no less relevant to our own times. 'We must be on our guard, above all', he wrote, 'against all yearnings for the de-complication of literature and life, for Homeric or religious warmth, for uniformity and wholeness' (Musil 1913b).

The western philosophical tradition began with the idea that insight or knowledge about the nature of things could somehow be applied by human beings to the shaping of their lives. For Plato, the paradigm of such knowledge or insight was geometrical proof. The applicability of knowledge, particularly *de rerum naturae*, to life was equally important for many others in antiquity, including non-Platonists such as Lucretius. This philosophical ideal reawoke in late medieval Europe, and was partly responsible for the creation of modern science in the seventeenth century. But Newton's achievement transformed our knowledge about the nature of things, as well as our conception of knowledge. This transformation has been described in many ways, and there is much controversy about which of these ways is best. But from at latest 1687 or so, knowledge became irrevocably theoretical. A gap opened up between knowledge and the shaping of individual human lives, a gap that has grown steadily wider over the centuries since then. The old philosophical ideal of applying knowledge to the shaping of practical life seemed doomed to irrelevance. Its vigorous revival by the Enlightenment led only to the Romantic reaction, whose most persuasive argument was the obvious gap between the desiccated world portrayed in our increasingly technical knowledge and the rich intuitive awareness in which we live our actual lives (the *Lebenswelt*, as philosophers like to call it when dwelling on this contrast).

This gap between knowledge and life split the thinking world into two warring camps, which have gone by many names; 'Enlightenment' and 'Romanticism' were among the early examples. Each side tried to bridge the gap between knowledge and life, to bring them back together, but from different ends, in different directions. One side insisted on *life*, and sought either to disqualify the new kind of knowledge from serious relevance for life, or to tame it somehow, to bring it within the ambit of practical and intuitive life, in the manner of Goethe and Schelling. The other side insisted on the new *knowledge*, rather, and required life to adjust; this was the stance of Diderot, the *Encyclopédiste* Enlightenment, and the positivist tradition. In various ways, nineteenth- and twentieth-century western intellectual life hinged on the conflict between these two stances.

This book is about one brief but important episode in this conflict – the attempt to revive a radical version of Enlightenment in Central Europe between the wars. The acknowledged philosophical leader of this movement, Rudolf Carnap, was long portrayed in philosophical history as a technocrat who cared only about knowledge and not about life. Recent work is discrediting this view. Still largely unknown, however, is the strategy Carnap proposed in his later years for overcoming the gap that has split the thinking world since Newton (or before). Carnap's proposal, while firmly anchored in the Enlightenment tradition, was strikingly new. It is also quite different from anything that has occupied the philosophical limelight during Carnap's time or since. The purpose of this book is to describe that proposal, to make it more explicit than Carnap did, and to bring it back into philosophical discussion. To motivate that proposal, the book will focus primarily on the path by which Carnap got there himself – it will examine his early career, from his student years in Jena before the First World War to the inter-war years in Vienna and Prague, up to his departure for the United States in 1936.

Central to the story is a dialectical relation between two kinds of conceptual system, the evolved systems of intuitively available concepts interwoven with ordinary language, and the constructed systems of scientific and mathematical knowledge. The story proceeds in two main stages. In the first stage, Carnap moved steadily toward the rejection of all vestigial inherited ordinary-language concepts, and sought to code all genuine knowledge within a fully explicit logical system. This idea reached its high point during

Carnap's Vienna years (1926–31). It was epitomised in the Vienna Circle project of 'rational reconstruction', in which evolved concepts of ordinary language were to be progressively replaced by the well-defined concepts of a logical system. This project began to fall apart around 1930, under a number of external influences and internal controversies. The Circle split into 'left' and 'right' wings. Carnap was able, in 1931–2, to rescue a form of 'rational reconstruction' on a completely different basis, rejected by the 'right' wing but embraced by the 'left', that was set forth in his *Logical Syntax of Language*, published in 1934. The present book focuses largely on Carnap's development to that point.

However, it does so from a later viewpoint. For the story has a second stage that begins in 1934, when a *contrary* motion set in. Carnap's conception of the relation between evolved and constructed languages became less rigid. The absolute break between the two was softened and relativised. Even in the *Syntax* itself, ordinary language had been conceived as a system of rules, though too complex to be readily codified. It was thus a 'calculus' of the same basic kind as constructed languages. The trend toward sharp distinctions that had characterised the development to 1934 gives way to a pragmatic recognition of the dynamic character of *both* ordinary language *and* constructed systems, and the dialectical relation between them. This change of view brought about the replacement of 'rational reconstruction' by the conception of 'explication' central to the present book. Unlike rational reconstruction, explication no longer envisaged one-way replacement of the ordinary, intuitive world view by a scientific one, but a dialectical interchange between the two kinds of system. Our practices and our values reside within an intuitive *Lebenswelt* that can be progressively improved, whose quality can be raised piecemeal through explicative replacement of its concepts by constructed ones, but we decide what replacements to undertake from the overall standpoint of the *Lebenswelt*, our practical concerns and our values.

In reconstructing this story, I have benefitted greatly from the recent revival of interest in Carnap and logical empiricism among analytic philosophers. This book aims not only to assemble what others have done over the past decade or two (particularly Richard Creath, Michael Friedman, Warren Goldfarb, Thomas Mormann, George Reisch, Alan Richardson, Thomas Ricketts, and Thomas Uebel) into a connected story, but adds an archival dimension of unpublished materials that greatly benefit the coherence of that story. The book attempts a synthesis of the work done so far, adding an overall motivation and sense of direction that perhaps makes more sense of the parts. In doing so it adopts a perspective more decidedly aligned with the later Carnap. This perspective derives largely from one of Carnap's students, Howard Stein. It was his class on Carnap at the University of Chicago, twelve years ago, that first set me on the path resulting in this book, and he has given me the benefit of his vast learning and his penetrating insight ever since. He read several versions of many chapters, including the entire penultimate draft, and forced me to rethink countless basic issues. I am very grateful to him for his obstinate unwillingness to tolerate sloppy thinking or imprecise language. Whatever merits the book may have are due above all to his continued interest in it over a long period. Michael Friedman was unfailingly generous in supplying comments and discussion on a wide range of issues, despite often disagreeing with my conclusions (even sometimes my premises). He also read many versions of this book over many years, and his thorough reading of the penultimate version saved me from many errors. And Steve Awodey, my co-author in a series of papers about Carnap and Gödel, played a critical role in helping me to understand the full ramifications of the basic logical issues involved at several key junctures of the story told here. Readers of those papers will recognise a number of motifs from them in Chapters 7–9 below. It is doubtful whether I could have got the story completely straight, in those chapters, without the help of a subtle but ruthlessly sceptical logician. Erich Reck read through the entire final version at lightning speed, though with his customary thoroughness, and made a number of very helpful last-minute suggestions, leading me to correct a number of possibly misleading formulations. I am grateful more generally for discussions and correspondence about the subjects of this book, over the past twelve years, with all those named above in this paragraph as well as Michael Beaney, Graham Bird, Jacques Bouveresse, Bernd Buldt, Tracy Dennison, Gary Ebbs, Greg Frost-Arnold, Daniel Isaacson, Gottfried Gabriel, Daniel Garber, Clark Glymour, Peter Hylton, Richard Jeffrey, Leonard Linsky, David McCarty, Sheilagh Ogilvie, Chris Pincock, Michael Potter, Eric Schliesser, Barry Smith, Michael Stölzner, William Tait, Hanneliese Carnap Thost, Pierre Wagner, Gereon Wolters, and Sandy Zabell. Audiences at a number of institutions where parts of chapters were given as papers, at various stages, have helped with questions or objections, especially at the Universities of Chicago, Indiana, Jena, Manchester, Oxford, Paris, Pittsburgh, Purdue, Stanford, and Vienna. The students who attended a class on Carnap, jointly taught with Steve Awodey at the University of Konstanz in the summer semester of 2003, helped similarly. Research assistance at various stages by Melissa Feinberg, Leslie Hudson, and Myra Awodey facilitated the seemingly endless process of composition. Two anonymous readers for Cambridge University Press made a number of useful suggestions that have greatly improved the book. I owe a particular debt to Professor Juha Manninen of the University of Helsinki for his aid in obtaining a copy of Carnap's letters of the late 1920s and early 1930s to Eino Kaila. I am also grateful to the staffs at the Archives of Scientific Philosophy at the University of Pittsburgh and the Special Collections Department at the University of California at Los Angeles, especially Brigitta Arden, Charles Aston, Gerald Heverly, Lance Lugar, and Jeff Rankin, as well as to Brigitte Parakenings of the Philosophisches Archiv at the University of Konstanz Department of Philosophy. Their unfailing helpfulness and their detailed knowledge of the holdings in their respective archives has made it possible to use those documents far more extensively and efficiently than I could have done unaided. Finally I thank the people at Cambridge University Press, especially Hilary Gaskin, Jodie Barnes, and Ann Lewis, for their heartwarming demonstration that for all the hand-wringing about its imminent disappearance, the traditional standard of competent workmanship in academic publishing stubbornly retains its niche in our world.

Note on the style of citation

Carnap's works are listed in Part II of the Bibliography along with all other published sources, but are cited in the text by date only, without Carnap's name. All other authors are cited by name and date. Unpublished sources are cited by abbreviated individual document name (e.g. 'ASP 1929a'), keyed to the list in Part I of the Bibliography, where full document locations, headings, and dates (where available) are given. Transliterations from Carnap's Stolze-Schrey shorthand are my own, though I have consulted those done by others where they were available. All translations from German are also my own. Where published translations are available, these are added to the relevant bibliographical reference, and referred to after the citation of the original, following the letters 'PT' for 'published translation' (e.g. 'Helmholtz 1878a, p. 235, PT p. 354'). Note that some quotations from Carnap's unpublished English-language writings (especially the unabridged original version of his autobiography) come from texts that were never edited by a native English speaker, and are often somewhat clumsy or even incorrect in their usage. Carnap would not have liked this, but no other option seemed feasible. My attempts to edit these passages soon came up against the question of where to draw the line, and it seemed better to leave them completely unedited than to make arbitrary ad hoc decisions about particular passages in isolation, and in the absence of general guidelines discussed and agreed by a group of informed scholars.[1]

---

[1] The unabridged autobiography itself will be subject to such a process and published, before long, in the *Full Circle* series (Open Court Publishing Company) edited by Steve Awodey.

Introduction

A certain recurrent, perhaps inextinguishable human ambition found its classic expression in the eighteenth-century Enlightenment, especially in the circle around the *Encyclopédie* of Diderot and d'Alembert: the ambition of shaping individual and social development on the basis of better and more reliable knowledge than the tangled, confused, half-articulate but deeply rooted conceptual systems inherited from our ancestors. The Enlightenment is identified with the idea that improved knowledge can be an instrument of individual and social liberation. People of whatever class or culture, given access to this knowledge and the tools to use it critically, are able in this view to emancipate themselves from their culture of origin and belong to a cosmopolitan republic of letters. Individuals who join this culture are better informed about the contexts of their lives, this story goes, and so are better able to make informed life choices and to take genuine civic responsibility. And societies composed of such citizens can use this knowledge to build pluralistic institutions that enable all their members to develop and pursue their aspirations autonomously. The cosmopolitan culture embodying this programme of life guided by better knowledge has never been entirely well defined, and even in the eighteenth century it took on a number of national guises. But these shared a common inheritance from classical antiquity, as well as a growing trans-national corpus of scientific (and, in the broad sense in which it was then still used, 'philosophical') knowledge, of political commentary, of literature, art, and music. These national variants of Enlightenment also shared many basic values, especially a basic respect for empirical knowledge and a striving for greater objectivity – the desire to overcome the limitations inherent in one's particular local point of view. While poverty and circumstance temporarily prevented the masses from participating in this cosmopolitan culture, the goal was to make it universal, and to enable everyone to participate without regard to

I

sex, race, or economic resources. Only the full participation of most citizens in this cosmopolitan culture, it was thought, could ultimately guarantee the viability of the envisaged democratic states of the future.

The Enlightenment was followed by an equally emblematic reaction against it, beginning in Germany: the Romantics rejected the cosmopolitan vision, and wanted no part in a cosmopolitan republic of letters. They resurrected pre-rational intuition, primal myth, the pre-articulate sense of belonging, the infinite yearning that could not be put into words. This was a kind of 'knowledge', they said, without which all explicit knowledge in the conventional sense was empty and lifeless. Music, mysticism, art, spontaneous and untutored inspiration were more reliable sources of truth than deliberative science and worldly knowledge. The local and authentic was exalted at the expense of the cosmopolitan and artificial. The spread of cosmopolitan knowledge to the masses was to be discouraged, as folk culture had more integrity than a deracinated, impersonal knowledge imposed from above. Economic growth, democratic politics, and urbanisation were also frowned on, as they tended to break down traditional, organic communities and rooted belonging. Like the Enlightenment, Romanticism was (in some of its versions, at least) a doctrine of liberation. But personal and social liberation had to be guided by flashes of inspiration, by poetry, art, and intuition rather than discursive knowledge. Romanticism, by its very nature, took very different forms in the various nations to which it spread; it was even less homogeneous than the Enlightenment.

But both these movements, the Enlightenment and Romanticism, still mark out their respective attitudes toward universal, cosmopolitan knowledge. Under various names, both traditions are very much with us today. On the worldly plane of government and commerce, in most western countries and all English-speaking ones, Enlightenment ideas have gone almost unchallenged as the dominant public ideology. In those countries, nearly all streams of political and social thought have proceeded from Enlightenment assumptions; Mill, Disraeli, and Marx were all on the side of science, progress, and the widest possible diffusion of cosmopolitan knowledge. Only in German-speaking Central Europe did Romanticism have any appreciable influence in the public sphere through the nineteenth century. This influence intensified toward the end of the nineteenth century, and became especially pronounced at the beginning of the twentieth.[1] The German Youth Movement, which had no parallel outside

---

[1] Otto Weininger is an example of this trend who has become known among English-speaking scholars because of his influence on Wittgenstein (Monk 1990); see also Sengoopta (2000).

Central Europe, was a neo-Romantic glorification of the 'natural' and primitive, in rebellion against the stuffy, materialistic petit-bourgeois culture of the post-1871 *Gründerjahre* that the young Nietzsche had eloquently complained about (Laqueur 1962). Thomas Mann's wartime diatribe against 'Western' – Enlightenment – civilisation is an indication of the tight grip that Romantic categories retained on a considerable proportion of the German educated classes.[2]

But the apogee of Romantic influence in German-speaking intellectual and public life came after Versailles. Much has been made of figures such as Heidegger, Carl Schmitt, or Ernst Jünger, but the phenomenon as a whole and its social context have yet to be adequately studied.[3] Spengler's *Decline of the West* was just one pinnacle in the vast neo-Romantic, anti-Enlightenment literature that appeared between 1918 and 1933. Another was the three-volume indictment of intellect, *Der Geist als Widersacher der Seele* (*The Intellect as the Enemy of the Soul*) by Ludwig Klages, whose taxonomy of human character had enjoyed wide popularity. Walter Rathenau, a finance mogul and minister in the Weimar government, wrote best-selling books whose tendency was hardly different. The cult following inspired by sages such as the poet Stefan George, and their impact on the writing of history, has often been noted.[4] Explicitly anti-scientific and anti-modern ideologies such as those of Rudolf Steiner enjoyed wide currency and even attained a degree of public acceptance. The atmosphere is well captured, and pitilessly satirised, in Musil's great novel *The Man without Qualities*.

The Vienna Circle is impossible to understand outside this very specific cultural context. The Circle reasserted Enlightenment values against this comprehensive Romantic fervour. It countered with an equally comprehensive programme of re-Enlightenment. Unlike previous German movements that had taken the Enlightenment partially on board – especially the venerable tradition of German classicism deriving from Goethe, Schiller, and Humboldt, within Kant's philosophical framework – the Vienna Circle resolved to accept no compromises. Everything was to be rethought from

---

[2] His *Betrachtungen eines Unpolitischen* (*Considerations of an Unpolitical Man*) (Mann 1918) returns constantly to the contrast, which had become a cliché by then, between German *Kultur* (which was inner, deep, and authentic) and Western *Zivilisation* (which was social, superficial, and artificial). Mann later changed his mind about the political burden of the book, and eventually became a supporter of the Weimar republic.

[3] A brief overview is provided by Hepp (1987). A well-informed recent study on one particular aspect is Noll's (1994) intellectual history of the Jung cult, painted against a broad panorama in Part I, Chapters 2–5, though the main focus here is on the period *before* 1914. Wolin (2004) offers a welcome broad perspective, whose overall diagnosis seems accurate. But his focus on only a few major figures somewhat obscures the major differences between France and Germany.

[4] E.g. by Gay (1968), though without being adequately placed in this wider context.

the bottom up. To begin with, the basis of scientific knowledge itself – the backbone of the cosmopolitan ideal – had to be reconstructed. The older Enlightenment philosophies of Mill, Comte, or Mach had been glaringly unable to cope with recent advances in the sciences. Instead, the Vienna Circle turned to Bertrand Russell, to Russell's student Wittgenstein, and to scientific thinkers such as Helmholtz and Poincaré. Russell had taken the lead, even before the First World War, in drawing attention to the wider implications of scientific knowledge, especially for traditional beliefs. He was a hero and role model for many younger intellectuals between the wars, even on the continent. In their philosophy as in their politics, the Vienna Circle sought to out-Russell Russell.[5]

On this basis, the Vienna Circle wanted to create a new kind of intellectual culture that would be adequate to scientific knowledge and democratic society. They wanted to replace the culture of German classicism, underpinned by Kant, with something better and more durable, something more unequivocally 'enlightened', though equally nourishing. The Vienna Circle was, in its way, the explicit voice of modernism. It preached a comprehensive, root-and-branch reformation of human mental and social life, and allied itself with movements in science, literature, politics, social thought, art, and architecture sympathetic to the idea that human life and culture must adjust to changed conditions of society and knowledge in the modern world.

The Vienna Circle hardly had time to plant its flag, though, before it fell victim to the political cataclysm heralded by the upsurge of Romanticism in the early twentieth century. The members of the Circle and its pendants in other Central European countries were scattered to the winds, and could only regroup in North America some years later. On the other hand, the Nazi disaster, though it dealt German universities a blow from which they never recovered, discredited Romanticism. The political and intellectual elites of the German-speaking states that emerged from the ruins of 1945 were thoroughly imbued with the ideals of cosmopolitan knowledge and scientific progress. Whatever attraction Romanticism had once enjoyed outside Germany also evaporated, and the scientific culture enjoyed unprecedented prestige, particularly in America, due not least to

---

[5] In the letter accompanying his *Aufbau* (1928a), Carnap says to Russell that he has here embarked on the programme sketched in Russell's *Our Knowledge of the External World*, but has carried it through more radically and consistently, so that he sees his book as '*Russellischer als Russell*' ('more Russellian than Russell'). In an earlier letter, he alludes to Russell's pacifist activities during the war, and remarks that it is surely no coincidence that philosophers disciplined by the rigour of logic and natural science are also those who oppose war and oppression. See below, Chapter 5.

the prominent role of science and technology in winning the war. The Enlightenment was riding high. Nearly all developed countries underwent enormous expansions in their higher education systems, and the value of knowledge was unquestioned. Nor was this just an artefact of the Cold War; this basic value was shared across the Iron Curtain. Nearly all political ideals that regarded themselves as 'progressive' – whether socialist, communist, or liberal – were squarely in the Enlightenment camp. Even most conservatives embraced the basic tenets of the Enlightenment.

The Vienna Circle and its allies, now established across North America, benefited hugely from this surge of public confidence in cosmopolitan science. They and their students became the dominant force within the American academic discipline of philosophy after 1945. By 1960 they had largely displaced the previously dominant pragmatists and more traditionally minded philosophers such as Carnap's Chicago colleague Richard McKeon. Philosophers such as Wilfrid Sellars, who did not share many 'logical empiricist' views (as they were now called), adapted their tone and vocabulary to the new outlook. In America, at least, 'analytic philosophy' came to be identified with Russell, early Wittgenstein, and – particularly – logical empiricism. It was seen as something of a technical subject, both scientific in its own approach and concerned largely with the workings of natural science. 'Philosophy of science is philosophy enough', Quine had said. He and Thomas Kuhn would later be regarded as having overthrown logical empiricism, but they themselves focused mainly on hard science, so the basic tenor and approach survived even if the doctrinal details changed. Nor was the influence of logical empiricism confined to academic philosophy; across the human and social sciences, its acolytes attempted to clean house, sometimes in rather crude and unreflective ways.

THE DECLINE AND FALL OF LOGICAL EMPIRICISM

But half a century has now passed since analytic philosophy established itself as the mainstream in English-speaking countries. We now live in a very different world. The shock of the Holocaust has worn off, science and technology are no longer universally admired, and higher education is starving, in most countries, rather than opulently expanding. The idea of a cosmopolitan Enlightenment is viewed with scepticism or indifference. And so analytic philosophy, too, is in decline. Though still quite well represented in philosophy departments at leading universities, its broader significance in its English-speaking heartlands is diminishing. It has less importance in the wider world of academic or educated discourse than at any time since the 1920s, and much less than competing forms of general thought or reflection – whether or not these describe themselves explicitly as 'philosophy'. The decline in external influence is reflected within the discipline itself; analytic philosophy lacks a clear agenda. There is little agreement even about the problems it should be addressing or the questions it should be asking. Though it would be premature to pronounce it dead (it is most lively in certain specialised areas such as the philosophy of biology or of physics, and has claimed a niche within cognitive science), the general pattern is one of fragmentation, mutual alienation among its component groups, and the loss of a recognised centre of gravity – with respect not only to doctrine, but also to terminology, the canon of essential texts, and basic standards of rigour and clarity.

In the face of these developments, most analytic philosophers have striven to distance themselves from logical empiricism. From the beginning, in the 1920s and 1930s, dissenting voices within analytic philosophy had opposed the modernism and the scientific orientation of the Vienna Circle – Wittgenstein himself among them. But as fashions began to change in the 1980s, these internal dissenters were rapidly outflanked within the wider intellectual community, especially in the humanities, by more radical anti-modernists from other philosophical traditions. The earlier critiques of logical empiricism by Quine and Kuhn, though generally accepted within analytic philosophy, left the way open to more radical opposition by figures such as Rorty, Putnam, and a host of social-constructivist historians and sociologists of science. Some of these more radical critics have sided openly with the very metaphysical traditions the Vienna Circle originally attacked. The distinction between analytic philosophy and other philosophy has become blurred, then, and somewhat arbitrary. At present, analytic philosophy is no longer even clearly defined.

In the wider intellectual world, meanwhile, the reaction against 'logical positivism' is even more pronounced. Despite recent historical interest in the movement,[6] it is still regarded with almost universal disdain. It functions in the humanities and social sciences as a kind of 'other', against which almost anyone's own position may be defined or identified. The baleful influence of 'logical positivism' was felt so widely that it is now a recognised term of abuse in almost every field outside natural science. In

[6] Book-length studies include Coffa (1991), Uebel (1992a), Haller (1993), Stadler (1997), Richardson (1998), Friedman (1999, 2000), Mormann (2000), and Verley (2003). In addition, there are numerous conference volumes and journal special issues devoted to logical empiricism e.g. Giere and Richardson (1996), Parrini, Salmon, and Salmon (2003), Awodey and Klein (2004), as well as a growing number of contributions to the major journals. Cambridge Companions to Carnap and to Logical Empiricism are in progress. A 'Vienna Circle Institute' – in Vienna, but with international membership – organises regular conferences and has produced a steady stream of publications since about 1995.

economic methodology, for instance, 'logical positivism' is something like original sin (Blaug 1980, pp. 1–10; Hands 2001, pp. 72–88). 'Behaviourism' (regarded as a psychological version of 'positivism') is synonymous with backwardness in cognitive science (e.g. Lowe 2000, pp. 41–4). In the study of history, 'positivism' is the one thing all can agree on rejecting.[7] And even a textbook on research in social work can organise itself conceptually around the nemesis of 'logical positivism' (Tyson 1995). This widespread rejection in turn exacerbates the embarrassment felt by analytic philosophers and redoubles their hurry to disavow any residual connection with the barbaric past. In an overview of the work in philosophy of language and mind over the half-century up to the 1990s, for instance, Tyler Burge blames the present lack of interest in analytic philosophy among the wider intellectual public on the intolerance of the logical empiricists (Burge 1992, p. 3). A reference work on twentieth-century philosophy of science claims that the death of logical empiricism 'was due not only to the dispersal of its members, but to a widespread recognition of the defects of its ideas' (Hanfling 1996, p. 193). In another recent history of analytic philosophy, the movement is not credited with much originality, and appears only briefly.[8] The general attitude is perhaps best summed up by Richard Rorty. 'Most of us philosophy professors now look on logical positivism with some embarrassment, as one looks back on one's own loutishness as a teenager' (Rorty 1998, p. 32).

This book will argue that these – understandable – responses are seriously misguided. The 'logical empiricism' they reject was never propounded by any of its leading figures, whose actual doctrines have been largely ignored. This book will try to spell those doctrines out. It will focus on the particular case of Rudolf Carnap, generally acknowledged the philosophical leader of the group.[9] It will try to state Carnap's main ideas clearly, and explain how they developed. As we will see, these ideas bear little resemblance to

---

[7] Logical empiricism as applied to history is – somewhat unfortunately – associated largely with a series of papers by C. G. Hempel which generated lively discussion in the 1950s and 1960s, but are now regarded by both philosophers and historians with little interest. Two quite different appraisals of this development are offered by Danto (1995) and Dray (2000).

[8] Chapters 12 and 13 of Soames (2003) discuss 'logical positivism' – which Soames does not regard as much of an advance over Russell and the *Tractatus* (pp. 257–8) – but this discussion uses A. J. Ayer's *Language, Truth, and Logic* as its main text. This (as we will see below, pp. 34–5) is rather like relying solely on texts of Wolff for a discussion of Leibniz.

[9] Though I would not go as far as Quine, who claims, 'The significance of the Vienna Circle, as a concerted movement, can be overestimated. We are told of the evolving doctrine of the Circle when what is really concerned is the doctrine of an individual, usually Carnap . . . When one speaks of the Vienna Circle or logical positivism, one thinks primarily of Carnap. We do better to think of him as Carnap' (Quine 1984, p. 325). Carnap himself certainly did not see matters in this light, and even the present portrayal of Carnap will at certain points require supplementation from other Circle members, particularly Neurath, along the lines suggested by Thomas Uebel (2001).

the crude caricature of them prevalent in the literature. Even some of Carnap's closest interlocutors – including Ayer, Hempel, Popper, and Quine – misrepresented fundamental aspects of Carnap's mature view. Carnap, it will turn out, clearly anticipated the recent anti-modern (or 'post-modern') critiques, and took account of them; he had after all confronted many of the same Romantic, anti-modern ideas in Weimar Germany. He welcomed Kuhn's introduction of a historical dimension into the philosophy of science, and regarded it as complementary to his own work (Reisch 1991). Indeed, he himself published *The Structure of Scientific Revolutions* as part of the *Encyclopedia of Unified Science* he edited. And the famous 'two dogmas of empiricism' Quine attributed to Carnap in 1951 had in fact, as we will see, been decisively abandoned by Carnap two decades previously, in the early 1930s.

WHY IT MATTERS: OVERCOMING TWO BASIC OBSTACLES TO ENLIGHTENMENT

It would hardly be worth the trouble of excavating Carnap's ideas, though, if it were only a matter of correcting past misunderstandings, and presenting Carnap as a forerunner of present fashions. Much more is at stake. The conceptual framework he created is still the most promising instrument, I will argue, for the very purpose he invented it to serve, in the somewhat utopian Vienna Circle context of the 1920s and early 1930s: it is still the best basis for a comprehensive and internally consistent Enlightenment world view. It is still the best hope we have of addressing the fundamental obstacles facing any attempt to formulate a coherent position of Enlightenment today. Because two such obstacles in particular have dogged the Enlightenment from the beginning, and have often seemed utterly fatal to any revival of Enlightenment ideas since then, their exposition will provide a useful context for introducing some of Carnap's basic ideas.

First obstacle. What *is* the 'knowledge' that the Enlightenment regarded as so critical to individual autonomy and social improvement? Can it be defined, even loosely, for practical purposes? To begin with, what *qualifies* as knowledge? And then how does all the knowledge that qualifies fit together? (Should it be classified according to human cognitive capacities and activities, in the manner of Bacon, d'Alembert, or Comte? Or does knowledge cohere in a more structural and hierarchical system of categories, deduced 'logically', as claimed by Aristotle, Leibniz, or Kant?) Behind this latter question lay the further problem of what constituted *important* knowledge.

The paradigm of important knowledge for the original Enlightenment was Newton's *Principia*, but much else qualified as well. The role of the *Encyclopédie* was, after all, to expound the important knowledge, to organise it, display its interconnections, and draw attention (where this was possible without attracting censorship) to its implications for everyday life and widely held beliefs. But what *made* knowledge *admissible* to the *Encyclopédie*, and what gave some of it a particular *importance?* There was more agreement on the first question than on the second. What made knowledge *admissible*, all agreed, was its *empirical* character. Locke and Bacon were the most frequently cited authorities on the subject of what this empirical character consisted in. Locke's *Essay*, in particular, was regarded as spelling out the implicit epistemological programme of Newton's *Principia*.

But this very answer also made an answer to the other question (what makes some admissible knowledge *important?*) very difficult. For the very paradigm of 'important' knowledge, in Enlightenment eyes – the *Principia* (theoretical knowledge, that is, the sort Kant thought essential to science) – was also a kind of knowledge that Locke's empiricism could not account for. No amount of empirical knowledge, as Hume later argued, could add up to causal knowledge or knowledge of universal laws. Nor could the classificatory approach of the *Encyclopédie* explain the central importance of theoretical knowledge. Most worrying, for the empirical criterion, was mathematics, which played so large a role in theoretical knowledge, and was not based on observations at all. So here was an impasse at the very heart of the Enlightenment project.[10] John Stuart Mill's mid-nineteenth-century attempt to develop a resolute mathematical empiricism served only to highlight the inadequacy of this view, and called forth Frege's withering critique in the 1880s.

Second obstacle. Despite this difficulty in formulating an adequate criterion of knowledge, *scientific* (and especially theoretical) knowledge occupied an exemplary place in the Enlightenment canon. But this very exaltation of science exposed the Enlightenment to the *other* fundamental challenge it has faced: its apparent blindness to the moral and affective context of knowledge. One of the most effective rhetorical devices Romanticism deployed against the Enlightenment, from the outset, was its complaint that Newtonian optics had 'unwoven the rainbow'. If scientific knowledge, especially of the Newtonian kind, were to be given precedence, as the Enlightenment proposed, then – so the Romantics claimed – human relations with

---

[10] This impasse was, of course, addressed and in some ways overcome in Kant's critical philosophy. But in the century after Kant, as we shall see below, his main influence was in a direction quite contrary to the intentions of the Enlightenment in the sense discussed here.

nature, and with other humans, were robbed of their spontaneity and subjective authenticity. For giving such priority to science would degrade our
subjective perceptions to the status of 'mere appearances', while impersonal scientific formulas specify the 'underlying reality'. The first generations of Romantics were anxious, therefore, to reinterpret science so as
to minimise the scope of this implication. Science was to be restricted to
what was directly and intuitively commensurate with human subjective
experience (this was Goethe's scientific project, hugely influential in the
nineteenth century). Other Romantics pursued the alternative strategy of
trying to show that science applied only to a superficial, worldly reality,
while human subjectivity had access to other, ideal realms of which science
knew nothing. Though not designed explicitly to cater to this demand,
Kant's distinction between 'understanding [*Verstand*]', the human rational
faculty that we employ in creating and understanding science, and 'reason
[*Vernunft*]', a broader kind of rationality that encompasses the moral, spiritual, and aesthetic (as well as *Verstand* as a subordinate part), was seized
on by Romantics and Idealists and employed to portray the Enlightenment
as having truncated human rationality to a merely scientific rump, and as
having ignored everything of genuine human importance.

This portrayal was in a sense highly unfair. It is true that the 'importance' of knowledge to the original Enlightenment had been a largely cognitive matter, a measure of explanatory power or fecundity, of the wide
range of intuitively unrelated phenomena that could be accounted for by
a single, compactly presented equation. Newton's *Principia* was, again,
paradigmatic. The motions of all the planets, the phases of the moon and
its trajectory through the sky, the rotation of the earth, the seasons, the
tides, the flatness of the poles could all be precisely deduced from the
law of gravitation (in conjunction with Newton's three laws of motion).
No other branch of knowledge had ever been able to offer such pregnant,
such 'teeming' truths, as Locke had put it.[11] And yet not only Locke, but
the *Encyclopédistes* themselves, were willing to grant 'importance' to many
other kinds of admissible knowledge, including literary, artistic, and moral

---

[11] Locke gives two examples for the 'teeming truths' that, 'like the lights of heaven, are not only
beautiful in themselves, but give light and evidence to other things that without them could not be
seen or known'. The first is 'the discovery of Mr. Newton, that all bodies gravitate to one another,
which may be counted as the basis of natural philosophy'; the second is 'our Saviours great rule,
that *we should love our neighbor as ourselves*' – by this rule alone, Locke says, he thinks 'one might
without difficulty determine all the cases and doubts in social morality'. This passage from Locke's
posthumously published treatise *The Conduct of the Understanding* is quoted by Howard Stein (1993),
p. 196; as Stein points out, according to the 'official' doctrine of the *Essay*, morality, unlike natural
philosophy, *is* capable of being made a science, so this late passage represents a major step toward
admitting natural philosophy to an equal status.

knowledge – all these are covered at length in the *Encyclopédie*. Empirical 'admissibility' of knowledge, and even 'importance', were in practice defined very broadly indeed.

Still, the Enlightenment had undeniably insisted that all thought and action must pass muster before the stern tribunal of scientific knowledge – the better and more reliable knowledge on the basis of which our lives and societies were to be reconstructed. Whatever cannot hold up its head before such scrutiny should humbly submit to the lower status due to it in the kingdom of knowledge. This insistence has exposed the Enlightenment to much obloquy, giving it the appearance of defending a desiccated or shrunken portrayal of human reason against a more humane ideal of a reason that encompasses ethical, political, emotional, and spiritual existence as well as the capacity for scientific knowledge. The Enlightenment need not have allowed itself to be backed into this corner. Mill, rightly worried about this perceived narrowness, supplemented his inheritance of Bentham's cold-blooded scientific asceticism with some of Goethe's generosity of spirit. But behind the Enlightenment's rhetorical failings on this front is a genuine philosophical omission that Mill, for all his efforts, could no more supply than his predecessors: the absence of a clearly defined relation between the scientific *knowledge* to which the Enlightenment gives such weight and the *practical realm* (including here, for brevity, everything 'non-cognitive'): the ethical, political, spiritual, artistic realms whose undoubted importance Romanticism has so effectively played off against their supposed neglect by the Enlightenment.[12]

To summarise: two fundamental flaws have undermined the Enlightenment: (1) it has no criterion for genuine knowledge; and (2) it does not tell us how such knowledge is to relate to the practical realm, broadly defined. What has seemed impossible for the Enlightenment tradition, above all, is to solve *both* these problems jointly. Any attempt to solve the first seems to *obstruct* a solution to the second, and vice versa. The clearer the criterion for knowledge, the harder to relate knowledge to practice. And the more relevant knowledge is for practice, the looser and fuzzier it becomes. The Enlightenment has generally been able to overcome one of these obstacles only by forfeiting any hope of overcoming the other. The following two sub-sections will examine these two obstacles in turn, and introduce some basic Carnapian ideas by showing how they *can* – unlike

---

[12] Again, Kant had indeed specified such a relation. But neither Mill nor other nineteenth-century supporters of Enlightenment would have recognised the Kantian legacy (see below) as consistent with their goals.

past Enlightenment programmes – address these obstacles not just singly, but jointly.

The first obstacle to Enlightenment: no criterion for knowledge

The problem

The Lockean or Baconian empiricism of the *Encyclopédistes* could not provide an adequate criterion of knowledge for the reason already mentioned: it was unable to account for mathematics, or for the central importance of mathematics in scientific knowledge. Moreover, it put the burden of fitting all of knowledge together either on a speculative taxonomy of human cognitive faculties or on the mechanical programme, which had to be accounted equally speculative as it could not be applied to any actual knowledge. The effort to overcome these problems by Enlightenment-minded thinkers over the next century took two main forms: the 'positivist' tradition following Comte and Mill, and the Kantian tradition.

Nineteenth-century positivism, from Comte to Ostwald, grappled earnestly with these challenges but made essentially no progress beyond the generation of the *Encyclopédistes*. Strenuous efforts to portray mathematics as in some sense empirical served only to discredit positivism with serious mathematical minds and with subsequent thinkers influenced by Frege or Husserl. And Ostwald's classification of the sciences (Ostwald 1905) was by his own admission (Ostwald 1914a, pp. 58–60, 1914b, p. IX) identical to Comte's; though he was aware of Frege's and Russell's work, he seems not to have considered it relevant to the unity of science (Ostwald 1914c). While the cultural agenda of positivism had a fundamental importance for later movements (such as the Vienna Circle), its philosophical achievement was limited to the repeated demonstration that strict empiricism has little to contribute to understanding the character and foundations of mathematics or to the problem of the structure and unity of knowledge.

The Kantian tradition was far richer, more influential, and was composed of many more subgroups. In the eyes of those who remained loyal to the goals of Enlightenment after 1800, however, the Kantian tradition was also somewhat double-edged. In their view, although Kant himself adhered to Enlightenment values, his remedy was worse than the disease. His definition of scientific knowledge seemed to come at the price of complete ignorance about how things really are in themselves. And this ultimate ignorance licensed the possibility that accounts *other* than scientific knowledge (based, for instance, on the immediacy of our conviction of personal freedom) might be intelligible. Whatever his intentions, Kant's legacy in the nineteenth century (especially in German idealism and historicism) had been to split knowledge into two sectors: the natural sciences, based on a priori mathematical principles and justified by perceptual evidence, and the human sciences (*Geisteswissenschaften*) based on entirely different principles, such as the freedom of human action and the existence of cultures or communities of shared action-guiding values. The Enlightenment emphasis on the *unity* of knowledge – the cognitive as the *conscience* of the practical – was thus lost. Natural science, though reliable knowledge, was quarantined as largely irrelevant to human political, ethical, and spiritual concerns ('practical' concerns, in the broad sense adopted here).

Still, Kant's approach to defining knowledge not only accommodated mathematics much better than positivism could, but led to a more principled way of interrelating the parts of knowledge by the categories of pure reason. In the second half of the nineteenth century, Hermann von Helmholtz, leveraging and extending this structural approach, inspired a new school of scientific neo-Kantianism that restored the unity of knowledge, at least as a goal. This movement, influential in the 1870s, had waned by 1900, displaced by schools of neo-Kantianism that no longer aspired to the unity of knowledge in the Enlightenment sense. Indeed, leading representatives of these later schools were known for their theories of the *distinctness* of the human sciences from the natural sciences.[13] Nonetheless, the earlier, Helmholtz-inspired tradition of scientific neo-Kantianism was the basis for the Vienna Circle version of Enlightenment in the 1920s.

It is here, in the early Vienna Circle, that the first criteria for knowledge as a single, uniform deductive system were put forward that overcame the obvious shortcomings of both the positivist attempts of Comte, Mill, or Mach and of the post-Kantian separation of human from natural sciences. The criteria advanced by the early Vienna Circle, culminating in Carnap's first major book *The Logical Construction of the World* (known as the *Aufbau*, after its German title), turned out, ultimately, to be defective. Carnap himself moved on to a very different approach in the early 1930s, as we will see. What remained constant through this transformation, though, was the basic idea that knowledge can be reconstructed and unified within a standard logical language.

---

[13] This is especially true of Heinrich Rickert and the 'southwest' school of neo-Kantians, who were known for their emphasis on the distinctness of the human sciences (especially history), and of Dilthey, associated mainly with neo-Kantian historicism. The 'Marburg' school, in its early phases (before 1920), advocated more of a programme of unity on a very rationalistic basis; see below, Chapter 2, pp. 81–8 and Chapter 3, pp. 105–8. Later this changed, when one of its leading representatives, Ernst Cassirer, developed his philosophy of 'symbolic forms', in which natural and human sciences employ different 'conceptions of truth' (e.g. Cassirer 1929).

This idea led to a radically different form of empiricism from that of Locke, Hume, or Mach; its historical importance is well known. But the real potential of the reconstructive idea lay not in this historical importance but in the – largely untapped – main use for which it was invented. This was its use as both a diagnosis of past improvements in knowledge and as a programmatic tool for future improvements. This use had a name, *rational reconstruction*.

A way of addressing the first problem: rational reconstruction

The rational reconstruction programme was perhaps the most radical version ever proposed of an idea that went back to the Enlightenment, but emerged most explicitly in the engineering and revolutionary spirit of the École Polytechnique in the early nineteenth century (Gillispie 2004), and was elaborated in the works of Condorcet, Saint-Simon, and especially Comte. For a democratic, post-revolutionary society to cohere and survive, these writers thought, the conceptual structure of traditional society had to be replaced by a completely new one based on natural science, as well as on an extension of natural science into the human sciences. The Vienna Circle's version of this programme was more radical in two respects: first, the new conceptual structure to replace traditional language and thought was to be unified not merely by a system of classification, but by strict *deduction*; second, they specified an actual deductive *system*, i.e. Russell's theory of relations as employed in a constitutional system such as Carnap's *Aufbau*. This made rational reconstruction incomparably more powerful than past versions of this idea; it meant that particular rational reconstructions of folk concepts could be exhibited and discussed in the controlled and precise way characteristic of scientific discussions. The new, reconstructed concepts could still be described or explained or gestured at in ordinary language, or even in traditional philosophical language.[14] But such forms of discourse can only be a more or less inaccurate approximation, a user interface for human users of genuine knowledge, whose precise and canonical statement is in the standard logical language.

Rational reconstruction both interpreted the *history* of knowledge, and programmatically charted the *future* of knowledge, as the progressive

---

[14] In the *Aufbau*, Carnap explains the actual steps of the constitution system in four languages, the canonical one being the symbolic construction. The other three are intended as 'auxiliary languages to help out', i.e. to gesture at what was going on, in three different ways: ordinary language, a realistic language such as might be used in the natural sciences, and a language of 'fictive construction' (1928a, §95) – i.e. a quasi-Kantian language such as that used by Hans Vaihinger. See Chapter 6 below for more details.

replacement of our intuitive notions by more useful, more consistent, more precise concepts. We can, for instance, replace our vague, subjective, intuitive sense of 'hot' and 'cold' with the precise, quantitative concept of temperature, which we can define intersubjectively by reference to measurement devices. The quantitative concept also gives us many capabilities the vague ones lacked. It provides, for instance, an outside, objective standard by which to judge subjective feelings; instead of just saying 'I feel hot' or 'I feel feverish', I can take my temperature. In this way rational reconstruction provides a framework of objectivity that enables us to escape from a merely subjective view of the world. But the replacement process is piecemeal and iterative: temperature remains to be explicated within a more general framework of concepts. Conversely, fruitful concepts are often developed long before we can understand how to fit them into a larger scheme or framework of knowledge (1928b, pp. 7–8). We sometimes find solutions before we fully understand the problems they solve (1928b, p. 6). Carnap's example for this is the seventeenth-century concept of the derivative of a function as a way of expressing the rate of change of a magnitude, which was used successfully by generations of physicists and mathematicians, but only *understood* – rationally reconstructed – by Cauchy and Weierstrass a century or two later (1928b, pp. 6–7).

Rational reconstruction, then, is an iterative, step-by-step (though not always tidy or unidirectional) process of replacing intuitive, initially rather vague concepts by more precise ones. In each step, there will be gaps, points not fully explicit, that have to be left for later reconstruction in the next step; there will also be backward steps, mop-up operations. We still use ordinary language for practical communication, and for practical decision making. But the effect of rational reconstruction is to improve or upgrade the ordinary language, step by step, by replacing its loose, soft concepts with harder and more explicit ones – with the Comtean ideal of complete replacement still in mind as the ultimate goal.

The best known and most elaborate rational reconstruction of this early period was Carnap's own *Aufbau*. It reconstructed (among other things) the informal concept of 'empirical knowledge'. Carnap realised, after a few years, that he had failed. Even the more modest goal of explicating the concept of 'empirical content' became a lifelong, ultimately losing, struggle for him. In the light of this negative outcome, it is tempting, in retrospect, to say that Carnap had been over-ambitious. But just this was characteristic of the Vienna Circle's entire programme: a utopian conviction that the world could be changed – that we need not accept the conceptual structure handed down to us. For the Vienna Circle, rational reconstruction was a central component of its extremely ambitious wider cultural and political agenda. The particular goal was to define knowledge precisely, but for the purpose of *using* it to rid humanity of the ghosts holding us in thrall to the ancient superstitions of traditional society as well as the unreflective conformities of modern societies.

The Vienna Circle's campaign for Enlightenment obviously had somewhat different preoccupations than its eighteenth-century ancestor (Uebel 1998), especially given the background of social and political revolution in Europe between the wars. But the basic attitude that ordinary language, popular culture, and traditional superstition could not and should not guide rigorous, dispassionate, objective science was the same in the Vienna Circle as it had been among the *Encyclopédistes*. From this utopian viewpoint, our existing, intuitive conceptual apparatus, expressed and embedded in natural language (and then continually reinforced by that language) was a relic of past mentalities, and had above all to be *overcome*, stepped back from, put at arm's length. One could not be rid of it all at once; rational reconstruction could only be piecemeal. But the important question was not how to *accommodate* the vague, soft concepts of ordinary language but how to *change* them. And for *this* question, the existing categories of natural language and the existing conventions of everyday life had no privileged status.

The same applied to the subjective feelings of understanding that accompany natural language, and are reinforced by it. These subjective associations were regarded as flexible and adaptable, capable of adjustment to whatever kind of language they developed around. After all, experts in a particular field (e.g. mathematicians or pianists) develop 'intuitions' (physical and mental) about things non-experts utterly fail to grasp even after hours of explanation (Bereiter and Scardamalia 1993).[15] Indeed, Carnap sought to replace or supplement natural language even as a medium of everyday communication; he had been an active member of the Esperanto movement from the age of 17 (ASP 1908a).

So the central thrust of rational reconstruction was not to clarify the conceptual scheme embedded in, and reinforced by, natural language, but to decide what to *replace* that inherited scheme with. The question was

---

[15] One might say that the Vienna Circle extended to language what Miguel Nicolelis, of the Center for Neuroengineering at Duke University, was quoted in the *New York Times* as saying about physical tools: 'Every time we use a tool to interact with our environment, such as a computer mouse, car, or glasses, our brain assimilates properties of the tool into neuronal space. Tools are appendages which are incorporated into our body schema. As we develop new tools, we reshape our brains' (Blakeslee 2003). This conception of the relation between the mind's subjective consciousness and its cognitive or cultural tools (linguistic or sensory) originates with Helmholtz (Gregory 1998; also below, Chapter 3).

not how to do justice to our existing intuitions, but to decide – from some overall viewpoint resting at any given moment, of course, partly on intuitions – what intuitions we *want*; which ones to keep and which to supersede.[16] This was not a theoretical task, or a therapeutic task, or even really an analytical task, of disentangling confusions of usage and meaning. Even at this early stage it was seen – appropriately to its origins in the École Polytechnique – as more of an *engineering* task.[17] The first obstacle to Enlightenment, then (its lack of a clear definition of knowledge), had not been overcome, but it had been stated much more precisely. It had been reformulated as the problem of the *logical* structure of knowledge (in the new, precise, Fregean sense of 'logic'). The problem of defining knowledge had been turned into a question (not easily soluble, it turned out) of the deductive – and inductive – relations between theory and evidence, while the unity of knowledge became a question of the deductive relations among the sentences and concepts of different sciences.

The second obstacle to Enlightenment: knowledge and the practical realm

The problem

In one of the oldest stories our religious traditions have handed down to us, the Tree of Knowledge destroys unselfconscious innocence; eating of its fruits poisons higher and nobler aspirations. What Max Weber called *Entzauberung* – the breaking of the spell, the dissolution of mystery – is associated in many people's minds with the diabolical power of mathematical science to *reduce* the richness of the experienced world to a few basic forces operating on a formless soup of invisible particles, and thus to make the experienced world we live and love and work in seem an illusion. Edmund Husserl spoke for many when he saw a crisis of western science in its reduction of the enormous richness of qualitative conscious experience

---

[16] This *voluntarism* at the core of Carnap's conception has been well described by Richard Jeffrey: 'Carnap's voluntarism was a humanistic version of Descartes's explanation of the truths of arithmetic as holding because God willed them: not just "Let there be light", but "Let 1 + 1 = 2" and all the rest. Carnap substituted humanity for God in this scheme; that's one way to put it, a way Carnap wouldn't have liked much, but close to the mark, I think, and usefully suggestive. Item: Descartes was stonewalling, using God's *fiat* to block further inquiry. It is not for us to inquire why He chose 2 instead of 3. But for our own *fiat* the question is not what it was, but what it will be: choice of means to our chosen ends . . . Philosophically, Carnap was a social democrat; his ideals were those of the Enlightenment. His persistent, central idea was: "It's high time we took charge of our own mental lives" – time to engineer our own conceptual scheme (language, theories) as best we can to serve our own purposes; time to take it back from tradition, time to dismiss Descartes's God as a distracting myth, time to accept the fact that there's nobody out there but us, to choose our purposes and concepts to serve those purposes' (Jeffrey 1994, p. 847).

[17] A more detailed discussion of 'rational reconstruction' is to be found in Chapters 6–8 below.

to the 'Galilean' model of science, whereby all the phenomena are reduced to a skeletal mathematical essence (Husserl 1936, e.g. p. 38).

But this perennial Romantic complaint was exacerbated further when gradually, after 1800, the Enlightenment changed its character from opposition movement to new establishment. The adoption of scientific reason as an official ideology by the agencies of authority – by the state, the professions, industrial corporations, the education system – gave rise to what Horkheimer and Adorno later called the 'dialectic of enlightenment'. This was the perverse process whereby scientific standards of evidence and the scientific style of thought become identified with *what is* rather than with *what might be* or *should be*, the aspiration for something better. Scientific standards, and the Enlightenment itself, came to be identified with the corrupt, unjust, unreflective world we live in. Worse, they seemed to block all recourse to any alternative conception. The Enlightenment had turned itself, to all appearances, from an ideology of revolution into the ideology of the status quo.[18]

This view of the Enlightenment, given greater currency today by Foucault and others, is now so deeply ingrained that rejection of the Enlightenment's heritage by thinking people, especially in the humanities, has become almost a default habit of mind.[19] The Vienna Circle, in this atmosphere, is hard to take seriously. And indeed, though the programme of rational reconstruction, as just described, may be a useful basis for overcoming the *first* obstacle to Enlightenment (i.e. supplying a criterion of knowledge), it seems almost calculated to make this *second* obstacle insuperable – to *aggravate* the tension between knowledge and the practical realm. Rational reconstruction inserts a rigid barrier between a tightly regimented, symbolically sanitised version of knowledge and the higgledy-piggledy world of human life, experience, action, and engagement. Indeed, it was precisely for this reason that Horkheimer and Adorno aimed their critique at the Vienna Circle version of Enlightenment – the rational reconstruction programme epitomised the 'dialectic of enlightenment', in their eyes, and took it to an extreme.[20]

---

[18] Horkheimer and Adorno (1947); this is of course a somewhat oversimplified version of their view, or perhaps a lowest common denominator of different interpretations, of which there have been many. Two opposing, but complementary, ones are to be found in Habermas (1985, Chapter V) and O'Neill and Uebel (2004).

[19] See the acute commentary of Wolin (2004) on the twentieth-century intellectual background to this process.

[20] The breakdown of the initially cordial relations between the Frankfurt School and the Vienna Circle in the 1930s, and its philosophical background, is described in detail by Dahms (1994), with further discussion in O'Neill and Uebel (2004).

But like most critics of the Vienna Circle, Horkheimer and Adorno focused on a superficial version of the rational reconstruction programme and completely failed to notice the new phase the Vienna Circle had entered after 1932. This is generally called the 'syntax' phase (somewhat misleadingly, since the specifically 'syntax' element of this view soon dropped out; see below, Chapter 10). The governing principle of this new view was Carnap's 'principle of tolerance', according to which the standard language (in which knowledge is to be reconstructed, as before) is no longer fixed. It is freely choosable: 'everyone should construct his logic, i.e. his form of language, as he likes' (1934a, p. 45; PT p. 52). There is no longer a 'correct' language. Philosophical arguments about whether some particular logical principle, e.g. the law of excluded middle, is 'true' – 'really' qualifies as 'logic' – are pointless. Languages can be, and have been, set up with or without such a principle. Why not try out different languages and see how they work? The only criterion Carnap required of a candidate language was that its rules be precisely specified. And the only way of judging the merits of a language was pragmatic. Its usefulness for some human purpose was the only ultimate criterion. Whether a realistic or idealistic language is to be preferred, Carnap said, for instance, should be regarded not as a philosophical but as a practical question. We should not regard it as an argument over *what is*, but as an argument over how we *want* to set things up (1934a, p. 42; PT pp. 46–7). And once we have left the illusory safe harbour of 'correctness', 'the open sea of free possibilities' lies before us (1934a, p. vi; PT p. xv).

To understand the full scope and revolutionary implications of this idea, we have to go beyond Carnap's own explicit formulations, and perhaps even beyond anything he actually thought. Certainly he did not immediately recognise (and never made quite explicit) the mutual feedback introduced by the principle of tolerance – the 'dialectic', in a different sense from Horkheimer's and Adorno's[21] – between the theoretical and the practical. Such a dialectic is unquestionably present at the heart of Carnap's post-1932 framework, but it is unclear to what extent he himself fully appreciated the implications of this. In this dialectical perspective, the chosen language becomes the standard of what counts as knowledge (of what counts as meaningful, of which knowledge is a subset). And knowledge, which presents itself to us in the chosen language, has for Carnap the indispensable social and personal uses the Enlightenment had always claimed for it. But on the

---

[21] A dialectic in Plato's, not in Hegel's, sense. Attention was first drawn to this dialectical structure of Carnap's later thought by his student Howard Stein (1992).

other hand, the criteria for *choosing* the language are *practical*. Knowledge shapes our practice, in other words, and practice shapes our knowledge. Interpreted or extended in this dialectical sense, the later Carnap, unlike Hume or William James, regards reason not as the slave of the passions, but an equal partner. Reason informs the passions (and the rest of life – the realm of 'practice'), and the passions inform reason. Neither is subordinate.

Explication as successor to rational reconstruction

With the embrace of tolerance Carnap gave up his previous hope that there could be a single, permanent logical framework for the whole of knowledge. This hope, on which the rational reconstruction programme had rested, was a legacy of the classical logicism of Frege and Russell, in which logic had been uniquely and unambiguously characterised – though Carnap had relied not on Frege's or Russell's own characterisation, but on Wittgenstein's conception of logic as a necessary artefact of representation. Even this necessity, however, was now given up. There was no longer any such unique characterisation of logic; the 'open sea' contained an infinity of possible logics. A logic was now characterised simply as a set of rules, the formation rules and transformation rules for a 'calculus'. But though these rules were now a matter of free choice, there at first remained the distinction, as sharp as Frege's or Wittgenstein's (though the sharpness was later softened, as we shall see) between concepts *within* such a rule system and those outside it. The idea of 'truth' or 'existence' henceforth applied, strictly speaking, only within such a system, and had a clear meaning only relatively to it. Such concepts could be employed in the *external* discourse of pragmatic decision *among* frameworks only to the extent that this external discourse had been regularised and disambiguated on the model of the rule-bound calculi we use it to talk *about* (1950a).

In this new, implicitly dialectical conception, the applied discipline of 'conceptual engineering' – the successor to philosophy – still seeks to improve our understanding by piecemeal *replacement* of vague concepts with more precise ones. Explication, the main task of conceptual engineering, consists in the replacement of a particular vague concept – an *explicandum* – by a more precise or useful one, its *explicatum*. The first step is the *clarification* of the explicandum, the establishment of some basic agreement, among those who use the vague concept, about what they mean by it, or what aspect of it to make precise. The next step is a proposal for its replacement, a proposed *explicatum*, which should have the most important uses agreed on in the clarification stage, but need not have all of them. The very process of explication may, indeed, show that the explicandum's various uses cannot, in fact, be combined in the same concept.[22] The explicatum should, wherever possible, be expressed in a language framework that makes precise and transparent its relation to a wide range of other concepts.[23] Many disciplines – especially those usually considered 'scientific' – use provisionally canonical languages[24] in which they expect, or sometimes require, explications to be framed.

On the one hand, then, are frameworks of (relatively) precise, hard concepts, on the other hand is the activity of practical decisions among such frameworks. These decisions are at best partly extricable from the entire world of practical decisions, which are generally conducted in ordinary pre-systematic language, i.e. in softer, less precise concepts. They may be hardened up, just as, in the perspective of rational reconstruction, the concepts of ordinary scientific language were progressively upgraded and replaced. But in the new perspective, such progress is no longer a one-way street. The practical realm kicks back. Ordinary language is still to be overcome and improved, but is also (at whatever stage it has reached in that improvement process) the *medium* of practical reflection, the medium *within* which we choose among theoretical frameworks.

There are three levels of language engineering or language study, in Carnap's mature conception: *syntax* considers languages as pure calculi, in isolation from anything extra-linguistic they might be thought of as representing; *semantics* considers languages as representing extra-linguistic states of affairs, but still in isolation from actual uses of language by humans; and *pragmatics* considers languages in relation to their use contexts and their users.[25] Each of these three (syntax, semantics, pragmatics) can be considered as *engineering* activities (the creation or discussion of new or improved languages) or as *empirical* studies (of existing languages). The engineering activity Carnap called 'pure' syntax, semantics, or pragmatics; the

---

[22] A striking instance of this in the case of a simple physical concept, that of 'rotation' (in the context of general relativity), is given by David Malament (2002).

[23] The most extensive discussion of explication by Carnap himself is Section I ('On Explication') comprising the first six chapters of *Logical Foundations of Probability* (Carnap 1950b); further discussion in Stein (1992) and Carus (2004). The latter papers take a broader view of explication than is usual in the literature, e.g. Beaney (2004), Maher (forthcoming).

[24] Such provisionally canonical languages have been called 'paradigms' by Thomas Kuhn (1962). While Kuhn himself (along with much of the intellectual world) thought he was 'refuting' logical empiricism, Carnap (editor of the series in which Kuhn's book appeared) thought Kuhn's book was fundamentally compatible with his own view (Reisch 1991). As Michael Friedman remarks, 'the accepted conventional wisdom concerning the relationship between Kuhn's theory of scientific revolutions and logical empiricist philosophy of science is seriously oversimplified and fundamentally misleading' (Friedman 2003, p. 19).

[25] The trichotomy of terms derives from Morris (1938) and has become standard in linguistics. However, the significance of these terms in Carnap's philosophy is entirely organic to his own development.

empirical study he called 'descriptive' syntax, semantics, or pragmatics. (Linguists generally engage in the *descriptive* syntax, semantics, and pragmatics of already existing natural languages, logicians in the *pure* syntax and semantics of constructed languages.) Among the traditional sectors of philosophy, epistemology and methodology belong to pragmatics, while whatever remains of metaphysics and ontology belongs to semantics – though this now becomes a matter of *deciding* which entities to make fundamental to a language framework, given our knowledge, rather than *finding out* what those entities are or might be.

The ideal of explication differs not only from previous philosophy, and from Carnap's own previous framework of rational reconstruction, but also from most *present* analytic philosophy. It differs from Quine's influential programme, for instance, encapsulated in Neurath's metaphor of reconstructing the boat of our conceptual scheme on the open sea, without being able to put it in dry-dock and reconstruct it from new materials. In Carnap's framework, our collective mental life is not – to adopt the metaphor – all in the same boat. It consists rather of a give and take between two kinds of communicative devices that operate in different ways. Carnap's boat is only one of these two parts, not both. It is the medium of action and practical decisions, in which vague concepts of ordinary language have a continuing, perhaps essential, role. This is not, in Carnap's terms, a proper linguistic 'framework' at all. It is a medium not for the pursuit of truth but for getting things done, and it is well adapted to this purpose. To improve it further, we chip away at it and replace its components, a few at a time, with better ones – and this reconstruction, it is true, we carry out at sea. But the better components we acquire from the ports we call at, where we go shopping for proper linguistic frameworks. We take on board better materials and better navigational instruments that help us to reach whatever ports we hope to visit in future – where we can again bring on new and improved materials and instruments. Sometimes, the improved instruments will so influence our knowledge of where we are going that the whole plan of the journey will be revised, and we will change course. But the decision what port to head for next we have to make on board, in our pragmatic vernacular, with whatever improvements we have incorporated up to that point.

Carnap's ideal of explication is one of continual give and take between harder and softer concepts, between our common speech, our medium of practical and political activity, on the one hand, and our formal theories and frameworks on the other. We can weigh the merits of those frameworks rationally; this is the fundamental difference between Carnap and Quine.[26] As social animals carrying out practical and social tasks, we employ an action-oriented discourse that is (perhaps necessarily) vague and full of inconsistencies, even if improved and simplified as in Esperanto. (It is a compromise, like the well-tempered tuning system of keyboard instruments – which is not perfectly 'clean' for *any* particular key.) Viewed as a candidate for employment in the realm of truth, it is a mess. But despite that we are capable, *within* this realm of action, of *writing down* precise rules for proper conceptual frameworks (not perfect ones, but *better* ones), and of using those hard concepts as *tools* to improve our messy lives and practices. We can raise ourselves up out of the mire of soft concepts by clinging to frameworks of hard concepts.

Explication as a way of addressing the second problem

The Carnapian ideal of explication does not itself *resolve* the tension between scientific knowledge and other values, but it is the most promising framework, I will argue, for seeking such a resolution today. It places the pursuit of knowledge and the pursuit of the good in a coherent and mutually indispensable relation to each other (a dialectical relation, in the interpretation offered here). It offers a broad scaffolding for a conception of reason (of *Vernunft*, to speak with Kant) that is adequate to the frightening power and scope of our knowledge, and that can make more precise and applicable the idea of knowledge as a 'conscience of the species' in the way the Enlightenment conceived it. The ideal of explication neither portrays science as a dominant and threatening father-figure or super-ego, as in the Romantic parody, nor as irrelevant to our higher and more exalted concerns.

Perhaps the simplest way of bringing out these practical merits of Carnap's ideal of explication – in a way he himself never did – is to compare it to *other* ideals of 'reason' or 'rationality' (ideal frameworks for the coordination of knowledge and the practical realm). To avoid needless proliferation of cases, I will restrict myself here to just two such alternative ideals, but two that have the merit of being well known and widely used: that of Quine and that of Habermas. (This also has the advantage that I can assume

---

[26] It is also the major difference between Carnap's view and that of the later Wittgenstein, at least as it is understood by W. W. Tait (1986, 2001) and Erich Reck (1997). The fundamental difference between Carnap and Quine is *not*, in fact, that Carnap needs an *antecedent* analytic-synthetic distinction, as is often thought (e.g. by Friedman (1999), Chapter 9, and Hylton (1998), pp. 49–50); see Awodey and Carus (2004). All Carnap needs is (a) a distinction between a realm of theory (where framework-relative truth and confirmation are the criteria) and a realm of action (where usefulness is the criterion); and (b) the possibility of choosing among frameworks of truth-pursuit from within the action-bound context of our practical lives.

acquaintance with them; the brief sketches of these ideals below will be fully comprehensible only to those who have encountered them elsewhere.) Though both are situated, broadly speaking, within the Enlightenment tradition, they represent extreme cases, responding disproportionately to the first and the second of the above two obstacles to Enlightenment, respectively. Carnap's more balanced ideal avoids the excesses of either extreme, I will suggest, and is able to overcome *both* obstacles jointly.

Quine's ideal descends from the logical universalism of Russell and Frege.[27] For Quine, there is no stepping outside the 'conceptual scheme' in which our 'mother tongue' places us. We complicate and sophisticate that scheme by means of our science, but we can never be in a position to choose our language, for that would require an Archimedean vantage point outside language, which is impossible. What meta-theory there can be, Quine thought, must be stated in the terms of the unified science it is about. How does this relate to the ordinary language people actually use in real life, the 'mother tongue' whose content, Quine maintained, only behavioural evidence manifested in speakers can tell us? Ordinary language is obviously not the unified science in which theory and meta-theory are to be framed. To bridge this gap, Quine fused ordinary language and an idealised language of science into a single, seamless, all-encompassing 'conceptual scheme'. The unity of this conceptual scheme is not a contingent, empirically observed continuity between different kinds of usage or dialect within a used language; it is a unity by definition. Users of ordinary language can improve the precision of what they say by 'regimenting' it into the more exact and unambiguous terminology used by scientists. And whatever in actual speech cannot be regimented (or accommodated to the canonically regimented statement of our knowledge) – i.e. whatever contradicts or falls outside the language of unified science – is simply not part of the conceptual scheme. It is part of observed linguistic behaviour, but makes no contribution to the picture of the world conveyed by the scheme. So the canonical statement of the scheme is the scientific one, of which ordinary language is a kind of interface for everyday use.[28]

Meta-linguistic or philosophical considerations must themselves, then, be stated within the terms of this scheme. Semantic ascent (from language to meta-language) enables us to refer to words and linguistic artefacts just

---

[27] That it actually *is* a logical universalism – of the kind first diagnosed by van Heijenoort (1967) and further discussed by Goldfarb (1979) – is suggested by Hintikka (1990); in his response, Quine (1990) somewhat testily disputes this classification, without offering much by way of argument.

[28] Quine's ideal is thus a more direct descendent of the Vienna Circle's earlier 'rational reconstruction' ideal (above, pp. 14–17) than Carnap's own ideal, which, as we saw (pp. 17–23), *rejects* that earlier view.

as we can use those words to refer to objects in the world. But whatever we say in the meta-language must be part of the scheme canonically stated in the scientific object language: 'This ascent to a linguistic plane of reference is only a momentary retreat from the world, for the utility of the truth predicate is precisely the cancellation of linguistic reference. The truth predicate is a reminder that, despite a technical ascent to talk of sentences, our eye is on the world' (Quine 1970, p. 12).

There is of course much more to be said about this view than these few brief paragraphs might suggest, but even from this summary we can see how Quine's ideal of reason would apply to a controversy such as that about the 'unity of science'.[29] While it would be a vast over-simplification to sort the positions taken by various philosophers on this issue into those who favour and those who oppose the unity of science, the Quinean ideal can accommodate only the former. It simply cannot recognise those who reject the unity of science, since in Quine's conceptual schemes, science is unified by definition. The unity of science is – not to put too fine a point on it – *analytic*! It is true by definition; there is no way of raising a question about it. In stark contrast, Carnap's ideal of explication can easily accommodate such questions; the suggestion that there is a fundamental 'disunity of science' is simply a different proposal about how to set up the scientific language. The merits of such proposals would be discussed and judged, in Carnap's ideal, according to their utility in understanding the relations among various parts of knowledge. It is one of the great merits of Carnap's ideal that it does not simply *exclude* radically dissenting views but accommodates them easily and naturally. This makes discussion possible, at least in principle; it makes it possible to agree on what one is disagreeing about, rather than just shrugging in perplexity and putting disagreements down to a clash of 'ultimate commitments'.

Quine's ideal framework, moreover, has no resources for making any sort of *normative* claim or recommendation. When Quine denied, for instance, the distinction between analytic and synthetic sentences, what exactly was his claim? That this distinction was not in fact used by scientists? This is

---

[29] Even Carnap and the Vienna Circle were well aware that 'unity of science' could be understood in a number of different senses (e.g. conceptual unity and unity of laws); see Creath (1996). Some scientists have taken strong positions on this issue, e.g. E. O. Wilson (1998) with his notion of 'consilience', and have provoked equally strong responses, e.g. Rorty (1998). Philosophical papers and books that have generated significant discussion over the past two decades include Kitcher (1989), broadly on the side of unity; Dupré (1993) and Giere (1999), with rather different positions, broadly against unity. A sense of the range of issues involved can be gained from Galison and Stump (1996), most of whose contributors are against unity.

empirically false.[30] That it is not used in ordinary life? This is equally false.[31] That the distinction does not 'exist', in some ultimate sense? Carnap would heartily have agreed (Awodey and Carus 2004, p. 206). That it *should* not be used? But what is this if not a proposal that the scientific community should adopt a different language? According to Quine, though, we *cannot* step outside our language and choose a different one.[32]

At the other extreme from Quine is Habermas. Quine, as we saw, all but *eliminates* the practical realm from consideration; the 'conceptual scheme' we are trapped in is a system of knowledge only, and essentially of scientific knowledge.[33] Habermas proposes, in contrast, to confine scientific knowledge to a corner, while other 'knowledge-constitutive interests', especially 'practical' and 'emancipatory' ones, have pride of place.[34] Habermas explicitly offers a full-scale account of a larger version of 'reason' or 'rationality' (*Vernunft*) that goes beyond scientific knowledge. Though his account is not substantive, like Kant's, but procedural, it is not procedural in the Vienna sense of *logical* 'procedures'; rather in the sense of sociopolitical debating 'procedures'. The characterisation of knowledge is thus

[30] An example Carnap often cited was Einstein's claim that Hilbert's axiomatic method, which distinguished sharply between the pure geometric calculus and a physical model, had been indispensable for the development of the theory of relativity (Einstein 1921, pp. 3–6).

[31] An obvious, mundane example is the frequent discussion among business people, looking at their monthly or quarterly results, whether some particular trend represents real activity or is merely an artefact of their accounting system.

[32] Carnap, naturally, maintained that Quine's strictures were better described as *proposing* a form of scientific meta-language or a more informal code of conduct for discourse about science. He said this most explicitly in the discussion after a colloquium given by Quine at the University of Chicago in 1950, reported by Howard Stein (1992, pp. 278–9). According to Stein, Quine was willing, at the time, to accept this description.

[33] Gila Sher (1999), exploiting a tension within Quine's conception pointed out by Dummett (1973), proposes a version of Quine's ideal that would remove this limitation, and actually make it a framework for an overall theory of rationality (1973, p. 516) – one not so dissimilar, it turns out, to Carnap's ideal of explication. This may perhaps be taken as showing how right Ricketts (2004, p. 200) is to emphasise the 'overwhelming similarities' and continuities between Carnap and Quine. But it also increases the pressure on Quine (or rather on Sher, speaking for Quine) to clarify the status of Quine's denial of 'the' analytic-synthetic distinction, as queried in the previous paragraph, and so explain how his conception actually *differs* from Carnap's. Sher's reconstruction of a Quinean ideal also suffers from an inevitable arbitrariness since it is not built from the ground up but is an edited version of Quine, whose own intentions it in some ways undermines. It is Quine with epicycles, while Carnap's ideal has a Copernican simplicity that makes the relation between theoretical and practical starkly clear.

[34] The following sketch of Habermas's ideas focuses on the broad continuities in his writings from *Erkenntnis und Interesse* (Habermas 1968a) to the present. There are clearly important differences between that earlier book and his more recent turn to 'universal pragmatics' and the theory of communicative action; e.g. the earlier 'knowledge-constitutive interests' give way to a broader 'communicative competence' based on ordinary language and more universal patterns rather than being rooted in specific disciplinary cultures. But these differences do not much affect the points to be made here.

essentially still a classificational one based on human capacities and faculties, like that of the *Encyclopédie*. Habermas shares Horkheimer's 1930s ambition of finding a basis on which to criticise and remedy the Vienna Circle's perceived reduction of human reason to a merely 'instrumental reason'.[35]

Though Habermas (1985, pp. 130–57) thinks that Horkheimer and Adorno went too far in their rejection of the Enlightenment, he also believes they were right to claim that its modern heirs have tended to confine reason to a merely 'technical' or 'functional' remainder, thus excluding it from the practical (especially any wider public) realm. His account of 'communicative rationality' addresses that deficit, in a spirit of constructive engagement with the Enlightenment rather than its rejection (Habermas 1981). Communicative rationality is Habermas's candidate, in other words, for Kant's *Vernunft*, while 'instrumental rationality' corresponds to *Verstand*. Communicative rationality, for Habermas, is what results from uncoerced interaction in an 'ideal speech community', in which interested and strategic communication is excluded in favour of purely disinterested and 'rational' discourse, where the standard of 'rationality' is both historical and quasi-naturalistic: a sociological account of the development of 'rationality' in the modern world, based on Weber, Durkheim, and Parsons (though with a strangely reduced and restricted role for science), is superimposed onto a developmental account of individual human rationality and self-determination derived from G. H. Mead and Piaget.

Quine's ideal of reason is practically the definition, then, of what the Kantian tradition culminating in Habermas has striven to *overcome*. A Quinean conceptual scheme embodies a purely 'instrumental' (or 'technical', or 'functional') rationality, which regards everything that is not part of the scheme either as reducible to its canonical – scientific – standard or as nonsense. This is just the view that Horkheimer and Adorno attacked in the *Dialectic of Enlightenment*, and for Habermas it represents a colonisation of the *Lebenswelt* by instrumental reason (whose proper realm is limited to

---

[35] Reason that is appropriate for determining means *once the ends are given* – i.e. to govern action that is purely instrumental or '*zweckrational*' in Max Weber's sense. Habermas, following the Frankfurt School, classifies all of natural science as instrumental in this sense. It thus seems quite doubtful that Habermas or any of his followers would accept Michael Friedman's (2001, pp. 54–6) proposal to associate Carnap's 'internal' questions with 'communicative reason' and Carnap's 'external' questions with 'instrumental reason'. On the contrary, it is precisely the questions 'external' to a given language framework that can be said to be a matter of public discussion, while those 'internal' to a language framework are essentially technical questions – precisely those that Habermas regards as the province of 'instrumental rationality'.

the sphere of 'instrumental' action).[36] Surely these Habermasian strictures must apply also to Carnap, who had after all been one of Horkheimer's and Adorno's *actual* targets? But that was the *textbook Carnap*. In fact, Carnap's ideal of explication, as described above, gives the practical realm not only an explicit place in the larger picture, but an equal and indispensable place beside scientific knowledge. The 'practical' and 'emancipatory' knowledge-interests are acknowledged as having equal weight in deciding which language(s) to use for knowledge, and must of course have *at least* equal weight in arriving at any decision about the more general language to use in practical deliberations.

The 'dialectic of enlightenment' is overcome, in Carnap's ideal of explication, precisely through the clear *separation* of the basic theoretical structure of science from its use in society and even by scientists (the distinction between its semantics and its pragmatics, as the late Carnap would have said). This *liberates* scientific knowledge from any particular historical form or social use. What knowledge 'is', in the ideal of explication, is not the significance it is given by any particular social configuration, an establishment or a state. Scientific knowledge is a group of theoretical claims confirmed or tested to some degree by the procedures agreed by the present practitioners of a particular branch of knowledge.[37] The implications drawn from these theories for social, political, ethical, aesthetic, or other purposes – even by the present practitioners of that branch of knowledge – are as contestable as any other social or political issue. Such implications may or may not result from the choice of the larger language of practice in which they are drawn. They may result from the choice of language in which the scientific theories themselves are framed, but as we have seen, even that is contestable – 'conventional', that is – in the sense that those participating in a discussion must (at least provisionally) *agree* on that choice. In an idealised model of such an agreement process one might imagine a literal 'convention' in which all concerned in the issue came together to agree, uncoerced, on constitutive language rules.[38]

For Habermas, the language in which the community speaks is taken for granted; it is accepted more or less uncritically from our ancestors, in all its social embeddedness.[39] For Carnap, the language is within our

---

[36] This is a theme throughout Habermas's work; one early formulation is Habermas (1968b); a later, more extensive and definitive one is Vol. 2, Part VI (pp. 171–293) of *Theorie des kommunikativen Handelns* (Habermas 1981), as well as the concluding pages of that volume.

[37] The procedures are agreed (and enforced), but not the interpretation of the result.

[38] Jeffrey (1994) suggests such a scenario; see Chapter 11, pp. 292–309 for more details on this idea.

[39] Habermas draws extensively on Austinian ordinary-language philosophy, and for these purposes situates himself within that tradition (Habermas 1988, Chapter 4 and 5; 1999, Chapter 2).

control. And the choice of language is an indispensable part of the envisaged dialogue; it is precisely here that practical and emancipatory concerns find their application. Nor does the choice of a language of science uniquely determine a conception of 'reason' in any larger sense. Any number of such conceptions are possible and so – extrapolating Carnap's linguistic pluralism to this even more underdetermined realm – any number of such conceptions may co-exist within a single society. Carnap's ideal framework thus also escapes one of the objections most frequently levelled at Habermas's view: its lack of provision for radical pluralism, and its explicit use of the history of rationality in European societies as a model for 'communicative rationality' more generally (e.g. Strong and Sposito 1995).

Habermas's ideal of reason, though it addresses the second of the two obstacles to Enlightenment (the relation between knowledge and the practical realm) is all but silent about the first obstacle (the lack of a criterion for knowledge). Indeed, Habermas is not, and has never really been, interested in knowledge as such. His interest is in specifically *emancipatory* knowledge, by which he means knowledge of the critical social sciences (sociology, political science, political economy). These are to be modelled on what philosophy had traditionally stood for; they are to be a kind of 'policy studies' to motivate enlightened political action and overcome false consciousness by means of *Ideologiekritik*. But what the Enlightenment called knowledge, and what it had in mind as 'important' knowledge, is of little interest to Habermas. He leaves that to 'technical' experts, and distinguishes it sharply from both emancipatory knowledge and hermeneutical (historical, anthropological, literary) knowledge. No doubt the 'technical' experts will have their own criteria and procedures, but these do not concern him, as this form of knowledge is, in his view, of little human and social interest. His view of knowledge is, as we saw, static and classificatory. In his later work, consistently with this, he has given up all attempts to articulate any conception of knowledge at all outside the context of a social theory.[40] The concept of 'communicative action' becomes primary, while knowledge is derived, as just a particular kind of communicative practice. Conceptual engineering is restricted to the *pragmatics* of languages (to use Carnap's terms) – and there just to what evolves socially. No self-conscious, purposeful *engineering* is really permitted; the entire Vienna Circle project of 'conscious shaping of life' ('*bewußte Lebensgestaltung*') is lost. The direction of change is from the pragmatic to the semantic, from practice to theory,

---

[40] As he spells out in Habermas (2000), pp. 8, 14–15; 'epistemic rationality' becomes a specific subform of communicative rationality more generally (Habermas 1999, pp. 107ff.).

with no feedback in the other direction. It is an opposite one-sidedness to that of Quine (or of the Vienna Circle's original 'rational reconstruction' programme). To be sure, the emphasis on rationality and rational communicative procedures makes this a different, a more Kantian approach to the 'social construction of science' from Bloor's 'strong programme' or other post-Kuhn proposals for social constructionism.[41] Habermas's conception of knowledge is clearly not *anti*-rational or even anti-modern, as he has often made clear (e.g. Habermas 1985).

But this primacy of communicative practices still leaves Habermas without a knowledge criterion. His mutual isolation of technical, historical, and emancipatory knowledge leaves him without an *overall* criterion to determine, of any given piece of knowledge, which of those categories it belongs in. There are only the 'justificatory practices of a language community' (Habermas 1999, p. 244), which for Habermas (unlike, say, Rorty) can certainly be 'rational' by virtue of their roots in culture and history. But what about *new* language communities, or combinations of old ones that have no obvious traditional home? To cite a concrete example: open any issue of a demography journal from the past few decades, and you will find that some papers employ *only* strict procedures of measurement or statistics, while others engage *only* in hermeneutic investigation of cultural patterns of household formation and family life. But there are also papers that try to do *both*, and to relate these approaches to each other in different ways. There is significant controversy between the two approaches, and how (if at all) they are to be related to each other.[42] So by what standards is the work in these journals to be judged? Communicative rationality gives no answers here; it can only talk about the historical and social legitimation of standards such as 'empirical adequacy' *within* mathematical natural science on the one hand, or *within* hermeneutic human sciences on the other. But this does not answer the question. For what we are faced with here – and this is typical of current social and human sciences – is a clash between these two *different* historical standards of 'empirical adequacy'.

Carnap's ideal of explication, in contrast to Habermas's, can accommodate such a situation. It portrays the clash of standards not as a blind social process, but one over which the participants can assert a degree of control. The question is a practical one of choosing a language for a certain purpose. The disputants each have desiderata for this language, which they

---

[41] Bloor (1976) is the classic founding text for the 'strong programme' of 'social construction of knowledge'. Bloor's ideas derive from late Wittgenstein, as some of his later writings (e.g. Bloor 1996) make more fully explicit.

[42] See, for instance, Kertzer and Fricke (1997).

are presumably capable of expressing to each other in a mutually comprehensible language (an everyday language of practice, in this case, upgraded by some knowledge of statistics, demography, and other social sciences). Once this preliminary clarification is done, the Carnapian approach is to step back and look at the desiderata in a larger framework. The goal is to develop a mutually agreeable language that is not so rigid that it excludes either approach but not so loose that it fails to satisfy each party's standards of 'empirical adequacy'.[43] This is not simply a mechanical task of pasting together two incompatible languages; it obviously requires creative ingenuity – this is conceptual engineering. The outcome depends on the quality of this engineering. Occasionally a perfect synthesis can be found, but usually the solution in such cases is something of a compromise, which in practice fails to satisfy at least a few disputants on the fringes. These can then go on arguing, demanding that the compromise be reviewed, or they can walk out and start a new discipline. Such an engineering failure can always be attributed to the impossibility of the task, but it can never be known for certain whether better engineering might not after all have done the trick in the end.

The Carnapian ideal to be reconstructed in this book avoids the pitfalls, then, of both these kinds of Enlightenment accounts of reason: those that focus entirely on the first obstacle and ignore the second (like Quine), and those that focus entirely on the second obstacle and ignore the first (like Habermas). The Carnapian ideal of explication addresses *both* these fundamental problems, jointly and equally.[44] It does not focus exclusively on the first, as Quine does, reducing reason entirely to the cognitive or 'instrumental'. But it also avoids an exclusive focus on the second, and proposes no particular conception of reason or *Vernunft* that would introduce a standard of objective truth or correctness into ethical, political, or other practical discourse. It imposes only minimal constraints, and otherwise gives free rein to a broad pluralism about what such a larger version of reason might be.[45]

---

[43] An attempt to devise such a solution in a particular, hotly disputed case (somewhat related to the above example of demography) is to be found in Carus and Ogilvie (forthcoming).

[44] Not in its actual articulation by Carnap himself, but in its implications, which it is the task of this book to draw out and make explicit. Though Carnap was personally more aware of the second obstacle than Quine or many other scientific philosophers, his actual published writings reflect mostly a preoccupation with the first obstacle.

[45] This enables it, as we will see in the concluding section of Chapter 11, to suggest a resolution of the well-known Rawls–Habermas debate about the degree to which political pluralism is compatible with reason.

HOW CARNAP'S IDEAL OF EXPLICATION ESCAPED NOTICE

To claim that Carnap's ideal of explication is uniquely able to provide the Enlightenment tradition with a programme for the future – and especially that it provides tools for breaking out of the 'dialectic of enlightenment' – is admittedly rather startling. To many it will sound incredible, given the image of 'logical positivism' as something like the *antithesis* of all utopian aspirations. It is true, certainly, that many over-zealous acolytes were all too willing, in the 1940s and 1950s, to use ideas and slogans associated with the movement in restrictive and intolerant ways, curtailing discussion and imposing rather complacent values in the name of value-free inquiry. But no movement should be judged by the followers who only jump on board opportunistically when its ideas are fashionable. A closer examination shows that there is no necessary connection between the narrow restrictiveness often associated with logical empiricism and its actual doctrines, stripped of their heavy-handed rhetoric. If we look at Carnap's ideas afresh, with an open mind, we find that the Vienna Circle's utopian aspirations remained central throughout Carnap's later years. He downplayed this guiding spirit after he moved to the USA. But his later conception still embodied the aspirations behind the earlier ideas that are the main focus of this book. Above all, the ideal he propounded – and continued to develop further in his last years – is applicable, as I have been suggesting, well beyond the issues he himself explicitly addressed.[46]

But how could Carnap's ideas be so radically misunderstood, even by some of his closest associates? This does admittedly stretch credibility to such an extent that it has to be addressed here, even if just in a few preliminary paragraphs whose full significance will only become apparent in later chapters. The main culprit, it seems, was the cultural difference between Central Europe and the North America to which Carnap emigrated in 1936. But mistakes of rhetorical and political strategy also contributed, as well as bad luck.

The Vienna Circle was not the only Central European movement to lose a good deal in translation when it was exiled to North America in the 1930s. Other exemplars of European 'modernism' had much the same problem. The ideas of the Bauhaus, for instance, or of psychoanalysis are often wrongly assumed to have had the same significance in the Weimar Germany or *fin-de-siècle* Vienna where they originated as in the wartime and

---

[46] See especially Chapter 11, pp. 292–309 for a sketch of how this ideal can be employed as a conception of reason in the full sense (not confined to 'instrumental' reason), in competition with the Kantian conceptions of Rawls and Habermas.

post-war North America to which they emigrated. It is certainly true that some of the same people were involved, and that they physically moved across the ocean. But these people often had only an imperfect understanding of the society to which they had emigrated in middle age. Their command of English was sometimes shaky. And despite a recognisable continuity of message and rhetoric, much of its intended significance was lost on their new audiences. The message became a different one, flatter and more superficial than its old-world predecessor.

In the particular case of the Vienna Circle, certain assumptions about the broader cultural and ethical context of their philosophical project were so obvious to them they were never made explicit in their writings. But for this very reason these assumptions remained foreign to their North American interlocutors. And this in turn made Vienna Circle views look even more superficial than they had seemed in their original European context. Their reception in Central Europe had already been grossly distorted by the highly adversarial context in which they had been enunciated. The Vienna Circle had come across, in this charged atmosphere, as a rabble of shallow and rather obtuse political sloganeers, the very antithesis of the cool, rational, scientific approach to social and cultural problems they advocated and tried to exemplify.

In this respect the Vienna Circle was its own worst enemy. Its initial propaganda in the late 1920s had gone far beyond what its actual philosophical achievements up to then could possibly have justified. It is hard to fault the motives of those involved; they correctly saw themselves as participating in a life-and-death struggle for the future of German and Central European civilisation. Like many others, they misjudged how quickly the crisis would occur and how weak democratic institutions really were in Central Europe. But they understood that the obstacles to those institutions lay deep in the culture, especially the culture of the educated. Neurath's propaganda campaign of simple slogans, calculated to signal a clear position and rally those of scientific inclination to an identifiable side, was never congenial to most of the remaining Circle. Carnap in particular often worried about the misleading superficiality of such pronouncements, though he was willing to compromise for the sake of political expediency in what he agreed was a desperate situation.

The original philosophical platform of 'rational reconstruction' could not begin to justify the rather inflammatory claims made for it. But beginning in 1931, Carnap developed the quite *different* platform of his 'syntax' view, as briefly sketched above, which in fact came much closer to providing a basis for many classical Vienna Circle positions. Though this became the springboard for Carnap's entire later development, it was only partially assimilated by the remaining Vienna Circle. Here bad luck, in the form of selective mortality, played a spectacularly unfortunate role. Hans Hahn died, at just this time, and Moritz Schlick was assassinated on the main staircase of Vienna University by a deranged student. Political developments added to the bad luck. Neurath fell afoul of the Austrian authorities and was unable to return home from Moscow; he got as far as the Netherlands, and had to stay there. Philipp Frank and Carnap, both meanwhile in Prague, saw the situation deteriorating there and emigrated to the USA, following Feigl. Their philosophical allies Reichenbach and von Mises emigrated from Berlin to Istanbul, Hempel to Brussels. Amidst this upheaval the continuity of discussion was interrupted; physical communication itself became difficult. The timing could not have been worse for the reception and discussion of Carnap's new philosophical platform.

But this already hopeless situation was further aggravated by a more insidious influence. Because of their greater skill in English prose and better access to publication outlets, English-speaking philosophers dominated the discussion of 'logical positivism' in the 1930s and 1940s. By far the most accessible source for the doctrines of the Vienna Circle, for several decades after the mid-1930s, was Ayer's *Language, Truth, and Logic*.[47] This book was published in 1936, two years after *Logical Syntax*. Carnap is acknowledged in the preface as the philosopher to whom Ayer owes most and with whom he agrees most closely. But his book completely ignores Carnap's new 'syntax' platform.[48] It is essentially a popularised account of the pre-1930 Vienna Circle position (the *Aufbau* and the *Tractatus*), hardly acknowledging the major obstacles to such a view that had long been discussed in Vienna. Even in 1930s Oxford, where Vienna Circle ideas were discussed intensively, they were hardly grasped.[49] And then after 1950, Quine was able to convince the world he had 'overthrown' Carnap's 'verification theory of meaning', pinning on Carnap a view he had not held for twenty years. Popper's *Logic of Scientific Discovery*, originally published in 1936, became well known in English translation in the 1950s. It portrayed the Vienna Circle in similar terms, also ignoring Carnap's new 'syntax' platform. And Popper continued all his life to ignore Carnap's devastating critique of the

---

[47] Astonishingly, this book is *still* taken as the main source for the doctrines of 'logical positivism' in a major new two-volume history of analytic philosophy (Soames 2003).

[48] *Logical Syntax* is cited once (p. 95), but there is no discussion of its main themes, and the principle of tolerance – the central doctrine of the book – is not even mentioned.

[49] To judge by the reminiscences of Isaiah Berlin (1973), at least; see also the confusions by prominent Oxford figures such as Ayer and Urmson mentioned below. Ayer, at least, was certainly present during most of the conversations recounted by Berlin.

falsifiability criterion,[50] on which Popper had based, and went on basing, many wide-ranging claims.

In the few cases when the 'syntax' programme *was* discussed, it was so badly garbled that the philosophical public could be excused for ignoring it. Ayer's 1937 paper 'Verification and Experience', attacking the 'syntax' programme, betrays as little understanding as his history of twentieth-century philosophy forty-five years later, in which he polishes off the 'syntax' programme in less than two pages without even mentioning the principle of tolerance (Ayer 1982, pp. 134–6).[51] J. O. Urmson, the author of a once widely read survey, *Philosophical Analysis: Its Development Between the Two World Wars*, admits that his critique is based largely on Ayer's 1937 paper (Urmson 1956, p. 123), and he certainly repeats Ayer's misunderstandings (as well as, again, omitting all mention of the principle of tolerance), adding an Oxonian tone of ridicule to his account. Popper, it is true, praised the *Logical Syntax* as 'one of the few philosophical books which can be described as of really first rate importance', avowing his 'firm conviction that, if ever a history of the rational philosophy of the earlier half of this century should be written, this book ought to have a place in it second to none' (Popper 1963, pp. 202–3). He even said that the book 'marks the beginning of a revolution in my own philosophical thinking' (1963, p. 203). However, he too ignored the principle of tolerance, and never mentioned the book's logical pluralism. What he did find there, amazingly, was 'the doctrine of the one universal language' (1963, p. 205)! Such remarks raise the question how closely Ayer, Urmson, Popper – or other ill-informed contemporary and next-generation critics of the 'syntax' doctrine[52] – read the book before pronouncing so confidently on its supposed doctrines.

---

[50] The critique in question, of which Carnap reminded Popper in his reply (Carnap 1963, p. 879) occurs in §§25–6 of 'Testability and Meaning' (Carnap 1936–7), published soon after the German original of *The Logic of Scientific Discovery*. Oddly, Popper's attitude toward 'Testability and Meaning' was enthusiastic, as in his view it represented a partial acceptance by Carnap of Popper's criticisms.

[51] Though he does, perversely, attribute to Carnap a coherence theory of truth – presumably because he had failed to note that the requirement of translatability into the 'formal mode of speech', in *Logical Syntax of Language*, applied only to the philosophical *meta-language*, not to the language of science itself, which Carnap of course recognised as containing 'object sentences', i.e. sentences that refer to things. See below, Chapters 9 and 10; specifically in refutation of charges such as Ayer's, see Carus (1999).

[52] Richard Rorty, for instance, equates '*the* logical syntax' of language (emphasis added), for instance, with 'the syntax of a "logically correct language"' (Rorty 1967, p. 5), thus projecting the transitional doctrine of 'Unity of Science' (1932b; see below, Chapter 9) onto the syntax *book*, which of course takes an entirely different view, embracing the principle of tolerance and eschewing 'correctness' altogether. Rorty then compounds this error by claiming that 'Carnap's only procedure for deciding whether a given language was "logically correct" was whether or not its sentences were susceptible to verification (or confirmation)' (1932b, p. 6). Rorty's teacher Wilfrid Sellars, who unlike all the above certainly *had* read the *Syntax* carefully, nonetheless misunderstood it in bizarre and convoluted ways too complex to detail here; see Carus (2004).

It is hardly surprising that, after this string of misfortunes, the 'syntax' doctrine had little impact. Carnap's own attitude, it must be said, reinforced this neglect. Soon after the publication of the *Logical Syntax*, Carnap embraced Tarski's semantics, apparently leaving the 'syntax' doctrine behind.[53] And just as he embarked for the United States in 1936, he also embarked on a ten-year project to elaborate a system of semantics. On the basis of this programme, he then spent most of his remaining career attempting to develop an inductive logic. These projects were, in fact, very much in the service of the ideas Carnap had conceived in 1931–2. But this completely failed to come across, in the American context. On the contrary, he was regarded in Chicago as a narrow technician with little interest in broader questions.[54] Carnap knew, of course, that the focus of the Vienna Circle on combating metaphysical obscurantism had less relevance in the post-war USA than it had had in inter-war Vienna or Weimar Germany. But although he remained politically aware during his American years, and involved in radical politics,[55] he made no effort whatever to connect these activities with the philosophical work he was publishing. Even in his autobiography in the Schilpp volume, his formulations are very careful, and the chapters describing the roots of his convictions in the German Youth Movement and social democracy were omitted from the published version. It seems that under the conditions of McCarthyism in the 1950s, Carnap was careful not to associate his academic work with anything that might attract unwelcome attention from authorities or university administrations. He was right to be concerned; the FBI did in fact spy on him extensively, as George Reisch (2005, pp. 115–19, 271–6) has recently established. His outward withdrawal from the ambitious utopianism of the Vienna Circle into technical detail was not, then, an accident.

But the occlusion of the utopian element in logical empiricism also meant that when a new generation of rebellious young people came along, in 1968, logical empiricism had little to offer them. It seemed to have no bearing on the larger questions they were asking, and was regarded as out of date even by professional philosophers, who had moved on to Quine

[53] In his *Introduction to Semantics* (1942), Carnap stated unequivocally that 'most of the earlier results [in *Syntax*] remain valid' (1942, p. 246), and listed the specific passages that required revision. But perhaps because of the split in the Vienna Circle's ranks at the Paris conference in 1935 over this issue, the difference between the 'syntax' view and Carnap's later view was somewhat exaggerated in retrospect. In any case, the general perception (e.g. by Ayer and Urmson in the above-quoted texts) was of a fundamental break.

[54] His sometime student Richard Jeffrey said, 'What Carnap was doing wasn't seen as philosophy by most of the faculty; they regarded it as a kind of engineering. And Carnap seemed perfectly content with that description' (personal communication).

[55] This has now been shown in detail by Reisch (2005, Chapters 1–2).

and Kuhn, or perhaps Popper. (In Britain, they had moved on to ordinary language philosophy some time earlier.) The idealistic young of 1968, whose fervour Carnap recognised as a kind of American equivalent to the German Youth Movement he had himself been so involved in before 1914,[56] did not perceive logical empiricism as even having any relevance to their concerns. They were attracted to more explicitly utopian frameworks of thought, especially various forms of Marxism.

PURPOSE AND APPROACH OF THIS BOOK

But the millennial enthusiasm of the 1960s is now also a thing of the past. The Marxist ideas so popular then have fallen into disrepute along with the Enlightenment more generally, and Romanticism is once again in the ascendant, enjoying an unprecedented popularity among English-speaking academics. As in 1920s Germany, science is in disfavour, the social and human sciences are striving mightily to distinguish themselves from the natural sciences, universal human rights and pluralistic democracy are questioned, the local and authentic is preferred to the cosmopolitan and artificial. So the Vienna Circle's reaffirmation of an Enlightenment world view against Romanticism has an urgent relevance now, ironically, that it never possessed in its post-war heyday. For the minority of intellectuals who still identify with the Enlightenment tradition, Carnap's ideal of explication provides a framework of discourse in which a utopian partisanship for reason and Enlightenment can co-exist with a pluralism more radical and fundamental than that envisaged by liberal political philosophers such as Rawls.[57]

To serve that purpose, though, logical empiricism has to be placed in a larger context than the narrowly technical one in which it has usually been discussed in the recent literature. Its relevance to larger issues, past and present, needs to be made clear. The bulk of this book is devoted to showing in some detail how Carnap's ideas arose in the context of the larger currents of thought in nineteenth- and early twentieth-century Europe. But the main thread is to chart his path toward the ideal of explication, as sketched above. I take the story from his philosophical beginnings, around 1910, through his arrival at the principle of tolerance and its first systematic exposition in the *Syntax*, in 1934, and a little beyond that. Though he does not mention explication by name until 1945, and does not describe it in

[56] Personal communication from Carnap's daughter, Hanna Carnap Thost.
[57] This is discussed at greater length in the final section of Chapter 11 below, with specific reference to the well-known Rawls–Habermas debate.

any detail until 1950,[58] all the tools required for it are essentially available by the late 1930s.

This task is more delicate than it may appear. The ideal of explication, the standpoint toward which this earlier development is to be seen as progressing – and from which particular steps in that development are thus to be judged – was never fully enunciated by Carnap. It requires excavation. It is not straightforwardly available from the published (or, indeed, unpublished) writings. It was something toward which Carnap approached, in his later years, but which never quite crystallised, probably not even in his own mind. Carnap's focus was not on the exposition of this unifying vision, this evolving *general* programme of explication, but on the *specific* projects of language engineering that exemplified it. So absorbed was he in these specific projects that for most of his career, up to the 1940s or so, he would scarcely have recognised the present account of his own broader programme. He was more interested in getting something *done* with his ideas, *applying* them, than with spelling out the programme that governed this work in the trenches.[59] Also he preferred to get his ideas across by example rather than by precept; 'by their fruits ye shall know them' was his pragmatic conviction.

But the fruits were meagre; most of Carnap's particular engineering projects have not survived him. Though he made numerous contributions to logic and the foundations of probability, none of his larger projects has been carried on by anything remotely resembling a 'Carnap school'. Though his spirit may, in a sense, be said to have animated a whole

---

[58] In Section I ('On Explication') comprising the first six chapters of *Logical Foundations of Probability* (1950b).

[59] This is well described by Carnap's student Herbert Bohnert, who rejects McKeon's characterisation of Carnap as the archetypally 'meroscopic' ('part-seeing', in McKeon's terminology, as opposed to holoscopic or 'whole-seeing') philosopher, and gives the following parable: 'Picture a *very* holoscopic mind. Suppose it is a very powerful one. After a survey of the whole scene it would, of course, form plans. The plans would require deep study in certain areas. The deeper study would reveal broader promises and puzzles. Interrelationships would be perceived. Plans and studies, by interaction, would quickly become global. Science would have to be unified, language systematized, the foundations of reasoning and experience scrutinized. Many specialized, meroscopic jobs would have to be done. Some could be done best by the mind itself – like constructing the needed overall conceptual framework – but time is limited. Minds must organize. A journal must be started. A manifesto of the new plan must be issued, congresses scheduled, an encyclopedia planned. Delays must be expected, of course. Wars. The interaction of minds is uncertain; the interaction of groups is unguided. In the meantime, the mind applies itself to those very special but very basic jobs which few but it can perceive as essential and promising. This brings the mind fame as a great specialist . . . At some point, of course, the whole plan is seen as unlikely to progress beyond its most initial phases in the time the mind sees as available to it. But then it was never unaware of possibilities. As a holoscopic mind, it understands its predicament perfectly. It still likes the plan. It proceeds in its painstaking work as if it had millennia' (Bohnert 1975a, pp. XLIII–XLIV).

generation of scientifically oriented philosophers in the United States, that generation took its actual doctrines and its philosophical priorities more from Carnap's antagonist Quine than from Carnap himself. Certainly his specific engineering projects are now, where not rejected as mistaken, hardly regarded with much interest.[60]

Carnap's larger programme of explication and pluralistic language engineering is also neglected. But that programme *is* of lasting value, I claim, even if every single one of his particular language projects and theories is abandoned.[61] This case cannot, of course, be made with precision. A programme of this kind inherently does not, in Carnap's somewhat misleading idiolect, concern matters of 'cognitive significance' – by which he meant that whatever case can be made is not internal to any particular linguistic framework, but pre-systematic and (in the broadest sense) pragmatic.

Carnap's development up to 1935 has been much studied in the past fifteen years (after several decades of almost complete neglect), and without the pioneering work of Richard Creath, Michael Friedman, Warren Goldfarb, and Thomas Ricketts, among others, this attempt to put together a continuous story of Carnap's development in the 1920s and 1930s would have been completely unthinkable.[62] What it adds to their work on early Carnap is threefold. First, it adds an archival dimension. To their analyses of the published writings, it adds the perspective of Carnap's unpublished correspondence, lecture notes, drafts, and manuscripts.[63] Secondly, it uses

---

[60] See Zabell (2005), however, who stresses the continuities between Carnap's programme and current Bayesianism.

[61] This value judgement raises a somewhat delicate issue regarding the proper task of philosophical interpretation, in that it defends certain aspects of the late Carnap's position to the neglect of others; Carnap himself would not have taken kindly to such a summary judgement on language projects dear to his heart. But for all their inherent interest, and possible potential for the future, most of Carnap's projects have not been carried on. An important exception is the inductive logic (see previous footnote); and very recently, new efforts have begun to reconstruct the *Aufbau*, avoiding Goodman's criticisms (Leitgeb 2007 and forthcoming). The approach taken here, however, will be not to assume the success of Carnap's particular projects, but to *bracket* them – and especially to show that the value of the overall programme or meta-framework for inquiry does not depend on the success of any particular language project pursued within it.

[62] We are long past the days when Ina Carnap wrote to Feigl wondering who might be willing to preserve the papers on the Vienna Circle Carnap says he has in storage ('He is sure that someday someone might be interested in it'), and Feigl responded, 'It would be nice to find somebody who could give a more detailed account of the development of our ideas in the 1920s and early 1930s than is contained in Kraft's book. My own recollections are dim and confused by now, and I doubt that I would do justice to what was going on in the discussions concerning the foundations of mathematics. I guess that there is no one else left who could do the job' (ASP 1962a).

[63] These are mostly located at the Archive of Scientific Philosophy at the Hillman Library, University of Pittsburgh, and at the Department of Special Collections, Young Research Library, University of California at Los Angeles. A number of smaller collections of papers have also been used; Part I of the Bibliography lists only those documents specifically referred to in the text of this book.

this more comprehensive view to show how Carnap's writings during this period fit into the overall story of his development. Particularly in the years 1928–32, leading to the syntax phase, the development was very rapid, and positions were often left behind even before the writings setting them out had been published; this has sometimes led to interpretive misunderstandings. Thirdly, this book takes the view, represented particularly by Howard Stein (1992) and Richard Jeffrey (1994) – both students of Carnap – that the later Carnap is the more interesting, and that his later position is the one toward which the earlier writings were headed. (This was, of course, Carnap's own view.) Thus, while pursuing a generally historical strategy for understanding the later Carnap's philosophical vision, the book is unashamedly teleological, in that it regards the ideal of explication as the vanishing point over the horizon toward which the earlier work was progressing.[64] Though this standpoint will be directly sympathetic, perhaps, only to those who share it (i.e. to those who still cling to Enlightenment values), it may at least prove useful to those who, without sharing Enlightenment values, will be surprised to find in Carnap a version of Enlightenment with which, from their own standpoint, dialogue is possible.

---

[64] Carnap's own later view does not, therefore, quite define the *telos* implicit in the 'teleological' standpoint of the present critical interpretation, which seeks rather to distinguish what can be salvaged, and is of permanent value, in Carnap's later view from what has, perhaps, less prospect of survival – and to put more emphasis on the former than has been customary. An interpretation of this sort must be guided by two not always fully compatible standards: that of accuracy, or faithfulness to the textual evidence, and that of attractiveness as a philosophical position in the present context. Accuracy is not completely well defined; sometimes there will be conflicting textual evidence, and in these cases the teleological approach will of course be inclined to follow the reading that maximises attractiveness. This danger is unavoidable in any writing on past philosophers that is motivated by more than purely historical or antiquarian interests – though of course one hopes that awareness of the danger may help to mitigate it.

CHAPTER I

The cultural inheritance

Among the words it is impossible to translate from German, *Bildung* occupies a time-honoured place as one of the most enigmatic. Depending on the context, it can mean 'education' (or 'educatedness'), 'formation', 'culture', 'shaping', or 'development'. Used abstractly and generally, it means something like 'personal development' or 'self-cultivation' (Bruford 1975), with an emphasis on mental (or spiritual) dimensions of development. It has a centrality among German-speakers that has no direct parallel in other European cultures;[1] especially its emphasis on inner and personal, rather than worldly and social, development is hard to convey outside the German context. Though it has been much eroded, this orientation is not entirely gone, and the vestiges that remain can remind us how much more pervasive and unquestioned such ideals would have been to a sensitive and intellectually inclined German boy growing up a century ago.

In Carnap's case, *Bildung* was even more central than to others of his generation, for educational thought was in the family. His grandfather Friedrich Wilhelm Dörpfeld (1824–93) was a well-known educational thinker, whose writings still belong to the canon of German educational classics.[2] Dörpfeld's eldest daughter Anna, Carnap's mother, wrote a memoir of his life. Carnap's autobiography begins with a recollection of watching his mother write this book.

It will be argued here that Carnap's entire philosophical project can best be understood within this specifically German cultural context. The programme of the Vienna Circle, from his perspective, was at bottom an attempt to provide a basis for a new comprehensive ideal of civilisation

---

[1] Norbert Elias takes this as the starting point, and one of the central questions to be explained, in his classic treatise *On the Civilizing Process* (Elias 1939); he later revisited the question in his book *Über die Deutschen* (Elias 1989).

[2] They were collected into a twelve-volume edition after his death, and he has been the subject of an extensive secondary literature. A selection of Dörpfeld's writings, with a biographical sketch, a bibliography of the literature on him, and an introduction to his ideas, is given in Dörpfeld (1963).

(a new *Bildungsideal*) to compete with the inherited German ones. It was the attempt, in fact, to provide a *Bildungsideal* adequate to modernity – to the ethos and requirements of science and democratic society. The remainder of this chapter will focus on the ideals Carnap encountered *before* he began to articulate any such new programme. First we look at the ideals Carnap grew up with at home. Next, we focus on the German Youth Movement (*Jugendbewegung*), which presented him with a quite different ideal, also very German, drawing heavily on Romanticism. This movement was shattered by the First World War, the major formative experience of Carnap's generation. After the war and the German Revolution, one part of the Youth Movement turned explicitly political. Carnap sympathised with this camp in principle, and involved himself in radical politics. But like Condorcet and Comte in response to a previous revolution, Carnap came to see political activity as remaining at the surface, while the fundamental problems could only be addressed by forging a new *Bildungsideal* that was more adequate to democratic, post-revolutionary modernity.

DÖRPFELD AND THE GERMAN EDUCATIONAL TRADITION

Carnap's grandfather Dörpfeld belonged to a line of German educational thought that goes back to Johann Friedrich Herbart (1776–1842), a philosopher and educator who had been a student of Fichte but then rejected German idealism. Fichte's or Hegel's transcendental freedom of the subject, Herbart said, left no room for social influences – especially systems of knowledge and values – on the development of individual human minds. Herbart stressed that the human individual was socially situated, and always to some degree the product of environmental factors assimilated during childhood and youth. While he agreed with Kant that we are ignorant of the nature of things in themselves, he objected to the subsequent idealistic exaltation of philosophy on this basis, and thought metaphysics must always take the results of empirical science as its starting point and ultimate standard of adequacy. Though the empirical science of the physical world cannot tell us what is ultimately real, Herbart thought perhaps a future empirical science of psychology could do so, and accordingly tried to develop a rigorously mathematical psychology based on a conception of conscious events as epiphenomena of what he called the 'reals', which he conceived as unchanging Leibnizian monads exerting various forms of 'pressure' on each other. This could also provide the basis, he thought, for a mathematical theory of learning processes that could become the basis for a proper science of education. Herbart resisted the subordination of education to other priorities, whether religious, political, or intellectual. Individual self-development through informed interest in higher knowledge and art was an ultimate good in itself, not merely desirable because of instrumental properties it might possess for church, state, or even academic disciplines. Herbart was, then, along with Fries, a representative of something closer to the western Enlightenment during a time when the German intellectual world had swung far in the direction of Romanticism.[3]

The 'Herbart school' of nineteenth-century educators, to which Carnap's grandfather belonged, did not maintain this quasi-Enlightenment standpoint in anything like its original form. Indeed, the 'Herbartians', including Dörpfeld himself, interpreted Herbart's emphasis on the situatedness of the individual mind in terms of original sin, and thus assigned a much more central place to religion in education than Herbart had. Within these confines, however, Dörpfeld remained quite faithful to many of Herbart's doctrines. He is best known for his resistance, along Herbartian lines, to the bureaucratisation and centralisation of Prussian primary and secondary education (Tenorth 2003).[4] And his more strictly pedagogical writings are very much in Herbart's spirit, e.g. a diatribe against the educational shibboleth of what he called 'didactical materialism' – the idea that the worth of an education could be measured by the amount of material 'covered'. In opposition to this Dörpfeld insisted, again following Herbart, that the student completely understand whatever was taught, and be given ample opportunity to reflect on what had been learned or discussed, so as to integrate it with what he or she already knew previously.

This approach also shaped Carnap's own primary education. After his father's death in 1898, he and his sister were taught at home by their mother. 'She regarded it as especially important that everything that was learned was really and completely understood by the child and was thoroughly digested and connected with other knowledge. Above all her aim was to stimulate our own thinking.' To ensure this outcome, the lessons took up only an hour a day, and the children were then left to read and think for themselves;

---

[3] Heesch (1999) is a useful introduction; Herbart's ideas also had a more direct influence on scientific thinkers, including Mach, Frege, and Riemann; Gabriel (2001) argues that Frege derived his basic notion of numerical statements as statements about concepts from Herbart; E. C. Banks (2005) skilfully teases out the precise elements in Herbart's thought that were suggestive to Riemann. Lenoir (2006) makes a plausible case that Herbart also exercised a strong influence on Helmholtz.

[4] What he proposed instead was local school councils within the framework of the (Lutheran) parish, an idea rejected by more radically secular and liberal voices like Friedrich Albert Lange, who was closer in spirit to the western Enlightenment (Tenorth 2003, pp. 235–6). On Dörpfeld's ambivalent political and social conservatism, see Beeck (1975), a very thorough and well-documented study.

'we learned much in an informal way', Carnap recollects, 'e.g. by observing plants and animals during our daily walks in the woods'. Also his mother was always available and never impatient, he says, 'when I approached her with my incessant questions [and demands] for explanations of all things which I saw'. Here too the Herbartian approach was in evidence: 'But she did not simply feed me ready-made answers; her main aim was rather to help me find my own explanations. For example, she might just mention a few facts unknown to me and then say: "The rest of the answer you can now think out for yourself"'. Carnap even, rather charmingly, suggests that his mother's emphasis on this distinction formed the basis for his own later insistence on distinguishing between logical and factual sentences:

Was it perhaps here that in my thinking the germ was created for the distinction between two kinds of knowledge, that which one can find by thinking alone, and the other which needs factual information? In other words, the distinction between logical and factual truth, which in my philosophical thinking later played such a fundamental role. (UCLA 1957b, pp. A11–12)[5]

Carnap's mother also 'did not like to give a child an order without giving the reason for it' (UCLA 1957b, p. A13). On the other hand, she did not regard social conventions, such as table manners and other such arbitrary rules 'as having any moral significance, to be accepted by children on authority, but rather as mere conventions which for practical reasons one has to comply with' (UCLA 1957b, p. A13). Therefore, while 'she often tried to give a rational justification for conventional conduct', if there was no good reason, she would be quite frank about that, 'she would admit that there was none, but that nevertheless it would be better to follow the customs in order to avoid hurting other people's feelings or getting into difficulties' (UCLA 1957b, pp. A13–14). On the other hand, she also modelled to her children a critical attitude toward such conventions; if there was a good reason to break one of them, then she did:

For instance, she let us children run around naked on the back porch; this was at that time rather unusual; but she had heard from other progressively thinking parents that it was good for the children's health. In my inclination to pursue a new idea to its radical conclusion, I asked her why we should dress at all, why we could not just as well walk around naked all the time and everywhere. She replied

---

[5] Note that in this and subsequent quotations from the original, uncut version of Carnap's autobiography, the English is often quite unidiomatic. Some of these passages are directly transcribed from dictation, with no editing. In other passages, Carnap incorporates suggested edits from various sources; unfortunately, most of those to whom Carnap circulated the raw typescript (including Mia Reichenbach, Peter Hempel, Herbert Feigl, and his wife Ina) were also not native English speakers.

that there was nothing wrong in this in itself, but that other people would not like it, and therefore it would be better not to do it. (UCLA 1957b, p. A14)

'She took the same attitude', Carnap adds, 'toward the conventions of language. When I said "er esst" in analogy to "ich esse" and "wir essen", then she told me, of course, that one says "er isst".' But when he asked for the reason, she said there was none; 'it just happened to be the general custom' which it was better to go along with in the absence of a good reason. This attitude to conventions – explicitly applied to language itself – deeply impressed Carnap, and he himself draws a connection between it and his later philosophical 'voluntarism'; 'I believe that the attitude of my mother toward social conventions was of great influence for the development of my own attitude and also for my philosophical thinking':

Because of this casual attitude of hers toward customs, conventions, and traditions, I never had the widespread reverence toward the sanctity of traditions, which is such an obstacle in the way of cultural progress. I believe that regarding the forms of customary language as sacrosanct is for some contemporary philosophers a serious impediment in their philosophical thinking, because it leads to a strong emotional inhibition against even considering problems of language planning. (UCLA 1957b, A15)

Having been so thoroughly imbued with the Herbartian spirit, in a household so self-consciously suffused with *Bildung*, it is not surprising that Carnap's initial career choice was to be a teacher. In Jena, where he went to university, he studied with the dominant presence in the education department, Wilhelm Rein (ASP 1966b), generally regarded as the last major figure of the Herbartian school. Rein played down the religious dimension that had been so important to Dörpfeld, and brought the social embeddedness of the individual into the foreground. Rein was also a notable influence on some of the important figures in the new movement of *Reformpädagogik* ('reform education', a form of 'progressive education') including Hermann Lietz, the founder of the experimental school Wickersdorf near Jena, and Wilhelm Flitner, Carnap's friend and contemporary, who was instrumental in the founding of the Jena *Volkshochschule*, a college of adult and further education, in 1919. Jena had already been a world leader in adult education, as the founder and owner of the Zeiss optical works, Ernst Abbe, and his successor Siegfried Czapski (Flitner and Wittig 2000), had given special attention to providing their employees with opportunities for mental and physical self-improvement.

Carnap and his mother were immediately at home in these circles. While Jena was a different and more cosmopolitan environment, a prism of emerging modernity (Werner 2003), the Dörpfeld family background, though rooted in the provincial Rhineland, afforded sufficient perspectives to allow a rapid assimilation. Though Carnap had never known his grandfather personally, he felt as if he had, through his writings (some of which his mother read aloud to the children), through his mother's memoir, and especially through her teaching practice. The other important role model for Carnap was 'Onkel Wilhelm', Dörpfeld's eldest son, who after training as an architect became a well-known archaeologist – first Schliemann's professional conscience, and later the founder of the German Archaeological School in Athens. He directed excavations at Troy, Olympia, Tiryns, and Athens, and became one of the originators of scientific archaeology, developing procedures to ensure that a site yield maximum information (Goessler 1951). Despite the many controversies he was embroiled in, often opposing the amateurish methods of more traditional archaeology, he became the leading inspiration to a whole generation of archaeologists. One of his many admirers was Wilhelm II, who invited him to dine in the palace in Berlin, at his summer residence in Corfu, and even after he had been deposed, for a long stay at Amerongen. It was Onkel Wilhelm's house that the Carnaps lived in when they moved in 1909 from Wuppertal to Jena, where Carnap finished school and went to university. Some years before that, the family had also visited Onkel Wilhelm in Greece, and was given a grand tour around many of his excavations, also observing him at his current dig in Leukas.[6] For all his many honours, and his enormous fame, Wilhelm Dörpfeld was – as many different accounts agree (von Rohden 1940, pp. 29–30) – entirely unpretentious and without vanity, focused on his work and devoted single-mindedly to the search for truth, accessible and friendly, generous in recognising the merits of others, even critics and rivals. This larger-than-life figure gave the young Carnap a model for extending the family's educational orientation in a somewhat different direction, leadership in the realms of intellect. Both his grandfather and his uncle, Carnap said, were 'highly revered by my mother', and he himself admired them because in their respective fields 'they did not simply follow traditional ways but searched for their own new paths' (UCLA 1957b, p. A7).

Given that Carnap was brought up in a deeply religious culture, the Herbartian framework it was presented in enabled him to retain much of its ethical substance while sloughing off the doctrinal packaging.[7] There was ample room for wider horizons, and the intellectual underpinnings

---

[6] This trip is reported in some detail by Carnap's sister in Kaufmann (1940).

[7] This process was very gradual; Carnap's attachment to some form of religion lasted at least well into the war (ASP 1911a, 1916a, 1917b); in ASP 1920d, his exit from the church is reported as news.

could be replaced while the basic values remained unchanged. Even within the realm of religion itself, what mattered was its relevance to an outlook, a way of life. For both his parents, Carnap said, 'their faith was a living force which permeated their whole life and determined their decisions in all practical questions'.

While I grew up, my mother often explained to me that the essential point in religion was not to believe certain things, but to live the right life. And for the decision in all moral questions regarding right and wrong, she referred not to any authority, either the parents or the word of God, but rather to one's own moral insight, the 'voice of conscience'. This was one of the cornerstones of her brand of Lutheran Protestantism. (UCLA 1957b, p. A8)

Her father, moreover, like a good Herbartian, 'had always strongly emphasised that in the education of a child's character, the moral principles should be based only on the child's own conscience and not on God's will'. Dörpfeld had thought the church 'made a very serious mistake by making ethics dependent on theology', because this caused young people to lose their moral orientation if they began to doubt the doctrines. Carnap's mother explained her father's ethical ideas to her children, but whether or not they understood all this, 'the practical attitude of my mother, aside from any philosophical reasoning, was very influential in our lives' (UCLA 1957b, p. A9):

What convictions, including religious beliefs, anybody had, was for her a morally neutral matter, as long as he would seriously search for the truth and in the forming of his convictions follow his best insight. This attitude led to a high degree of tolerance . . . I think it was chiefly due to this tolerant attitude of my mother that later, when I abandoned my religious beliefs, I could do so without an internal crisis. (UCLA 1957b, pp. A9–10)

Carnap's father was also very religious, and though he had died when Carnap was seven years old, a strong sense of identification remained. Johann Sebulon Carnap had been an autodidact, who was taken out of school at age ten and sent to work at the loom (the Carnaps were ribbon-weavers) and in the fields: 'With great energy he used the evening hours for acquiring an education by himself, in many fields of knowledge, including foreign languages'. He also prospered and was able to build up a considerable business, which also earned him respect in the community, where he was 'cheerful, extraverted, sociable, and energetic'. But he 'never tried to conceal his modest origin. His esteem of other people was based only on their character, not on their social position' (UCLA 1957b, p. A2). Carnap's father appears to have represented to him a sense of *Bodenständigkeit* or rootedness in a particular local tradition, a very German sense of regional identification, and he was proud that his father was a man of the people. He evidently identified with – and saw his father as an archetypal embodiment of – the character of the 'Bergisches Land', the former Dukedom of Berg, along the right bank of the Rhine across from Cologne, which had become part of Prussia after 1815:

> The men of this region were known as having a strong sense of external and internal independence. Here the Reformation was not established from above by the authorities, but was carried through by the people themselves. Until 1813 this meant a permanent struggle and resistance against the Catholic regime of the region. Therefore the people themselves had to organise both their church and their school communities and to take care of their own education. For many generations there had been quite a number among the peasants and craftsmen who eagerly read books on religion, philosophy, science, and history, and then gathered in the evenings in small groups to discuss their problems. The vivid interest which these people took in their religion and their way of life could sometimes not be satisfied by merely accepting the Lutheran doctrine. The Reformed Church, which was strongly influenced by Calvinist ideas, had many adherents. About the year 1742 some members of this church, among them two ancestors of my father, found the worldly life in the great city of Elberfeld too sinful and intolerable. Eventually a group comprising about fifty families emigrated to the other side of the mountain and founded the town of Ronsdorf, which they called their 'Zion', devoted to a new and better life. (UCLA 1957b, pp. A5–6)

Carnap concludes this remarkable passage (of which the parts on the 'Bergisches Land' are a précis of the corresponding pages in his mother's biography of her father) with the even more remarkable declaration: 'I believe there is still a trace [of this impulse] in me, derived from the strivings of these people for the realisation of a visionary aim, and from their missionary spirit, although . . . transferred to secular aims and, in accordance with my more contemplative than active temperament, not expressed in practical activities' (UCLA 1957b, pp. A6–7).

It has been speculated that Carnap's later anti-metaphysical attitude might be viewed as a sublimated form of the puritanical German Pietism in which he had been raised (Gabriel 2004). But while suggestive, this would seem to miss more interesting ways in which Carnap's early education prefigures his later philosophy. From the passages just cited it seems obvious that what Carnap mainly admired in the puritanical tendencies of his ancestors was nothing in those views themselves but rather the fierce independence of mind and missionary spirit they showed (as well as Carnap's characteristically German attribution of personal characteristics to his rootedness in a regional tradition). The actual *content* of his early religious beliefs came from his mother's family, with its intellectual sophistication, its broad horizons, and its commitment to *Bildung*. And here, among the Dörpfelds, the religious content took a back seat to the ethical commitment. The attitude to beliefs was pragmatic, and the essential component of religion 'was not so much the acceptance of a creed, but the living of the good life' (1963, p. 3). Creeds were regarded with extreme tolerance, far removed from any puritanical fastidiousness. This culture inherited from Herbart and the German classics made it easy for Carnap to maintain the ethical substance of his family's values while shedding the religious packaging.

The first step in this process, after abandoning the mythological features of Christianity as a child, he says, was to adopt 'a kind of pantheism', derived, as he says, 'less from the works of Spinoza himself than from those of men like Goethe, whose work, personality, and *Lebensweisheit* (wisdom of life) I esteemed very highly' (1963, p. 7). This too 'had more an ethical than a theoretical nature; that is to say, it was more a matter of the attitude toward the world and fellow human beings than of explicitly formulated doctrines' (1963, p. 7). Nonetheless,

I was also influenced by the pantheism of Gustav Theodor Fechner, the physicist and philosopher who is known as the founder of psychophysics. My mother liked to read at that time his little-known religious-philosophical works; it was characteristic for her attitude toward religious questions that she did not find any difficulty in reconciling Fechner's pantheism (or panentheism) with her own Lutheran-Protestant faith. (1963, p. B20)

'I relinquished my religious beliefs by a gradual development', Carnap says, 'a continual transformation in which some new features came slowly into focus and others faded away'.

It was not, as I had often seen it with others, a matter of a sudden and violent rebellion with vehement emotional upheavals, where love is transformed into hatred and reverence into contempt and derision. I think this is chiefly due to the influence of my mother's attitude. Since childhood I had learned from her not to regard changes of convictions as moral problems, and to regard the doctrinal side of religion as much less important than the ethical side. (1963, p. B23)

This underlying ethical continuity also sheds light on a fact which, Carnap says, 'seems to me personally of great importance': 'This is the fact that my abandonment of my religious convictions led at no time to a nihilistic attitude toward moral questions. Although, of course, with the belief in immortality also the aim of obtaining "eternal salvation" disappeared, I did not change my attitude with respect to practical moral questions' (1963, p. B23).[8]

This is all the more remarkable since, after the move to Jena in 1909, Carnap was exposed to ideas at school that would never have been discussed at his school in Wuppertal; 'here a much freer atmosphere prevailed in the school and among the pupils'. He joined a 'Scientific Club', a forum 'where we pupils gave talks and held discussions'. Here he first came across the 'strange but fascinating heretical views of the iconoclast Ernst Haeckel, who on the basis of the theory of evolution attacked the dogmas of the church'; Haeckel, of course, was living in retirement right there in Jena. He was controversial, Carnap says, 'admired by some of us, hated by others' (A17). It was here, then, that Carnap first encountered a more radical form of Enlightenment. And though he immediately became its partisan, this caused no break with the ethical traditions he had been brought up in. This new influence will be discussed in the next chapter. Meanwhile, we turn to a quite different influence that he *also* encountered in Jena, when he enrolled in the university there the following year (1910), and whose roots in German Romanticism would appear to make it quite antithetical to everything his family stood for: the German Youth Movement (*Jugendbewegung*).

JUGENDBEWEGUNG AND SERAKREIS

The Youth Movement that began around 1900 in the wealthier suburbs of Berlin has hardly begun to be understood.[9] It would appear to be the first example of something that has become quite familiar in post-1945 industrial societies: a large-scale rebellion of well-off adolescents against the perceived conformism of their parents and teachers to the rigid norms of the society into which students were being socialised.[10] But it also had some specifically German features. Drawing heavily on German Romanticism, with its ideal-isation of medieval and primitive societies, the Youth Movement appealed

---

[8] Indeed, he says, 'My moral valuations were afterwards essentially the same as before'. There follows, in the published version of Carnap's autobiography, a brief and extremely low-key attempt to state the essentials of this 'implicit lasting attitude'. Though this statement is so bland as to descend almost into the anodyne, it does begin with the credo of *Selbstbildung* in the tradition of German Classicism: 'The main task of an individual seems to me the development of his personality' (1963, p. 9).

[9] Laqueur (1962) is a serviceable basic introduction; Aufmuth (1979) and Bias-Engels (1988) add some interesting details, but to my knowledge no attempt has yet been made to explain why the Youth Movement was specific to Germany, notably lacking parallels in western countries during this period.

[10] According to his daughter Hanneliese (personal communication), Carnap himself remarked on this resemblance during the 1960s.

to teenagers who perceived only complacent materialism and monotony in the mass society around them. They yearned instead for the heroic ideals and the simplicity of bygone ages, the stability of traditional society, contact with nature, and the simple life of peasants. In the late 1890s a group of schoolboys in the wealthy Berlin suburb of Steglitz began to arrange expeditions to the countryside, where they took long walks together. They sang as they walked, and carried as little as possible in their knapsacks; the idea was to adapt to local conditions, eat the plain food of the local peasantry, abstain from 'city' vices such as alcohol, coffee, and tobacco, and sleep in barns or under the open sky. The group called itself the *Wandervogel* ('bird on the move'). They hoped that direct contact with nature would heal them of the decadent and over-indulgent habits of urban civilisation, and would correct the one-sidedness and overspecialisation inherent in modern life. They wanted to be 'whole human beings', overcoming the alienation described in an oft-quoted passage from Hölderlin:

It is a cruel thing to say, and yet I say it because it is the truth: no people are more cut off from themselves than Germans. You see workmen but no human beings, thinkers but no human beings, priests but no human beings, masters and servants, youths and staid, respectable people, but no human beings . . . (quoted by Laqueur 1962, p. 5)

As the movement became national, it also developed its own culture and terminology, along with certain standard rituals and practices, a press (mostly consisting of local newsletters), and a special repertoire of songs (to be sung on the trail), collected in the anthology that became synonymous with the movement, *Der Zupfgeigenhansl*. It also split, as such movements do, into rival factions. The original leader, Karl Fischer, was strongly opposed to assimilation of the *Wandervogel* into the adult-supervised world of school and sport. Some of his lieutenants were more in favour of compromise. Tensions also increased as the burgeoning movement caught the attention of people with quite different agendas.

Members of the *Wandervogel* who went on to university sought to continue their activities, and pursue their new-found way of life, in the new surroundings. As university social life had been dominated, up to then, by the older fraternities or *Burschenschaften*, whose main occupations were drinking, smoking, card-playing, and fencing, the first requirement for the new arrivals was to create an alternative focus of social life. The *Akademische Freischar* ('free academic troupe') founded at the University of Göttingen in 1907, filled this gap. By 1912, both the *Freischar* and the *Wandervogel* had grown significantly, but there was no official connection between them,

nor a national organisation to adumbrate the different local manifestations
of what its participants felt to be a single movement.

The following year offered the perfect opportunity for such a gathering.
To commemorate the centenary of the Battle of Leipzig, the turning point
of the 'wars of liberation' against Napoleon, there was to be a patriotic
festival to dedicate a monument in Leipzig on 13 October 1913. What better
opportunity could there be for a counter-festival? Local representatives
of the *Wandervogel*, the *Freischaren*, and related groups converged on a
mountain in Lower Saxony, the 'Hoher Meißner', for a celebration of unity
on 12–13 October. A steering committee met nearby to found a national
umbrella organisation. This event was a huge success, with around four
thousand participants, from all over Germany and Austria. Press coverage
was largely positive, impressed by the discipline and order maintained,
the pristine state in which the forests and meadows were left, and the
absence of drinking, smoking, fighting, and other vices (Messer 1924, p. 25).
The meeting of the group leaders, though far from harmonious, did issue
in a group statement,[11] and an agreement to meet again and formulate the
bye-laws of the new national organisation. All who participated (including
Carnap) reported a rush of identification, pride, and solidarity.

A central role at this event had been played by one particular charismatic
figure, Gustav Wyneken. Wyneken had been a student of Hermann Lietz,
had joined him in starting the Wickersdorf school, and had become an
important voice in the educational reform community, founding and editing the journal *Die freie Schulgemeinde*. Wyneken had seen in the Youth
Movement an opportunity to create something that had never existed in
the world before, he said, a culture of youth. The world up to then only
had room for children and adults; there was the idyllic world of childhood
and the serious world of adult pursuits. Adolescents, emerging from the
former, were pitched into the latter without any scope for connecting their
dreams and ideals to anything in the real world. To enable them to do this,
he thought, it was essential for them to participate actively in the creation
of *their own culture*, a new 'youth culture' (*Jugendkultur*) subject to constant
change and renewal as successive generations took possession of it. Wyneken
was influenced by Nietzsche and the German idealist tradition, but also by
a broad education in many literatures and a cosmopolitan spirit that was
quite at odds with many of the more *völkisch* (nativist, organicist) Youth

---

[11] The famous 'motto of the Hoher Meißner': 'Free German Youth desires, of its own determination
and under its own responsibility, to shape its life with inner authenticity [*Wahrhaftigkeit*]. It stands
united for this inner freedom under all circumstances' (Messer 1924, pp. 19–20; Gustav Wyneken
apparently drafted these words).

Movement groups represented at the Hoher Meißner. When he addressed the assembled throng there, he warned them against a superficial patriotism that made war with neighbouring nations seem inevitable. We have to stand for an idea, he said, not for a nation; we have to take up the inheritance of Fichte and of Gneisenau, who had said that if the Germans could not liberate their own lands from Napoleon, then the English should come in and impose a free constitution. Wyneken urged the assembled young to stand up for German freedom, to remember the Hambach festival of 1832, and to understand 'German-ness' in such universal terms, not in a racial or other exclusive sense.

It was this strand of the *Jugendbewegung* that Carnap identified with. It would appear not to have been the mainstream. When the Movement as a whole came under attack soon after the Hoher Meißner event because of Wyneken's supposed subversive activities,[12] he and his organisation were quickly sacrificed, and excluded from the new steering committee (though the resulting left–right split in the movement was overcome when Wyneken was readmitted in 1917). The Wyneken-inspired 'Meißner formula' (note 10 above) was watered down. The mainstream, if there was one, would appear (to the best of our rather fragmentary knowledge) to have been represented rather by figures such as Hans Blüher, one of the original Steglitz partici-pants in the *Wandervogel* who went on to write prolifically about the Move-ment and other cultural questions. Blüher is hard to classify in categories we can now easily recognise. An ardent anti-feminist and anti-Semite whose heroes were Nietzsche and Otto Weininger, he outraged many by suggest-ing that sublimated (or less-than-sublimated) (homo)sexuality or pederasty provided much of the impulse behind the *Wandervogel*. Male bonding of a quasi-sexual kind, he thought, especially between a (male) leader and (male) followers, was the bedrock of any important social movement or institu-tion, especially the nation, but also of revolutionary movements. Though a firm believer in the organically grown folk culture and the destiny of the Germans, he abhorred everything bourgeois, and shared with revolutionary socialists the hatred of bourgeois stability, of plodding routine, of anxiety about money and material possessions. During the war he wrote a num-ber of pamphlets and articles developing a contrast between two kinds of

---

[12] In the Munich parliament, representatives of a Catholic party denounced Wyneken and his new, student-edited magazine *Der Anfang* as a threat to the church, the school, and the family. It was clear, they said, that the purpose of the *freideutsche* 'youth culture' was to undermine 'every positive religion as well as patriotism . . . the connection with Monism and monistic tendencies is obvious' (Messer 1924, p. 27). The Bavarian government immediately banned *Der Anfang* and other movement writings, even the *Zupfgeigenhansl*, for 'immorality'. Students were prohibited from participating in certain aspects of the movement, and even the *Wandervogel* itself was banned in some towns.

people he called *die Intellektuellen* and *die Geistigen* (the intended contrast is hard to capture in English; perhaps 'intellectuals' and 'creative spirits'). The latter, he thought, were the creative inventors of new ideas and new realms of thought, while the former, the intellectuals, simply reproduced mindlessly the creations of the *Geistigen*. The intellectuals were no better than assembly-line workers, in his view. Though supposedly using their minds in their work, they were completely passive, no better than bourgeois craftsmen, and their frenetic journalistic activity was entirely mechanical, not animated by any inner life. Carnap paid close attention to these articles (even in the trenches, during the war, he avidly followed as much of the *Jugendbewegung* press as he could get his hands on), and sent them on to his friends, repeatedly asking for responses. He particularly recommends Blüher's essay on 'intellectuals' and *Geistige*; 'this piece seems to me very important', he writes, 'as it expresses his view with particular clarity' (ASP/WF 1916d). And 'these are ways of thinking that we urgently have to engage with' (ASP/WF 1916b). Among the pursuits Blüher had dismissed as merely 'intellectual' and morally deadening were the natural sciences, indeed the whole approach to *Wissenschaft* (serious knowledge, scholarship) as practiced at universities, which he thought a bourgeois perversion of the healthy, natural use of the mind in contemplative spiritual exercises and the creative ecstasy of poetry and inspired philosophy such as that of Plato or Nietzsche. (Blüher might be seen as a kind of proto-Heidegger; certainly his ideas grew in the same soil.)

It is hard to know, in the absence of more detailed biographical research, just how aware Carnap was, before the war, of these tensions among the various influences on him, and within the Youth Movement. It seems more likely that the war itself, and the reflection it provoked (see next section), stamped these differences on his mind. Before the war, Carnap had been preoccupied with discovering himself, emerging from his shell. Before Jena, it seems, he had been a rather shy, introverted, mathematically inclined student with yearnings but little social involvement (ASP 1908a). In Jena, he blossomed, found himself not just able to participate as an equal but even to lead. He was able to test his opinions in discussion and find that he was often better-informed than his peers, and that they respected him. Nor was this new-found social ease confined to a purely intellectual context; he was soon playing a leading role in the local group that spearheaded the *Jugendbewegung* in Jena, the 'Sera Circle' organised by the publisher Eugen Diederichs.

Diederichs, his publishing house, and his Sera Circle also exemplify the pre-1914 eclecticism of the Youth Movement and the version of 'modernism' it represented.[13] Diederichs published *both* Wyneken *and* Blüher, as well as many others associated with the Movement. What united its various strands was then (before 1914) still more important than what divided them. 'Instead of following the traditional value standards, we strove to find our own ways of life', said Carnap, forty years later. And speaking of the impressively colourful and heterogeneous ranks of different local groups at the Hoher Meißner (where he attended as part of the Sera contingent):

For the first time the unity of the great German Youth Movement became visible, which, in spite of all the differences between the groups, was inspired by a common aim. The aim was to find a way of life which was genuine, sincere, and honest, in contrast to the fakes and frauds of traditional bourgeois life; a life guided by our own conscience and our own standards of responsibility and not by the obsolete norms of tradition. (UCLA 1957b, pp. B31–32)

The common enemy of Wyneken, Blüher, and other strands within the Youth Movement was the rigidity of bourgeois convention. As we saw, Carnap had learned at home to regard social conventions with casual scepticism, even disdain. Now he learned, from Diederichs and the Sera-Kreis, not just that one could reject or ironically distance oneself from existing conventions, but also that one could invent *new* ones. The human race could invent its own modes of social life and civic cohabitation.

The Sera group organised excursions and processions to the hills around Jena in which improvised rituals, often drawing on archaic elements as well as traditional dances and costumes, played a central role. At Midsummer, for instance, a huge bonfire was built on a lonely hilltop after sunset. After the carefully orchestrated and ritualised feasting, dancing, and singing, couples jumped over the flames together holding hands, until the fire died down amidst the murmur of quiet conversation. As the sun appeared on the horizon, over the hills, the antiphonal hymn to the sun by St Francis of Assisi was intoned, with Diederichs himself in the lead. Carnap much admired his creativity in making such events memorable (UCLA 1957b, p. B33).

This attitude toward creating new conventions would prove to be of fundamental importance to Carnap's philosophy through all its phases. And though the Youth Movement 'did not leave any externally visible achievements', Carnap later wrote, 'the spirit that lived in this movement,

---

[13] Diederichs called his publishing house a 'Versammlungsort moderner Geister' (meeting place of modern spirits); on the agenda implied here see Werner (1998; 2003, Ch. III) and Hübinger (1996a). The essays collected in Hübinger (1996b) and in Ulbricht and Werner (1999) shed light on Diederichs in a wider cultural and intellectual context.

which was like a religion without dogmas, remained a precious inheritance for everyone who had the good luck to take an active part in it. What remained was more than a mere reminiscence of an enjoyable time; it was rather an indestructible living strength which forever would influence one's reactions to all practical problems of life' (UCLA 1957b, pp. B34–5). Moreover, it was something he missed throughout his subsequent life:

After the war . . . the same spirit was still alive in the life of my newly founded family and in the relationships with friends. When I went to Vienna, however, the situation was different. I still preserved the same spirit in my personal attitude, but I missed it painfully in the social life with others. None of the members of the Vienna Circle had taken part in the Youth Movement, and I did not feel myself strong and productive enough to transform single-handedly the group of friends into a living community, sharing the style of life which I wanted. Although I was able to play a leading role in the philosophical work of the group, I was unable to fulfil the task of a missionary or a prophet. Thus I often felt as perhaps a man might feel who has lived in a strongly religious [and] inspired community and then suddenly finds himself isolated in the Diaspora and feels himself not strong enough to convert the heathen. The same feeling I had in a still greater measure later in America, where the power of traditional social conventions is much stronger than it was in Vienna and where also the number of those who have at least sensed some dissatisfaction with the traditional forms of life is smaller than anywhere on the European continent. (UCLA 1957b, p. B35)

Into this idyllic dawn of a new world erupted the unheralded disaster of August 1914 and the Great War.

WAR AND REVOLUTION

Carnap presents himself as having gone to war dutifully, with little awareness about the larger context of the events he was participating in: 'The outbreak of war in 1914 was for me an incomprehensible catastrophe. Military service was contrary to my whole attitude, but I accepted it now as a duty, believed to be necessary in order to save the fatherland' (1963, p. 9). By the time he and his Sera friends got around to volunteering, every nearby recruiting station had vastly over-filled its quota. But, determined not to shirk the general duty as ivory-tower intellectuals, he and his friend Flitner made a systematic search throughout the region. Carnap was quickly snapped up for his skiing ability, and began the war on ski patrol in the Carpathians (Flitner 1986, pp. 181–8). Within a year he was transferred to the western front, where he was in the thick of the action, and fought in some of the bloodiest engagements (ASP 1940a). Many of his friends and acquaintances, including Sera friends and at least one of his half-brothers, were killed. He was himself wounded, in France, and was awarded the Iron Cross on 24 September 1916 (ASP 1916b).

The subsequent change in his attitude appears to have mirrored that of the whole country, in which initial passiveness gave way, by the end of 1917, to a loss of confidence in the authorities, and by mid-1918, to an active desire for radical change. From June of 1917, Carnap was stationed in Berlin, where he worked on wireless technology at an army research facility. Here he was able to experience everything from the July crisis of 1917 through the collapse and the revolution at first hand. By the time of his arrival, information had become easier to obtain – especially in Berlin – than in the first years of the war, and dissent was already expressed more widely and openly. The left of the social democratic party (the SPD) had stopped voting in favour of new war credits even in 1916, and by early 1917 the split had become irremediable. In April, the anti-war wing officially became a separate party, the 'independent social democratic party' (USPD). At that point, the wartime consensus (the so-called *Burgfrieden* maintained among the parties since the autumn of 1914) collapsed, and the simmering disagreements between social democrats and the military about the conduct and aims of the war came at least partly into the open. The resulting instability gave rise, among the right, to the legend of the 'stab in the back' that was supposedly responsible for the German defeat.

The starting point of Carnap's political development during this period would appear to have been close to the Wyneken wing of the *Freideutsche Jugend* (the *Freischaren*, i.e. youth-movement oriented students). So it is a little surprising to hear how radically unpolitical he nonetheless still evidently was:

Before the war I, like most of my friends, had been uninterested and ignorant in political matters. We had some general ideals, including a just, harmonious, and rational organization within the nation and among the nations. We realized that the existing political and economic order was not in accord with these ideals, and still less the customary method of settling conflicts of interest among nations by war. Thus the general trend of our political thinking was pacifist, anti-militarist, anti-monarchist, perhaps also socialist. But we did not think much about the problem of how to implement these ideals by practical action. The war suddenly destroyed our illusion that everything was already on the right path of continuous progress. (1963, p. 9)

It was only when he came to Berlin in mid-1917, though, that he had 'the opportunity to study political problems by reading and talking with friends' (1963, p. 10). He noticed that the USPD was the only party that opposed the war, and that in other countries as well, 'the labor parties were the only large groups which had preserved at least a remnant of the aims of internationalism and of the anti-war attitude'. Accordingly, he 'began to study the ideas of the socialist workers' movement in greater detail' (1963, p. 10). As before, this was part of an evolution within the Youth Movement as a whole. In Berlin, he says, 'I took part in the discussions of a group of young people, most of whom came from the Youth Movement. We tried to clarify our *Weltanschauung* and to draw the consequences for contemporary political problems, especially of the war, and of the future after the war' (UCLA 1957a, p. C3).

Carnap also brought his wider circle of Youth Movement acquaintances into the discussion, seeking to make it more systematic:

I also began to send out circular letters to a circle of friends and acquaintances in order to further the discussion of political problems. The letters did not contain any revolutionary propaganda. They were based on facts like declarations by the German government which paid lip service to the ideal of a peace by negotiation or declarations by leaders of the workers' movements in various countries, and resolutions at some of the international labor conferences. To the communication of these facts I added some comments concerning the attitude of various circles in various countries, in order to convey an understanding of the causal connections, and finally suggested some questions for discussion. The participants were asked to write down their views, objections, or questions. Although the letters did not contain any secret material, some of the material was of a kind not published by the newspapers. My more or less implicit criticism of the attitudes of the governments and especially of the German government was rejected by some of the participants, and some even declined to take any further part. (UCLA 1957a, p. C4)

In the autumn of 1918, some of the folders containing Carnap's letters together with accumulated responses were accidentally forwarded to someone at the front, and fell into the hands of the military censors. Carnap had to stop the project, but was able to escape punishment, as the commanding general of the Berlin region, which was responsible for ordering Carnap to desist, did not issue the order in the usual way, and pass it down the ranks. Instead, a high-up police officer stopped by in Carnap's office, in civilian clothes, asked some questions, and showed Carnap the order without issuing it to him. 'I don't know', Carnap writes, 'whether further disciplinary steps would have followed. But soon thereafter came the collapse of the front, the revolution, and consequently freedom of speech' (UCLA 1957a, p. C5).

Even before that stage had been reached, Carnap had found other outlets for his new political enthusiasm. He had joined the USPD on 1 August

1918 (ASP 1918a). He read widely in the underground political press, and evidently used his contacts in the Youth Movement to participate directly in one of these organs, the *Politische Rundbriefe* published irregularly from 5 October 1918 by Karl Bittel, a leader of the Youth Movement in Stuttgart before the war, who had been at the Hoher Meißner in 1913, and had even then represented the most politically conscious and active wing of the *freideutsche* (*Freischar*-oriented) movement.[14] During this period, his political orientation, though certainly at the left of the then-current German spectrum, was not orthodox Marxist, did not toe the 'Spartakus' line of Rosa Luxemburg and Karl Liebknecht, and was not by any means uncritically admiring of Lenin's revolution in Russia. If anything, Bittel tended more to a libertarian socialism of the kind promoted by Gustav Landauer, whose book *Aufruf zum Sozialismus*, Bittel wrote, 'towers above the rest of the German socialist literature, from an intellectual point of view. At the same time, it is *the* book for *freideutscher* socialism: *against* Marxism, materialism, centralisation, state socialism and *for* communal cooperative socialism in the spirit of brotherhood' (ASP 1919b, p. 124). Carnap heavily underlined these words in emphatic agreement.

Bittel makes the transition of the Youth Movement into politics the explicit mission of his *Politische Rundbriefe*: 'This was the point of the preparation in our communities of self-shaping [*Erziehungsgemeinschaften*]: to dedicate ourselves to these ideals in our own private lives and that of a small circle of friends. Now it is critical to apply them in public life' (ASP 1918b, p. 1). Carnap underlined these words in agreement, as well as several other passages of Bittel's opening editorial, including this one: 'Politics, therefore, is not to be anything that lies inertly beside our inner world, unrelated to it, but rather something *that flows with necessity from the will to realise our true being*' (ASP 1918b, p. 2).

Carnap must have been involved with the planning of Bittel's enterprise, for this same first issue contains a contribution by him, the first instalment of a well-informed article on various conceptions of world government (ASP 1918b, p. 4; continued in ASP 1918c). The reading, thinking, and discussions of the past year also issued in a more thorough and wide-ranging statement of the position he had reached by October 1918, an essay he wrote for the *Politische Rundbriefe* called 'Germany's Defeat: A Senseless Misfortune, or Are We Guilty?' (ASP 1918c). For reasons that are unclear, it was not published. Perhaps events moved too swiftly: though evidently

---

[14] Bittel was associated with the cooperative movement; Bittel and Carnap had presumably met at the steering committee meeting at Schloß Hanstein the day before the main festivities at the Hoher Meißner in 1913 (cf. Messer 1924, pp. 25, 75).

largely written by 26 October, the surviving copy is cobbled together from at least two different typescripts, and is dated 29 October. It is marked for the printer; evidently Carnap intended to publish it. But that same morning, he would have heard the news that Germany had become a constitutional monarchy. By evening, all was again cast into doubt, as Wilhelm II, after signing the constitutional changes, fled Berlin to join Hindenburg's military headquarters in Belgium. And the Naval command, in direct repudiation not only of Wilson's conditions for a cease-fire, but also of its own new democratic government, issued orders for a last, desperate stroke against the English. It was against this order that the mutiny broke out among the sailors in Kiel and other northern ports that led directly to the German revolution over the following days.

Carnap's essay on 'Germany's Defeat' begins by denying that what is currently most dreaded in Germany – the military defeat and the imposition of Wilson's conditions – is to be regarded as a misfortune. A detailed and well-informed discussion of Wilson's Fourteen Points concludes that every single one accords not only with justice but with principles that 'we' – the readers of the *Politische Rundbriefe* – can all accept (if we try to take an objective rather than a parochially national point of view – which, Carnap points out, even academics seem to be having some difficulty with recently). The peace likely to be imposed by France and England will be more onerous than a Wilson peace. But Carnap puts much hope in the League of Nations, which he predicts will eventually ease the burden of the worst provisions. Only one of these is genuinely a misfortune, and will weigh heavily on Germany's future in the short and medium term: the burden of substantial, possibly crippling, reparations payments (ASP 1918c, pp. 9–10).

After this diagnosis of the present situation, Carnap steps back to view it in a broad historical perspective. We are at a critical juncture in the development of civilisation over the past several thousand years, he says – the development that began when humans were first able to produce more than they needed for immediate survival. For the first few thousand years of this development, while the rule of law was developing *within* certain societies, war was still the ordinary way of settling differences *among* societies, though the idea of a world order goes back to antiquity, and has frequently been articulated in recent centuries, e.g. by Kant. This war is a turning point, Carnap says. It has made these ideas of a world order an urgent priority in the minds of many, and has at last brought them into the realm of practical proposals. At this turning point from one dispensation to another, the war represented the last, desperate, dying struggle of the old, anarchic principle of national assertion, against the new principle of subordination to a universal order. At such a transition point there is much confusion; both principles are present everywhere in varying proportions. What seems like bravery and legitimate national assertion of power to some will seem like lawless trespass to others. Germany is the tragic case where national assertion was paramount in the minds of most citizens, while the outside world saw it as a rogue state that had to be brought under control. This difference is perhaps due to Germany's history, and its geographical position in the centre of Europe, which gave its ruling classes a more war-like and aggressive character than those of other countries, where the ideas of enlightenment, justice, international law and order arrived earlier (ASP 1918c, pp. 13–14).

But not only the ruling class is at fault. The remaining citizens are also to blame, for they knew better, but failed to seize the reins of government over the past century. They could have done so, 'but the nation of thinkers and poets was too unpolitical to give such questions its full attention, let alone to impose its own solution'.

This too is understandable. Indeed, it derives from a national character that we esteem highly and that has made this nation capable of magnificent achievements in other aspects of civilisation. Understandable, but not excusable. World history is the ultimate tribunal [*Die Weltgeschichte ist das Weltgericht*], and its judgement is ineluctable. Our generation and the next have a heavy burden of penance to bear. (ASP 1918c, p. 14)

The objection that Germany was not the sole cause of the war carries little weight, in Carnap's view, as the 'frame of mind [*Geistesverfassung*] in Europe that made the world war inevitable and then made its termination impossible until now', draws its 'principal nourishment from Germany' (ASP 1918c, p. 16). The academics and intellectuals bear a special responsibility for this, Carnap says, because of their reluctance to dirty their hands with politics, resulting from their failure to find the right balance between the active and the contemplative life. Addressing the *freideutsche* readership of Bittel's *Rundbriefe*, Carnap goes on to ask:

And what is *our* share in Germany's guilt? We do feel a solidarity with the entire German people, i.e. we feel an inner sharing of fate and guilt. But in a more specific sense we feel connected to those among the people who sympathise with us in mode of life, attitudes, and convictions – with people who share the life of the *mind*. *What is their share in* [*Germany's*] *guilt?* Their indifference toward political life has various grounds. Of the two polar forces of mental life – *action and contemplation*, which somehow have to find a yet unknown synthesis – the second, quietist, mystical one has perhaps exercised too strong an influence on German people. At this point we ourselves don't know how to find the right balance between these two forces, and yet we must reach the damning verdict: disharmony [in this respect] is [a grave] fault [*Disharmonie ist Schuld*]. (ASP 1918c, pp. 15–16)

And this imbalance between the poles of action and contemplation 'belongs to the most fundamental problems, whose solution must urgently concern us [*deren Lösung uns am Herzen liegen muß*]' (ASP 1918c, pp. 15–16). But we who are involved in the life of the mind have also failed, Carnap goes on, to combat those tendencies in our own ranks – within the human sciences (*Geisteswissenschaften*) – that complacently accept the past stages of the human race as prescriptive for all eternity. We have allowed an interpretation of history to arise that confers legitimacy on the way things are, 'without measuring them against the standard of an objective value'. And from this an ethic has prevailed that makes the interests of the national state and its absolute power the paramount consideration, without understanding that any single state is only a small part of a larger whole. That such irresponsible ideas are preached not only by politicians but even by leading professors of the human sciences 'is an especially heavy burden on our – the intellectuals' – balance sheet of guilt and our responsibility for the future' (ASP 1918c, pp. 16–17).

And what should be our response to this situation? Above all, we should not fall into complacency. Having learned his lesson that things will not come right of their own accord, but need conscious intervention and sustained effort, he has a sense of urgency:

The greater the fault, the more urgent the task. Let us not evade the sense of guilt nascent [*aufkeimend*] in us! But let us also not collapse into bitterness or resignation. There is neither sufficient reason nor enough time for this. The time is upon us, for the next years will be decisive in every respect for shaping the world-system and for shaping the reconstruction of peoples.

And how, in particular, should we go about restoring the balance between action and contemplation? How should we correct the irresponsible tendencies of the human sciences in Germany? Carnap's answer is political involvement, but politics understood in a *very* broad, almost universal sense:

The experience of recent years has led us to give one particular relation a special significance, i.e. that of politics, in the broadest sense. If we believe that this is where we must now apply the lever, we have no fear that by doing so our sphere of activity will be too narrowly circumscribed or too one-sided. For everything belongs to politics, in our view, that has some connection with the public social life of people [*mit dem öffentlichen Gemeinschaftsleben der Menschen*], not only the spirit that animates the society but also its structure . . . So all vocations – education and maintenance of bodies and minds, research into the interconnections of nature, mind, and world events, shaping of things or human relations according to inner conviction, production and distribution of the objects that body and mind require for life – are specialised functions according to their kind, but by their effects they are contributions to the same project. (ASP 1918c, pp. 17–18)

'Politics' in this sense meant 'everything . . . that has some connection with the public social life of people', which includes practically all human activities. But – and here is the key to this conception of 'political involvement' – for all these activities to work together, it was essential to arrive at a 'form of community [*Gemeinschaftsgestalt*]' that could serve to coordinate them so as 'to remove [these tasks] from the realm of chaotic whim and subordinate them to goal-oriented reason [*der chaotischen Willkür zu entziehen und der zielbewußten Vernunft zu unterwerfen*]' (ASP 1918c, p. 18).

This, as we will see in more detail in the next two chapters, is a clear echo of the scientific positivist 'engineering attitude', descended from the Enlightenment via Comte and Ostwald. In Carnap's case, though, it was combined with a more radically voluntarist, Romantic, and utopian streak he derived from his experience with the Youth Movement and its conviction that the world could be remade. Carnap's mental coming of age, then, combined two elements that are usually opposed; it combined Haeckel and Wyneken, so to speak, or Mach and Landauer. While it was not uncommon for members of his generation to be *exposed* to these antagonistic ideologies, it was rare for anyone to retain both. One had to take sides. They were – indeed still are – regarded as utterly incompatible. But in Carnap, the German Romantic and utopian influence from the Youth Movement, especially the parts of it that had moved to the radical left after 1917, co-existed with a scientific positivist version of the Enlightenment-oriented educational tradition stemming from Herbart. Most of those under the influence of the Youth Movement tended to reject the science-oriented Enlightenment tradition, while those who clung to the latter rejected the uncompromising, wild Romantic yearning for utopia.

It is this assimilation of opposed cultures in obvious tension with each other, I suggest, that drove Carnap to develop a sequence of viewpoints, over the next half century, that tried to do justice to a much wider range of sympathies and ideas than philosophers have usually done. Each of the main works – *Der Raum*, the *Aufbau*, the *Logical Syntax, Meaning and Necessity, Logical Foundations of Probability* – is a synthesis, attempting to bring together perspectives (often more than two) that were regarded as fundamentally opposed. The surface personality of these works is austere, modernist, almost self-parodyingly deliberate and methodical, deceptively plain. As Carnap grew older, this self-effacing mask of impersonality became more pronounced, froze almost into a mannerism. But the overall perspective he reached in his maturity, I will argue, did in fact succeed in attaining the goal of his youth: laying the intellectual foundations for a new *Bildungsideal* adequate to the modern world. He did not articulate it as a *Bildungsideal*, of course. But closely related perspectives *were* elaborated in this form by other Central European intellectuals of his generation. Two of particular relevance, who were exposed to the same contradictory influences, traumatised by the same war, and similarly anxious to do justice to both scientific positivism and Romanticism, were Carnap's acquaintance Richard von Mises and the novelist Robert Musil. Their writings can help cast light on, and provide texture for, Carnap's more abstract and impersonal stance. Musil in particular developed a perspective that not only has many points of contact with Carnap's, but is deeply compatible with it.[15] 'All spiritual daring is now to be found in the exact sciences', Musil had said, for instance, 'It is not from Goethe, Hebbel, or Hölderlin that we [i.e. we modern artists and writers] will learn, but from Mach, Lorentz, Einstein, Minkowski, from Couturat, Russell, Peano' (Musil 1912, p. 1318). It has been suggested, in fact (Mormann 2001), that Carnap's philosophy is best seen as a sketch for a 'science of possibilities' or *Möglichkeitswissenschaft* of the sort Musil envisages in Chapter 4 of the *Man without Qualities*, where the theme is the 'sense of reality' and its less common companion, the 'sense of possibilities', which might be defined, Musil says (Musil 1931, p. 16; PT p. 11), as 'the ability to consider what could just as well have been the case, and not to take what is more seriously than what is not'.

The consequences of such a creative tendency can be remarkable, of course. Unfortunately it often makes what people admire seem wrong, what they prohibit seem permissible, or both seem indifferent. Such possibility-people [*Möglichkeitsmenschen*] are enfolded, it is said, in a gossamer cocoon of mist, imagination, dreaminess, and subjunctives . . . When they are praised, these fools are sometimes called idealists, but this obviously covers only the weaker variant of the species that has no grasp of reality to begin with or sulkily avoids it – the variant in which the missing sense of reality, in other words, is actually a shortcoming. But the possible extends beyond the dreams of mentally deficient persons. It extends also to the aspirations of God that have yet to awaken [*die noch nicht erwachten Absichten Gottes*].

---

[15] Musil actually read the *Logical Syntax* and considered proposing it (somewhat ironically) as the 'best new book of the year' of 1934 in response to a query from a literary magazine.

CHAPTER 2

The intellectual inheritance: positivism and Kantianism

Kant and Goethe were the fixed points of the German intellectual firmament in Carnap's generation. Both had to be absorbed and digested by anyone with pretensions to *Bildung*.[1] And both were common property among the factions; the two antagonistic traditions heroically or perversely combined by the young Carnap each had their own versions of Kant and Goethe. One theme in the following two chapters will be the exact sense in which the young Carnap can be called a 'Kantian'. As we will see in the present chapter, that is not a straightforward question; a wide range of philosophies offered themselves as Kantian or neo-Kantian, including some now classified as 'positivist'. Before we can begin with Carnap's own development, then, we must cast a glance at the intellectual surroundings he grew up in, particularly the aspects of Kant that made such widely divergent interpretations possible, and the subsequent rise of various neo-Kantian schools (such as the so-called 'Marburg school') following the Kant revival in the 1850s by the great physicist and physiologist Hermann von Helmholtz. As we will see, the ambition to create a scientific philosophy was widely felt on both sides of the divide – among positivists no less than among neo-Kantians. But no new synthesis was forthcoming; the obstacles were too great.

POSITIVISM

Even before he went to university, as we saw, Carnap had been influenced by Ernst Haeckel, whose side he had taken in a school discussion group. It was an exciting time to be in Jena. Haeckel had just founded the German Monist Association there in 1906, attracting much attention. A professor of comparative anatomy in Jena, he had previously made himself notorious as the

---

[1] Gustav Mahler always carried *Wilhelm Meisters Wanderjahre* with him on concert tours, for instance, and read aloud from the *Critique of Pure Reason* to Alma when she was in labour.

pre-eminent importer of Darwin's ideas into Germany. At a 1904 congress of free-thinkers in Rome, he had been ceremonially named the 'anti-pope'. Now, since the phenomenal success of his book *The World-Riddles* (*Die Welträtsel*) (1899), criticisms of Haeckel's reckless impiety issued forth from every corner of German intellectual life, especially from theologians. In this book, Haeckel had sought to refute Emil Dubois-Reymond's (1872) diagnosis of 'The Limits of our Knowledge of Nature'. Within the mechanistic framework, Dubois-Reymond had argued, there were certain ineluctable limits to scientific knowledge. Later (1880), partly in answer to an attack of Haeckel's on his earlier article, he had listed seven unsolved 'world-riddles'.[2] Haeckel's *Welträtsel*, without challenging mechanism, declared all seven of them soluble. His case was rhetorically persuasive, or at least provocative, to a wide public, but was not regarded as convincing by most scientists or philosophers.[3] The declaration of '*ignorabimus*' ('we will never know') by Dubois-Reymond, a leading scientist and close friend of Helmholtz, had given ammunition to all the romantic, mystical, anti-scientific currents of Wilhelmine Germany; Haeckel's rebuttal correspondingly drew their ire. The religious biologist Johannes Reinke, for instance, demanded in the upper house of the German parliament that the newly founded Monist Association be banned (Eisler 1910, p. 144). But for all this controversy, the young Carnap evidently had no hesitation about where he stood.

Of greater influence on his thinking, however, was Haeckel's successor as head of the Monist Association, Wilhelm Ostwald, who was awarded the Nobel Prize in Chemistry in 1909 for his work on catalysis, chemical equilibrium, and the speed of chemical reactions. Though Mach and Haeckel were still alive, and still writing, it was Ostwald, above all, who continued their tradition – of scientific thinking as an integral and vigorous part of general culture – into the twentieth century. In 1906, at the age of fifty, he had resigned his Leipzig professorship and began devoting himself full time to his 'project of enlightenment' (Ostwald 1908, Preface), with a ferocious energy over an astonishing range of activities. He took over the chairmanship of the Monist Association in 1909. In his lectures on *Naturphilosophie*,

---

[2] (1) the nature of matter and energy; (2) the origin of motion; (3) the origin of life; (4) the apparently purposeful arrangement of nature; (5) the origins of simple perceptions and of consciousness; (6) the origin of language and of rational thought; (7) the apparent freedom of the human will. Of these, he thought (3), (4), and (6) difficult though soluble, in the light of Darwin's new theory; (1), (2), and (5) he thought insoluble; (7) he discussed at length but without a definite resolution.

[3] His main device for explaining the origin of sensation and consciousness, for instance, was to attribute a kind of primitive volition and proto-consciousness to elementary particles. As Dubois-Reymond himself had already pointed out (1880, pp. 71–2), this did nothing in itself, without further explanation, to solve the problem.

considered important enough by Lenin to be subject to detailed refutation in *Materialism and Empirio-Criticism*, he had consciously tried to revive the idea of a *Naturphilosophie* and rescue it from its idealist associations. In 1902 he founded a periodical, the *Annalen der Naturphilosophie*, and was able to persuade a glittering array of well-known scientists to contribute, as well as many promising younger thinkers. (Philipp Frank's first publication appeared there (1907) as did, in its very last issue (1921), the *Tractatus Logico-Philosophicus*.) Ostwald also included an extensive book review section in each issue, nearly all written by himself, that covered an enormous variety of scientific, philosophical, and socio-political fields, from Marx to William James to technical monographs on scientific subjects. He also founded the famous *Ostwalds Klassiker der Naturwissenschaften*, perhaps the best-known series of scientific classics ever published, and again was able to persuade leading scientists from all fields to select important texts, introduce them, and annotate them for non-specialist readers.

Ostwald was a far more sophisticated thinker, and a more important scientist, than Haeckel, but his more general and philosophical writings often did not match the care and rigour of his work in physical chemistry. Unlike Haeckel, he responded to Dubois-Reymond's challenge by attacking the mechanical world view itself head on. He did this at one of the plenary sessions of the 1895 annual meeting of the German Society of Scientists and Physicians in Lübeck with a programmatic talk entitled 'Overcoming Scientific Materialism' (Ostwald 1895). The reification of matter and its hypostatisation as the sole reality in the mechanical world view, he said, had been understandable in the seventeenth century, but was ultimately a metaphysical superstition that was becoming less and less plausible every year. No comprehensive mechanical explanation had been forthcoming for heat, radiation, electricity, magnetism, or chemical reactions (Ostwald 1895, p. 16). It was very doubtful that there was an ether of the kind required as a medium to propagate electromagnetic waves (Ostwald 1895, p. 18). In the twenty-three years since Dubois-Reymond's famous talk, Ostwald continued, none of its critics had questioned its main premise – mechanism. This, Ostwald maintained, is why no one had been able to refute him. 'But if this foundation collapses, and we have seen that it must, then the *ignorabimus* falls with it, and science once again has free rein' (Ostwald 1895, pp. 19–20). What Ostwald proposed as a replacement of mechanism was his own doctrine of 'energeticism', in which energy replaced matter as the single substance of the world, and became the basis of his monism. Though this doctrine played a brief role for a few years after 1895 in stimulating the development of thermodynamics (Hiebert 1971, p. 68; Deltete 1999), it is now regarded as an eccentric curiosity. Indeed, Ostwald's energeticist ideas are less remembered than Boltzmann's (1896) and Planck's (1896) refutations of them.

For all his rather fanatical attachment to 'energeticism', however, Ostwald's broader philosophical perspective was very much that of classical positivism in the French and English style. Though well read in the German classics and of broad culture, he had a scientist's contempt for the specifically philosophical tradition since Kant. The 'system of the sciences' at the basis of his *Naturphilosophie* was explicitly identified with that of the positivist tradition descended from Comte. Ostwald's enthusiasm went far beyond the borrowing of ideas; he became so fascinated with Comte himself that he wrote a biography of him (Ostwald 1914a), and also translated and edited the early essay Comte referred to as his *opuscule fondamentale*, the 'Plan of the Scientific Work Necessary for the Reorganisation of Society' (Comte 1822). As we will see in Chapter 3, there is good reason to think that Ostwald's (and thus Comte's) conception of a 'system of the sciences' had a significant influence on Carnap's early efforts to construct such a system.

Haeckel and Ostwald saw their monism, then, as the direct heir of the genuine, radical Enlightenment of the *Encyclopédistes* that had been handed down, in direct apostolic succession, via Condorcet, to the 'ideologues' during the French Revolution (Baker 1975, pp. 112ff.), thence to Saint-Simon, and finally to Comte. The German version of the Enlightenment, the *Aufklärung*, was held to be a pale shadow of this great tradition. Its leading figures – Gottsched, Wolff, Lessing, Nicolai, Kant – had been careful not to offend the authorities too brusquely. They had contented themselves with a muffled version of the Parisian original. Even Kant, whose answer to the question 'What is Enlightenment?' is perhaps even now the most widely cited text on that question, fell short in their eyes.

Kant had undeniably, they thought, been a Janus-faced figure. Facing in the western direction (toward Edinburgh, London, and Paris), he certainly shared certain 'Enlightenment' sympathies, broadly speaking. He regarded Newtonian science as the paradigm of knowledge and had little patience with widespread eighteenth-century conceptions of teleological providence or natural religion. However, he also seemed to face in a nearly opposite, anti-'Enlightenment' direction, which was to prove at least equally influential. He had explicitly announced in the introduction to the *Critique of Pure Reason*, after all, that he had 'had to limit knowledge to make room for faith' (Kant 1787, BXXX; PT p. 117). And his dualism of the 'intelligible' and 'sensible' worlds, especially in the *Critique of Judgement*, had become the foundation for German Idealism and Historicism, and thus opened the notorious abyss between the natural and human sciences in the nineteenth century that broke apart the (*Encyclopédiste*) Enlightenment consensus on the unity of knowledge.

Kant's ambivalence with respect to the Enlightenment and scientific thinking was a commonplace among late nineteenth-century philosophers, even among many who called themselves 'neo-Kantian', such as Lange, Paulsen, or Vaihinger. It was certainly a commonplace among the Monists. One of its more vivid expressions is to be found in Haeckel's famous book on the 'world-riddles', where he compares the scientific monist 'Kant I' to the anti-scientific dualist 'Kant II'. When this philosopher, 'the most highly regarded modern thinker', is praised, Haeckel says, it is essential to clarify whether Kant I or Kant II is meant, and he helpfully supplies a table in two columns, contrasting Kant I on the left with Kant II on the right, point for point (Haeckel 1899, p. 415; omitted from PT).

KANT'S TWO LEGACIES

A convenient way of marking this ambivalence is provided by Kant's own metaphor of the 'Copernican revolution'. One of Kant's signal philosophical achievements was a genuine Copernican revolution along the lines he himself describes (Miles 2006), the incorporation at the most general level of the observer into the observed process – of the human knower, that is, into the theory of knowledge:

Up to now it has been assumed that all our knowledge must conform to the objects; but all attempts on this basis to find out something about them a priori through concepts, something that would extend our knowledge, came to nothing. So let us see, for once, whether we can make better progress in the tasks of metaphysics by assuming that the objects have to conform to our knowledge. This certainly better accommodates the required possibility of a priori knowledge of them, giving us knowledge of objects before they are given to us. This case has the same character as the first thoughts of *Copernicus*, who, after making little progress in the explanation of celestial motions when he assumed that the entire celestial host revolves around the observer, tried to see whether he could not do better by letting the observer revolve, and leaving the stars in peace. (Kant 1787, B XVI; PT p. 110)

It is fair to regard this 'Copernican revolution' as setting the agenda, in one way or another, for much of philosophy for the next century or two. Certainly it set the agenda for Carnap, as we shall see. But Kant's way of carrying out this programme carried within it the seeds of future dissension. His legacy splintered into many contending schools in the generation after him, with each party claiming to represent (or diagnose, or overcome) the true Kant. These contending parties can be grouped, very roughly, by their attitude toward the 'Copernican revolution'. On the one side were those (mainly scientists and mathematicians, but also a few philosophers such as Fries and Herbart) who regarded it as a challenge or a programme for scientific and mathematical research, so as to be able to understand it naturalistically. On the other side were those, especially German idealists, historicists, and *Naturphilosophen*, who saw the 'Copernican revolution' not as a step toward a more naturalistic epistemology, but rather as a return to a more organic and anthropomorphic conception of nature, restoring the human perspective to cognitive sovereignty rather than regarding it as part of larger natural processes. This side saw Kant's central achievement as not a 'Copernican revolution', but an 'anti-Copernican counter-revolution'. It is probably fair (though of course controversial) to say that Kant's texts lend themselves to each of these two interpretations and continuations, and that there is an anthropomorphic dimension even to the 'Copernican revolution' itself. Within Kant's own intricate system, the two strands of his legacy that were to fall out so spectacularly in the following generation were inextricably entwined. Indeed, it could be said that the leading lights on both sides sought to explicate or reinterpret Kant precisely so as to *extricate* the 'Copernican revolution' from the 'anti-Copernican counter-revolution' (or vice versa). The following sketch has no ambition of wading into the shark-infested waters of Kant interpretation, but merely to indicate how such radically divergent interpretations were possible and, in a way, inevitable.[4]

The 'Copernican revolution'

One thing Kant had seen more clearly than his predecessors was that syllogistic logic was inadequate to account for the reasoning that led from Euclid's axioms to Euclid's theorems (Friedman 1992). So to answer the question 'How is pure mathematics possible?' not only the axioms of time and space had to be accounted for, Kant thought, but the reasoning that led from axioms to theorems also needed to be explained and justified. His solution, given in his language of human mental faculties, had two parts. The

---

[4] The secondary literature on Kant is, of course, vast. In the present sketch I have been guided largely by the writings of Michael Friedman and by Graham Bird's new comprehensive commentary on the first Critique, *The Revolutionary Kant* (2006); these readings appear now to supersede the more traditional interpretations by Strawson, Adickes, and others. However, given the need to fit the picture of Kant sketched here into an early twentieth-century context, the Kant interpretations of various neo-Kantians, especially Lange, Vaihinger, Natorp, and Cassirer, have also been taken into account.

first part concerned the axioms of space and time. These, Kant said, were imposed on the substrate of the world – whatever was out there, the *Ding an sich* (thing in itself) – by the structure of our sensory apparatus (the 'pure forms of intuition' arrived at in his transcendental aesthetic). The second part concerned the reasoning from axioms to theorems. Since pure syllogistic logic was inadequate to account for this reasoning, Kant thought it could not be purely 'analytic', but must result from the ability of the human intellect to 'synthesise' or bind together not only various observations into empirical concepts, but also empirical concepts into theoretical concepts. The human intellect could, in Kant's (1783, §36, p. 77; PT p. 111) terms, construct 'formal nature' ('the sum-total of the rules governing all appearances') from 'material nature' ('the sum-total of appearances'). This was Kant's double-barrelled 'Copernican revolution'; our scientific knowledge results from observations, necessarily projected by our sensory apparatus into a certain (precisely specifiable) framework of space and time, gathered and synthesised by our intellects into concepts and mathematical theories.

In this framework, Humean scepticism was accommodated while the security and objectivity of Newtonian science – *relative* to the world of appearance – was preserved. The link between the ultimate reality to which we have no access and its aspect facing toward our human-specific perceptual apparatus has for Kant (as it had for Berkeley) the nature of a *sign* or symbol, since it does not *resemble* its 'original'. The symbolic perceptual language in which we grasp the sensible aspect of inaccessible reality is *constituted* by certain structural parameters of our perceptual apparatus, the pure forms of intuition, which are thus *fixed* features of the world of appearance (the aspect facing us, the only possible object of our knowledge). In addition to this, and quite separately from it, we assemble and give *form* to (impose *patterns* on) the signs so received, by means of our *intellectual* apparatus, which shapes the rather chaotic world of signs mediated by 'material' nature into 'formal' nature. Kant's synthesis, then, required his dichotomy between intuition (*Anschauung*) and understanding (*Verstand*), neither of which was complete in itself: 'Thoughts without content are empty; intuitions without concepts are blind' (Kant 1787, B75; PT pp. 193–4).

This 'Copernican revolution', though originally stated (and at first interpreted) largely in the psychologistic language of mental faculties,[5] lent itself,

---

[5] For Kant's own purposes (whether or not a parallel version of Kant's system could be developed without this feature), 'thoughts' and 'concepts' are two-sided; they are *both* human faculties *and* the objective content generated or manipulated by those faculties: 'the job of the senses is to intuit, that of the understanding is to think. To think is to unify mental images [*Vorstellungen*] within a consciousness' (Kant 1783, §22, p. 61; PT p. 98). Gary Hatfield concedes that, despite Kant's efforts

over the course of the nineteenth century, to non-psychologistic reinter-pretation. This proceeded on two fronts, corresponding to the two parts of Kant's system: (1) the *axioms* of geometry (and of mathematical science more generally) had to be decoupled from intuition, and (2) *deduction* had to be decoupled from the 'synthetic' activity of the intellect. The latter project was essentially the task of logicism; intellectual 'synthesis' became dispensable as the basis of deduction once the logical and mathematical system became a (more or less) gap-free system of mechanical procedures, one that the human intellect could follow (and use, to discover and under-stand results), but which did not *require* human intellection to operate or to guarantee its accuracy and reliability. For if logic is understood in this Fregean sense, then it *does* make possible each step of the reasoning from axioms to theorems – just what Kant had discovered syllogistic logic unable to do. Frege's own primary intentions or motivations, as far as we can now reconstruct them, seem not to have included the elimination of Kantian 'synthesis'. But his polemics against 'psychologism' – of which he offered a more precise concept than the philosophical literature since Herbart[6] – provided a model for distinguishing more generally between subjective mental grasp or production ('synthesis') of deductive relations and their objective validity, independent of any human mind or conviction.

In any case Frege's own philosophical views are not canonical or nor-mative for the overall development in the late nineteenth century of what Howard Stein calls 'a second birth' of mathematics.[7] There were many aspects to this movement of ideas: geometry came to be understood in terms of groups of transformations, and was progressively axiomatised; analysis became comprehensible in terms of natural numbers. These and

---

to separate 'transcendental psychology' from 'empirical psychology' (Hatfield 1990, pp. 84–7), in 'his account of the possibility and limits of knowledge, Kant adopted the psychological vocabulary of his contemporaries' (Hatfield 1990, p. 83). And this was how Kant was generally understood; according to Hatfield, 'virtually every reading of the [first] *Critique* in the first hundred years after its publication was "psychological" in one way or another'; he includes not only Fries and Herbart, but also Fichte and Hegel in this diagnosis (Hatfield 1990, p. 110).

6   To whom Hatfield (1990, p. 118) attributes the first articulation of a notion of 'psychologism', especially in relation to Kant. Certainly Herbart's textbook of 1813 clearly distinguishes mental faculty from content: 'All of our thoughts can be regarded from two sides; on the one hand as an activity of our mind, on the other with respect to *what* is thought by it. In the latter perspective they are called *concepts* [*Begriffe*] which, as it designates what is *grasped* [das *Begriffene*; the intended coordination is lost in English], reminds us to abstract from the ways and means by which we receive, produce, or reproduce the thought' (Herbart 1813, pp. 81–2).

7   'Mathematics underwent, in the nineteenth century, a transformation so profound that it is not too much to call it a second birth of the subject – its first birth having occurred among the ancient Greeks . . . As to the "second birth", I have to emphasise that it is *of the very same subject*' (Stein 1988). See also Tappenden (2006).

many other developments had what I am here calling the 'logicist' tendency of integrating large parts of mathematics into a single logical system whose basis was something simpler and more elementary than the natural numbers themselves. As this integration progressed, the Kantian invocation of intellectual 'synthesis' as the basis for mathematical deduction looked more and more superfluous.

But this entire effort of decoupling deduction from 'synthesis' was only one of *two* nineteenth-century projects that explicated and naturalised Kant's 'Copernican revolution'. The other project – decoupling the axioms from intuition – was equally important. It too began with scientific and technical developments whose philosophical implications were long not made explicit. These were of two very different kinds: First, the development of non-Euclidean geometries by Gauss, Bolyai, and Lobachevsky – alongside the (perhaps equally important, but at first quite separate) development of projective geometry. Of perhaps even greater importance, though, was a development that actually goes back to Kant himself, and specifically to his 'Copernican revolution'.

The 'Copernican revolution' was something quite new on the philosophical scene; there had been nothing like it in the (*Encyclopédiste*) Enlightenment framework of ideas. Nor had it been assimilated by the western heirs of that tradition; it played no role whatever in the positivism developing in France and England. Where it did play a central role was in Germany; it had set the agenda for the first generation of investigators in what can appropriately be called 'naturalistic epistemology' – early nineteenth-century German physiology of sense perception. The leading figure was Johannes Müller, whose student Hermann von Helmholtz carried on his work, and associated it explicitly with Kant's 'Copernican revolution' as the foundation of a more general world view continuous with the Enlightenment. It was Helmholtz's 1855 lecture 'On Human Vision' that finally brought the western Enlightenment or positivist stream of thought (which had by then become widespread among scientists even in Central Europe) together with Kant's 'Copernican revolution'. The philosophical 'neo-Kantianism' inspired by this lecture (Köhnke 1986, pp. 151ff.; PT pp. 96ff.) can be regarded as the beginning of a distinctively German or Kantian version of positivism, exemplified by such figures as Benno Erdmann, Richard Avenarius, Hans Vaihinger, Friedrich Albert Lange, Friedrich Paulsen, and others. In their writings, as in Helmholtz's, Kant was portrayed as very much a part of the mainstream Enlightenment. Lange, for instance, sought to complete what, in his view, Kant had intended but left only half finished: 'to destroy metaphysics' (Lange used the word 'metaphysics' much as the

Vienna Circle later would; he meant by it particularly the 'scholasticism' to which he thought Hegel had 'regressed'):

I regard every sort of metaphysics as a kind of madness, with only an aesthetic and subjective justification. My logic is the calculus of probabilities, my ethics are social statistics [*die Moralstatistik*], my psychology rests entirely on physiology; I seek, in short, to remain entirely within the exact sciences. (quoted by Köhnke (1986), p. 233; PT p. 151)

These first neo-Kantians wanted to found a 'scientific philosophy', and in the first issue of their new journal – the *Quarterly Journal of Scientific Philosophy* (*Vierteljahrsschrift für wissenschaftliche Philosophie*) – its editor Avenarius spoke for the whole movement when he suggested that philosophy must rid itself of 'those unconscionable pseudo-problems [*Scheinprobleme*]' that had dogged philosophy throughout its history: 'Without it ever being asked whether these questions have a legitimate origin, they reproduce themselves down the generations in traditional philosophy, creating nothing but confusion and a waste of energy' (quoted by Köhnke (1986), p. 391; PT p. 254).

The 'anti-Copernican counter-revolution'

This entire tradition of post-Helmholtz scientific philosophy can plausibly be regarded, then, as a legacy of Kant's 'Copernican revolution'. But Kant's nineteenth-century influence extended in other directions as well, including those we included above under the label of an 'anti-Copernican counter-revolution', which exploited the anthropomorphic or anthropocentric dimension in Kant's system. The main feature of Kant's thought that made this anti-Copernican heritage possible was the unknowability in principle of ultimate reality, the *Ding an sich*. This leads directly to an important departure in Kant's thought from the *Encyclopédiste* Enlightenment, which had striven to take the new knowledge provided by Newtonian and post-Newtonian science literally, and to seek out its direct, unmediated implications and applications for practice, for belief, for social, cultural, and political life. Kant returned, in this respect, to an earlier – Cartesian and Leibnizian – preference for a foundation, a framework or structure of ideas and concepts not themselves part of our knowledge of the world, but essential to the correct understanding of that knowledge. He returned to a framework or structure, that is, of 'first philosophy' – though not in the Cartesian sense (perhaps more in Aristotle's original sense). Though Kant retained the Cartesian idea of a metaphysics of nature, he also greatly diminished its importance. What he did retain was the essential idea of an integrative framework, indispensable to the correct understanding of the *place* of scientific knowledge in the larger scheme of things. Perhaps it is not quite appropriate to call this 'first philosophy' any more; the Cartesian ideal of *deriving* all science from first principles is marginalised. But in another way the appellation 'first philosophy' still seems right (as the logical empiricists would have agreed), since the framework in which we are to understand science is given by the overall perspective in which Kant diagnoses the (synthetic or analytic, *a priori* or *a posteriori*) status of various kinds of knowledge – a transcendental or meta-scientific perspective whose canons of reasoning (*Vernunft*) were ultimately not constrained by science itself.

These features made Kant's framework very attractive to those who were opposed to the *Encyclopédiste* way of thinking, who felt threatened by the unrestricted scope of science, the idea of the 'unity of science'. Many were appalled at Buffon's argument, for instance, that human beings were part of the animal kingdom, and that animals were part of the material world, governed by laws of nature (though of course Aristotle's conception had not been far from this). Many of Voltaire's, Hume's, and Diderot's writings, and many articles in the *Encyclopédie*, addressed the moral, political, and spiritual consequences of the prospect that such natural explanations would be forthcoming. The project of the *Encyclopédie* itself grew out of the conviction that the whole of knowledge, in all its departments, had to be cleansed and reinvented in the new framework of the Newtonian–Lockean philosophy. On this basis there could then be a mutual interpenetration of theoretical and practical knowledge to further the material and cognitive progress of humanity.[8]

It is perhaps not surprising that this new picture, frightening and unfamiliar in many respects (as it still is!), did not remain fashionable among European intellectuals for long. They soon demanded a buffer against the impact of science, and the Kantian philosophy seemed to offer such a buffer. The whole blame for these later uses of Kant's ideas should not be laid at Kant's own door, especially since they were often combined with other ideas, especially those of his erstwhile students Herder and Fichte (both of whom he had attacked in print) and of Goethe, who eloquently articulated the German and romantic rebellion against Newtonian science and its spiritual consequences. So although Kant himself is not wholly to blame for these uses, his ideas did play a central role in the general retreat from the Enlightenment's effort to frame a scientific world view, and in

---

[8] d'Alembert *Preliminary Discourse* (1751) e.g. pp. 42–3; see also the translator's footnote 59 on p. 49.

the effort (which he would have deprecated strongly) to insulate or cushion the familiar *Lebenswelt* from any sort of direct confrontation with the burgeoning enterprise of knowledge.

This basic post-Kantian strategy for insulating the familiar *Lebenswelt* from direct confrontation with science is still with us. It was not confined to German idealism or historicism. It survives, for instance, in John McDowell's contrast (taken from Wilfrid Sellars) between a 'realm of law' and a 'space of reasons' (McDowell 1996),[9] or in Richard Rorty's denial that 'the natural scientist gets closer to the way things are in themselves than the carpenter, the moralist, or the literary critic' (Rorty 1998, p. 38). The 'way things are in themselves' continues to play the central negative role in these views, long after the underlying Kantian and post-Kantian apparatus has wilted away.

During much of the first half of the nineteenth century, idealism dominated German philosophy and even for a while, in the form of Schelling's *Naturphilosophie*, German science. By the 1840s, however, the positivist current among western scientists had spread to Germany. The result was a progressive alienation between science and philosophy, which Helmholtz saw it as his role to overcome. And he succeeded, to the extent that a generation of post-Helmholtz scientific neo-Kantians, espousing a new form of positivism, had by the 1880s gained a foothold even in German philosophy departments. It was not to be expected, however, that philosophers could tolerate such an austere doctrine for very long. By the end of the century, the neo-Kantian movement had backed away from it, yielding once again to the attractions of 'first philosophy'. Friedrich Albert Lange, who had obtained a chair in Marburg not long before his tragically early death, was succeeded there in 1876 by Hermann Cohen, who was soon joined by Paul Natorp. Their 'Marburg school' of neo-Kantianism (which counted Ernst Cassirer among its illustrious students), though nominally loyal to Lange and Kant, was (as Moritz Schlick would point out[10]) in some ways closer in spirit to Hegel.

NEO-KANTIANISM: HELMHOLTZ AND THE MARBURG SCHOOL

The Marburg school was clearly of significance in Carnap's early development; the names of Natorp and Cassirer are invoked frequently

---

[9] Oddly, Sellars framed this distinction within Carnap's semantical framework, which he however misunderstood quite seriously; see Carus (2004). McDowell's claim that he is building on the Kantian tradition is disputed by Friedman (1996).

[10] In a review of Natorp's book *Die logischen Grundlagen der exakten Wissenschaften* (Schlick 1911, p. 257).

in his notes and even in his early publications. As we will see later, it is sometimes difficult to determine exactly what form the influence took. To assist that discussion in the two following chapters, the present section will focus on aspects of the Marburg view that arose in direct confrontation with the preceding generation of (scientific) neo-Kantians, especially Helmholtz himself.

Helmholtz

From the Marburg perspective, the Helmholtzian view left no room for meta-theoretical discourse:

Taken as an expression of the 'species-specific organization [of the nervous system]', the a priori truths become a special class of psycho-physical 'realities'. But they are thereby inescapably integrated with and subordinated to the conditions of the knowledge of reality, rather than being able themselves to ground and criticize this knowledge. (Cassirer 1912, p. 255)

For Cohen and his students, the discourse in which they sought to discuss scientific knowledge, a kind of discourse that is 'able . . . to ground and criticize this knowledge', could not be 'inescapably integrated with and subordinated to the conditions of the knowledge of reality'. Any meta-science or philosophy must be *first* philosophy; it must come *before* 'knowledge of reality' and could not be 'integrated with' or 'subordinated to' it.

   For Kant, the possibility of such a 'superordinate' realm of discourse ('metaphysics') had rested on the existence of genuine synthetic a priori knowledge, of which, he had assumed, pure mathematics and pure natural science were clear examples. But now the analysis of perception carried out by Helmholtz and others had cast those clear examples in doubt, by showing that perception itself did not automatically supply or presuppose any particular axioms of geometry or mechanics.

   Helmholtz had agreed with Kant (and Berkeley) that the qualities as 'given' to us in experience are produced by our nervous systems in response to some external object or process to which we have no direct access. They give us not a 'picture [*Abbild*]' of their respective objects, whatever those are, but rather a 'sign [*Zeichen*]'. Recent advances in physiological optics and acoustics, then, reinforced Kant's 'Copernican revolution'. Specifically, they had shown that the qualities produced in conscious experience depended on the type of nerve cell conducting them, not on the category of external stimulus.[11]

---

[11] This 'law of specific nerve energies', propounded by Helmholtz's teacher Johannes Müller, remains a cornerstone of perceptual physiology (Gregory 1998, p. 97).

Helmholtz's own research, building on this insight, had shown how much processing remained to be done to produce a world of reasonably stable objects in time and space out of these qualitative raw materials. The phenomena of perceptual constancy could not be explained by afferent nerve impulses alone, but evidently involved the *construction* of an *integrative* representation of the environment using perceptual inputs as constraints. This construction requires many sorts of conscious and unconscious (or pre-conscious) inference. The perceptual constraints supply the parameters of a vast learning process, in infancy, by which specific nerve-cell responses to different wavelengths of sound and light are put together, with other stimuli, into an integrated internal representation of external processes. Then as language and thought are added, in childhood, the representation is completed by cultural and individual creative processes, e.g. of inductive inference, extrapolative and interpolative. The culturally transmitted enterprise of science is a more precise and self-conscious extension and articulation of this creative process.

On the surface it might seem that Helmholtz's discoveries reinforce not only Kant's 'Copernican revolution', then, but also the transcendental aesthetic and the 'pure forms of intuition'. But for Helmholtz the mere perceptual qualities themselves do not supply enough inherent structure to impose binding constraints on the explicitly articulate *science* of objects in space and time. The axioms of geometry and mechanics are not forced on us by our perceptual systems, Helmholtz maintained, but can be chosen self-consciously by us to maximise the fit between our scientific theories and the observations or experiments we undertake to confirm or test them. The 'forms of intuition' are simply the qualitative 'feel' of sense perceptions to our subjectivity, including their qualitative spatiality and temporality:

Kant's doctrine of the a priori given forms of intuition is a very happy and clear expression of the actual relations. But these forms must be empty of content, and must be free enough to accommodate any content whatever that is capable of occupying the relevant form of perception. But the axioms of geometry limit the spatial form of intuition so that every thinkable content can no longer be accommodated within it . . . (quoted by Koenigsberger 1903, vol. 2, p. 160)

Tools developed by Gauss and Riemann for the exploration (*Auffindung*) of all logically possible consistent geometries had shown that we have considerable liberty in defining spatial relations. And, Helmholtz argued, Lipschitz had demonstrated 'the transferability of the general principles of mechanics to such [non-Euclidean] spaces . . . so that the series of sense impressions that would be generated in them can be completely given, whereby the intuitability of such spaces . . . is shown' (Helmholtz 1878a, p. 235, PT p. 354; he illustrated this qualitatively for a particular case with his story of the mirror-world in Helmholtz 1870).[12] Thus, by empirically and conceptually analysing the perceptual process that Kant had still regarded as simple and unanalysable (and thus also as fixed), we are able to move beyond Kant and see that although qualitative spatiality itself is synthetic a priori, no particular geometry is.

The structure we discern in experience, then, is put there by us, as Kant had said, though not built *in* to experience in the fixed and inescapable way Kant had described. We impose structure on experience in flexible and adaptive ways (whether consciously or pre-consciously) that allow us to revise our impositions in response to external stimuli and internal desiderata. These higher-level impositions or constructions – from ordinary concrete physical objects generated by largely unconscious processing to the patterns we hypothetically extrapolate by precise and deliberate scientific theories – are constrained by the lower-level qualitative inputs, but go beyond them. We give names to these patterns, treat them mentally just like ordinary physical objects or processes; we call them magnetic fields or sound waves, and can use these 'objects' in predicting and manipulating our environment just as effectively as, or even more effectively than, we use ordinary physical objects.

On the other hand we *also* now know, Helmholtz said, how our visual and auditory organs respond to and process those waves and fields. We can thus distinguish a 'reality' that is 'behind' the qualities we subjectively perceive. This 'reality', even if we have no qualitative access to it, is just as applicable to practical tasks as the concrete physical objects generated pre-consciously by our perceptual systems. We have no idea of the ultimate, essential nature of this 'reality'; we know only the patterns among the observable qualities. But we can also *relate* these patterns to the *production* of qualities by our sensory systems. Just as *within* the qualitative world we can cross-check the reports of one sensory system by those of another to distinguish exogenous from endogenous reports (or can internally cross-check a single sensory system by transporting our viewpoint to achieve different perspectives), so we can cross-check our sensory sign system as a *whole* against the processes exciting it, and determine whether the patterns

---

[12] Helmholtz himself, of course, did not think that *all* the possible spaces envisaged by Riemann were candidates for physical geometry, but only those of constant curvature; see Helmholtz 1870 and the discussion in Friedman 1997, pp. 33–5. When he refers to 'such spaces' in the quotation above, he thus means only non-Euclidean spaces of constant curvature.

we observe in the 'reality' issue from within the sensory system itself or from an extra-sensory environment.

So although we have no idea what the object of our perceptions ultimately 'is', Helmholtz says, we know that its behaviour must be *structurally* analogous to whatever it is that our sensory systems respond to. And because our conscious and unconscious impositions on the system of perceptual signs are not fixed but revisable, we can triangulate from different perspectives on the patterns we discern in those signs. This gives us reason to think that the patterns reside at least partly in the objects or processes (whatever they are) in *response to which* our systems produce those signs, and not only in those systems themselves. So there is no completely inscrutable *Ding an sich*, as Kant had said. Our structural knowledge of sign-behaviours is genuine knowledge of an extra-sensory environment, whatever it is, not just a projection by an internal system. 'So even if our sense impressions in their qualities are only *signs*, whose special nature depends wholly on our internal organisation, they are nonetheless not to be dismissed as empty appearance, but are in fact a sign of *something*, whether it is something existing or something occurring; and what is most important, they can depict the *law* of this occurring' (Helmholtz 1878a, p. 227; PT p. 348).[13]

This turns 'Kantian humility' about the *Ding an sich* (Langton 1999) into a more specifically 'ontological humility' about the *qualitative* (and thus also substantial or essential) *nature* of the ultimate constituents of our world. It is no longer a theory of 'the' *Ding an sich*; it is a *rejection* of any such thing. It blocks the use of an inscrutable 'how things really are in themselves' as the basis of any 'anti-Copernican counter-revolution'. The 'antinomies of reason' invoked by Kant to argue that the *Ding an sich* was completely inscrutable are rediagnosed as conflicts between our

---

[13] The spirit of just this view was well expressed many years later by, for instance, Hermann Weyl (who actually refers back to Helmholtz in this context, though he uses modern axiomatic language): 'A science can determine its subject matter only up to an isomorphic representation. In particular, it is altogether indifferent toward the "essence" of its objects of study. What distinguishes the real points of space from number triples or other interpretations of geometry can only be *experienced* in immediate, live acquaintance . . . It is mysticism to expect of scientific knowledge that it reveal – to acquaintance – a deeper essence than that openly available to acquaintance. The conception of isomorphism pinpoints the unquestionable and ineluctable limit to knowledge' (Weyl 1926, p. 22). Weyl goes on, in this passage, also to describe a view of the *Ding an sich* that is very consistent with what Helmholtz had formulated half a century earlier. Although we do not know the 'essence' of the *Ding an sich* – whatever is behind the appearances – we know something about its structure, he says, since we know that the experienced world must be isomorphic to it. For (in Helmholtz's words, which he quotes here) 'if different perceptions urge themselves on us, we are justified in concluding that there is a difference in the real conditions' (Helmholtz 1878b, p. 656, quoted by Weyl 1926, p. 22). Weyl concludes, very much in Helmholtz's spirit, 'Though we are not *acquainted* with the things in themselves, we *know* as much about them as about the appearances'.

pre-scientific, intuitive conceptions[14] and our precise, scientific ones. So for Helmholtz our knowledge, though merely structural, takes *precedence* over our intuitive conceptions. There is no antinomy, since our knowledge has become a binding constraint on the development of other systems of thought, such as those for practical reason (which he thinks may require 'metaphysical' principles). Intuitions that conflict with our available knowledge must give way, and accommodate that knowledge, take it provisionally as given. This is just the criterion for 'Enlightenment' advanced at the beginning of this book. In Chapter 3 below, we will encounter this same attitude in the first philosophical notes of Carnap's to have been preserved.

The Marburg school

Cohen's response to this Helmholtzian programme was to concede that subjective intuition can impose no structure of its own. This meant abandoning the central Kantian idea that 'pure forms of intuition' (space and time) impose 'subjective condition[s] of sensibility' (Kant 1787, B42; PT p. 177) on our understanding. But instead of concluding from this, with Helmholtz, that there is *no* synthetic a priori knowledge of geometrical or other axioms, Cohen subordinated subjective intuition to the pattern-imposing 'synthetic' activity of the intellect. The work of the transcendental aesthetic was taken over by the categories of the understanding.

This might indeed appear almost to be a return to Hegelian idealism. Kant's entire dialectic between the two poles of his system, active intellect and passive experience, would appear to be undermined, as would his connecting link between sensibility and understanding. The 'myth of the given' was so completely rejected, in this view, that the raw material 'synthesised' by thought was all but *created* by thought. But although the Marburg school called its approach 'logical idealism', a distinction was maintained between a realm of experience (*Erfahrung*) and one of intellect (*Denken, Synthesis*). And although 'experience' in the sense in which Kant had taken it over from Locke and Hume – perception (*Wahrnehmung*) – was regarded as structureless and thus not constraining theory, something like its role in Kant's bipolar system was taken, for the Marburg school, by the experience codified into and subsumed by scientific theories. This they now called 'experience [*Erfahrung*]'. Thus for them Kant's two poles were now *both* located within what Kant himself had called 'intellect' or 'understanding'. One of them *they* called 'intellect' (transcendental logic, the spontaneous

---

[14] The word 'intuition' is used here in the modern colloquial sense, not in Kant's technical sense.

creation in thought of pure mathematics) and the other they called 'experience' (scientific theories). The 'empirical' element in the latter was now seen as a matter of progressively imposing categories of *thought* (such as 'factuality', 'concrete existence', 'location in space-time', etc.) onto the flux of qualitative, subjective sense experience – which is, notoriously, 'blind', and thus highly malleable by the synthetic faculty. The Marburg philosophers drove a wedge, that is, between Kant's 'perception [*Wahrnehmung*]' and his 'experience [*Erfahrung*]' (Kant 1783, §§18–20, pp. 53–8; PT pp. 92–6). Experience in this sense was largely *independent* of perception, whose role in knowledge became marginal. Kant's 'material' nature ('i.e. according to intuition, as the sum-total of appearances') was not abolished, but lost its independence, and its critical role of providing content to 'formal' nature ('as the sum-total of the rules governing all appearances, insofar as they are to be thought of as arranged into an experience'; Kant 1783, §36, p. 77; PT p. 111). Formal nature becomes independent of material nature and essentially steps into its role as the provider of empirical content to pure thought. So the Marburg school not only conceded to Helmholtz that perception cannot, as Kant claimed, impose a grammar of its own ('forms of pure intuition') on the world of experience; they went further, and turned this Kantian idea upside down. While Helmholtz thought material nature *constrained* the theoretical free creations of the intellect, singling out empirically reliable ones, the Marburg philosophers thought the understanding could progressively exhaust material nature, which they thus essentially *subsumed* within formal nature without residue. This is how space and time become – not forms of pure intuition, as in Kant, nor a matter of empirical physics, as in Helmholtz, but – categories of the understanding.[15]

Science is not *about* facts of perception, Cohen said, it is about certain constructs of the intellect, abstract objects that resemble nothing in our perceptual experience. Theory-independent facts, even if they were possible, would be entirely irrelevant to science. To begin with, the Marburg philosophers argued, following Poincaré, that sense experience does not

---

[15] Interestingly, Kant himself had warned against such a step, which he attributed to Plato, who, he wrote: 'no doubt had some inkling of the question . . . "How are synthetic statements a priori possible?" in an obscure sort of way. Had he guessed, back then, . . . that there are in fact a priori *intuitions*, but not of the human understanding, only *sensible* ones (under the name of space and time), and that therefore all objects of our senses are only appearances, and even their forms . . . are not those of the things themselves, but of our subjective sensibility, which therefore hold for objects of experience, but not one step further, then he would not have looked for pure intuition (which he needed, to make sense of synthetic a priori knowledge) in our god-like understanding and its original images of all essences, as independent objects, thus lighting the torch for wild speculation' (Kant 1796, p. 380; PT p. 433).

have the precision required by theory.[16] And 'factuality' is itself a category of *thought*:

> Reality, factuality is . . . a determination of thought, and one of highest complexity. Only the comprehensively determined would be an absolute fact; but comprehensive determination contradicts the incompletable character peculiar to empirical knowledge. Facts are not given, nor are they in the absolute sense even accessible to empirical knowledge. (Natorp 1904, p. 6)

There is no 'given', there are no 'facts' of perception, for what perception purports to reveal only gives the pursuit of scientific knowledge its *direction*. Knowledge is an *intellectual* function, the progressive unfolding of creative thought. Nor does this synthetic thought process *operate upon* 'given' or 'perceptual' elements. Kant had seen that genuine knowledge involved the synthetic creation of new concepts, but had undermined this 'radically idealist insight', in Natorp's view, by taking such synthesis to act upon (and bring to synthetic unity) mental representations (*Vorstellungen*), for he thereby portrayed them as 'given' and pre-existing prior to an act of synthesis (Natorp 1910, p. 46).

The facts of interest to science are not gained passively or receptively by the sensibility, in the Marburg view; they are *sought out* by the scientific intellect to answer questions of theory, and thus essentially created by theory.[17] The objects of scientific knowledge were thus explicitly equated with Platonic ideas; they were infinitely distant ideal points to which knowledge aspires (e.g. Natorp 1910, pp. 16ff., Natorp 1921, p. 426). Kant's manifold of experience was replaced by an idealised 'completed physics', to which human theories approximated more and more closely, but which they could never reach. The Marburg school called this view a 'genetic' conception of knowledge, in which our concepts (and categories) are not fixed but evolve over time and converge on, though they never reach, a perfect – ideal – fit with their (evolving) objects. Natorp summarised and reiterated this

---

[16] As Natorp put it, 'The quantitative as well as the qualitative determination of the sensible always remains . . . by its nature vague, for in every series of sense impressions (e.g. a tone or color series) the distance between the members of the series can be made so small that each member is indistinguishable from the one next to it in the series, but distinguishable from, say, the second or third in line from it. The very nature of the sensible thus excludes a definiteness of the sort required and posited by thought' (Natorp 1904, p. 5).

[17] In the first edition of his major work *Kants Theorie der Erfahrung* (Cohen 1871), Cohen concludes a paragraph on scientific experiment as follows: 'And so it turns out that the science that most loudly takes its stand on experience [i.e. natural science] in fact constructs that experience, and that it can only arrive at a priori knowledge through this *generation of experience* to its design' (p. 11; my emphasis). The case where an experiment *refutes* a theory was not considered; indeed, the first real attempt to justify this extremely rationalistic view of scientific facts with actual reference to experimental science was Chapter 5 of Cassirer's *Substance and Function* (1910).

conception in three answers to the objection, 'But are facts not after all determinate *in themselves*, even if they are not so for us?'

First, it is knowledge that must determine a fact in the first place; nothing is determinate for knowledge that knowledge has not itself determined. Second, only from the viewpoint of achieved knowledge does it make sense to talk about what might be determinate in itself, i.e. from the viewpoint of its final result, its infinitely distant goal. And third, since our knowledge always remains conditioned and limited, anything we might want to say about things determinate in themselves, from the standpoint of our knowledge, will always remain as conditional and limited in its validity as our knowledge more generally. (Natorp 1910, p. 97)

What remained of Kantian intuition (*Anschauung*) was an empty shell, leaving its trace in the *empirical* content of *theoretical* physics, accumulating along with changes in theory.[18] Obviously this idea faces (at least!) all the same challenges in identifying the 'empirical content' of theoretical physics as Carnap's (or Reichenbach's) later attempts to address this question – but with the additional handicap that the 'empirical' could only be defined by reference to the 'theoretical' itself; there is no independent factual realm (and not even, it seems, any room for empirical laws or generalisations – e.g. statistical correlations such as that between smoking and lung cancer).

Helmholtz's methodology of science (like that of most scientists, steeped as they were in the 'naturalistic' view Cohen was criticising) appeared, to the Marburg philosophers, to assume that the *objects* of science can be assumed to pre-exist: he presupposed that they were the objects we encounter 'receptively' in the world of subjective experience. But this fell back into the characteristic error of naturalism, they said, i.e. the error of presupposing theory-independent facts. The 'objects' of science, even of the science of perception, must be ideal objects, theoretical posits, constructions of the intellect (like electrons or gravitational fields). They could no more be the apparent objects of subjective perception, in the Marburg view, than science itself can be built from perceptions.[19]

The status of philosophy in this scheme was not straightforwardly foundational, as in Descartes or even vestigially in Kant; the Marburg

---

[18] Experiments, for Natorp, have no significance in the absence of theoretical questions: 'The experiment always answers a previously asked question, i.e. it decides a previously entertained hypothetical possibility' (Natorp 1910, p. 89).

[19] The object of scientific knowledge is seen as defined, at each stage, by the overall system of knowledge itself: '*What* is given can only be defined from the viewpoint of achieved knowledge' (Natorp 1904, p. 6). '"Things" . . . turns out more and more, the clearer it is grasped in its actual content, to be a metaphorical expression for law-governed, permanent interconnections among phenomena, and thus for the constancy and continuity of experience itself. To attain this substantiality and continuity (that is never fulfilled in any object perceptible to the senses), thought sees itself led to a hypothetical substratum of empirical being that has no other function, though, than to represent the enduring order within this being' (Cassirer 1910, pp. 366–7; PT pp. 276–7).

philosophers often warn against trying to pre-empt scientific findings by pure thought alone. The special task of philosophy was, rather, to 'assert the final unity of culture as against, or rather amidst, the whole variety of its special manifestations', and 'possibly even to find the law according to which it unfolds in all these different directions' (Natorp 1909, p. 217). This was to be found in Cohen's 'principle of the origin' (Natorp 1910, pp. 22–6), the synthetic unity of the intellect (Natorp 1910, pp. 26–7), to which the categories and the principles of science were ultimately to be traced. Sometimes, instead of 'unity of culture', the Marburg philosophers said 'unity of science [*Einheit der Wissenschaft*]' (Natorp 1909, p. 235). This is not to be confused with either d'Alembert's earlier, or the Vienna Circle's later, programmes of the 'unity of science'. The Marburg version of 'unity' extends only to knowledge that 'objectivizes', not also to knowledge requiring introspection (e.g. psychology; Natorp 1912, pp. 134 ff.), and philosophy has the task of adjudicating this boundary at the 'transcendental' meta-level (Natorp 1909, pp. 265ff.). (Even this degree of unity was too much for most contemporary neo-Kantians; see below, pp. 105–8. And Cassirer's later conception of 'symbolic forms' also put greater emphasis on the role of philosophy in delineating the *different* 'conceptions of truth' (Cassirer 1929) within different kinds of knowledge.)

So although philosophy did not itself *supply* the first principles of science, in this view, philosophy is indispensable to the right *understanding* of science, its place within the whole of culture. Philosophy gives us a framework of thought independent of, and prior to, science by which we can determine which 'conceptions of truth' or 'modes of knowing' are appropriate to which inquiries. This is what 'transcendental' meant, to the Marburg philosophers; '"transcendental" . . . is the name given by Kant to the way of looking at things that starts out not just with objects but also with our *way of knowing* objects in general' (Cassirer 1912, p. 255). And this transcendental discourse dealt mainly in synthetic a priori knowledge (synthesised by the intellect, not by pure intuition). Helmholtz, they thought, had failed to recognise this; his 'naturalistic' analysis of the human 'mode of knowledge [*Erkenntnisart*]' had missed the 'logical' presuppositions of any such explanation:

For it is always a certain category of objects and a certain form of interaction among them that has to be presupposed here to explain the process of knowledge. But the question about the being of the object remains indefinite and insoluble until there is an answer to the question about the kind of knowing on which what we know about the object depends. (Cassirer 1912, p. 255)

The 'kind of knowing' might, after all, be synthetic a priori. So philosophy (as *opposed to* science) was transcendental in this sense, and indispensable for a correct understanding of the unity of cultural striving, especially for a correct understanding of natural science within this unity: 'The actual object of *philosophy* is accordingly not the "organisation" of nature, nor that of the "mind"; its sole and original task is, rather, to determine and expose the "organisation" of *knowledge of nature* [*Naturerkenntnis*]' (Cassirer 1912, p. 255).[20]

What the transcendental method afforded, in particular, was a standpoint from which not only to criticise Helmholtz's methodological ideas, but also to show that he had misunderstood the wider significance of his physiological findings. The Marburg view, as we saw, required theories to be mathematical and left no room for empirical generalisations or statistical correlations. Empirical concepts appearing in such statements were to be regarded as resulting only from intellectual operations:

The 'facts' of natural science are henceforth valid only insofar as they can be guaranteed by certain and exact *judgements*. But this sort of certainty is only attainable if the particular scientific judgements are anchored in the general basic judgements of mathematics. The order of *certainty* proceeds from mathematics to physics, not the other way around. (Cassirer 1912, pp. 255–6)

So Helmholtz's physiological studies of perception could not have the significance he attributed to them; indeed, his claim that these findings undermined Kant's argument for the existence of synthetic a priori sentences rested on a vicious circle:

---

[20] Cassirer makes this fundamental difference between 'pure thought' in the realm of transcendental logic, and the application of this thought to the empirical realm, very plain: 'The analysis of knowledge does not operate in a realm in which there is talk of some sort of existing realities and their causal interrelations, but it develops, rather, prior to all such assumptions about the reality of things, a general ideal interconnection of truths and the relation of their interdependence. The pure meaning of these truth relations must be ascertained before any sort of application is to be made to existing things' (Cassirer 1912, pp. 256–7). Natorp regarded this distinction as identical to Plato's between dialectic and science: 'According to [Plato], science that relates directly to an object, e.g. mathematical science, proceeds from certain *presuppositions* (hypotheses), by which it is undergirded on something like a trial basis, without making any attempt to justify them for itself. From these it proceeds downwards in secure procedures to the consequences, and proves its theorems – in the sense, but only in the sense, that they correspond to the original presuppositions and are thus correct if the presuppositions are. The justification of the presuppositions falls to another, more fundamental science; *Plato* calls it dialectic . . . So science remains autonomous within its realm. But this realm remains, at the same time, strictly limited. The validity of its basic assumptions is not, within science as oriented directly to objects, in question at all. All its statements are only meant conditionally. So it makes sense that the justification itself of those basic assumptions should be reserved as a peculiar task for a different science, a science of a completely different kind and at a different level' (Natorp 1910, pp. 12–13).

the very concept of object, which physiology also presupposes, can only be pre-cisely and securely fixed in the language of mathematical physics. The concept of perception reduces to that of 'stimulus', which in turn reduces to the general concept of motion. (Cassirer 1912, p. 256)

But where is the circle? Helmholtz had of course never claimed to have a mechanical account of perception. And on what other grounds should perception or 'stimulus' otherwise have been 'reducible' to concepts of motion? Cassirer's accusation of circularity rested, rather, on the idea that motion is itself an imposition of thought ('if [the concept of motion] is used not with the vagueness of a popular slogan but in the precision of its scientific meaning'). So mechanics was a construction of pure thought, of 'mathematical, i.e. *ideal* basic assumptions' (Cassirer 1912, p. 256):

What motion 'is' cannot be articulated any other way than in concepts of magnitude; but these in turn presuppose for their understanding a basic system of the pure science of magnitudes. Thus the principles and axioms of mathematics become the actual foundation that have to be assumed as invariant in order to give any scientific assertion about reality its foothold and its point [*Halt und Sinn*]. (Cassirer 1912, p. 256)

This applied, in particular, to the choice of physical geometry;[21] 'it has been shown again and again', Natorp said, 'that after an appropriate choice of physical principles *every* empirical observation can be made consis-tent with *every* geometry'. So the choice of geometry 'must certainly be reached independently of empirical observation', i.e. by 'pure thought' alone (Natorp 1910, p. 302). And while Euclidean geometry was not a necessity of pure thought (as the existence of non-Euclidean geometries showed), it remained a necessary pre-condition of any experience (Natorp 1910, p. 316). So although he was wrong about the reasons for this, 'Kant was entirely right to claim that geometry is grounded, and cannot help being grounded, in assumptions that are not given by experience, but must be presupposed, since it is they that make experience as science possible' – among them the assumptions that space is three-dimensional and Euclidean (Natorp 1910, p. 318).[22]

---

[21] Despite disclaimers about pre-empting scientific findings by pure thought alone, the meta-level, 'transcendental' determination of the method and tendency of different sectors of knowledge made it possible, in the Marburg view, 'not just to prescribe but also to judge [*richten*]' the results and activities of working scientists (Natorp 1909, p. 240).

[22] Natorp's argument for this is roughly as follows: it is a necessity of *pure* thought that the space-time framework for *empirical* thought, and thus physical geometry, must be *Eindeutig* (non-ambiguous), and three-dimensional Euclidean geometry is the only candidate that meets this condition. This assertion is based on a somewhat obscure 'proof' (pp. 306–7) that would appear to assume what it sets out to prove.

So although the Marburg philosophers had dispensed with pure intuition, they had an equally reliable source of synthetic a priori knowledge in pure thought – the unfolding of the 'origin' of all principles of science as well as the philosophical diagnosis of the 'organisation' and unity of knowledge. And in their writings on that 'organisation', their central concern, for all their attention to natural science, was to *confine* its scope within the various manifestations of culture. Though their conception of this unity was more 'rationalistic' or 'top-down' than that of Kant, and involved no fundamental discontinuity between 'natural sciences' and 'human sciences', like the view of the rival neo-Kantian 'southwest school' of Windelband and Rickert, the Marburg philosophers did not think the unity of knowledge derived from a conceptual or methodological unification. They were, as they called themselves, idealists. There was no need to develop a 'scientific world view' of the kind sought by the *Encyclopédistes* or the positivists, they thought, since science could be safely quarantined; the larger concerns of human moral, political, and spiritual existence could be shielded from it. For the Marburg neo-Kantians, 'transcendental' meta-scientific discourse was not just separate from, but antecedent to, the discourse of science itself. At the 'transcendental' level, the *scope* of scientific knowledge could be determined and limited.

THE SURVIVAL OF THE ASPIRATION FOR A SCIENTIFIC PHILOSOPHY

Looking back in 1884 on development of the neo-Kantian movement he had set in motion three decades earlier, Helmholtz was less than happy about its development:

At the beginning of my career I was more of a believing Kantian than I am now; or rather, I believed then that what I wanted to see changed in Kant were peripheral details that hardly fell into the balance against what I still estimate highly as his main achievement; until I subsequently found that the strict Kantians of the present fix their attention – and think Kant at his most highly advanced – on precisely the issues regarding which he had not (in my view) overcome the insufficient knowledge of his time, particularly its metaphysical prejudices, and did not quite achieve the goal he had set himself. (Helmholtz 1884, pp. VI–VII)

The 'main achievement' of Kant's that Helmholtz had in mind here was the 'Copernican revolution' – the basic idea that our sense data are signs of something to which we have access only via those signs, and that the basic sign vocabulary is 'spontaneously' produced by our nervous system.

Helmholtz accepted the Kantian doctrine, then, that there are transcenden-tal 'forms of intuition' (like qualitative spatiality) – that we employ in all empirical judgements and are not based on facts of perception (Helmholtz 1878a, pp. 228–30, 248). But he also thought that the empirical and con-ceptual analysis of perception, to which he had devoted the better part of his career, was an intellectual advance over Kant, one of the utmost philosophical importance:

> I believe that we must regard the dissolution of the concept of intuition into the elementary processes of thought as the most critical step forward in recent times. Its absence underlay Kant's conception of the axioms of geometry as transcen-dental propositions. In particular, it was the physiological investigations of sense perception that led us to the elementary pre-verbal processes of knowing, which remained unknown and inaccessible to philosophy while the latter restricted its investigations to what could be expressed in language. (Helmholtz 1878a, p. 244; PT p. 364)

For Kant himself, Helmholtz's critics were quick to point out (e.g. Cohen 1885, pp. 222–38), the 'Copernican revolution' and the 'anti-Copernican counter-revolution' were inextricably interconnected. The fundamental difference here was that the critics, especially the Marburg school, wanted to *preserve* this interconnection, while Helmholtz and his philosophical followers wanted to overcome it; they wanted to *detach* the 'Copernican revolution' from the 'anti-Copernican counter-revolution':

> No essential component of the Kantian system would be lost thereby; on the contrary, the system would improve in consistency and comprehensibility, as the proof of the possibility of metaphysics, resting essentially on the persuasive power of the axioms of geometry, would be dropped . . . As *Kant's* critique is directed everywhere else against the admissability of metaphysical reasoning, it would seem to me that his system would be freed of an inconsistency if one were to give up the a priori origin of the axioms, and a clearer concept of the nature of intuition would be gained. (Helmholtz 1878b, p. 642)

But Helmholtz underestimated the magnitude of the task. He did not realise that, to reintegrate his own 'clearer concept of the nature of intu-ition' into a restored synthesis on the pattern of Kant's, it had to be brought together with the clearer understanding of reasoning that derived from Dedekind, Frege, and the mathematical unifications of the later nineteenth century. Though far more sophisticated than Mill, Helmholtz himself had attempted to ground arithmetic on a quasi-empiricist view (Helmholtz 1887); this paper had appeared in the same Festschrift as a not dissimilar paper by Kronecker (1887). It was in response to these two papers that

Dedekind published 'Was sind und was sollen die Zahlen?' (Dedekind 1887, p. III, first footnote). But the two sides of the explication of Kant had not arrived at a new synthesis, even by the first decades of the twentieth century. Those philosophers who appreciated Frege's decoupling of deduction from the synthetic activity of intellect, and his refutation of Mill's mathematical empiricism, were – like the Marburg school – largely uninterested in empirical facts. And those who *were* interested in empirical evidence, and who followed Helmholtz's decoupling of the axioms from intuition, like Mach, Petzold, or even the early Schlick and Reichenbach, had little appreciation for the idea that logic (and thus mathematics) could be a largely mechanical system of rules, independent of the human intellect for its functioning. Russell was on both sides of this divide, but he too had not brought them together (though as we will see, some of his ideas would prove very important to Carnap). The aspiration survived for a new synthesis on the model of Kant's, purged of the remaining anthropomorphism of Kant's faculties of synthesis and pure intuition. But no one had come along yet with a sufficiently strong commitment to *both* sides of this explication – the empirical and the logical – to bring them together.

CHAPTER 3

The grand plan of a 'system of knowledge': science and logic

In a letter written to a friend from the western front, in 1916, Carnap already expresses his impatience at the barriers between science and philosophy. Asked to recommend readings on the foundations of science, he admits that 'what the physicists have written about the foundations of physics will *hardly* satisfy a philosopher . . . Even a mind as sound as Mach's frequently makes me shake my head' (ASP/WF 1916c). He concedes that a 'non-specialist' like Natorp or Wundt might actually be preferable, though he hasn't read them yet. Poincaré and Helmholtz are singled out for favourable mention.

By 1920 he had read a good deal more, but remained unhappy with the gap between philosophy and science. The sciences that proceed mathematically have developed very rapidly in recent years, he says, 'without devoting much time to the critical appraisal of the foundations and methods of this construction'. Both sides are to blame:

Part of the blame rests with philosophy, which has often failed to comprehend the viewpoints of those rapidly developing sciences; on the other hand, part of the blame goes to the sciences, which were occupied more with conquering new territories than with securing and carefully integrating what had been gained. In short, through the fault of both sides a mutual alienation developed. (ASP 1920d, pp. 1–2)

On reflection, though, he continues, the fault is really on neither side, but inherent in the situation. To explain this he employs a military metaphor that came naturally to his generation:

What happened was unavoidable given the rapidity of an advance in mobile warfare: communications broke down between front and staff. To the philosophers at headquarters, in the absence of bulletins [from the front], the situation became less and less clear; it is especially unfortunate that although Kant was still alive at the time of the first work on the fundamentally important non-Euclidean geometries, he received no bulletins about them – which [if he had received them] might have been of great benefit both to his system and to those geometries. At the front, the lack of communication could have been even more damaging if there hadn't fortuitously been a few leaders who made up for their lack of strategic schooling with native insight and clearsightedness: thanks to men like Gauss and Helmholtz as well as Riemann and Hertz, among many others, who combined outstanding talent in their specialties with great system-building power and a sureness of instinct for the big picture, by and large the right paths were followed. (ASP 1920d, p. 2)

But, he adds, 'in the long run it can't go on like that'. Already, the danger signs are obvious, and even the participants have begun to realise that all is not well:

For some time now in geometry, more recently also in arithmetic and analysis, and now in physics as well, it is becoming clear that at certain points the bulletins from the front don't at all fit with the official map at headquarters. After making do for a while with saying, at headquarters, 'they don't themselves seem to know where they are!', and at the front, 'what do we care about the outdated map back there!', the insight is dawning that neither accusation is altogether unjustified: the exact sciences often work with concepts (which in some cases turn out to be their most important ones) whose meaning they can't give precisely; and on the other hand the traditional methods of philosophy can't help much with this. (ASP 1920d, pp. 2–3)

In response to this situation, some participants have begun to work on a new 'comprehensive map' that will satisfy both sides, and will accurately reflect the real state of knowledge. Carnap wants to join this effort, he says, and contribute his labours to the construction of a 'system of knowledge' (*System der Wissenschaft*) with 'logically consistent foundations and systematic construction of concepts' that is also 'capable of comprising all the insights of the special sciences and of presenting them with the greatest possible simplicity and unity' (ASP 1920d, p. 3).

It might appear, then, that the Vienna Circle's conception of the 'unity of science' is already present here in the early Carnap. But we find in this very letter that when Carnap is thinking of 'philosophers', he specifically has in mind Natorp, Cassirer, Nelson, and Husserl. Still, they are not the only ones at work on the great project of a new 'comprehensive map'; from the other side there are also mathematicians at work on it (Carnap mentions Klein, Frege, Russell, Couturat, and Hilbert) and 'physicists' (Mach, Dühring, Poincaré, Weyl, and Ostwald). Carnap sees his own role precisely in the mediation between the philosophers and the scientists, who despite their common effort at a new map are still apt to misunderstand each other due to the long separation, during which they developed different and inconsistent terminologies and even concepts (ASP 1920d, p. 3).

The idea of a comprehensive, architectonic 'system of knowledge' or 'system of the sciences' can be understood in many different ways. The Baconian, classificatory approach of the *Encyclopédie* was carried forward by Comte and other nineteenth-century positivists. But the encyclopaedic impulse is equally to be found in German idealism (Hegel) and in the Romantics (Novalis). And the idea of systematising all knowledge goes back to antiquity. We already find it highly developed in Aristotle, whose logical works, and whose system of categories, provided the template for similar efforts over the next two millennia. Leibniz added the idea of mapping the whole of knowledge in a single inferential, at least partly *deductive* structure, a 'universal characteristic' or *calculus philosophicus* – though this idea was neglected until revived two centuries later by Frege. Kant's systems of pure intuition and categories of the understanding were developed within a 'transcendental' logic concerned primarily to identify the synthetic a priori components of knowledge and show how they could be applied to experience.

Which of these many possible conceptions of a 'system of knowledge' are we to regard as the early Carnap's central aspiration? The answer seems to be that he saw it as his role to bring several of these conceptions *together*. Because of the persistent misunderstandings and conceptual differences, both apparent and genuine, 'someone who has a partiality for and understanding of *both* philosophy *and* the exact sciences can be particularly useful as a helper' (ASP 1920d, p. 3). Beyond these different conceptions of 'system', Carnap also wanted more generally to bring together two kinds of philosophical perspective that are usually regarded as antagonistic – a kind of 'empiricism' and a kind of 'rationalism'. The 'empiricist' side drew on the positivist tradition of Comte, Mach, and Ostwald, and was reinforced by the scientific ethos of his training in experimental physics. The 'rationalist' side drew on a Leibnizian conception of a deductive *calculus philosophicus* that Carnap derived from Frege. The latter's *Begriffsschrift* offered a way of implementing such a Leibnizian dream where earlier logical systems had failed. Logicism, therefore, meant far more to Carnap than just the reducibility of arithmetic (and thus analysis) to logic; for him logicism was the key to the realisation of a 'system of knowledge'. It offered the prospect of succeeding where Leibniz, d'Alembert, Kant, and Comte had failed.

Both the 'empiricist' and the 'rationalist' components were indispensable to the comprehensive 'system of knowledge' Carnap needed to support the utopian goals he had laid out in 1918, in the service of a new 'form of community' (*Gemeinschaftsgestalt*) that could serve to coordinate all human activities so as 'to remove [them] from the realm of chaotic whim and subordinate them to goal-oriented reason' (above, Chapter 1, pp. 62–3).

THE SCIENTIFIC TEMPERAMENT

Life in the trenches was not only horrible, but also very boring, and afforded a lot of time for reading. Apart from Einstein's publications on general relativity, Carnap kept up on all the novels and other new publications from the various factions of the Youth Movement, and participated in long-distance epistolary discussions of books agreed on by a group of friends. One of these texts was Goethe's *Theory of Colours*,[1] and Carnap's response to it shows that his characteristic aversion to ontological disputes, already apparent, was deeply rooted in scientific considerations. In a letter of 1916, written at the front, he responds to a friend's Goethean complaint about Newton's 'epistemologically monstrous notion . . . that a mechanical process, ether waves, should be more real to the person experiencing them than the colour he sees – that being the most real of all, to which everything else has to be reduced in order to be graspable, explainable'. Carnap denies that degrees of reality are involved: 'Such a reduction does not seem an "epistemological monstrosity" to me, for it doesn't claim that the mechanical phenomena are *more real* than the non-mechanical ones derived from them'. Carnap is with Aristotle here, basically; he maintains, against Goethe's conflation, that something can be immediate to our subjective consciousness (and thus 'first or best-known to us') without therefore being 'first in nature'. There is no reason for physics to restrict its conception of nature to the effects on the perceptual organs by which those occurrences become known to us:

For the *contents of sensation*, all physical qualities have equal rights (weight, tone, color). But since *physics* has the task of describing natural processes as simply as possible, it is undeniably a big step forward for it when it has e.g. succeeded in portraying acoustical phenomena as pure processes of motion (specifically as vibrations of bodies) that are knowable, measurable, and countable, and with which, while we abstract from physiological effects, *no* (that is the important

---

[1] The Goethe–Newton controversy continued to appear in Carnap's writings as the case where 'the battle between qualitative and quantative method' had found its 'classical form, so to speak' (1926, pp. 52–3; 1966, pp. 109–12). Goethe's approach is regarded as a *methodological* mistake, not as 'meaningless' or 'metaphysical'; it is taken to be the same methodological mistake that Planck discerned in Mach, that of anthropomorphising science by insisting on the fundamental or essential nature of our evolved sense modalities, at the expense of theoretical unity. However, when Carnap comes to ask the question what *motivates* this mistake, in Goethe and others who say that quantitative physics fails 'to really help us *understand* nature' (1966, p. 109), the answer is his chapter on 'The Magic View of Language' (1966, pp. 115–21).

thing!) other qualities are intermixed than those of bodily motion (mass, spatial coordinates, temporal coordinates). A longitudinal vibration in the air of frequency 435 [cycles per second], regardless of how it is induced, and the sound wave of the pitch 'a', don't just match, they are identical. The fact that motion-processes and pitches affect different sense modalities is no business of physics. (ASP/WF 1916b)

This response to Goethe's scientific views corresponds almost exactly to that of Helmholtz, and thus locates the young Carnap rather precisely on the German intellectual terrain of the early twentieth century. Helmholtz's well-known commentary on Goethe[2] – deeply respectful (as Carnap was) of the artist and sage, even of the practicing scientist, while critical of his *conception* of science – had spelled out a little more explicitly the view Carnap advocates to his friends:

But this step into the realm of concepts, which has to be taken if we want to ascend to the causes of the appearances of nature, repels the poet. In his poetic works he clothed the mental content of those appearances in the most compelling sensual presentation, without any conceptual intermediation. The greater the sensual vividness of the presentation, the greater was his fame. The physicist on the other hand wants to lead him into a world of invisible atoms, motions, attractive and repulsive forces that work according to laws but are all mixed up in a barely penetrable tangle. For the physicist the sense impression is no ineluctable authority; he investigates its justification and asks whether what the senses declare to be similar is really similar and what the senses declare to be different is really different, and often arrives at a negative answer. (Helmholtz 1853, pp. 18–19; PT p. 13)[3]

Carnap calls his view at this time – for reasons to be discussed in the next chapter – an 'idealistic conception [*idealistische Auffassung*]'. We hear more of it in a letter Carnap addressed in 1921 to one of his youth movement friends, Wilhelm Flitner, who had recommended a book by Friedrich Gogarten, *The Religious Decision* (*Die religiöse Entscheidung*). This book, Flitner had thought, contradicted Carnap's 'idealistic conception' because in contrast to that view, Gogarten portrays a 'gaping rift between cultural occurrence and divine occurrence' in the vivid terms 'of a person strongly gripped by certain experiences' (ASP 1921f, p. 2). But having now read the book, Carnap denies that it reveals any new 'region of reality [*Wirklichkeitsbereich*]'

---

[2] Which Carnap had read, and still referred to half a century later (1966, p. 111).

[3] Helmholtz concludes this passage by referring to the philosophical implications of his own research, as described above: 'The results of this test available so far show that while the sense organs report external processes to us, they display them to our consciousness in completely changed form. Thus the quality of sense perception depends less on the peculiarities of the perceived object than on those of the sense organ that receives the report.' See also Helmholtz's earlier remarks on Goethe (Helmholtz 1852, p. 601).

that would show his 'idealistic conception' to be one-sided or incomplete. Of course, he admits, Gogarten could respond that Carnap is simply blind to the realms of which he writes: 'So to him, my failure to see would not be an objection, but would merely show that I (so far) don't belong to the elect'. So there is a stand-off between these positions; how should one go about deciding it?

Initially, only the relativist view is possible: he admits that he can't make the other reality visible to me, I have to admit that I can't refute it; so each of us can initially maintain his position. But surely there has to be a way of getting beyond such relativism (which my belief in rationality can only allow as a temporary expedient) and arriving at an objective, generally binding knowledge. (ASP 1921f, p. 2)

Carnap gives a parable to show how that might come about. Imagine most people were blind, and only a few could see. There would be a similar stand-off regarding the existence of a visual world. But the blind could impose a standard for recognising the existence of such a world; they could say 'if you perceive more than we do, then you must discern more connections in things *that reach over into our world*, i.e. you must sometimes notice a connection as necessary that seems coincidental to us and surprises us'. The seeing person can do that; he can predict things about their commonly perceived (heard and felt) surroundings that the blind person can't; so the latter 'must acknowledge the peculiar perceptive powers of the seeing person' (ASP 1921f, p. 3). The same sort of standard can be generalised to cases that involve not a specific sense modality or immediate perception, but different learned interpretative capabilities, as Carnap illustrates with another parable. Take a completely unmusical person U, to whom a musical person M is incapable of explaining or showing directly what more there is to a melody than just a temporal series of pitches, or to harmony than combinations of simultaneous pitches.

But as soon as they both direct their attention to the consideration of history as a whole, it becomes clear that M can notice connections where U sees none. If they are presented with a musical work, say, M is capable of specifying its period and cultural context from the musical character he notices. These are connections that U can check. I'm not saying that for M and for us the point of musical activity lies in this sort of historical analysis. Certainly not. But the point is that M is *also* capable of making connections among things *in U's world* that remain unconnected for U. (ASP 1921f, p. 4)

This is the same demand, Carnap says, that I would make of Gogarten: show me what you can predict, by virtue of your vision, in the subset of your world that is accessible to both of us, that I am unable to make sense of without your vision. 'For me it is a kind of postulate or article of faith that everything that is to be called real in some sense has ultimately to stand in a determinate relation to my (unique) reality'.

Though the monism of this 'idealistic' conception was epistemological, without Haeckel's or Ostwald's ontological claims, it was no less monistic. 'I don't believe in the reality of occurrences that aren't connected both upward and downward by historical threads (which isn't quite the same as claiming causality in history, though I also believe in that)' (ASP 1921f, p. 4). In response to Gogarten's mystical dualism (e.g. 'so what happens in this moment . . . arises no longer from the context of happening and letting happen, determined by human beings, and also doesn't flow as a cause or in its consequences into the general development of world history'), Carnap replies: 'But for me even the particular moment, *every* moment, is part of history, however unique it may be and however utterly inexhaustible its content may be' (ASP 1921f, pp. 4–5).[4]

THE PHILOSOPHICAL SIGNIFICANCE OF LOGICISM

In the first piece of Carnap's philosophical writing I have been able to find, a dissertation written in 1920 to qualify for the secondary teaching certificate, on the question, 'Of what *philosophical* significance is the problem of the "Foundation of Geometry"?', he endorses Russellian logicism (i.e. including geometry): 'Recent work on the foundations of geometry and arithmetic has shown that the former science can be derived completely without use of intuitive elements from arithmetic, and the latter in turn from deductive logic' (UCLA 1920a, p. 1). But this is immediately qualified as follows:

It is specially to be emphasised that *deductive* logic is here the starting point, as represented in algebraic form – on the basis of an idea of Leibniz – by Peano, Russell, Couturat, Frege, and Schröder, among others. For this deductive sector certainly does not, as *Natorp* has shown [with references; see discussion below], comprise the whole of logic, which after all must specify the laws of deductive procedure in the first place, and which investigates the laws according to which 'any possible object of science forms itself into an object to begin with'. Deductive logic presupposes the objects as already given, so it can't be a primary sector of logic, but can only be erected on the solution to that primary task. (UCLA 1920a, pp. 1–2)

---

[4] Just as he would later say in the *Aufbau* (1928a, p. 253), contradicting Natorp, that any particular, however qualitatively inexhaustible, can be uniquely characterised ('constituted', in the later terminology) within the conceptual system of science.

This would seem to be incompatible with Frege and Russell, for whose universal view of deductive logic there was no room for a meta-logical, meta-systematic standpoint external to deductive logic.[5] But although Carnap was willing, in 1920, to acknowledge Natorp's claim to have 'shown' that deductive logic had to be constituted within something larger, on closer inspection it appears that only part of the argument by which Natorp reaches this conclusion could have been acceptable to Carnap, even then. The Natorp passage he refers to occurs in a critique of 'formalism', as Natorp calls Russell's view that logic and mathematics are identical, and that there is no more to mathematics than logic. Natorp criticises this idea on several grounds. First, he says it leaves logic without a starting point; it is circular because it uses logic to set up logic:

Logic is itself supposed to be a deductive science; but it certainly belongs to the task of logic to specify the laws of deductive procedure and the justification of the necessary and general validity [this procedure] presumes. But can the specification and justification of a logical procedure be undertaken by that procedure itself? That makes no sense, as the procedure of deduction would have to be assumed as already specified and justified in order to be able to provide the required specification and justification in a valid way. (Natorp 1910, pp. 5–6)

This could have been taken by Carnap, at this point, to reinforce his idea that a larger system of categories is needed, within which to ground logic and relate pure mathematics (and logic) to empirical sentences. But Natorp puts the main burden on a second and different argument that – mistakenly, as Carnap would have known[6] – regards Russell's logicism as equivalent to the idea that mathematics and logic are both formal in the sense that they express no judgements but are only purely mechanical derivations. Such a syntactic procedure, Natorp says, empties symbols of meaning, and without meaning they are not symbols; they are just marks on a page that stand for nothing.[7] The basic concepts and axioms of any discipline must have meaning, he says, as they are generated by the 'synthetic' faculty of

[5] As Warren Goldfarb says: '[In Frege–Russell logicism,] if the system constitutes the universal logical language, then there can be no external standpoint from which one may view and discuss the system. Metasystematic considerations are illegitimate rather than simply undesirable' (Goldfarb 1979, p. 353).

[6] Or at least have known soon after this; he did not read the *Principia* thoroughly until June 1920 (ASP 1920a).

[7] He refers here also to an early argument he had published to this effect (contrasting Whitehead's *Universal Algebra* and Russell's *Foundations of Geometry* unfavourably with Grassmann) in Natorp 1901b, pp. 282–3; Cassirer had also criticised Russell, along similar lines (Cassirer 1907), and later made the same anti-'formalist' point against Schlick's *General Theory of Knowledge* (Cassirer 1927, p. 136).

thought.[8] If they are treated as empty mechanical counters, then they bear no relation to a human understander, and cannot be grasped:

Whether this is supposed to be science or just a game, instructive or merely amusing, or both or neither, it is enough for us to declare that we do not understand the task of logic in this way. For what counts in logic as far as we are concerned is, first and last, sense [*Sinn*], understanding [*Verstehen*], and we confess frankly and freely that what we understand, concerning this entire activity, is not much or little but nothing at all. For an understanding of its point [*Sinn*] is given neither by the fact that the procedure corresponds to the rules set up, nor that the result sometimes (not always) coincides with something we otherwise already believe ourselves to understand. (Natorp 1910, p. 7)

Carnap would have known that Russell, like Frege, did not conceive logic as empty, but rather as completely universal, as applying to *everything*, and would have found it strange to contrast Frege with Russell in this respect. The Marburg school were apparently willing to assimilate Frege's project to their own aspiration of 'a purely logical foundation . . . of mathematics', in which its basic concepts are 'presented by logic' and its axioms are 'contained in the laws of logic or derivable from them' (Natorp 1910, pp. 1–3), while they thought Russell's almost identical project excessively 'formalist'. Russell sounded too friendly, in their ears, toward the 'empiricist, psychologistic, and nominalist view, as . . . represented by, say, *Helmholtz* and *Kronecker*',[9] while Frege had 'repulsed' this same empiricist conception 'in resoundingly effective argument' (Natorp 1910, p. 3). In praise of the *Grundlagen der Arithmetik*, Natorp goes on to say:

Very trenchant is above all the refutation of *J. Stuart Mill*'s attempted foundation of number on induction, as well as the defence against any derivation of number from properties of the things to be counted; no less trenchant is the denial of the unclear justification from 'intuition', the resolute return to the very laws of thought alone . . . (Natorp 1910, pp. 112–13)

The last point is a misunderstanding. Natorp, like Cohen and Cassirer, conceived of the 'laws of thought' as governing the spontaneous *activity* of

---

[8] Though Frege, like the Marburg philosophers, insisted that logic and mathematics have meaning, he also accepted an 'empirical source of knowledge [*sinnliche Erkenntnisquelle*]' (Frege 1924/5) as an *independent* source; this was denied, as we saw, by the Marburg philosophers. Also, Frege thought that whatever elements in mathematics were not logical must be 'intuitive [*anschaulich*]', but this was precisely the doctrine of Kant that the Marburg philosophers dispensed with.

[9] The dismissal of Helmholtz's view of mathematics, and particularly arithmetic, as 'psychologistic', was something of a commonplace among later neo-Kantians. In fact, Helmholtz's philosophy of arithmetic, though empiricist (certainly non-Kantian), was no more psychologistic (in the more precise sense introduced by Frege) than his philosophy of geometry, despite superficial appearances, as Robert DiSalle shows (DiSalle 1992).

the intellect (as governing a *process*, a constant striving for, and movement towards, synthesis),[10] while Frege's focus was the objective existence of the *objects* of thought and the *concepts* that bind them together.[11] This misunderstanding, in turn, prevents Natorp from seeing the point of Frege's classification of arithmetic judgements as analytic. What Frege must have meant by this, Natorp surmises, is that arithmetic is a 'pure act of thought [*reine Denkleistung*]', but one that, as Frege explicitly concedes, is not merely 'elucidative [*erläuternd*]' but 'constructive [*erweiternd*]'. Consequences are, in Frege's own metaphor, 'contained in the definition, but as the plant is contained in the seed, not as the beam in the house' (Natorp 1910, p. 113; Frege 1884, §88), Natorp says, and 'precisely this' – this conceptual fruitfulness of reasoning – 'is what in *Kant's* language is called synthesis'.

And that Frege really has synthetic judgements in mind (in *Kant's* sense) is confirmed by many things, such as his remark against *Mill*: two and a pair are by no means the same, as *Mill* oddly seems to suppose. That is, in *Kant's* language: the addition judgement [*Additionsurteil*] is synthetic. Two ones 'are' a two, not as if the concepts were identical or the second could be analytically derived from the first, but they are equivalent: whatever can be thought of as two ones, that same thing can be thought of as a two, but in a different, new logical conception, which is posited correlatively with the former, always *with* it, that is, but not *in* it. (Natorp 1910, pp. 113–14)

Again Natorp misunderstands. Frege's point about Mill (Frege 1884, §25) has nothing at all to do with a synthetic 'addition judgement' that Natorp connects it with. On the contrary, it *is* in fact deducible directly from Frege's definitions and axioms that one plus one equals two, so this sentence is *analytic*. Two is not one plus one 'in a different, new logical conception'; 'synthesis' has no role here for Frege. His point in the passage Natorp mentions is, rather, his familiar one that the concept 'pair of boots' and the concept 'boot' are distinct, and that the application of distinct concepts to the same phenomena can result in different numerical judgements. This is also not 'synthesis' for Frege, but the relation ('falling under') between

[10] Immediately following the passage just quoted, the words 'the "idea [*Idee*]"' are added as an appositive to 'the very laws of thought alone'; Natorp evidently regarded the 'laws of thought' as tantamount to 'the idea' (in the Platonic sense) from which thought emerges – what he also, following Cohen, calls 'the origin [*Ursprung*]'; see Chapter 2, p. 85. And Cassirer had said that, according to the critical philosophy, 'the truth value of knowledge . . . is not reduced to, or founded on its relation to, some external court of appeal, but emerges from the self-given, autonomous law of self-consciousness' (Cassirer 1922, p. 761).

[11] This is particularly evident in his famous remark 'The unifying power of the concept far exceeds that of synthetic apperception. The latter is incapable of joining the citizens of the German Empire into a whole, but one can certainly bring them under the concept "citizen of the German Empire" and count them' (Frege 1884, §48).

concept and object. And it was just this relation that Natorp objected to, regarding it as an uncritical acceptance of traditional Aristotelian logic: 'Though correctly wanting to take the numbers back to the pure basic laws of thought, [Frege] thinks he can simply take over the latter, at least the fundamental ones and those he needs for his purposes, from traditional logic' (Natorp 1910, p. 114). In Frege's view, Natorp says, it is 'presupposed as known and given what "X falls under the concept A" means', and this presupposition is 'altogether in the sense of traditional logic, i.e. in the sense of *Aristotle*', according to whom 'being contained in a concept' means 'the relation of the (given!) individual to the general [concept]' (Natorp 1910, p. 114). What Natorp objected to in Frege's logic, in other words, was that it took the objects of its universe of discourse as given, rather than recognising, in accordance with the 'genetic' conception of knowledge, that a particular object is always inexhaustible, never completely defined.

Frege's view of (genuine) concepts as unambiguous, objective, and well defined for every case (i.e. his adherence to the law of excluded middle for empirical as well as mathematical concepts) is incompatible, then, with the 'genetic' view of the Marburg school. In Michael Dummett's (1963) sense, the Marburg school is 'anti-realist' – it rejects excluded middle for objects in the universe of discourse – while Frege is 'realist'. In this respect, the young Carnap was Fregean,[12] though the monism we encountered in his 'idealistic conception' (on pp. 95–7 above) would seem to exclude a ('third') realm of thoughts that give meaning to sentences. And we saw in the present section that Carnap also rejected the Russellian classification of the principles of deductive logic as synthetic a priori; they were to be constituted, rather, within a wider kind of 'logic', presumably within a system of categories like that of Kant.

What were, then, the philosophical uses or implications of logicism itself for Carnap? That all of mathematics, including geometry, could be generated from logic was in itself of great significance, as it implied, for Carnap (here he followed Russell in extending Frege's argument for arithmetic to geometry), that all mathematics is analytic, and this robbed Kant's argument for the existence of synthetic a priori statements of its main examples, drawn from arithmetic and geometry. But Carnap thought that this logically constituted mathematics was 'abstract', had no content. It was not universal, as in Russell and Frege, but rather a 'pure relational structure,

---

[12] One might say that he was already, at this point, what Thomas Ricketts (1994) calls the Carnap of the *Syntax*: a 'relativised' Fregean, for though his conception of object is language-relative, the language frameworks he himself works with require excluded middle for object names. (Which is not to say that Carnap would – later – have refused to consider a language without excluded middle.)

whose elements are completely indeterminate' (see below, p. 110). This may seem surprising, for a student of Frege, but in fact Carnap was influenced much more by the *idea* of the logical unification of mathematics, the elimination of any specifically mathematical concepts or principles, than by the philosophical doctrines of any particular logicists. In the case of Frege, we have the evidence of Carnap's own notes on Frege's lectures (cf. also ASP 1919a). From these – which are among the very few sources on the development of Frege's doctrine after the discovery of the antinomies – it seems clear that the Frege Carnap encountered was not the Frege of the *Grundlagen* or the *Grundgesetze*. The constructive and ontological part of the system is absent, and only the inferential part is left; basic laws IV, V, and VI are omitted.[13] The system no longer builds up a particular domain of logical objects; it is applicable in principle to any domain. In these lectures, then, the early Carnap would have encountered a different Frege from the archetypal 'realist' familiar to philosophers of mathematics today (e.g. Dummett 1981, 1991).

Nonetheless, Frege's influence on Carnap was quite fundamental in at least three respects. First, there was Frege's advocacy and creation of a completely explicit, gap-free system of logic, and his demonstration that, relative to this system, arithmetic is analytic. Second, Frege influenced Carnap – early and late – by the stark contrast he drew between the explicit precision of his Begriffsschrift and the inadequacy of ordinary language for pure thought. A fully explicit logic such as his Begriffsschrift could be instrumental, Frege thought, in breaking the tyranny of inherited ordinary language over the human spirit:

> If it is a task of philosophy to break the dominion of words over the human spirit by revealing the deceits about the relations among concepts that often arise almost unavoidably through the use of language – by freeing thoughts from everything that sticks to them solely by virtue of the concrete make-up of the linguistic expression – then my concept-script, further developed for these purposes, can become a usable tool for philosophers. (Frege 1879, pp. VI–VII; PT p. 106)

Insofar as such passages can be read as suggesting that Frege relied on a 'third realm' of objective thoughts that were to be 'freed' from their imprisonment in the vagueness of ordinary language (e.g. Ricketts 2004a), Carnap's monism would, as we saw, have left no room for this. Nonetheless, his conception of the 'task of philosophy' as breaking 'the dominion of words over the human spirit' by 'revealing the deceits' of ordinary language, was strongly influenced by Frege's example. And it should be noted that,

---

[13] The fragment of the earlier logic presented in the lectures is complete, though, as Reck and Awodey (2005) point out; some of the earlier axioms are replaced by new inference rules.

despite his knowledge of Frege's platonic realism,[14] Carnap was inclined to interpret Frege in a more pragmatic vein. As he would later write, Frege had

> strongly emphasized that the foundation problems of mathematics can only be solved if we look not solely at pure mathematics but also at the use of mathematical concepts in factual sentences. He had found his explication of cardinal numbers by asking himself the question: What does 'five' mean in contexts like 'I have five fingers on my right hand'? (1963, p. 48)

Finally and perhaps most importantly, Frege influenced Carnap by reviving, and making feasible, the Leibnizian dream of unifying the whole of knowledge, constructing a 'system of knowledge', through logic. The original ambitions for Frege's Begriffsschrift (or for the project of which the booklet *Begriffsschrift* was the first step) had not been limited to logic and mathematics (Beaney 1996, pp. 38–41). The preface of the book in which it was first set out, and his earliest writings explaining and defending it, make clear that he had wider ambitions, comparable to those of Leibniz, for a universal language for the transmission of pure thought:

> In the arithmetical, geometrical, chemical symbols one can see realisations of the Leibnizian idea in particular areas. The concept-script proposed here adds a new one to these, in fact, the one situated in the middle, neighboring all the others. From this vantage point one can advance with the best hope of success toward filling in the gaps among existing symbolic languages, connecting their hitherto separated areas to a single region, and expanding it into areas that still lack a symbolic language . . . (Frege 1879, p. VII; PT p. 106)

In fact, Frege seems to have envisaged a larger framework, 'further developed for these purposes' of which the extant *Begriffsschrift* encompassed only a beginning[15] – a framework intended as a *lingua characterica*, not a mere calculus. This appears to have been overlooked, he says, perhaps due to the fact 'that in the execution I allowed the abstractly logical to step too much into the foreground' (Frege 1882, p. 98).

However, before 1922 Carnap did not cast Frege–Russell *deductive* logic in the role of addressing those wider questions (1963, p. 6). It seems plausible that he regarded Frege's Begriffsschrift, rather, as *part* of a full-blown *lingua characterica* in which Leibniz's larger aims (including the development of an instrument of discovery, and even of an international language!) could be

---

[14] In his own copy of 'Der Gedanke', an offprint sent him by Frege, the passage on the 'third realm' is heavily underlined with several question marks in the margin.

[15] 'The goal of my efforts is a *lingua characterica*, first for mathematics, not a *calculus* restricted to pure logic . . . A *lingua characterica* should, as Leibniz says, portray not words but thoughts' (Frege 1881, pp. 13–14).

realised. But deductive logic was not sufficient in his view, as we have seen, to determine 'the laws according to which any possible object of science forms itself into an object to begin with'. This had to be undertaken from within some wider framework governed, but not constituted, by deductive logic: 'Deductive logic presupposes the objects as already given, so it can't be a primary sector of logic, but can only be erected on the solution to that primary task.' And that task, for Carnap, was a matter of mapping the total conceptual space by a system of *categories* like that of Kant, who had claimed of his category system that it 'makes all treatment of every object of pure reason systematic, and supplies an indubitable guide or guiding thread . . . for it exhausts all components of the understanding, under which every other concept must be brought' (Kant 1783, §39, p. 84). For something to 'form itself into a possible object of science', then, was to fall under a category. In *Der Raum* (1922), as we will see (though not yet in 1920), this would become the task of mapping out the 'eidetic' space (the space of 'essences' or of non-factual truths) and subordinating the object in question to one of the basic features ('regions' or categories) of the overall 'system of the study of science [*System der Wissenschaftslehre*]' arrived at by 'formal ontology' (Husserl 1913, pp. 25–7).

For all this packaging, though, it is clear that Frege's logic, and logicism more generally, were envisaged as playing a central role in the revival of a Leibnizian, *deductive* 'system of knowledge' that could provide the basis for Carnap's conception of 'politics' in the widest sense. Most immediately, such a system was to provide a standard and framework for a *critical* attitude toward knowledge, and even toward scientific practice. Though science was the touchstone of knowledge (as well as the basis of social progress), Carnap also followed Ostwald in regarding the scientific *enterprise* as rather messy and inefficient. (He may also, following Ostwald, have thought this a major problem for the future, when that enterprise would have to be greatly expanded.) We have seen that he thought physicists do not really understand the foundations of their own discipline; if it hadn't been for the good instinctive judgement and broad scope of a few people like Gauss and Helmholtz (despite their 'lack of strategic schooling'!), he thought, science could easily have taken less productive paths than it did. In any case, the unreflective style that got us this far will not get us further; the cracks are already showing: 'In the long run it can't go on like that'. To ensure that progress continues, he implies, the officers at headquarters need to get better informed about what is happening at the front, and then need to *impose some order.*

The officer attitude toward scientific practice is evident in other ways during Carnap's early development. In 1919 he wrote a 'special subject essay [*fachwissenschaftliche Hausarbeit*]' in physics, of about sixty pages, surveying the literature on the assigned topic[16] and concluding that the widely and divergently ramified (*weitverzweigte*) empirical results do not add up to a unified picture; he makes various suggestions for imposing some degree of theoretical unity on the experimental findings reviewed (UCLA 1919a, p. 58). And in the last paragraph of the early paper 'On the task of physics' (published in 1923, but largely written in 1921), he claims to have shown

> which decisions have to be made and which criteria have to be specified to remove the judgement of a physical theory and especially the choice among several alternative theories from the realm of scientific instinct, which has always held sway here, and submit these matters *to the rule of conscious principles of the study of science* [*unter die Herrschaft bewußter Grundsätze der Wissenschaftslehre*]. (1923, p. 107)

The demand is for a meta-logical *lingua characteristica* incorporating 'conscious principles of the [scientific] study of science [*bewußte Grundsätze der Wissenschaftslehre*]' that would force scientific standards of rigor and precision onto the conduct of the scientific enterprise itself, rather than allowing 'the realm of scientific instinct' of the strategically unschooled practising scientist to prevail. This impulse evident in the early Carnap later found a more sophisticated and dialectical context in the ideal of explication.

WHICH CONCEPTION OF 'SYSTEM'?

The form to be taken by a 'system of the sciences' or a 'system of philosophy' was a central subject of discussion among the neo-Kantian schools in the first decades of the twentieth century. Indeed, this issue was among the defining differences between the Marburg school and the 'southwest' school headed by Heinrich Rickert. Where the Marburg school had taken the mathematical natural sciences as the paradigm of knowledge, the southwest school saw a fundamental distinction between the natural sciences and the human sciences, following Windelband's famous distinction between the ideographic and the nomothetic sciences (Windelband 1894), developed *in extenso* by Rickert in his book on *The Limits of Concept Formation in the Natural Sciences.*[17] This difference might not seem to have obvious political connotations, but during the First World War it certainly acquired them.

---

[16] The task (*Aufgabe*) set was 'The results to date of the theory of forced oscillations, especially those arising from impacts, are to be collected and critically reviewed' (UCLA 1919a, p. 1).

[17] The clash between these conceptions of 'system' is highlighted in Hönigswald (1912), a long and highly critical review of Cassirer's *Substance and Function* by a prominent member of the southwest school; Cassirer, Hönigswald argues, entirely fails to do justice to the special character (*Eigenart*) of history. A graduate student of Rickert's who took an interest in this debate, and gave a seminar attacking Cassirer's book along similar lines, was one Martin Heidegger (Denker 2002, p. 79).

The editor of the *Kant-Studien*, a prominent student of Windelband, published an article in that journal on 'The Concept of the Nation' in 1916. Here he employed the southwest-neo-Kantian device of 'particularity', to which only the human sciences have access, since the natural sciences generalise and therefore cannot capture the particular uniqueness of the individual case; he applied this idea to the nation rather than to the individual person. He applied it, in particular, to the German and Jewish nations, arguing that they should not mix or cohabit within the same territory. He claimed not to be anti-Semitic (he applauded Zionism, for its desire to separate the Jewish race and maintain its individuality), but argued that Jews should not have the right to practise professions or own property in Germany (Schlotter 2004, pp. 66–9). This was Bruno Bauch, soon to be Carnap's doctoral supervisor.

The obvious targets of this war-inspired effusion were the Marburg school, not only because Cohen and Cassirer were Jewish, but because Cohen had made the compatibility, indeed essential inner bond, of German and Jewish culture into one of his particular themes. He had gone so far as to proclaim – in a consciously anti-Zionist spirit – that Germany was the natural home of the Jewish diaspora worldwide, because of the cosmopolitan spirit of Kantian philosophy and Weimar classicism (Schlotter 2004, p. 65). The Marburg school were particularly outraged by Bauch's attack, therefore, and Cassirer wrote an uncharacteristically vehement response. Bauch, however, refused to publish it (it was not published until 1991), whereupon Hans Vaihinger, the founder and chairman of the Kant Society, relieved Bauch of his editorship, in the hope of avoiding a split. Bauch, however, attracted widespread sympathy, and went on to found a rival 'German Philosophical Society' on the grounds that the Kant Society had become a Jewish cabal, and that Jewish censorship was intolerable (Schlotter 2004, pp. 69–71 and Chapter 10, pp. 75–85).

Carnap had been in Freiburg during the academic year 1911–12, had attended several of Rickert's lecture courses, and been enthralled (Gabriel 2004, p. 6). We find scattered references in Carnap's early works to Rickert, Hönigswald, Bauch, and others of the southwest school. And Bauch had, after all, been Carnap's doctoral supervisor. So it may seem reasonable to conjecture, as Thomas Mormann (2006) recently has, that it is *Rickert's* conception of 'system' (esp. Rickert 1921) that we should attribute to Carnap in his development of the *Aufbau* system, rather than the positivist one, the Marburg one, or the deductive-Leibnizian one derived from Frege. Mormann acknowledges that these other elements are present, but argues that Rickert's was the key to Carnap's project of achieving a synthesis among all these conceptions. In particular, he thinks, it explains the comprehensiveness of the constitution system, especially its inclusion of cultural objects and values (1928a, §§150–2); it explains Carnap's emphasis on the constitutional system's ability to construct both the *general* concepts of natural science and the *individual* concepts of the cultural sciences (§§12 and 158); and it explains the interpretation, suggested by Carnap himself (§42), of the relation between quasi-analytically constituted concepts and their objects as Rickert's relation between *Gelten* (holding) and *Sein* (being); the concepts 'hold' of their objects (1928a, p. 177).

However, Carnap's relation to the southwest school has to be seen in the context of his own intellectual development during and after the war, which brought about a sharp disillusionment with the German humanistic tradition. As we saw at the end of Chapter 1, Carnap specifically blamed 'those tendencies in our own ranks – within the human sciences [*Geisteswissenschaften*]' for the war – tendencies that, he thought, complacently accepted the past stages of the human race as prescriptive for all eternity, and had allowed an interpretation of history to thrive that confers legitimacy on existing social and political arrangements. Clearly he had the German historicist tradition in mind here, and very likely also its chief philosophical spokesman – Rickert. However enthusiastic he may have been about Rickert in 1911, things looked different in the cold post-war light of *Neue Sachlichkeit* and the realisation that historicism was 'an especially heavy burden on our – the intellectuals' – balance sheet of guilt and our responsibility for the future' (ASP 1918d, pp. 16–17). Indeed, Rickert may well have been of interest, not as a positive influence, but now as a target of refutation. Carnap may indeed have been influenced by Rickert in the vast scope he gave the *Aufbau* system, its inclusion of cultural objects and of values, and its reconstruction of the relation between *Sein* and *Gelten* – but the point was precisely to demonstrate that all these matters *could* be accommodated within a unified system *without* imposing Rickert's fundamental discontinuity between natural and human sciences.[18] Everything

---

[18] Although the Marburg school was less suspect in this regard, any distinction Carnap may have recognised between these neo-Kantian schools in the first years after the war had evidently diminished in significance by the Vienna Circle years. In a list compiled in Dessau of metaphysicians 'according to their degree of badness' (UCLA 1929b), Kant, Natorp, Cassirer, Windelband, and Rickert are all at the same level, less bad than Hegel or Heidegger, and even than Husserl (or indeed Klee and Kandinsky, who are grouped with Husserl as exemplifying 'analysis of consciousness in metaphysical form', though not as flagrantly as Heidegger or Bergson). Still, the Marburg and Southwest philosophers are judged worse than the 'realists', among whom Carnap lists Driesch and Nicolai Hartmann as representatives of the aggravated form, Russell and Reichenbach as more modest offenders.

Rickert had claimed to be beyond the reach of science Carnap was bringing within a single unifying framework with a single universe of discourse (*Gegenstandsbereich*).[19]

In the light of Carnap's larger political and cultural goals, Mormann's interpretation seems implausible. But it still remains a little puzzling, in the light of Bauch's political role, why Carnap should have chosen him as his supervisor. We do know that Bauch (indeed philosophy) was not his first choice (1963, p. 11). Practical convenience might have played a role; Carnap was not physically present in Jena while he wrote his dissertation, so it probably made little sense for him to switch universities. But we have no real evidence bearing on this question; its resolution will have to await further research. Though Carnap's new-found political orientation was diametrically opposed to Bauch's, their relations seem to have been and remained cordial, if somewhat distant. Carnap himself remained close to the Kant Society and published in the *Kant-Studien* as well as in Vaihinger's *Annalen der Philosophie*.

---

[19] Mormann's only textual evidence for Rickert's direct influence on the *Aufbau* project is Carnap's use of the term 'chaos' in the first sketch of the system, entitled 'Vom Chaos zur Wirklichkeit', supposedly an echo of Rickert's (1921, p. 50) use of this word in his *System der Philosophie* (Mormann 2006, p. 175). It is argued in some detail below (Chapter 4, pp. 125–7) that this terminology actually derives from a quite different source – Vaihinger's *Philosophy of the As If.*

Carnap's early neo-Kantianism

What sort of Kantianism is available to someone who holds that all mathematics, including geometry, is analytic? A version of Helmholtz's view, presumably – that the qualitative properties of spatiality, though not the axioms of geometry (which are underdetermined by qualitative spatiality), are synthetic a priori on the basis of something like pure intuition. And this is indeed what we find in the early Carnap. Even before the 1920 dissertation, it seems that his interpretation of Kant was largely naturalistic and Helmholtzian. As he recounts from his student days:

> Once I gave a report in Bauch's seminar on this view of Kant [that the geometrical structure of space is determined by the form of our intuition]. I tried to show that it seems possible to generalise this conception considerably, because I saw an analogy between space on the one hand and systems of other features of sense qualities on the other. In particular, I tried to show that the three-dimensional structure of the system of colours, ordered according to their similarities, is determined by the form of our colour intuition in the same way in which the three-dimensional structure of space is determined by the form of our spatial intuition. (UCLA 1957a, p. B2)

What about the Marburg school? Carnap accepted its notion of the 'object-creating function of thought', as we will see below (p. 153). And we saw in Chapter 3 that Carnap, quoting Natorp, was willing to countenance some form of 'transcendental logic' which 'investigates the laws according to which "any possible object of science forms itself into an object to begin with"', since 'deductive logic presupposes the objects as already given'.

A closer look at the 1920 dissertation will help to determine his attitude toward the Marburg conception more precisely. Carnap's procedure here does seem, on the surface, to follow the Marburg idea of empirical knowledge as attained by starting with the most general mathematical ideas and then successively adding constraints or 'determinations', i.e.

'narrowing down' the most general ideas by applying further categories of the 'synthetic' faculty of the intellect. As in Natorp, pure reason generates an abstract and general science of magnitudes of the kind Grassmann had developed (though Carnap's geometrical – Russellian – logicism constructs this science of magnitudes, in turn, from arithmetic and thus logic). Carnap calls this 'abstract' geometry, and contrasts it with 'pure' geometry and with 'physical' geometry. The passage where he compares the three nods unmistakeably toward Marburg:

This differences [among the three] can be made clearer if we look, e.g. at the different meanings of 'straight line'. Abstract geometry means by 'straight line' an . . . ordered continuous series, i.e. a pure system of relations whose elements are completely indeterminate. If on the other hand we take the basic configurations of spatial intuition, the points of 'ideal space', as the elements, then abstract space becomes pure space. A straight line is now a spatial curve with certain attributes, not one observed in nature, but the straight line that Euclid – or better, ordinary projective geometry – speaks of. Physical geometry, finally . . . treats of spatial relations in nature; by a 'straight line' it means a certain line (i.e. one-dimensional manifold) of physical space, more precisely of bodily space, which is never actually precisely given in nature, but can be defined asymptotically by conditions of increasingly precise approximation. (UCLA 1920a, p. 5)

But Carnap carefully avoids taking sides here between Kant himself and the Marburg school, regarding the 'pure forms of intuition'. To obtain 'pure' from 'abstract' space, we take the domain of 'basic configurations [*Grundgebilde*] of spatial intuition' as elements of the 'pure system of relations whose elements are completely undefined'. This sounds more like Kant, but Carnap hedges his bets by adding, as an appositive, 'the points of "ideal space"', and then making explicit that a straight line of 'pure' space is *not* 'one that is perceived in nature [*eine in der Natur wahrgenommene*]'. This certainly does not represent an unambiguous commitment to the Marburg conception of space and time as products of intellectual 'synthesis', but leaves the door ajar to this view, as does the name 'pure space' itself (in *Der Raum*, a year later, it would become 'intuitive space'). In any case, there can be no doubt that this is a Kantian view of one stripe or another, not an empiricist one such as Mach's (1902, pp. 320–422). This is affirmed a few pages later when Carnap returns to the relations among the different kinds of space:

An [abstract space] is a logical system of relations among indefinite elements. It says: in case certain relations, specified purely formally, hold [*gelten*] among the elements of a set, then certain theorems hold for this system. If we then put in place of those elements the points of an ideal space of our representation [*eines idealen Raumes unserer Vorstellung*] and assume those relations as unproved axioms, then those theorems hold here as well: we then have the pure geometries. But what motivates [*was veranlaßt*] us to accept, and what justifies us in accepting, these assumptions? The motivation is given by the task [*Aufgabe*] of constructing the systems of physical geometry. The logical justification for asserting the axioms and claiming their apodeictic certainty rests on the fact that they are not founded on experience but are a priori knowledge. (UCLA 1920a, p. 13)

The characterisation of 'abstract space' is Russellian and if-then-ist. And the motivation Carnap gives here for even bothering with 'pure space' is pragmatic and scientific, more in accord with Helmholtz than with later neo-Kantian views. But the conclusion sounds Kantian. And what does seem very much in accord with a specifically Marburg intellectualism is what comes next: the most general concepts of 'abstract' geometry are narrowed down, analyzed into sub-concepts compatible with certain 'specialising constraints [*spezialisierende Voraussetzungen*]' (UCLA 1920a, p. 7) deriving from considerations relevant to 'pure' and 'physical' space but not themselves empirical, i.e. the axioms of 'pure' geometry and, then, various meta-'physical' principles. We begin with the most general concept of *function*, 'because if we start there we can obtain the objects of the mathematical sciences by a uniform procedure [*in geschlossenem Fortgange*]'.[1] A fold-out table at the end of the dissertation shows a hierarchical 'system of the logical and mathematical sciences'; at the top are 'functions', branching down we come, via 'functions with several arguments', then 'truth-functions with several arguments/*relations*', to 'binary relations', 'asymmetrical relations', 'intransitive asymmetric relations/ordered series/*ordinal numbers*', and thence finally to real numbers and the continuum, and continua of three dimensions. These structures of 'abstract geometry' each have application instances, either to pure 'spatial figures [*räumliche Gebilde*]' to obtain 'pure geometry', or to moving bodies, to obtain 'physical geometry'. The 'specialising constraints [*spezialisierende Voraussetzungen*]' of 'pure geometry' (i.e. a selection of Hilbert's axioms) further constrain the possibilities, as then does a series of further restrictions arising from various regulative principles of physics: the 'principle of the impenetrability of three-dimensional bodies' confines us to projective spaces of three

---

[1] 'Following *Frege* we conceive a function in its most general sense as an "unsaturated" expression with one or more open places ("argument places"), which has a particular meaning (a "value"), when objects step into those places. If this meaning is not another object but a "truth value", i.e. either the True or the False, then we have a particular kind of functions, the "truth functions". As *Frege* shows, concepts are functions of this kind with *one* argument, and relations are functions of this kind with several arguments' (UCLA 1920a, p. 2).

dimensions;[2] the 'principle of the motion of bodies in continuous trans-formations [*Grundsatz der Bewegung der Körper als stetiger Transformation*]' further confines us to metric spaces; the 'principle of rigid bodies [*Grundsatz des starren Körpers*]', finally, to metric spaces of constant curvature.

Moreover, Carnap appears to concede to the Marburg approach that intuition (*Anschauung*) is not the ultimate standard of knowledge (though as we saw, 'pure' space seems to rely on pure intuition for its construction). The context is his refutation of the idea that 'only Euclidean geometry can ground experience [*Erfahrung begründen*]'. 'Such a view', he says, 'must not only be logically refuted, but its genesis must be psychologically explained' (UCLA 1920a, p. 30). Though there is no exact psychological theory about the relative difficulty of attaining 'intuitive representations [*anschauliche Vorstellungen*]' of spaces with different curvatures, some kinds of space are evidently more difficult for humans to develop an intuition of than others. In some cases, such as the space of variable curvature required by general relativity, it seems to be attainable 'only through somewhat longer, more thorough acquaintance with the geometrical relations obtaining in it'. But this requirement of a 'longer acquaintance', someone might object, indicates 'that it would then merely be a matter of the conceptual *knowledge* of the geometrical relations in that space, since of course no long theoretical acquaintance is necessary for the development of an intuitive image' (UCLA 1920a, p. 31). His response to this objection might once again, at first sight, seem to put him near the Marburg school:

The answer to this is that theoretical acquaintance is needed because it is a matter of spatial relations whose departure from the accustomed Euclidean geometry only becomes apparent in the observation of very large areas, which we are not accustomed to imagine, and even there [they depart from the Euclidean] to such a tiny degree that it is hard for us to distinguish these spatial relations reliably from the almost identical ones of Euclidean space. (UCLA 1920a, p. 32)

The use of theory can distinguish different kinds of space where the dif-ferences are too fine for sense perception to distinguish – this sounds like an echo of Natorp's argument for the genetic conception of knowledge (Chapter 2 above). But in fact this passage neatly illustrates the *limits* to Carnap's acceptance of the Marburg viewpoint. For the basis of the 'psy-chological explanation' he goes on to give for the widespread prejudice

---

[2] This is because the most general 'pure' geometry for him, at this point, was projective geometry of *n* dimensions; he appears to have taken this over from Russell (1897). A few weeks after writing this dissertation, he realised that it should be *topological* space of *n* dimensions, and *Der Raum* reflects this change; see below, pp. 121–2, 131–8.

against non-Euclidean geometries in intuitive representation (*anschauliche Vorstellung*)[3] is 'habituation [*Gewöhnung*]'. Furthermore: 'This impossibility of imagining [non-Euclidean spaces] does not exist. We are only the victims of habit. To imagine the relations within a non-Euclidean space is not impossible, just difficult' (UCLA 1920a, p. 30). This is essentially the view of Helmholtz, not of Natorp.

And although Carnap endorses Natorp's statement that 'after an appropriate choice of physical assumptions *every* [set of physical observations] can be made consistent with *every* geometry'[4] (Natorp 1910, p. 302, quoted by Carnap, UCLA 1920a, p. 20), he actually interprets that statement in a way that goes directly counter to Natorp's intentions, as he must have realised, though he innocently says 'as it is presumably meant': 'i.e. that (a) physical assumptions, (b) physical observations, and (c) the geometrical system mutually determine each other by functional relations'. If we take Natorp this way,

. . . then with the same justification with which Natorp sees (b) and (c) as independent variables that determine (a), we can regard (b) and (a) as independent variables uniquely determining (c). The possibility of both views is a consequence of the fact that the functional relation involved is a purely logical (not a causal or other) relation. (UCLA 1920a, pp. 20–1)

He then pushes this to a point where it explicitly contradicts Natorp:

So the claim in *Natorp*'s next sentence ('thus the choice of assumptions for geometry has definitely to be arrived at independently of physical observations') not only does not follow from the previous sentence, but in fact its diametrical opposite follows: 'so the choice [of assumptions for geometry] does not have to be [arrived at] independently [of physical observations]'. (UCLA 1920a, p. 21)

Empirical evidence had a different status here than for Marburg. For Carnap, it was not only equal and fully independent (he goes out of his way to emphasise the *symmetry* between theory and evidence, given a geometrical framework), but had the final word.[5] While a choice of (b) and of (c)

---

[3] Among those who maintain this prejudice, Carnap explicitly footnotes Natorp (1910) and Bauch (1911).

[4] Though he also corrects it: 'rather than "after [*nach*]" it should, more correctly, read "by means of [*durch*]", for *after* that choice every set of observations can no longer be made consistent with every geometry' (UCLA 1920a, p. 20).

[5] This is especially clear from his rejection of Natorp's criticism of Gauss's attempt to determine the curvature of our space by measuring the sum of the angles between three hilltops: 'Since he [Gauss] decided (implicitly) to retain the physical assumptions . . . he was right to attribute to his experiment the significance of finding out the "correct" geometry. The accusation that this was a mistaken empiricism, levelled at him by *Natorp*, is therefore not justified. Of course Gauss could also, if his measurements had given a positive result, have altered the physical rather than the geometric

determine (a), and (b) and (a) determine (c), there was never any question, for Carnap, that (a) and (c) could determine (b). Moreover: 'This gives not just a negative definition for the role of observations, for the limitation described also gives positive suggestions'. The 'determinations' that narrow down the most general, abstract mathematical structures are both (ordinarily) *occasioned* and, in their final application to nature, *determined* by empirical evidence:

. . . the occasion for deriving precisely this system as a special case from the next one up *can* be empirical; and the claim that precisely this system is applicable to nature *must* be based on observations (presupposing certain basic physical assumptions, whose validity does not rest on experience). (UCLA 1920a, p. 37)

Carnap accepts from the Marburg school a certain primacy of theory; in fact, as we shall see, he accepts their view of the 'object-creating function of thought' (below, p. 153). But he rejects their scepticism about theory-independent evidence, which remains for him the ultimate *arbiter* of theory. And in the historical development of physical theory, he points out (UCLA 1920a, pp. 21–3), the interplay among physical theory, physical evidence, and mathematical geometry was not lopsidedly determined or driven by one of the three; the mathematical development of non-Euclidean space was a rather late development, though crucial in bringing about the realisation that the answer to the question which space is 'the space of our intuition' is not obvious, but must be investigated empirically. He leaves no doubt where he stands, in the end: 'The battle now was over the issue of whether this question should be decided by observation or by speculation' (UCLA 1920a, p. 23).

There are residual signs of ambivalence about the relation between 'pure' and 'physical' geometry, which indicate that his thought was developing as he wrote. While 'pure geometry' is in the foreground, Carnap carefully avoids commitment whether it is constituted in pure intuition (as in Kant and Helmholtz) or created by the intellect (as in Natorp). Its role in physics is a little ambiguous; while we know the axioms of pure geometry with 'apodeictic certainty', this apparently tells us nothing about their applicability to physical space, where, as we saw, they are subject to the ultimate tribunal of observational evidence. Still, we are told that 'The motivation is given by the task [*Aufgabe*] of constructing the systems of physical geometry'. And 'it is to be stressed', Carnap says in one passage, 'that the

---

assumptions. In any case such an experiment has the significance that it tests the agreement of our present geometry and our present physics, and that it either confirms that agreement or overthrows one or the other of the two systems (whichever we choose)' (UCLA 1920a, p. 19).

geometry applied to experience does not have physical space as its object, as one might think, but pure space' (UCLA 1920a, p. 13). This would seem to indicate a relation of successive application among abstract, pure, and physical geometry (as we later find in *Der Raum*; see below, pp. 127–35), and is consistent with the above-quoted passage in which physical geometry 'treats of spatial relations in nature' and yet what it means by 'straight line' is something 'which is never actually given precisely in nature, but can be defined asymptotically by conditions of increasingly precise approximation' (above, p. 110). But in the fold-out chart, 'pure geometry' and 'physical geometry' are displayed as two completely separate and independent application instances of *abstract* geometry. This approach, not really supported in the text of the dissertation, would indicate a more definite Marburg influence. As the chart is referred to in the text, it may reflect an earlier position.

How should we characterise the Kantianism exhibited here? Though there is certainly an influence from the Marburg philosophers, especially Natorp, it is outweighed by the evident continuities with the first generation of more scientifically oriented neo-Kantians. Like Helmholtz, Carnap appears to have regarded Kant as – in spirit – unequivocally opposed to all first philosophy, and wanted to make Kant's system internally consistent by eliminating the aspects due merely to 'the inadequate development of the special sciences in Kant's time'. Carnap seems to have regarded himself as part of the broadly Helmholtzian project of 'explicating' (as he might later have said) Kant's Copernican revolution by detaching the axioms from intuition and deduction from synthesis (see Chapter 2 above).

Poincaré and Dingler

Throughout the 1920 dissertation, Carnap refers frequently to Poincaré, whom he had read even before the war. Some notes he took in 1914 indicate what had immediately impressed him. His summary of *Science and Hypothesis* is unexceptional:

Basic idea: The basic laws of mathematics and mechanics stand over and above 'true and false'; they are conventionally stipulated, because the most *convenient* forms of the empirical and mathematical laws can be represented by means of them, i.e. because they are the most opportune. (ASP 1914a)

In the preface to his German translation, Friedrich Lindemann excerpted fourteen of Poincaré's most sharply epigrammatic formulations to give the reader a flavour of the book. Of these, Carnap copied out two. The first is predictable: 'Experience can serve as the foundation of the principles of mechanics and nonetheless can never contradict them' (Poincaré 1904, p. 107). The second is Poincaré's own summary of the basic idea of his book: 'What science can attain to is not the things themselves but only the relations among the things; apart from these relations there is no knowable reality' (Poincaré 1904, p. XIII). This, he says, is what we will find out after we have reviewed all the sciences from arithmetic through geometry and mechanics to electrodynamics and experimental physics. This view is familiar from Helmholtz (above, Chapter 2). But it was also taken by neo-Kantians as consistent with their own position. The neo-Kantian Friedrich Kuntze, for instance, in a memorial address to the university of Berlin after Poincaré's death, summarised his *philosophical* achievement in these words: 'To pinpoint Poincaré's philosophical importance in a single sentence, one might say that he comprehensively broke the transcendental faith of the exact sciences and thereby made room once again for Kant's idealism'. There are two aspects to this, says Kuntze: a negative one which 'teaches the unknowability of the innermost essence of all the concepts from which mathematical science constructs itself, such as mass, force, energy', and a positive aspect which 'gives our knowledge [*unserem Erkennen*] the task of discerning relations and nothing but relations' (Kuntze 1912, p. 338).

Such an interpretation of Poincaré (shared by Natorp and Cassirer) is, at very least, extrapolative and controversial,[6] especially the first, negative aspect. What does Poincaré mean when he says we 'cannot know the things themselves' or 'a reality completely independent of the mind which conceives it, sees or feels it, is an impossibility' (Poincaré 1913, p. 14)? He does not mean that there is such a thing as Kant's unknowable *Ding an sich*. Poincaré means, rather, that our tools for knowing are not only natural (not only our direct sense inputs) but also artificial, i.e. linguistic; they contain a large element of arbitrary decision (like the units of measurement). *What we know* presents itself to us ineluctably with an admixture, in the terms, of such linguistic conventions.[7] And it is true that his conventionalism

---

[6] The interpretation of Poincaré's philosophy is still controversial; McLarty (1997) goes furthest in absolving Poincaré of any metaphysical prejudices against concept formation, even in logic. On the other side, though few would today go as far as Kuntze or Natorp, Friedman (1999, Chapter 4) maintains that 'Poincaré's conception of arithmetic is extremely close to the original Kantian conception of arithmetic' (1999, p. 83). As Goldfarb points out, though, 'in Poincaré's hands the notion of intuition has little in common with the Kantian one. The surrounding Kantian structure is completely lacking; there is no mention, for instance, of sensibility or the categories' (Goldfarb 1988, p. 63).

[7] Indeed, Poincaré thought innovations of language were the essential contribution of mathematics: 'mathematics is the art of giving the same name to different things . . . This is one of the characteristics

regarding the axioms of geometry and the laws of mechanics was a *conservative* conventionalism, one in which human 'convenience' tended to be defined rather statically (hence his insistence that no matter what form our future physics may take, we would choose to express it within the framework of Euclidean geometry). Implicitly at least he did, therefore, impose limits of a kind on human knowledge. But this conservatism fell far short of a Kantian belief that we had no choice in the matter of our geometry *at all*, or that it was irrevocably hard-wired into the human mode of processing sense data. On the contrary, his characterisation of the conventions as 'disguised definitions' indicates that he saw geometry and mechanics *not* as synthetic a priori but, rather, as analytic – though (here the conservatism again) not quite freely stipulated, rather dictated or tightly constrained, in an almost Wittgensteinian way, by the 'practice' enshrined in our 'form of life'.[8]

This also casts a rather different light on Poincaré's theme – the central idea, as he says, of *Science and Hypothesis* – that we cannot know the things themselves but only the relations among things, which are the only reality available to us. It seems that what Poincaré means by this is closely akin to the 'ontological humility' introduced by Helmholtz in his version of the *Zeichentheorie* (Chapter 3 above) which he described in words not so very different from Poincaré's:

Our sensations are effects brought forth in our organs by means of exterior causes, and how such an effect manifests itself depends of course quite essentially on the nature of the apparatus on which the cause operates. Insofar as the quality of our sensations gives us information about the peculiarities of the exterior process that excites it, it can count as a *sign* of that process, but not as a *picture*. For one expects of a picture some sort of similarity with the pictured object . . . But a sign need have no similarity of any sort whatever with that of which it is the sign. The relation between them is only that the same object, working its effects in the same way, produces the same sign, and that unequal signs always correspond to unequal causes.

To the popular view, which naively and complacently assumes the full truth of the pictures that our senses give us of things, this remainder of similarity that we recognise may seem rather paltry. In truth it is not; with its aid something of the greatest significance can be achieved: the representation of the regularities in

---

by which we recognise facts which give a great return: they are the facts which permit of these happy innovations of language. The bare fact, then, has sometimes no great interest . . . it only acquires a value when some more careful thinker perceives the connection it brings out, and symbolises it by a term' (Poincaré 1914, p. 34). This idea would, of course, be of great importance to Carnap after 1932.

[8] It also seems that (like Russell) he *did* regard certain basic mathematical (or logical) principles as synthetic a priori, such as the principle of induction. As in Russell's case, though, it is not entirely clear what is meant by this. See the discussion by Warren Goldfarb (1988, pp. 63ff.).

the processes of the real world . . . So even if our sense impressions in their qualities are only *signs*, whose special nature depends wholly on our internal organisation, they are nonetheless not to be dismissed as empty appearance, but are in fact a sign of *something*, whether this is something existing or something occurring; and what is most important, they can picture the *law* of this occurring. (Helmholtz 1878a, p. 222; PT pp. 347–8)

Poincaré himself makes his meaning even more explicit in a chapter of *The Value of Science* entitled 'Is Science Artificial?', in which he discusses the thesis of the Bergsonian Édouard LeRoy to the effect that 'the facts of science and, *a fortiori*, its laws are the artificial work of the scientist; science therefore can teach us nothing of the truth' (Poincaré 1913, p. 112), and especially LeRoy's 'paradoxical' affirmation 'that *the scientist creates the fact*' (p. 115). But this, it turns out, even for Le Roy refers not to ordinary 'crude' facts, but only to the 'scientific' fact. Poincaré shows that no unambiguous boundary can be drawn between these informal categories, and that, moreover, which of them a fact belongs in is language-relative. So:

All the scientist creates in a fact is the language in which he enunciates it. If he predicts a fact, he will employ this language, and for all those who can speak it and understand it, his prediction is free from ambiguity. Moreover, once this prediction is made, the question whether it is fulfilled or not evidently does not depend upon him. (Poincaré 1913, p. 121)

Poincaré and Helmholtz focus on different aspects of the interface between scientific knowledge and sense perception; Poincaré on the linguistic, Helmholtz on the processing of sense data. Yet it should be clear that, from the above perspective, their views are in harmony.

And it is very much in this spirit, not that of Kuntze or the Marburg school, that Carnap understood Poincaré in 1920. In the above passage where Carnap explicitly disagrees with Natorp, he cites Poincaré in support of his point that 'we are only the victims of a particular habituation'.[9]

Poincaré has shown with an example how the observers in surroundings that behaved in a *physically* different way than what we are acquainted with . . . would necessarily arrive at a *mental image* of a non-Euclidean space . . . and thereby that our difficulties in imagining such a space are to be attributed only to our lack

---

[9] Only if they had grown up in, and become habituated to, those fantastic worlds (the non-Euclidean and four-dimensional) would creatures otherwise similar to us, Poincaré says, find it convenient to use those geometries; we, brought up in our own accustomed world, would stick with Euclidean geometry: 'Quant à nous, en face des *mêmes* impressions, il est certain que nous trouverions plus commode de ne pas changer nos habitudes' (Poincaré 1902, p. 94). The 'il est *certain*' expresses the *conservativeness* of his conventionalism.

of habitual observation of that sort of physical process, i.e. only to 'our different socialisation' – to purely empirical factors. (UCLA 1920a, p. 32)

Where Poincaré had taken our habituation to be so deep as to prohibit the adoption of a different geometry, however, Carnap took a more voluntaristic approach. While this was certainly rooted in his wider views of the social and (in a broad sense) 'political' role of his intended 'system of knowledge', it may have been further encouraged by Carnap's acquaintance, at this time, with Hugo Dingler. An early publication of Carnap's (not listed in the 1963 bibliography) was a favourable review, in a Munich newspaper, of Dingler's *Foundations of Physics* (*Grundlagen der Physik*) (ASP/HD 1921a). And Dingler (whose early work had been highly praised by Mach[10]) was the only author of this period with whom Carnap found himself in such close agreement that he had seriously considered a collaboration.[11] At first sight this seems puzzling; there is little in Dingler's philosophy of physics that would have seemed especially attractive to Carnap, now or later.[12] And though Carnap later acknowledged Dingler's influence,[13] he emphasised that 'I did not share Dingler's radical conventionalism and still less his rejection of Einstein's general theory of relativity' (Carnap 1963, p. 15). What he *was* attracted by, for a brief period in the early 1920s, was Dingler's extreme voluntarism, the most articulate expression on a theoretical or philosophical plane, in early twentieth-century Germany, of the practical and ethical voluntarism Carnap espoused (Chapter 1 above).

In his *Grundlagen der Physik* (the book Carnap had reviewed favourably), Dingler had laid down, for instance, the 'principle of stipulation [*Prinzip der Festsetzung*]' i.e. '*There is no other way to guarantee the general validity of a law other than its stipulation by the will*' (Dingler 1919, p. 13). And the 'principle of synthesis [*Prinzip der Synthese*]' said that in the construction of science '*as much as possible . . . is to be achieved by stipulations arrived at by ourselves and as little as possible by other sources*'. Dingler stressed, like Poincaré, that there were conventional as well as empirical elements

---

[10] In the preface to the seventh (1912) edition of the *Science of Mechanics*, Mach says, 'At age 74 years, struck down by severe adversity, I will no longer foment a revolution. But I hope for substantial progress from a younger mathematician, Dr. Hugo Dingler, who has . . . retained his free, unprejudiced sense for *both* sides of science [the empirical and the "empirio-critical"]' (Mach 1912, p. XXXI).

[11] 'Dingler and I gave up the earlier plan of a joint publication when we noticed, at a thorough discussion (September [1921] in Jena), that despite agreement in important fundamental questions our standpoints are after all too far apart' (ASP 1921f).

[12] The best overview is Toretti (1978); see also the collection edited by Janich (1984).

[13] In the original version of his autobiography, he went so far as to say he had been 'influenced by Poincaré and *especially* by Hugo Dingler' (my emphasis) (UCLA 1957a, p. D28).

in our knowledge, but also held, *unlike* Poincaré, that since the empirical parts are contingent and uncertain, and since we have full control of the conventional parts, we should minimise the role of evidence and *maximise* that of conventions[14] (Dingler 1919, p. 10); this is presumably what Carnap meant by 'radical' conventionalism. When he discussed the idea 'that (a) physical presuppositions, (b) physical observations, and (c) the geometrical system are mutually determined by functional relations' (pp. 113–14 above), Carnap sees Einstein as taking the path of changing (c) and requiring a non-Euclidean geometry 'if one regards one and the same measuring rod independently of its place and its orientation as a realization of the same distance' (Einstein 1916, quoted by Carnap in UCLA 1920a, pp. 19–20). Dingler, on the other hand, acknowledges all the same evidence and takes the path of changing (a):

he chooses – in the full consciousness of free choice – the Euclidean spatial system and decides to keep it no matter what experiences occur; this then determines the form of the natural laws. He opposes relativity theory from this standpoint, but only from the principle of simplicity, because it applies its corrections at the 'foundation of the building' (the Euclidean spatial system) rather than at the 'third floor' (the physical assumptions). (Dingler 1919, p. 20)

Although he rejected Dingler's conclusions, it seems that Carnap was inspired by the example Dingler set of discussing and appraising science from the viewpoint of a general *Wissenschaftslehre*. The article (1923) that was originally planned as a collaboration with Dingler (and drafted in 1921) is an expansion of the above quotation from 1920, contrasting Einstein's path and Dingler's as two different ways of interpreting the 'demand for maximal simplicity [*Forderung der Einfachstheit*]' – as applied *either* to the basic laws or axioms themselves, *or* to the whole of the resulting description of nature. The point of this article is to show that there is a trade-off between these alternatives, and that simplicity of the axioms (i.e. Dingler's choice) leads to a vastly more complicated overall description.[15]

In the draft of this paper from the summer of 1921, he begins by saying he will summarise his points of agreement with Dingler:

The goal here is above all to set up a clear *demarcation* [*Abgrenzung*] *vis-à-vis the empirical standpoint* claiming that physics can be built up on the basis of

---

[14] In which he included the laws of logic, e.g. the law of contradiction: '*the application of the law of contradiction rests on my free will* . . . and this is just what we called a stipulation [*Festsetzung*]' (Dingler 1919, pp. 14–15).

[15] In his notes for a 1934 Prague lecture course on 'Current Trends in Natural Philosophy', he says of Dingler: 'Exaggeration of a healthy basic idea [*eines gesunden Grundgedankens*]. One *can* stick to chosen basic laws; but that would be highly impractical [*unzweckmäßig*]' (ASP 1934b, p. 7).

experimental results alone, without setting up non-experiential principles. Against that it is to be emphasised that at two points in particular ['the basis of spatial determination and the causal law', to which in the published version a third is added, 'the stipulation of a norm for time-measurement'] stipulations must be undertaken that are subject to our free choice; that, more precisely, are in no way forced on us by empirical findings and thus can subsequently neither be confirmed nor refuted by them. The *choice of stipulations* is not, however, a matter of whim, but proceeds according to methodological principles . . . (ASP 1921c, p. 1)

It seems, then, that although Carnap was interested in a clear 'demarcation vis-à-vis the empirical standpoint', and was willing to go along with certain Marburg formulations of such demarcation, the main thrust of this *Abgrenzung* stemmed from Poincaré (and more radical conventionalists like Dingler). And his interest focused on the categorial framework and its 'methodological principles' by which the basic principles of science (perhaps, as we saw in Chapter 3, even deductive logic) were to be determined.

It is with all this in mind, then, that we should read the very Kantian-sounding conclusion in the final paragraph of Carnap's 1920 dissertation:

The special importance for philosophy of the problem treated here consists in this: that in *geometry* the system that forms the object of this science – or, according to our explanations, more precisely: the most general form of these different systems [i.e. projective space of *n* dimensions] – represents the transcendental-logical function of the a priori form of intuition and thus the condition of the possibility of any object of experience in general. (UCLA 1920a, p. 38)

A few weeks later, Carnap would realise that topological space of *n* dimensions, not projective space, was 'the most general form of these different systems', but even without that additional step, he had chosen a very general framework, one that he surely thought, when he chose it, on the basis of his reading of Klein and Russell was, in Russell's words, 'the [most general] qualitative science of abstract externality' (Russell 1897, p. 121). What he thought of as the a priori form of intuition, in other words, was almost exactly what Helmholtz continued to regard as a priori, even as late as 1878, in a reply to J. P. N. Land (who had raised this issue):

It is a misunderstanding on Professor Land's part, by the way, if he thinks I wished to raise any objection to the notion of space as being for us *a priori* and necessary or (in Kant's sense) transcendental, form of intuition. That was not at all my intention. Of course my view of the relations between this transcendental form and reality, as I will set it forth in the third section of this paper, does not quite coincide with that of many followers of Kant and Schopenhauer. But space may very well be a form of intuition, in the Kantian sense, without this form including the axioms. (Helmholtz 1878b, p. 641; PT p. 213)

This differs from Carnap's 1920 view only in that Carnap would have inserted 'specialising' (or 'more specifically metrical') before 'axioms' in the last sentence (because of his Russellian view of projective geometry as expressing only the most general 'qualitative' form of 'abstract externality'). In epistemology at least, Carnap picked up where Helmholtz had left off.

TWO KANTIAN QUESTIONS, AS FRAMED BY VAIHINGER

Given the above portrayal of the early Carnap – as a neo-Kantian who was closer to Helmholtz and Poincaré than to the newer southwest or Marburg schools – it is not surprising that two Kantian questions motivated much of his early interest in the precise relation between 'the immediately given [*das Unmittelbare*]' and 'rational ingredients [*rationale Zutaten*]':

(i) How is theoretical natural science possible? (How can we get from immediate acquaintance (*das Unmittelbare*) to universal laws?)

(ii) How (conversely) can the purely theoretical statements of science be applied to, or brought to bear on, subjective experience? (How can the 'rational ingredients' make contact with the subjective world of sensation? In Kantian terms, this is the problem of 'schematisation'.)

Though these questions had motivated Kant's 'Copernican revolution', and also been central for Helmholtz, they had been largely taken off the philosophical agenda again by Cohen and Natorp, who had subsumed Kant's 'material' nature so completely under 'formal' nature that little question could remain about the possibility of bridging the gap between them. For Carnap, on the other hand, these questions were central again. A 1920 letter to Hugo Dingler, for instance, lists a number of subjects (apart from an already sketched axiom system of kinematics)[16] on which he would like to work:

> The dependence of physics on the axiom of measurement;
> The point of, and justification for, the application of non-Euclidean geometry in physics;
> The axiom of congruence in physics; or: The methodological significance of the rigid body in physics;

---

[16] This sketch (ASP 1920b, mentioned in 1963, p. 11) was later worked out in some detail (ASP 1924a). The context of the list is a query whether any items on it might be acceptable as possible subjects for a physics dissertation in Munich under Dingler's supervision. He adds, at the end of the list, 'These are of course only a few examples off the top of my head to indicate roughly the field I want to work in. Many [other] questions deserving closer scrutiny are obviously worth considering.'

The relation between kinematics and experience;

The axioms of physics;

On the synthetic (in the sense of: non-empirical) method in physics;

The a priori character of the laws of physics;

The empirical and non-empirical moments in the law of the conservation of energy;

In what sense does the law of the conservation of energy have unconditional validity independently of all future experience?

On the relation between the theory of relativity and experience;

What grounds are ultimately decisive in deciding about the justification of a physical theory, with special reference to the theory of relativity?

(ASP/HD 1920a)

And in fact Carnap's main preoccupation during this entire period was the construction of a 'total system of all concepts' that would construct all concepts, including those of theoretical natural science, from a starting point in immediate acquaintance (see Chapter 5 below).

In one of the sketches toward this project, he analysed the totality of any given 'world picture [*Weltbild*]' into two major components: that expressing, or concerned with, values or sentiments (*Lebensgefühl*), and that expressing, or concerned with, beliefs or views (*Anschauungen*). The latter is the realm of judgement, he said, statements about it can be true or false, while the former is outside that realm. In Jena, before the war, he had learned from Herman Nohl, a pupil of Dilthey, that philosophical systems are to be regarded as expressions of *Lebensgefühl*, and cannot be rationally judged (Gabriel 2004). As we saw, he was not denying the practical significance of such expressions, let alone of *Lebensgefühl* itself; he recognised that it was connected to, or depended on, the realm of knowledge. Indeed he was convinced that knowledge could *transform* the realm of *Lebensgefühl* quite fundamentally.[17] His entire attention focused, therefore, on the realm of knowledge. Metaphysical philosophy, the attempt to frame questions of *Lebensgefühl* in theoretical form, could not in his view contribute much to this enterprise.

In Carnap's 1921 'idealistic conception' discussed in the letter to Flitner (pp. 95–7 above), he had proposed a criterion of objectivity to distinguish between the rationally criticisable and *Lebensgefühl*: experiences of the 'real' (as he had then put it) were those that could be intersubjectively described

---

[17] In this he differed from Dilthey and Nohl, perhaps because of the influence of Marxism during this period. His Bauhaus-lectures in 1929 point in this direction (cf. Dahms 2004). In his autobiography, he states his belief that 'all deliberate action presupposes knowledge of the world, that the scientific method is the best method of acquiring knowledge and that therefore science must be regarded as one of the most valuable instruments for the improvement of life' (Carnap 1963, p. 83).

and predicted. Gogarten's mysticism, discussed there, remained at the level of *Lebensgefühl* because it could not point to any aspect or part of the non-mystic's experience predictable or explainable only in mystical terms, in the way that the seeing person or musical person, in his examples, was able to predict events and processes that protruded into the blind or unmusical person's world of experience. Goethe's critique of Newton, too, inappropriately imposed considerations of *Lebensgefühl* on the realm of science, since for *physics*, i.e. for what was 'first in the order of nature', it is irrelevant that sound qualities and tactile sensations of vibration belong to different sense modalities; this is rather a matter of the 'first toward us', how things come to be known (to us). To conflate the 'first toward us' and the 'first in the order of nature', as Goethe had,[18] was to allow *Lebensgefühl* to dictate or constrain what could be rationally judged. Like the Marburg school, the young Carnap saw the power of science precisely in its ability to *liberate* us from the modalities of sense perception and, intimately bound up with them, the categories of everyday common sense. Contrasting the realm of perception and that of physical theory in 1921, he wrote:

The total separateness of these two areas cannot be emphasised strongly enough. The first contains the contents of sensation: colours, sounds, smells, pressures, sensations of warmth, etc. – none of which is even mentioned in theoretical physics . . . The epistemological question of the relation between the two areas is not at issue here. Whether (along phenomenological-realistic lines) one calls the contents of the first (e.g. the colour blue) 'mere appearances' and those of the second (e.g. the corresponding electromagnetic waves) 'reality' – or vice versa (along positivist lines) one designates those of the first 'the real given' and those of the second 'mere conceptual complexes' – about that question, physics doesn't need to be concerned . . . physics expresses itself neutrally with the help of purely formal correspondence-relations and leaves such interpretations to a non-physical investigation. (ASP 1921c, pp. 10–12)

At this point such a 'non-physical investigation' had not been excluded as meaningless. Although by the late 1920s the class of cognitively meaningful statements and the class of expressions of *Lebensgefühl* would be regarded as mutually exclusive, it seems that even at that later time (see Chapter 6

---

[18] A later example of this was Wilfrid Sellars's notorious idea of 'sensa', to which Carnap objected, 'In general I would emphasise that the acceptability of a theory formulated in terms of constructs is to be judged only by its efficiency in explaining and predicting observable events. If one theoretical system is simpler than another but leads to exactly the same predictions of observable events, then it is more efficient and therefore definitely preferable. It is certainly desirable that, for any phenomenon which we observe, there be a counterpart in the total theoretical system of science. But I do not see any good reason for desiring, let alone for requiring, that for certain events, e.g. sense-data, the counterparts in the theoretical system should be primitives rather than complex concepts definable on the basis of the primitives' (ASP 1954a, p. 4).

below) Carnap leaves room for *practical* external principles, of the sort that Helmholtz calls 'metaphysical hypotheses', to fill out provisionally what is not (yet) accessible to science, and to guide us in life meanwhile:

These hypotheses are even more essential for practical action [*das Handeln*] [than for science itself], because one can't always wait around for a secure scientific decision to be reached, but must make a decision, whether according to probability or according to aesthetic or moral feeling. In this sense as well, there can be no objection to metaphysical hypotheses. (Helmholtz 1878a, p. 239; PT p. 360)

In fact, Carnap was strongly influenced in the early 1920s by a philosopher who made this idea central to an entire system. This was Hans Vaihinger, the author of *The Philosophy of As If* (*Die Philosophie des Als-Ob*) (Vaihinger 1922). Vaihinger was also known as a Kant scholar, the author of a massive two-volume commentary on the *Critique of Pure Reason*, and the founder of the *Kant-Studien* in 1906 as an impartial, inclusive forum for Kantians of all persuasions, in contradistinction to the 'house periodicals' of the various schools, which rarely published dissenting views.

Vaihinger regarded himself as a Kantian, and as a disciple of Lange, but called his view 'idealistic positivism' or 'positivistic idealism'. What this name does not capture but which he himself acknowledged as essential to his philosophy is its conception of intellectual life as subservient to practical ends and thus, ultimately, to human passions.[19] Like Lange, Vaihinger was an enthusiastic Darwinian; language and thought had evolved, he said, as 'purposefully operating organic functions', i.e. survival mechanisms. Their products – theories and concepts – are to be understood within the entire economy of the human organism and not as existing primarily for the sake of accurate representation of something external (Vaihinger 1922, pp. 1–25). He was seen by many at the time as an ally of the American pragmatists,[20] and admitted the resemblance, but had a low opinion of William James and rejected his theory of truth. Unlike James, Vaihinger distinguished between truth and belief; what we *believe*, he thought, are useful fictions like Kant's ideals, and we believe them for practical reasons, even if we think they may well be false. Vaihinger's view of what we can actually know

[19] In this respect he endorsed Schopenhauer's subordination of reason to the will, though he was careful to note that he did not accept Schopenhauer's metaphysical theories. He regarded his view as continuous, also, with Kant's 'primacy of the practical', and this rather 'pragmatist' conception of Kant was also the one he argued for in his commentary and many articles about aspects of Kant's philosophy.

[20] Klaus Ceynowa (1993) argues that American pragmatism and Vaihinger's philosophy have a common origin in the psychological theories of Alexander Bain, which were directly and explicitly picked up by Peirce and James, and had quite independently been transmitted to Germany especially via the neurophysiologist Adolf Horwicz, whom Vaihinger acknowledged as an important influence.

to be true or false was radically positivist; without fictions, he thought, we are locked in a chaotic and utterly formless subjectivity of the present moment. And the quality of fictions was to be judged by their usefulness in the conduct of life, not by their truth. Even if some or all of our most useful and robust scientific fictions should happen to be actually true, he thought, there is no way we could know them to be so (Vaihinger 1922, esp. pp. 123–9).

Vaihinger's positive doctrines influenced Carnap less than the basic framework in which he articulated the Kantian questions (i) and (ii) above (Vaihinger 1922, esp. pp. 286–327). The 'idealistic conception' that Carnap advanced (in the letter to Flitner) against Gogarten's mysticism seems at least partly derived from Vaihinger. More specifically, the view expressed in an early set of notes toward the *Aufbau* (in April 1921; see Chapter 5 below) that all we know directly is the 'chaos of sensations [*Chaos der Empfindungen*]' is a direct echo of Vaihinger (Vaihinger 1922, e.g. p. 298), though Carnap seems to have thought from the beginning that Vaihinger's view of what could be gleaned or deduced from this 'chaos', by logic or phenomenological reflection or both, was too narrow, and that more could be achieved by these means. Throughout the early 1920s, Carnap refers to conventions and even scientific theories as 'fictions', most prominently in a paper that actually carries the word in the title: 'Three-dimensionality of Space and Causality: An Investigation of the Interrelation of Two Fictions'. This paper, written in the summer of 1922 (published 1924) represents the zenith of Vaihinger's influence on Carnap. It was published, not coincidentally, in the journal *Annalen der Philosophie und philosophischen Kritik*, which had been founded in 1921 by Vaihinger's chief disciple Raymund Schmidt to provide a forum for discussion of the 'as-if' philosophy. In the *Aufbau* itself, one of the four languages in which the construction is described (§95) is that of a 'fictional construction [*fiktive Konstruktion*]'. This has generally been taken to be Kantian language, which is approximately right. More specifically, it is Vaihinger's language, as the pragmatic dimension indicates; the fictions are chosen to suit the practical purpose of the construction. 'The practically suitable [*zweckmäßigen*] *fictions* arise from the purpose of the constitutions as rational reconstructions of the knowledge of objects' (§99). And at a deeper level, a certain fundamental pragmatism pervades Carnap's thought during this period, even (as we will see in Chapter 6) in the *Aufbau* itself.

Vaihinger's influence is most obvious in Carnap's way of articulating question (i) above ('How is theoretical science possible?'), as well as in his first attempts to answer it – the 'total system of all concepts' to be discussed in Chapter 5. Meanwhile, Vaihinger's influence extended also to Carnap's early attempts to confront question **(ii)**, in his doctoral dissertation and first book, *Space: A Contribution to the Study of Science* (*Der Raum: Ein Beitrag zur Wissenschaftslehre*) (1922) as well as other writings during this period. The next two sections will examine the evolution of Carnap's neo-Kantianism by comparing *Der Raum* (written in the spring of 1921) with the 1920 dissertation discussed above.

DER RAUM

Like the 1920 dissertation, *Der Raum* distinguishes three meanings of 'space': formal, intuitive, and physical space, corresponding to the three sources of knowledge Carnap then recognised: logic (the analytic), pure intuition, and observation. (In 1920 they had been called abstract, pure, and physical space – this is not just a change of name, as we will see; the definitions have shifted somewhat.) As in 1920, the third source of knowledge, observation, gets significantly more emphasis than was usual in the Kantian tradition. And as in 1920, the Helmholtzian distinction between the axioms of geometry and qualitative 'spatiality' is explicitly formulated:

Intuitive space is an order-configuration [*ein Ordnungsgefüge*] whose formal species we can conceptually outline, but as in the case of anything intuitively given, not its particular qualitative being [*sein besonderes Sosein*]. Here one can merely gesture at contents of experience [*Erlebnisinhalte*] . . . (1922, p. 22)

But what had been called 'pure geometry' in the 1920 dissertation acquires a somewhat different role, reflected in its new name, 'intuitive geometry'. In 1920, the axioms of 'pure geometry' had been considered 'a priori knowledge', and this licensed a claim to their 'apodeictic certainty'. Though the motivation for arriving at these axioms had been to construct systems of *physical* geometry, pure geometry itself had nonetheless still been a form of objective knowledge. In *Der Raum*, as we will see, this becomes hazier, and 'intuitive geometry' becomes more *subjective*. In the final section below, some possible diagnoses of this trend from 1920 to 1921 will be discussed.

The relation among the three kinds of space is also expressed somewhat differently in *Der Raum*. The terminology is a little confusing: 'The relation of substitution [*Einsetzung*] holds between the theory of formal space and that of intuitive space; between the latter and the theory of physical space the relation of subordination [*Unterordnung*] holds' (1922, p. 60). All Carnap means by this, though, is that in the first case a *completely* general structure is narrowed down to a particular category of possible applications, still general with respect to concrete instances, while in the second case this structure of (relatively limited) generality is applied to particular concrete instances.[21] His view of formal geometry is not axiomatic here, so he does not regard the theory of intuitive space as a *model* of formal geometry. What he calls 'formal' geometry was, rather, *constructed* by explicit definition from fundamental concepts and principles of logic. As such it was unambiguous (*eindeutig*); it could be applied to different cases but did not admit of different interpretations.

Where, then, did classical axiomatic geometry – geometry as it is ordinarily known, in the long tradition reaching from Euclid to Hilbert and beyond – fit in? There is a correspondence between 'formal' geometry and axiomatic geometry, Carnap tells us;[22] we can express the axioms 'formally' (1922, p. 1). But which axioms are we to choose? On the one hand, they should correspond with intuition, but on the other hand, they should be usable to establish a (spatial or spatiotemporal) framework for physical theory.[23] 'Formal' geometry itself does not constrain this choice. Nor does axiomatic geometry, of itself, give any basis for choosing any particular set of axioms from the infinite possibilities shown by Hilbert. And, as in the 1920 dissertation, Carnap rejects the possibility of arriving at 'the' empirically correct geometry solely by observation.

So Carnap began on the intuitive side, and here he relied on Husserl, who had sketched something like a categorial grammar of subjective intuition. Carnap used this sketch as a basis for the choice of axioms for physical geometry. (It was not supposed to *justify* the axioms; the point was to choose intuitively graspable ones. Physical theories expressed in terms of the chosen geometry are then justified inductively by observational facts.)

---

[21] The relation of formal to intuitive geometry *and* that of intuitive to physical geometry is 'that of a general rule to its *application*, but in different senses'; in the first case 'limitation of the general conceptual rule to a special case, which with respect to reality nonetheless enjoys generality'; in the second case 'application of this limited generality to a particular real case, in which there is no more generality'. He then explains the above terminology: 'Let this difference be designated by the expressions "substitution" and "subsumption", for in the first case something definite is substituted for indefinite relata, in the second case something really experienced is subordinated to a definite rule' (1922, p. 60).

[22] To modern ears this sounds odd; for us, axiomatic geometry *is* 'formal' geometry, and the Russellian constructions Carnap calls 'formal' geometry would be *models* of axiomatic theories. In the following passages, I use Carnap's own terminology.

[23] Michael Friedman attributes a somewhat different view to Carnap: 'The point of physical space, for Carnap, is . . . to order and arrange the objects of our actual experience of nature in the intuitive space we have already constructed completely a priori' (Friedman 1999, p. 48). But Carnap makes clear that intuitive space is to be adjusted to the requirements of physical space, not vice versa; e.g. the criteria for the choice of 'stipulations [*Forderungen*]' in the development of intuitive space are determined by the requirements for the study of physical space (1922, p. 29).

So Kantian 'pure space' of 1920 is replaced by the more subjective 'intuitive space' of 1921. The relevant idea of Husserl's, for this purpose, was that of 'eidetic' perception or instantaneous *grasping* of an experience in its particular qualitative nature, quite apart from any content it may have regarding something objective, or external to the experience (Husserl 1913). This is an elaboration on the Helmholtzian view Carnap had begun with in 1920; regarding our 'intuitive-spatial representations' of intuitive space, he now says:

Experience does not supply a justification [*Rechtsgrund*] for them; the principles are independent of experience, more precisely (as Driesch puts it): independent of the 'amount of experience', i.e. knowledge of them does not, as with empirical statements, become more secure with multiply repeated experience. For what we have here, as Husserl has shown, are not facts in the sense of experienced reality, but the essence ('Eidos') of particular given things, which can be grasped at once in their particular qualitative being by a single presentation. Just as I can tell – of three definite colour shades deep green, blue, and red – from a single experience, even just in imagination, that the first in its special quality is more closely similar to the second than to the third; so I find when I imagine spatial configurations that several lines go through two points, that on each of them more points are situated, that a simple line segment, but not a plane region, is divided in two by a point lying on it, etc. (1922 , p. 22)

It would be a mistake to trivialise Carnap's interest in phenomenology during this period.[24] Husserl's approach to 'eidetic perception' could be seen as the component of 'transcendental logic' that 'investigates the laws according to which "any possible object of science forms itself into an object to begin with"'. As such it would be the essential 'pre-logic [*Vor-Logik*]' (Driesch 1913, p. 24) required for the application of logic, in the version of phenomenology presented by Hans Driesch, whose *Ordnungslehre* was a significant influence both on *Der Raum* and on the *Aufbau*. In particular, phenomenology provided a tool for addressing question **(ii)** above (pp. 122–7): how could the purely formal relations of universal, completely general and completely unambiguous (*eindeutig*) 'formal geometry' apply to something as fluid and subjective as first-person spatial experience? Unlike

---

[24] The above terminology of 'substitution [*Einsetzung*]' (describing the relation of formal to intuitive space) and 'subordination [*Unterordnung*]' (intuitive to physical space) Carnap illustrates by analogy to Husserl's categories of 'formal ontology (the "mathesis universalis" of Leibniz), regional ontology, factual science' (1922, p. 61, referring to Husserl 1913, pp. 30–1. and 111–12. as well as Husserl 1900, pp. 221ff., where Carnap particularly notes Husserl's reference to Leibniz's *mathesis universalis* as the ideal to which his 'pure logic [*reine Logik*]' aspires). And in Carnap's copy of the Suhrkamp edition of *Scheinprobleme* (1966), where the editor Günther Patzig remarks (in his afterword) that while living near Freiburg in 1919–26, Carnap seems not to have sought or taken up contact with Husserl and his circle there, Carnap's note in the margin objects: 'doch' (ASP 1966c, p. 101).

the Marburg school, Husserl and Driesch had taken this problem seriously, and unlike Schlick (1918, p. 36), they had not simply thrown up their hands and declared that between theory and intuition 'the bridges . . . are demolished'.

Husserl's comprehensive programme of systematising subjective experience, particularly as it relates to the foundations of the sciences, would naturally have appealed to Carnap as a project consistent with his own effort to relate a 'total system of all concepts' (see below, Chapter 5) to subjective experience – to 'schematise' such a system. Carnap could have regarded Husserl's programme for a 'philosophy as exact science [*Philosophie als strenge Wissenschaft*]' (Husserl 1911) as a programme for an overall *calculus philosophicus* in which the sought-for 'principles of the [scientific] study of science [*Grundsätze der Wissenschaftslehre*]' could be made intuitively explicit, tested for consequences, and justified. Husserl had offered his programme of 'pure logic [*reine Logik*]' as the basis for a new kind of *Mathesis universalis*, with reference to Leibniz and Bolzano (Husserl 1913, p. 22; Husserl 1900, §§60, 67). While Carnap already regarded Frege's logic as the main tool of construction, it could not provide the objects or materials on which construction could operate.[25] Husserl's phenomenological inventory of our 'phenomenal syntax' by means of 'analysis of consciousness [*Bewußtseinsanalyse*]' could be used as a 'schematic' psychology to 'schematise' (in Kant's sense) the purely logical constructions of formal space in their application to physical space.

Husserl's radical critique of experimental psychology in 'Philosophy as an exact science' (Husserl 1911, pp. 302ff.)) did not mean he was anti-experimental. The Gestalt psychologists – who were certainly experimental – read Husserl's paper as a *constructive* proposal for experimental psychology, especially regarding the psychological foundations of mental content (Ash 1998, pp. 74–9). It seems Carnap also took Husserl this way, and from his viewpoint phenomenology had a number of advantages over other 'schematic' psychologies then available. Unlike the Marburg school, Husserl emphasised the subjectivity of experience. Unlike Schlick, or the empiricism to which most experimental psychologists still inclined, Husserl had by the time of the *Logical Investigations* (Husserl 1900) adopted a Fregean anti-psychologism in logic and mathematics. And finally, Husserl

---

[25] This conviction remained in place through the initial phases of the *Aufbau* project: 'To reconstruct reality [*Wirklichkeit*] structurally, we proceed from a number (as small as possible) of undefined basic concepts [*Grundbegriffe*] whose content can only be hinted at by phenomenological indication [*durch phänomenologischen Hinweis*] and basic relations among these' (ASP 1922d, p. ci); see below, Chapter 5.

showed a greater awareness even than most (pre-Gestalt) experimental psychologists of the complexity and composite character of intuition. He had learned from the century of empirical research after Kant that this crude traditional category was too vague for most purposes. 'Intimation of essences [*Wesenserschauung*]' is not in fact much more precise than Kant's 'intuition [*Anschauung*]', but Carnap could at least regard it as a stand-in or place-holder, and meanwhile he was satisfied that as a 'structural' subcomponent of *Anschauung*, directed only to 'essences' (1922, p. 23), it defined a sufficiently distinct subcategory of traditional Kantian *Anschauung*.[26]

So although it would be wrong to trivialise Carnap's interest in phenomenology, his adoption of Husserl's framework to choose axioms for intuitive space is somewhat provisional. And though Carnap did not himself think this the most interesting part of *Der Raum*, he did, in a 1921 letter (his first) to Bertrand Russell, accompanying a copy of the typescript, think it would be of most interest to Russell:

> What may interest you most in the present essay is probably the distinction between 'formal space' and 'intuitive space' as two quite different objects of a science of space. I believe I have shown here that although geometry can restrict itself entirely to treating a 'complex of relations' (geometry as the theory of formal space), on the other hand there is also a different geometry (i.e. as the theory of intuitive space) that cannot fully be derived from formal logic. (ASP 1921e, p. 1)

What did Carnap believe that he had 'shown'? It is not the first part of what he claims here, i.e. that geometry can be seen as completely formal; Russell himself had argued long ago, in *Principles*, that geometry was constructible from logic. Carnap must then have believed himself to have shown that there is 'another geometry (i.e. as the theory of intuitive space) that cannot fully be derived from formal logic'. How had he 'shown' this? He had started with a subset of Hilbert's axioms which, he said, could be taken as describing the *Wesenserschauung* of the ordinary human experience of objects in a local space. Depending on the conventions we adopt about the global extension of these principles, we obtain different metric geometries of constant curvature (Euclidean, Lobatschevskian, Riemannian). These geometries are arrived at differently from their counterparts in 'formal space'; they are not *constructed* from basic notions of logic (as formal geometry is), but *deduced* from intuitive axioms. On the basis of such axioms alone, though, we are unable to single out one of the geometries of constant curvature. We *can*

---

[26] This is also suggested by Driesch (1913, p. 119), a text to which Carnap refers in the section of *Der Raum* on intuitive space.

see them as special cases of a higher-dimensional structure,[27] or of more general – projective and topological – spaces of three dimensions. And using the results of formal geometry for this special case of intuitive geometry, we can combine these directions of generalisation and arrive at topological intuitive space of *n* dimensions, 'the most general structure built from intuitive components . . . the *most comprehensive intuitive space*, which carries within it – partly as components (*Teile*) and partly as specialisations (*Besonderungen*) (constraints (*Spezialisierungen*)) by means of further basic structures and basic relations – all other possible intuitive spaces' (ASP 1921e, p. 31). It may seem a stretch to call such a space intuitive,[28] but it is the lowest common denominator of spaces that *are* derived from intuitive axioms (ASP 1921e, p. 62). This, then, is what Carnap meant by saying that he had *shown* there to be 'another geometry (i.e. as the theory of intuitive space) that cannot fully be derived from formal logic'. An application instance of formal geometry could be arrived at by a different, axiomatic route. And if its axioms codified certain attributes of intuition, the chosen axiomatic geometry could claim to provide a 'schematisation' of formal geometry – an answer to question **(ii)** above (p. 122).

The choice of axioms for intuitive space made it locally Euclidean, but this did not, without further conventions, require space to be globally Euclidean. The intention was evidently to make intuitive geometry dovetail with the needs of physical geometry, specifically with the requirement that physical geometry be locally Euclidean but globally of variable curvature.[29] This is Carnap's solution to what has been seen (e.g. Friedman 1999, p. 48) as his central problem in *Der Raum*, 'to adapt Kant's notion of a form of intuition to the general theory of relativity'. The solution seems to have at least two obvious defects, which Carnap seems not to have considered. First, his procedure of construction is inadequate to the

---

[27] Such as, in the first instance, four-dimensional metric space. This of course exceeds the power of human intuition to conceive. 'But since four-dimensional structures of such regions are built up from intuitively given three-dimensional structures with the help of conceptual relations, a way of imagining them that is related to intuitive grasping, a composite of the intuitive and the conceptual, is possible here' (1922, p. 30).

[28] Carnap acknowledges the difficulty: 'Even this structure will be called an intuitive space, despite the impossibility of comprehending its figures, insofar as they are of more than three dimensions, in intuition, since firstly, all intuitable figures that we know in [three-dimensional metric intuitive space] occur in [*n*-dimensional metric intuitive space], and secondly because those higher-dimensional figures are also assembled from intuitive components' (ASP 1921e, p. 31).

[29] 'The reason we didn't stipulate more tightly constraining extensions, which would have brought us to the simplest of those extended structures, i.e. flat Euclidean space, will only become evident when we discuss physical space' (ASP 1921e, p. 29). Although 'this would certainly be possible', by changing the 'extensions' so that more of the 'principles' were to hold globally rather than just locally (ASP 1921e, pp. 29–30).

goal, for while a manifold with a Riemannian metric can be constructed within *n*-dimensional topological intuitive space, it cannot be arrived at from any subset of Hilbert's axioms. So the intended *connection* of the intuitive starting point with the Riemannian outcome is lost. And second, what is 'local' to human perception is not therefore 'local' at the infinitesimal level. To extend what we perceive around us *down* to the infinitesimal presumably requires as much supplementing by conventions as extending what we perceive around us *up* to infinite space.

All this was less important to him, though, than his entirely separate argument, in the subsequent section on *physical* space, that no *empirical* evidence could force us to accept any particular metric geometry, either.[30] In a sense, this section is mis-titled; it should perhaps have been called 'observational space', for it develops a conception of the observational facts relative to physics that is quite independent of intuitive space. Carnap calls these facts the *Tatbestand* – 'store of facts' or 'factual basis' – the 'empirical observations' in the 1920 dissertation, which we saw invoked against Natorp as the ultimate arbiter for the determination whether the framework of physical theory and the chosen geometry fit together. The factual basis (*Tatbestand*) that plays this role of arbiter – dependent on no convention, and thus the absolute constraint for any proposed combination of theory and geometrical convention – imposes the necessary conditions of experience: 'only the spatial determinations contained in the factual basis [can] be conditions for the possibility of experience' (1922, p. 65). These conditions are 'necessary', then, only in the sense that they are *not conventional*, as Carnap makes clear in the passage where the idea of the *Tatbestand* is introduced and motivated:

This connection between the freely chosen metric stipulation and the physical spatial structure resulting from it is central to this whole question and requires a more detailed discussion. Here we introduce an important distinction. It is a matter of dividing what is evident in actual experience into two components that arise from two different sources. The intended separation is related to that between content and form of experience, but not quite the same. For this latter distinction does not divide the evidence of actual experience into two parts, but names two components (or factors) by whose product each element of actual experience becomes possible to begin with; they cannot manifest themselves individually: unformed content cannot be exhibited [*ist nicht aufzeigbar*], but is a purely intellectual component. So instead of that we will undertake the division *within* the realm of form, between necessary and freely choosable [*wahlfreie*] form. The content that is – not unformed,

---

[30] As he says in the same letter to Russell: 'The most important results of my line of thought, though, are I think contained in the chapter about physical space' (ASP 1921e, p. 2).

but – available only in the necessary form will be called the *factual basis* [*Tatbestand*] of experience. It can be subjected to further, freely choosable formation. (1922, pp. 38–9)

The facts of experience, he argues in the section on 'physical space', are consistent with many different metrics; only their topological relations are invariant. Here he proceeds essentially as in the 1920 dissertation, but adds considerable depth and sophistication. First he shows in some detail how we can determine the curvature of a given space in nature by measurements, once we have chosen a measuring rod in that space, e.g. two marks on a metal bar. (Of course we must first hold the time variable constant, Carnap points out, since 'what we are here regarding as physical space is not actually the form of spatial occurrence, but rather just a three-dimensional projection of this form, i.e. of the four-dimensional space-time manifold' (1922, pp. 40–1).[31]) Then he reverses the procedure, and shows how we could first choose a geometry with respect to a given space and then find out the resulting measurements on physical objects. He does this by an extended example showing that all our everyday and scientific observations are compatible with a geometry that takes the surface of the earth to be flat (1922, pp. 47–54). Of course this requires that all the laws of physics be revised accordingly, and that light rays travel along circular paths – obviously too inconvenient for a useable physics, but all the laws still hold, on the basis of the same evidence, under the new geometry. The point is to show that we *could*, if we insisted, impose a different metric geometry on our experience. We cannot even say, as Helmholtz had tried to show, that we are limited to geometries of constant curvature. Carnap concludes with a discussion (pp. 55–9) of how these choices are in practice made within physics, focusing on the case of general relativity; here he essentially sets out the view contained in 'The Task of Physics' (1923), with its discussion of the trade-off between simplicity of axioms and simplicity of the overall system. He summarises the results as follows:

---

[31] 'Three-dimensional projections can be constructed in various ways by choosing three axis-directions. Under certain circumstances (i.e. when none of the three axes falls within the Minkowskian light cone), such a construction can be regarded as space' (1922, pp. 40–1). We can eliminate the ambiguity, though, if we restrict ourselves to spatial configurations that are independent of simultaneity, i.e. when undertaking the measurements (to determine the curvature, given a metric) we determine the mutual position of two bodies only when they are at rest with respect to each other. This is possible because in the required measurements only point-contacts are required, and these can be observed to hold for the duration of a measurement by observers stationed at each point of contact; 'thus by this precaution regarding the determination of the properties of physical space we free ourselves from the otherwise inevitably required consideration of the time determination' (1922, pp. 40–1).

In the factual basis [*Tatbestand*] of experience, we are given a three-dimensional topological space, but not a metric space, which can be arrived at only on the basis of a fixed measuring rod. We can choose freely either a measuring rod or a metric geometry, but it is best to proceed neither in one of these ways or the other, but to determine the measuring rod and its corresponding metric geometry so as to permit the factual basis to be represented in the simplest possible way. (1922, p. 59)

By distinguishing among three conceptions of 'space', Carnap thought he could eliminate the age-old controversy between mathematicians and philosophers, in which the latter insisted on Kant's view that the axioms of geometry were synthetic a priori and the former denied it. They are both right, he says, as they mean different things by the word 'space'. The mathematicians mean either formal space (Carnap mentions Couturat) or physical space (Riemann, Helmholtz, Poincaré), while the philosophers have intuitive space in mind.[32] For Russell, Carnap phrases this old controversy a little differently:

The dispute about whether this construction of geometry is possible on a purely logical foundation – or whether other elements are also required – is thus shown to be otiose: both sides are right, but they are speaking of different things. (ASP 1921e, p. 1)

But did he think the synthetic a priori structure arrived at by pure intuition prescribed the necessary framework for experience and thus for science?

MINIMAL KANTIANISM

The conclusion of *Der Raum* reads somewhat differently from that of the 1920 dissertation:

The principles of *intuitive space* are . . . a priori. According to Kant's well-known distinction between 'arising from experience [*der Erfahrung entspringen*]' and 'commencing with experience [*anheben mit der Erfahrung*]' this does not mean they are comprehensible without experience, but rather 'independent of the quantity of experience' (as Driesch puts it), and thus does not contradict the requirement that for intimation of essences [*Wesenserschauung*] experience must be given, either immediately in perception or mediately in imagination. In these principles of intuitive space we have before us the synthetic a priori statements claimed by Kant. (1922, p. 63)

---

[32] This diagnosis is really more appropriate to the 'pure' space of the 1920 dissertation, which *does* seem to be similar to what the Marburg school had in mind.

Carnap does mean these principles (*Grundsätze*) to be synthetic a priori 'in the Kantian, transcendental-critical sense'; they are 'necessary conditions of the object of experience, because dependent on the forms of intuition and thought' (ASP 1921c, p. 10; cf. Carnap 1923, p. 97),[33] as he put it in a paper written just after *Der Raum*. He makes explicit that the axioms of intuitive space have the requisite 'experience-constituting validity [*erfahrungsstiftende Geltung*]':

> The topological spatial relations that form the conditions of the possibility of every object of experience cannot be those of physical space, as the latter is not independent of the factual basis of experience, but represents only the real, not the necessary manifestation [*den nicht notwendigen, nur wirklichen Befund*] . . . The specifications [*Bestimmungen*] of topological intuitive space, in their independence from experience and in the generality they enjoy by virtue of the source by which they are known – and therefore also those of formal topological space, that general relational structure of indeterminate things of which topological intuitive space is a special case – can alone have such experience-constituting validity. (1922, p. 66)

How to interpret this rather convoluted passage? It is their 'independence from experience' and their *generality* that give the specifications of topological intuitive space their 'experience-constituting validity', and that make them the 'necessary conditions of the object of experience'. And this generality derives from 'the source by which they are known'. And that is? In the same sentence we are reminded that this generality derives from *formal* topological space, of which topological intuitive space is an application – and that the specifications of formal topological space (which share their 'independence of experience' with intuitive topological space and *are* (at least part of) 'the source by which [those of intuitive topological space] are known') *therefore also* have 'experience-constituting validity'. So although we are told that the specifications of intuitive topological space *alone* enjoy synthetic a priori status, we also find that this is so by virtue of two properties that they actually derive from the specifications of *formal* topological space – which, by the way, *share* in this experience-constituting validity. Only that they are of course not *synthetic* a priori. What exactly is Carnap getting at by the extremely odd way of presenting his conclusion? And what role does the Kantian framework actually still play in this view? The concluding paragraph of the book says:

> In accordance with the above considerations we must consent to the Kantian conception. The spatial configuration that possesses experience-constituting validity

---

[33] Once again, note the careful neutrality between the 'forms of thought' preferred by the Marburg school and the 'forms of intuition' of Kant and Helmholtz.

is precisely to be identified, in place of the one suggested by Kant, as topological intuitive space of arbitrarily many dimensions. Not only this configuration but also its underlying structure [*Ordnungsform*], *n*-dimensional formal space, are thereby declared to be conditions of the possibility of every object of experience whatever. (1922, p. 67)

Once again, this is very carefully hedged. Exactly the same phrase occurs in the final sentences of the two dissertations; both in 1920 and in 1921, the most general form of intuitive space is declared to be 'the condition of the possibility of any object of experience whatever'. But as we saw in the previous section, there has been a subtle change of emphasis in the understanding of this phrase. In 1920, the geometrical system whose object is 'pure space' was also said to represent 'the transcendental-logical function of the a priori form of intuition', and 'pure space' was accorded a *cognitive* status as the framework for the 'empirical evidence' constituting 'physical space'. In 1921, the emphasis in intuitive space has shifted toward *subjective experience*, with external reference to any physical reality bracketed, and the 'factual basis' (*Tatbestand*) of physical space available as raw material for inductive establishment of physical theories independently of intuitive space. 'So Kant's claim is correct, but not for the whole class of those statements he himself applied it to', Carnap writes in the conclusion to *Der Raum*, 'After all, statements about *physical* space are synthetic as well, but certainly not a priori, rather a posteriori, for they are based on induction' (1922, p. 64).

It would seem that, during this period between the two dissertations, Carnap came to think more and more that to regard the synthetic a priori as a form of *knowledge* (as opposed to a condition of subjective *experience*) was to give undue privilege to the human standpoint. As we saw, he had been influenced as a schoolboy by Haeckel, who had inveighed against the anthropomorphism and what he called 'anthropolatry' of idealistic philosophers who exalted the human viewpoint rather than adopting what Haeckel called a 'cosmological perspective' (Haeckel 1899, p. 14). But Haeckel had not applied this directly to Kantian synthetic a priori knowledge, which was intimately bound up with all the philosophy Carnap had been taught before the war. Even in Helmholtz and Lange it had played a certain role, as we saw.

While in 1920 he was still willing to call the specifications of 'pure space' *knowledge* – enjoying 'apodeictic certainty' – that now came to seem a mischaracterisation. Perhaps it was knowledge of a sort, but knowledge of the human perspective, not knowledge of the structure of the perceived world in which the human being lives. Helmholtz, despite having a view rather like this, had called it 'knowledge' nevertheless (though hesitantly, and only in certain contexts), and in 1920 Carnap had still been satisfied to do so as well. But by the time of *Der Raum*, it seems, he was only willing to go along with 'the Kantian conception' to a very hedged and limited extent. He was still prepared to allow the human perspective a minimal privilege; intuitive space was no longer a foundation for anything, but could be considered on its own. The components of spatial intuition could be inventoried and systematised in phenomenological style, without reference to anything external to them. The human perspective did, after all, somehow have to fit into a naturalistic picture of the world; there had to be a place within the naturalistic picture for human subjectivity. (There had to be a provisional starting point for the 'total system of concepts' he was already thinking about and that will be the focus of Chapter 5.) And in any case, our perceptual and intellectual apparatus, anchored in biology, is the conduit through which our knowledge has to pass. It is in this sense that the Kantianism of *Der Raum*, even more than that of the 1920 dissertation, can be called *minimal*. The privilege accorded the human perspective is reduced to the minimum degree that could reasonably be called Kantian at all.

CHAPTER 5

The impact of Russell

TOWARD A 'TOTAL SYSTEM OF ALL CONCEPTS'

Though Carnap had many different irons in the fire in the period before 1922, his main preoccupation was the development of a comprehensive system of knowledge: 'I worked on many special problems, always looking for new approaches and improved solutions. But in the background there was always the ultimate aim of the total system of all concepts. I believed that it should be possible, in principle, to give a logical reconstruction of the total system of the world as we know it' (UCLA 1957a, p. E4). We can trace the evolution of this idea, already visibly headed in the direction of the *Aufbau*, in several sets of notes from this period. Even in the earliest of these notes, dated August 1920 and headed 'Skeleton of Epistemology [*Skelett der Erkenntnistheorie*]', Carnap implicitly rejects both the Marburg and the phenomenological responses to Helmholtz's empirical investigation of perception:

The first given: experiences (facts of consciousness) . . . In some cases I can observe, rather than the experience itself, a particular aspect of the experience: its 'object'. (So not 'intentional relation'); these experiences we call 'ideas [*Vorstellungen*]'. Some ideas are particularly singled out (give the criterion!): 'sensations [*Empfindungen*]'. (ASP 1920c)

A few months later, in April 1921, he put down some further notes entitled 'Analysis of the World Picture [*Analyse des Weltbildes*]'. In a section that began '*The point of knowledge: bringing order to the chaos* of sensations', he wrote, after going through a 'progressive hierarchy of ordering [*Stufengang des Ordnens*]' – from groups or patches 'in the momentary visual field [*im Augenblicksgesichtsfeld*]' to enduring physical objects to 'regularity of succession: *nature*' – that this third stage permits extrapolation into the future: 'Every physical law is basically a claim about expected sensations!' But this 'logical' reconstruction or foundation was not the *practical* order of priority in real science: '*Retrospective shift of viewpoint*: The constructions

139

now go by the name "real world", the immediate by "just appearances" (and sometimes "illusions")' (ASP 1921a).

In a further set of notes, from July 1921, Carnap tried to make this sketched hierarchy of 'constitution' (not yet so named) more precise with an ad hoc notation to indicate 'identity of content [*Inhaltsidentität*]' between or among experiences – though the 'interpretation of that relation *as* identity of content' is a subsequently added 'rational ingredient [*rationale Zutat*]'. This gives us an idea what Carnap might have regarded at this time as the bedrock of the 'content' that gives a sentence meaning, in the context of his 'idealistic conception'. In the absence of the post-hoc rational interpretation, 'identity of content' is initially 'a non-definable relation of close resemblance interpretable only by pointing at experiences'. These notes, headed 'On the analysis of experiences [*Über die Analyse von Erlebnissen*]', struggle with the task of distinguishing the components in knowledge that are 'immediate [*unmittelbar*]' from those which are 'rational ingredients': Carnap searches for a criterion to determine which relations or distinctions among experiences and classes of experiences are genuinely and unquestionably 'immediate' or 'experiential [*erlebnismäßig*]' (ASP 1921d). From the Marburg point of view, such a search would have been pointless, as no such criterion is possible. *All* relations among experiences are 'rational ingredients' (which would be a pleonastic expression). But Carnap, as we saw, followed the earlier generation of scientific neo-Kantians in his focus on the precise delineation of the 'immediate' components of our knowledge from 'rational ingredients' (as well as the grounds for this delineation, and the nature of their interrelation).[1]

In the April 1921 notes (soon after the completion of *Der Raum*), these thoughts take a more explicitly pragmatic turn, perhaps under Vaihinger's influence, and consider what he would later call the 'pragmatics' of knowledge, including a clear distinction between cognitive and non-cognitive questions. On the motivation for his projected book, Carnap notes:

Value of error (= harmfulness of truth)

Two components of religion: (1) intuitive feeling of life as a totality [*Lebensgefühl*] (not judgeable), (2) views (connected to *Lebensgefühl*) (judgeable)

---

[1] The principal aim of the 1920 dissertation on geometry, for instance, was to make clear 'which a priori and which empirical elements turn up in each of these spatial systems' (UCLA 1920a, p. 37). And in the notes on 'Analysis of the world picture' (quoted in following paragraph), he writes: '*The point of knowledge: Bringing order to the chaos* of sensations . . . Important to distinguish: "the given" ("the original source") and "the added-in" ("construction"). So that when views are in contradiction it [can be] decided which of the two is at issue' (ASP 1921a). This pragmatic rationale for an analytic-synthetic distinction was to remain with him all his life.

(1) can be undermined simultaneously with (2): example: The effect of Darwinism on peasants (creation story, acts of the saints, etc.)

Solution: half-truth confuses, the whole [truth] enlightens.

Now what if one doesn't know whether one can penetrate (or <u>complete</u>) the whole [truth]?? (ASP 1921a)

A similar doubt is expressed in the 1921 letter to Flitner quoted in Chapter 3 above; after the remarks on Gogarten, Carnap says, 'Those are preliminary thoughts. Nor am I sure yet how to show that the proposed requirement is the criterion of objectivity for a kind of "seeing" that is inaccessible to us. I don't even know how far this requirement is justified' (ASP 1921f). It is, rather, a 'postulate or article of faith' for him, he says, that anything real must be accessible to (have a 'determinate relation' to) one's own single reality. This uncertainty would soon be resolved by one of the turning points of his career, but his 'article of faith' would survive the turning point, and would only yield over several years to the thought process that the turning point set in motion.

THE TURNING POINT: RUSSELL'S PROGRAMME FOR SCIENTIFIC METHOD IN PHILOSOPHY

In early 1922 Carnap read Russell's book *Our Knowledge of the External World as a Field for Scientific Method in Philosophy*. Its programme of 'logic as the essence of philosophy' struck just the right tone:

Philosophy, from earliest times, has made greater claims, and achieved fewer results, than any other branch of learning. Ever since Thales said that all is water, philosophers have been ready with glib assertions about the sum-total of things; and equally glib denials have come from other philosophers ever since Thales was contradicted by Anaximander. I believe that the time has now arrived when this unsatisfactory state of things can be brought to an end. (Russell 1914a, p. 13)

This appealed strongly to the young Carnap. The story of its immediate impact on him[2] is best told in his own words:

Whereas Frege had the strongest influence on me in the fields of logic and semantics, in my philosophical thinking in general I learned most from Bertrand Russell. In the winter of 1921 [-1922] I read his book, *Our Knowledge of the External World*

---

[2] 'My philosophical insights are usually gained not in moments of inspiration but rather through a slow process of growth and development. It is only on rare occasions when a book or a talk made a strong, lasting impression on me. This happened one day in the winter of 1921 when I was in bed with influenza reading Russell's book which had just arrived' (UCLA 1957a); also quoted by Mia Reichenbach; Coffa 1991, p. 208.

as a Field for Scientific Method in Philosophy. Some passages made an especially vivid impression on me because they formulated clearly and explicitly a view of the aim and method of philosophy which I had implicitly held for some time. In the Preface he speaks about the 'logical-analytic method of philosophy' and refers to Frege's work as the first complete example of the method. And on the very last pages of the book he gives a summarizing characterization of this philosophical method in the following words: 'The study of logic becomes the central study in philosophy: it gives the method of research just as mathematics give the method in physics . . . All this supposed knowledge in the traditional systems must be swept away, and a new beginning must be made . . . To the large and still growing body of men engaged in the pursuit of science, . . . the new method, successful already in such time-honored problems as number, infinity, continuity, space, and time, should make an appeal which the older methods have wholly failed to make . . . The one and only condition, I believe, which is necessary in order to secure for philosophy in the near future an achievement surpassing all that has hitherto been accomplished by philosophers, is the creation of a school of men with scientific training and philosophical interests, unhampered by the traditions of the past, and not misled by the literary methods of those who copy the ancients in all except their merits.'

I felt as if this appeal had been directed to me personally. To work in this spirit would be my task from now on! And indeed henceforth the application of the new logical instrument for the purposes of analyzing scientific concepts and of clarifying philosophical problems has been the essential aim of my philosophical activity. (Carnap 1963, p. 13)

One chapter of Russell's book, about the construction of the physical world from the phenomenal world, directly addressed Carnap's central preoccupation at this time: his 'ultimate aim' of 'the total system of all concepts'. Russell sketches how a construction could proceed using only his own logic of relations and of classes. For Carnap, this was the ultimate test for the 'logical-analytical method of philosophy'; if Frege–Russell logic sufficed for *this* purpose, then there was a prospect of constructing the whole of knowledge without needing much more in the way of *calculus philosophicus* or 'transcendental logic' than the principles of deductive logic and a specification of the given. The categorial system could be greatly simplified. The original dream of an all-encompassing system of concepts could be realised far more economically and elegantly than Leibniz or even Frege had imagined possible.

Russell's sketch, though, differs strikingly in several basic respects from what the 1921 Carnap would have found acceptable. Most egregiously, it is phrased in terms of ontological reduction – Occam's Razor is 'the maxim which inspires all scientific philosophizing' (Russell 1914a, p. 112); the idea of Russell's construction is to exhibit matter as it appears in physics 'as a logical construction from sense-data' (Russell 1914a, p. 106). This raises two questions: First, why did Russell's preoccupation with ontology not prevent Carnap from enthusiastically endorsing the 'logical-analytical method of philosophy'? And second, why did his acceptance of this programme nonetheless *harden* Carnap's rejection of ontological questions as a legitimate object of discourse?

From ontological humility to ontological disdain

It is sometimes said that the Marburg school rejected ontology (Richardson 1998, p. 122; Friedman 1999, pp. 152–62). But this is so, if it is, in a very different sense from that of the early Carnap. The Marburg school's rejection of fixed 'objects' of reality is not at all a matter of indifference or *disdain*, as we see in early Carnap, but is rather *asserted* as a claim about what is *not* real, and it is asserted, moreover, on the basis of considerations deriving entirely from 'logical', non-empirical, reasoning, i.e. from first philosophy. In comparison, Carnap's own view, though anti-ontological, was closer to Russell's raillery against the entire 'classical tradition' in philosophy:

> The original impulse out of which the classical tradition developed was the naïve faith of the Greek philosophers in the omnipotence of reasoning. The discovery of geometry had intoxicated them, and its *a priori* deductive method appeared capable of universal application. They would prove, for instance, that all reality is one, that there is no such thing as change, that the world of sense is a world of mere illusion; and the strangeness of their results gave them no qualms because they believed in the correctness of their reasoning. Thus it came to be thought that by mere thinking the most surprising and important truths concerning the whole of reality could be established with a certainty which no contrary observations could shake. (Russell 1914a, p. 15)

The function of 'logic' in the view of this tradition, said Russell, is essentially to buttress a certain selective scepticism: 'Where a number of alternatives seem, at first sight, to be equally possible, logic is made to condemn all of them except one, and that one is then pronounced to be realised in the actual world'. But:

> The true function of logic is, in my opinion, exactly the opposite of this. As applied to matters of experience, it is analytic rather than constructive; taken *a priori*, it shows the possibility of hitherto unsuspected alternatives more often than the impossibility of alternatives which seemed *prima facie* possible. Thus, while it liberates imagination as to what the world *may* be, it refuses to legislate as to what the world *is*. (Russell 1914a, pp. 18–19)

The Marburg school's 'logical idealist' arguments clearly fell into the category of 'the classical tradition'. Russell's own view, as expounded here, though, sounds remarkably consistent with the kind of ontological indifference or equivocation we observed in Helmholtz and early Carnap: pure reason, i.e. logic, can't *itself* tell us what the world is or is not. It can generate possibilities, which we can then offer up to the test of (consistency with) scientific reasoning and observation.[3] Despite the ontological focus of *Our Knowledge of the External World*, then, Carnap could not but feel liberated by the vistas Russell opened before him, and the light touch with which he flicked away the sceptical doubts in which two millennia of 'classical tradition' had entangled themselves.[4]

Which leaves the second question: Why did Carnap's Helmholtzian 'ontological humility' become self-conscious and explicit at this point? Why did his previous *indifference* toward ontological concerns now turn into a positive *rejection* of, *disdain* toward them? Of course Russell's manifesto legitimised Carnap's own combination of 'scientific training and philosophical interests' and also boosted his confidence in the 'view of the aim and method of philosophy which [he] had implicitly held for some time'. In particular, the ontological disdain implicit in his own developing views[5] now became more definite and self-conscious, and part of an explicit programme (see pp. 154–60 below). Beyond this, Carnap may have sensed that he of all people was ideally placed to benefit from Russell's call to arms, and was in a position, precisely *because* of his ontological disdain, to see the gaps in Russell's programme, and to be the one to complete it. He may have realised immediately that he was in a position to solve problems Russell was prevented from addressing precisely *by* his realism and his reductionist orientation. This was the subtext when, six years later, he sent the finished *Aufbau* to Russell:

I want to draw your attention straightaway to two points in which I have been compelled to depart from your conception. These points of difference do not, however, rest on differences in basic attitude, which seems to me to be entirely

---

[3] Howard Stein has pointed out to me that Carnap *also* took Russell's point in a direction which is *not* Russellian, but closer to Poincaré: 'logic reveals alternatives which might be regarded as *effectively equivalent*, differing merely in formulation, in *wahlfreie Form*, not in *Tatbestand*'. Unlike Poincaré, though, Carnap from his earliest writings sees the choices thus revealed as genuine *choices*, and as important ones for the progress of knowledge.

[4] Russell's influence on Carnap has recently been discussed by Pincock (2002), whose view of the matter is largely compatible with that put forward here, though Pincock glosses over the enormous changes in the *Aufbau* project between 1922 and 1928; see Chapter 7 below.

[5] He remarks in the autobiography (original version): 'one day a friend seemed somewhat disturbed by some formulations which sounded to him positivistic or even materialistic. I told him that indeed my conceptions about the foundations of science, especially mathematics and physics, were strongly influenced by physicists like Kirchhoff, Boltzmann, Mach, etc., but on the other hand, also by neo-Kantians like Natorp and Cassirer. When he asked me which philosophical position I held myself, I was unable to answer' (UCLA 1957a, p. E20; corresponds to 1963, p. 17).

shared between us. The differences arise, rather, precisely from my attempt to follow through on this basic attitude of yours more consistently than has been done so far. I therefore believe myself here to have been 'more Russellian than Russell'.

I placed a motto at the beginning of the book (p. 1) which I want to call the 'construction principle'. Now I believe you have violated your own principle by not constructing but inferring the heteropsychological (see §140). I believe myself, through the way described of constituting the heteropsychological (§57f., §§140–143), to have followed this principle. In the same way I believe myself, through strict adherence to the 'autopsychological basis' ('methodological solipsism'), to have followed your principle more closely than has been done so far. You yourself call the retention of the autopsychological basis desirable, but too difficult and hardly feasible. Through my system I believe myself to have shown its feasibility, even if I have to admit that there can be no question yet of a completely satisfactory implementation of the system in all respects.

The second point of difference concerns the realistic way of putting the question (see comments on the literature in §176). Here, too, I believe myself to have carried through your basic attitude more consistently by rejecting the (metaphysical) concept of reality. I believe that these questions about reality – and thus the entire philosophical controversy about realism – have no point or sense whatever [*überhaupt keinen Sinn*] (§§175–178 and part 2 of the pamphlet 'Pseudoproblems', which is also being sent to you). (ASP 1928b)[6]

By this time, Carnap had fully assimilated the revolution his thought had undergone in 1922, and the three sources of knowledge had been reduced to two (of which one had then, after Wittgenstein's influence set in, become entirely empty). Pure intuition had disappeared entirely; its vestigial, phenomenological form in *Der Raum* would be reclassified as non-cognitive. It was no longer a source of knowledge at all, and the sort of pragmatic device it had been moving toward becoming in *Der Raum* was reclassified, after Wittgenstein, as no longer articulable in language, as outside the realm of the cognitive. But this new (temporary) equilibrium of the Vienna years was not reached all at once; it would be a long and difficult and multi-dimensional development from 1922 to that point.

LOGIC AS THE ESSENCE OF PHILOSOPHY

The transformation of the two Kantian questions

The two questions behind Carnap's work in 1919–21 (pp. 122–7 above) were radically transformed in the months after he read Russell, as several manuscripts from 1922 testify. To understand the impact of Russell

[6] In his reply, Russell – tentatively – *agreed* that Carnap did in fact appear to be more Russellian than Russell!

on the Kantian questions of how to get from subjective sense perception to objective theories and vice versa, a certain aspect of Carnap's pre-1922 'idealistic conception' needs to be examined more closely. We saw above that he had introduced, in his 1921 proto-*Aufbau* notes, a makeshift symbolism for 'identity of content [*Inhaltsidentität*]' ('a non-definable relation of close similarity that can only be interpreted by pointing to experiences [*durch Hinweis auf Erlebnisse*]') between a current experience (*vorhandenes Erlebnis*) and the memory trace of a previous one. He worried about the 'experientiality [*Erlebnismäßigkeit*]' of this relation (which reveals itself *as* identity of content only by subsequent 'rational interpretation [*rationale Deutung*]') and its variants, and wondered, for instance, whether the inclusion relation between one experience and another (e.g. the relation between the experience of hearing a single tone and that of hearing a triad containing that tone) was genuinely an *experienced* inclusion, and whether it and its converse (distinguishing a single pitch within a heard triad) were genuinely distinguishable in experience (*erlebnismäßig verschieden*) (since one might think of a single tone as 'experientially implying' the triad, given that its overtones are physically present, however audible or inaudible they may be in a particular case) (ASP 1921d).

There were two problems with this approach. First, it involved the *analysis* of a momentary 'total experience', which Carnap regarded as problematic. It is usually said (e.g. Friedman 1999, p. 93) that he wanted to be adequate to the latest psychological theories, in this particular case, to Gestalt psychology. This may be true,[7] but it is clearly not the whole story. It seems, rather, that his psychological holism derived from Vaihinger's portrayal of subjective experience as an undifferentiated 'chaos' that could not assemble itself into an ordered 'reality' from elements of sensation or perception, but needed intellect-imposed 'fictions' to acquire any degree of coherence at all. This was his main reason for not constructing his 'total system of all concepts' along the positivist lines of Mach or Mill.

---

[7] It is unclear whether he was at this stage directly influenced by the Gestalt theorists. His own recollection (1963, p. 16) is evidently somewhat faulty, as the 'change of approach' he mentions was the one occasioned by Russell. He had certainly gone to psychology lectures in Jena before the war, though Wertheimer's key paper was published only in 1912 (Ash 1998, Chapter 8). In the *Aufbau*, Carnap cites no publications of the Gestalt psychologists from before the mid-1920s but does cite earlier philosophical arguments (by Schuppe, Gomperz, Schlick, and others) for psychological holism (Carnap 1928a, §67, pp. 92–3). On the other hand, he clearly alludes to the Gestalt theorists' 'phi-phenomenon' (the inability of experimental subjects to distinguish smooth motion from a closely spaced series of discrete displacements) in the 1922 manuscript *From the Chaos to Reality* (ASP 1922a, p. 3). It seems clear that Carnap had, in any case, assimilated the *philosophical* criticisms of associationist psychology (e.g. by Husserl, Driesch, Natorp, and Cassirer), and especially Vaihinger's view, even before Gestalt psychology became widely known (Ash 1998, Chapters 4 and 5, pp. 51–83).

Second, the analysis of a 'total experience' did not allow a straightforward application of ordinary deductive (Frege–Russell) logic, as the relations among sense data are vague, complex, and fuzzy. This was especially true if, as Carnap evidently thought, the 'logical' relations among sense data to be used in the construction should reproduce the actually experienced subjective relations among such data – otherwise the construction would not faithfully transmit (to higher levels of knowledge) the 'implications' of experience. Carnap needed a *starting point* for his project of a 'system of all concepts'. These 1921 notes, which try to use Hume's or Mach's starting point, soon dry up.

The different starting point Russell suggested to Carnap in late 1921 was based on what Russell, in *Our Knowledge of the External World*, called his 'principle of abstraction'.[8] Though used by Russell mainly to effect onto-logical economies (the substitution of equivalence classes – mere 'logical constructions' – for suspect 'fictitious metaphysical entities'; Russell 1914a, p. 134), two of these uses were directly related to Carnap's project: the suggestion that physical objects could be constructed as classes of their 'aspects' or 'perspectives' (Russell 1914a, Lecture 3; Russell 1914b), and the description of Whitehead's method of constructing the points and instants of physics from sense data by 'extensive abstraction', i.e. as the limit of successively enclosed or nested regions containing the point (Russell 1914a, pp. 114, 121).

Neither of these suggestions turned out to be directly usable for the solution of Carnap's problem (1928a, §124, p. 164). But the 'principle of abstraction' in conjunction with what Carnap called Russell's 'construction principle [*Konstruktionsprinzip*]' – 'Wherever possible, logical constructions are to be substituted for inferred entities' (Russell 1914b, p. 155) – gave Carnap the new starting point he needed. He seems to have seen immediately that, although Russell's particular suggestions would not serve his purposes, a formally similar kind of construction *would* make it possible to arrive at the kinds of discrete and atomistic sense-data needed for science. A form of 'quasi-analysis' appears in the first sketch of the *Aufbau* system (ASP 1922a, pp. 4–6), and the method was worked out in formal detail soon afterwards (ASP 1923a). Russell's 'principle of abstraction' suggested to him, in other words, how he could use ordinary Frege–Russell logic to

---

[8] This principle, introduced by Russell in *Principles* to support the reality of relations, and absent from *The Problems of Philosophy*, became something quite different in the 1914 lectures; it became, in fact, the central tool of philosophical analysis. It could, Russell now says, 'equally well be called "the principle which dispenses with abstraction"', and 'clears away incredible accumulations of metaphysical lumber' (Russell 1914a, p. 51). Interestingly, this idea, which represented such a momentous breakthrough for Carnap, had been suggested to Russell by Whitehead just as he was writing *Our Knowledge of the External World*, and is presented there only as a bare, somewhat confused sketch.

show the *logical equivalence* of a Gestalt-psychological starting point, suitably articulated, and a perceptual-atomistic starting point – and perhaps many others.

Both of the main obstacles to the 'total system of all concepts' that had stood in Carnap's way in the summer of 1921 (holistic perception; inapplicability of ordinary deductive logic to perception) had thus been overcome with the help of Russell's suggestions. But the new starting point thus adopted also had consequences well beyond the solution of two local problems in the construction of a system. It is no exaggeration to say that this was the point at which Carnap's minimal Kantianism and his ambitions for a *system* of knowledge flowed into the broader stream of empiricism to create something new, a 'logical empiricism', an empiricism with a 'structural' dimension absent in the previous empiricisms of Locke, Hume, Mill, or Mach, and even from the more recent, mathematically informed empiricisms of Schlick, Reichenbach, or Russell.

But this change was not instantaneous. It took Carnap several years to assimilate the full implications of the 1922 turning point that put him on the *Aufbau* path. The immediate impact was to put the idea of a 'total system of all concepts' on a new basis: Russell's logic, in conjunction with Husserl's phenomenology, gave him the tools for overcoming the hopeless isolation of Vaihinger's 'chaos of sensations' in the individual subjectivity. The programme was roughly this: Taking something like Vaihinger's 'chaos' as the immediately available 'primary world' of direct acquaintance, one could use phenomenological *Vor-Logik* to discern a minimal degree of structure *within* this 'primary world'. This minimum was sufficient, though, to serve as the basis for extending the primary world significantly beyond Vaihinger's confines (especially in its temporal dimension) by applying Russell's theory of relations to it. On this expanded basis of a primary world, a very small number of 'fictions' (in contrast to Vaihinger's unsystematic proliferation) suffices to construct an objective 'secondary world' or 'reality'. These few remaining 'fictions' were thus the categories or categorical principles by which subjective sensation is built up into an objective 'reality'.

The role of phenomenology in the early system

The above themes, accordingly, set the tone of Carnap's first sketches of the *Aufbau* system during 1922: the manuscript *From the Chaos to Reality* (*Vom Chaos zur Wirklichkeit*) and the paper 'Three-dimensionality of Space and Causality: An Investigation of the Logical Connection between Two Fictions' (published 1924). The influence of Vaihinger went beyond the titles; the opening paragraph of *From the Chaos to Reality* displays a streak of Vaihingerian pragmatism. It describes the practice-driven, non-intellectual 'irrational point of departure' of the investigation – the 'desire to overcome the inconsistencies in reality through the reconstruction of reality':

'Reality' is not given to us as something fixed, but undergoes constant correction. The epistemologist says that it is constructed, for the sake of a particular task it performs, from an original chaos according to ordering principles that are at first instinctive and required by the task itself. But this idea of a chaos is a fiction. We who now consider these things know nothing of an original chaos; we have no memory of having undertaken the construction of reality from any such chaos. What we experience is only an already ordered reality, whose order and plan is subject, nonetheless, to constant emendation. These emendations or corrections are usually occasioned by small inconsistencies [*Unstimmigkeiten*]. But there are also large inconsistencies, going right through the entire fabric of reality, that we feel the impulse to overcome by imposing an order of nature. It is this desire for a new order, for elimination of the large inconsistencies, that motivates epistemological deliberation and the fictions that occur in it – of a chaos as the point of departure and of ordering principles according to which the construction proceeded, proceeds, and ought to proceed. (ASP 1922a, p. 1)

'Reality' is a human construction, as in Vaihinger, but we have no immediate access to an unconstructed world, either. The early Carnap seems already to have had in mind something like Neurath's well-known maxim that we 'reconstruct our boat on the open sea', and cannot start with a blank slate. Nonetheless, we are capable of discerning 'inconsistencies [*Unstimmigkeiten*]' in the reality we live in and take for granted around us. We can tell that the construction is faulty. There are great cracks in the foundations, and the problem cannot be solved by local touch-ups. A full reconstruction is necessary, 'a completely new building from the cornerstone on up [*ein völliger Neubau vom Grundstein an*]'. This, then, motivates Carnap's suggestion that we accept 'the epistemological fiction of a construction beginning from the chaos [*des Aufbaus vom Chaos aus*]'. And he gives this 'fiction' a 'precise formulation':

We experience a reality and reconstructions of it; we extrapolate backwards these reconstructions of a largely ordered reality, i.e. we take reality as if it had resulted from an ordering construction process emerging from a disordered state. We reconstruct this fictive original state and undertake a thorough reconstruction so as to achieve a more unified system of reality. (ASP 1922a, p.1)

How to *arrive* at such a fictive confusion? Using phenomenological discernment, Carnap proceeds to abstract or isolate from our present 'already-formed reality' everything 'that points to an already complete order and

individual specification [*schon fertige Ordnung und Einzelbestimmbarkeit*]',
among which he includes:

> The distinction between the psychic and the physical, the configuration
> [*Anordnung*] of the latter in space, the integration [*Einordnung*] of both into the
> temporal series, the distinction among the various sense qualities, the conceptual
> definiteness of particular sense qualities on the basis of the quality-relation space
> [*des Qualitätsverwandtschaftskörpers*], e.g. the definiteness of a particular colour on
> the basis of its position in colour space, of a particular tone on the basis of its
> position in the scale. The *chaos* contains no identical elements, i.e. no elements
> that are individually identifiable and sustainable as 'these same ones' [*als diese selben
> festhaltbaren*]. (ASP 1922a, p.1)

To get beyond such a completely structureless 'chaos', of the kind Vaihinger himself portrays, we remind ourselves of the practical purpose of the
construction: 'For the chaos to be ordered at all [*überhaupt*], there must be
distinctions available within it that determine [*von denen es abhängt*] what
positions within the applied ordering scheme are put in correspondence
with the parts of the chaos [*Chaosteile*]' (ASP 1922a, p.1). Phenomenological reflection supplies this disaggregation into 'parts'. But where does
the ordering scheme to be coordinated with these parts come from? It is
clearly *brought to* the chaos from outside, and does not arise from within it.
These imported 'fictions' cannot be discerned within the 'chaos' itself, or be
derived from anything discernible from the 'chaos': '. . . the character that
these distinctions have with respect to each other can only be conceptually determined once this correspondence to the ordering scheme has been
established – and are only determinable and nameable by means of this
ordering scheme' (ASP 1922a, p. 2). There is nothing inconsistent in this;
the parts identifiable within the 'chaos' by phenomenological discernment
have no names in ordinary language, so we refer to them by names they
will be given at a later stage of the analysis, when an 'ordering scheme' has
been introduced. At the outset, 'on the basic level [*auf der Urstufe*]', not
only temporal ordering of experiences but even plurality of experiences is
to be eliminated or abstracted from, leaving only the present moment. But
phenomenological discernment makes it possible to distinguish, within this
present moment, a first basic distinction (*Grundunterschied*), between two
parts of the present experience, which Carnap provisionally calls the *live*
and the *dead* part of the experience (essentially Hume's impressions and
ideas):

> To specify what is meant by this we now have to use the words that are given
> these parts on a much higher level of the construction [*Aufbau*] in view of certain

interpretations and subordinations [*Einordnungen*]; but note that at this point it is only done to point to these parts of experience themselves, without here already presupposing or introducing the interpretations on which these expressions are based. By the live part we mean what is later called sense impressions [*Sinnesempfindungen*], by the dead part we mean the ideas [*Vorstellungen*]. (ASP 1922a, p.2)

Within the 'dead' part Carnap further distinguishes two distinct kinds of total experience,[9] the 'completed' ones (i.e. memory traces, in the retrospective or reconstructive conceptual interpretation) and those that lack this character of 'completion'. The central role played by phenomenological intimation or discernment in Carnap's approach at this stage is strikingly illustrated by his discussion of this property of 'completedness':

Now the property 'complete [*fertig*]' has a special peculiarity. The 'complete' component has an 'expandability [*Entfaltbarkeit*]', i.e. it can be decomposed into a manifold some of whose parts have the 'character of completedness' with respect to certain other parts, but not with respect to different other parts. In the retrospective language: When we direct our attention to the remembered component of present experience, this component reveals a wealth of memory traces of a kind such that, say, a certain one represents the memory of a certain previous experience, which thus reproduces the memory traces contained also in this second experience, which in turn are memories of a third experience, and so on. That this directing of attention and the unfolding of the completed component is also an event in time and doesn't belong to a *single* present experience should not disturb us here, as this duration (in contrast to the time span that forms the content of this unfolding process and is represented by the memory traces) does not become conscious in present experience, and so does not belong to it as a proper component at all, but only becomes known in retrospective psychological interpretation. (ASP 1922a, p. 2)

The relation of '"completedness [*Fertigkeit*]"-with-respect-to' is the basis for subjective temporal orderings of experience, and the individual experiences thus related become the basic elements of the system, the 'building blocks [*Bausteine*]' from which it is constructed. A number of relations among these building blocks (which would later, in the *Aufbau*, be called 'basic relations') are introduced, and the construction of qualities by quasi-analysis proceeds as we know it from the *Aufbau*.

Despite the 'fictional' nature of the original chaos and thus of the primary world or 'realm of experience', it seems clear that it nonetheless still has the character of a *foundation* on which the various possible 'realities' can

---

[9] He remarks that both of the living and dead parts still include 'that which is later subject to a separate treatment under the heading of accompanying emotional colouring and impulses of the will', as these aspects are at this point still undifferentiated.

(by using different possible extrapolations) be built. Phenomenological reconstruction plays the critical role of identifying the building blocks of the foundation.[10] The 'realm of experience' is 'given' (though there was some flexibility regarding its description), while the construction of a 'reality' on this basis is 'optional'.

Carnap specifically invokes Kant in this connection, distinguishing a primary world or realm of 'first-level experience' (*Erfahrung erster Stufe*), as 'experience that is shaped only by necessary form [*die Erfahrung, die nur notwendige Formung trägt*]', from secondary worlds of 'second-level experience [*Erfahrung zweiter Stufe*]', to which further non-'necessary', fictional elements or conventions are added.[11] This is the same distinction between 'necessary' and 'optional' form that we saw in *Der Raum* (Chapter 4 above, pp. 133–4) in the definition of the *Tatbestand*; the 'necessary' features of perception that were there regarded as 'conditions of all possible experience' were those that remain constant under topological deformations. Moreover, he emphasises that it follows from the optional nature of the second-level additions 'that *different* kinds of second-level experience, depending on the further transformations, can be generated from the *one and only* first-level experience'. In slightly different terms, applied to the constitution system:

The '*experience realm* [*Erlebnisbereich*]', as a first-order realm, is now completed by the addition of further elements to [form] a second-order realm, which is called '*reality*'. This completion occurs not in a unique way, but always with the reservation, as it were, that [such] an addition can later be corrected or omitted. So every addition occurs provisionally, to begin with. (ASP 1922a, p. 7)

These additions are governed by just two fictions, which Carnap here calls 'tendencies' or conservation principles, the '*tendency to conserve the uniformity of state* [*Tendenz zur Erhaltung der Zustandsgleichheit*]' and the

---

[10] It seems clear that Carnap no more intended the particular 'building blocks' identified in *From Chaos to Reality* to be a *uniquely correct* foundation than he later regarded the basis of the *Aufbau* to be.

[11] These quotations in this sentence are from the paper 'Three-dimensionality of Space and Causality: An Investigation of the Logical Connection Between Two Fictions' (1924), which was composed just after *Vom Chaos zur Wirklichkeit*. The passage reads as follows: 'The criticism that has been levelled at the Kantian conception of experience, especially from the positivist side, has taught us that certainly not all the factors contributing to form [*Formfaktoren*] to which Kant ascribes necessity deserve that ascription. (Sense) experience does necessarily exhibit a certain spatial and temporal order, and furthermore certain qualitative determinations of equality and inequality. But the gathering up of certain elements of experience into "things" with "qualities", as well as the ascription of certain elements of experience as "causes" of others, are certainly not necessary, i.e. a condition of every possible experience. It is rather a matter of free choice, *whether* this transformation [*Verarbeitung*] should occur and even to a great degree *how* it is to occur' (1924, pp. 106–7).

'*tendency to conserve the uniformity of process* [*Tendenz zur Erhaltung der Ablaufsgleichheit*]'. The first is a version of Mach's 'principle of continuity'[12] and is equated to (or offered as a version of) the category of substance; the second is an induction principle[13] and is equated to the category of causality. Apart from the phenomenological identification of 'building blocks' and the basic relations among them, within 'first-level experience' (and these were regarded as partly internal, as emerging from reflection on experience itself), these categories or tendencies are the only 'fictions' introduced into the construction from outside. This small number of 'fictions' Carnap is willing to regard as imposed by pure reason, and here there is a point of contact with the Marburg school, as Carnap fully acknowledges (though he rejects their elimination of the 'primary world'):

The neo-Kantian philosophy does not recognise the primary world, as its conception that the forms of second-level experience are necessary and unique [*eindeutig*] prevents it from discerning the difference between the primary and the secondary world. But its genuine achievement, which was to demonstrate the object-creating function [*gegenstandserzeugende Funktion*] of thought, remains intact, and underlies our conception of the secondary world as well. (1924, p. 108)

Despite his rejection of the Marburg school's 'necessary and unique' categories, then, there is a sense in which Carnap accepts their claim that any 'secondary world', any 'reality' – any world containing objects, of whatever kind – is created by the categories of reason. In the paper just quoted from, approximately contemporary with *From the Chaos to Reality*, he argues for a particular example of this. There can be neither causality nor more than two dimensions, he says, in any sense modality within the primary world;[14] the move from two to three (or more) dimensions *is* the move from the 'single given' to an 'optional reality'. And what he argues (this is the main point of the paper), is that '*the fiction of three-dimensionality of space is a logical consequence of the fiction of physical causality*' (1924, p. 129). The category of causation is fundamental, and is 'object-constituting' in the sense that one of its consequences is the three-dimensionality of the space in which physical objects are located.

[12] 'If a complex of elements persists throughout a temporal series, it is fictively supplied [*durch Hinzufügung fingiert*] as continuing to persist, if it then disappears' (ASP 1922a, p. 7).
[13] 'If the same variation series [*Veränderungsreihe*] of a complex of elements frequently occurs, it is fictively supplied as continuing in the same way if on another occasion it is interrupted by disappearance of the complex' (ASP 1922a, pp. 7–8).
[14] The restriction of the primary world to two dimensions is again argued on largely phenomenological grounds.

Logic and meta-logic

The argument by which Carnap reaches this conclusion is not only rather dubious (he would soon reject it; see below, Chapter 6), it is also not 'logical' in the sense that Carnap had now adopted Russell's slogan of 'logic as the essence of philosophy'. There was evidently still ample room for a not very well-defined meta-logic or 'transcendental logic' in which not only the principles of logic were specified, but also the universe of discourse (the 'basis', in Carnap's later terms) and the basic categorial principles ('fictions') of construction. Indeed, Carnap explicitly endorses the Marburg idea of the 'object-creating function of thought'. What had been unclear in the 1920 dissertation, and remained unclear even now, was not only the scope of this meta-logic, but also how it related to the logical object language. Russell had suggested that 'the study of logic becomes the central study in philosophy: it gives the method of research just as mathematics gives the method in physics.' And following Russell's example, Carnap was able to show to his own satisfaction that the traditional empiricist invocation of 'qualities' from which to construct 'objects' could be displaced by logical construction. *This* much 'transcendental logic' was clearly displaced by deductive logic. But what about the modes of reasoning by which the 'building blocks' were identified and defined, and by which the categorial principles of construction (as well as, on their basis, e.g. the three-dimensionality of physical space) were arrived at? These were forms of reasoning whose 'method of research' did not fall under the heading of what Russell meant by 'logic'. Where did they leave off and where did logic take over? This was not yet clear, and as Carnap worked through the construction of the *Aufbau* system, the boundaries would shift. Still, the impulse from Russell in 1922 had been of great significance; this step was the one that clearly laid out the terms within which he would work for the rest of his life.

SCIENTIFIC PHILOSOPHY: ERLANGEN AND THE WIDER WORLD

After the war ended, in 1918, Carnap had withdrawn, like many of his generation (especially of those associated with the *Jugendbewegung*) into rural seclusion. He had married and settled into the raising of children. Though he had remained in contact with a few people (especially his *Jugendbewegung* friends) and continued to toy with the possibility of an academic career, he was sceptical that the economic situation or his own eccentric interests would permit that course. But he had not withdrawn into an idyllic rural life from resignation, or out of a back-to-nature ideology of passive resistance, like many of his contemporaries (Hepp 1987, pp. 167–71). On the contrary, as we saw above (Chapter 1), Carnap thought that precisely its lack of balance between the active and the contemplative life had prevented the German intelligentsia from intervening more forcefully against the 'mental state [*Geistesverfassung*] of Europe that made the world war inevitable', a frame of mind that draws its 'principle nourishment from Germany'. The 'politics' in which Carnap now resolved to involve himself was a very high-level sort, though; politics was 'everything . . . that has some connection with the public social life of people'. And for all these activities to work together, it was essential to arrive at a 'form of community [*Gemeinschaftsgestalt*]' that could serve to coordinate them so as 'to remove [these tasks] from the realm of chaotic whim and subordinate them to goal-oriented reason [*der chaotischen Willkür zu entziehen und der zielbewußten Vernunft zu unterwerfen*]' (Hepp 1987, p. 18). This is the 'engineering cast of mind' at work (Hayek 1952).

Even such a rarefied and high-level form of 'politics', though, could not be pursued in a quiet corner; it needed to be shouted from rooftops. And for such large-scale proselytisation, a new *doctrine* was needed; after the turning point just described, Carnap felt he had found his task and his doctrine. So the time had come to make his programme known to the world, to take it to the people (the relevant people, at least) and campaign for it. The doctrine was essentially the one later associated with the Vienna Circle: The problems of the human race could be solved by reliable – scientific – knowledge, and a first, crucial step toward embarking on these solutions was to face up to the world as it is rather than deluding ourselves about it; a new *Sachlichkeit* (sobriety, unflinching acceptance of facts) was needed. Traditional philosophy, especially in the German tradition, was more of a hindrance than a help to this painful task; it held out the possibility of realms of being not accessible to science, or non-scientific ways of making the unknowable *Ding an sich* intelligible, or realms of empirical inquiry (e.g. history or psychology) incompatible with natural science. Carnap saw in his new 'total system of all concepts' a way of blocking all such claims – and thus of exposing as frauds the self-appointed prophets like Spengler, Heidegger, or Klages, who sought to delude people about the need for facing things as they are. Such directly political or cultural-political implications were rarely apparent on the surface; Carnap was acutely aware that he was working at a very high level.

This 'political' turn (in the broad sense of 'political' Carnap uses in 1918) of the tradition Reichenbach called 'scientific philosophy' (and von Mises, attempting to correct the usual narrow usage, called 'positivism'), and the form it took in the Vienna Circle, has often been misunderstood.[15] Whatever its particular nature and content, it grew directly out of a sense of Germany's responsibility for the war, and particularly a sense that German intellectuals had done too little to influence the general culture, or to shape the *Gemeinschaftsgestalt* – had been too introverted in their own affairs and not engaged enough with the common vernacular of their time and place: 'The significance of the task, and the responsibility that comes with it, have become clear to us by recognition of the guilt that we who participate in the life of the mind share for the fate of our people and of mankind, and not least for the catastrophe of recent years' (ASP 1918d, p. 18). The notorious militancy and enthusiastic missionary spirit of the Vienna Circle is part of this response to the war.

From before the armistice, then, Carnap had been searching for something like what he found in Russell three years later, something that would assign him his role in the drama of his times, and make him feel with conviction that 'To work in this spirit [would be his] task from now on!' When he found it, he was transformed almost overnight, it seems, from the recluse who had been gathering his strength to the missionary zealot. He immediately began to contact others whose philosophical views might be in some way close enough to his that dialogue was possible, and to organise a series of conferences at which his ideas for 'an all-comprehending conceptual space', or 'total system of all concepts' could be discussed. He saw these studies as falling into two categories, and by November of 1922 he was sending out mimeographed invitations to a corresponding pair of conferences, one on 'theory of relations as a tool for the epistemologist'[16] and another on 'construction of reality/structural theory of knowledge' (ASP 1922c, 1922d, 1923b); the main text for the second conference was Carnap's own sketch *From the Chaos to Reality*. The academy of the Kant-Gesellschaft in Erlangen made its rooms available, and the result was the Erlangen conference of 9–13 March 1923, which, as Carnap modestly says in his autobiography, 'may be

---

[15] Insofar as any wider perspective is discerned at all, it is seen in the *directly* political engagement championed by Otto Neurath (e.g. Cartwright *et al.* 1996); Carnap is viewed as a follower in this regard. Galison (1996), for instance, sees Carnap as having begun with a rather narrow focus, but after he had been in Vienna for a while, '[increasingly,] he had come to see this work [the *Aufbau*] in general, and the efforts of the Vienna Circle more generally, as part and parcel of a larger, critical, cultural movement'. As we have seen, this gets it precisely backwards; the system of the *Aufbau* was *conceived* in the service of a movement, which Carnap thereby (at least partly) *originated*.

[16] For this conference Carnap distributed mimeographs of some preliminary notes toward his *Abriß der Logistik*, mostly written during this period, whose declared purpose it was to make logic (particularly the theory of relations), hitherto employed only in the foundations of mathematics, a tool for all philosophers and scientists; its second half is entirely devoted to applications, in a wide variety of fields (1929, p. III).

regarded as the small but significant initial step in the movement of a scientific philosophy in Germany'. Hans Reichenbach, Heinrich Behmann, Paul Hertz, Kurt Lewin, and a number of others attended (Schlick was invited but unable to come), and the event appears to have been a coming to self-consciousness of a movement of 'scientific philosophy'; as Carnap said later, 'there was a common basic attitude and the common aim of developing a sound and exact method in philosophy. We were gratified to realise that there was a considerable number of men in Germany who worked toward this same aim' (1963, p. 14).

It was an enthusiastic but also rather chaotic meeting: 'Our points of view were often quite divergent, and the debates were very vivid and sometimes heated' (1963, p. 14). An example given by Carnap involves a debate 'on the question whether a momentary experience could contain sense-data as actual parts'. Hertz thought such components indispensable; 'Lewin rejected them emphatically from the viewpoint of Gestalt psychology'. Reichenbach intervened to claim that the dispute was merely terminological. Carnap, though, disagreed and thought a matter of genuine significance was involved; he tried to introduce quasi-analysis 'to do justice to the justified demands of both sides, by preserving on the one hand the experiences as indivisible units, but on the other hand constructing certain complexes of experiences which correspond to the traditional components' (UCLA 1957b, pp. D21–D22).

However, this attempt to mediate met with the same fate as Carnap's position paper *From the Chaos to Reality* – all but complete incomprehension. Though he was encouraged that so many people were working in the same general direction, Carnap was also disappointed that no one seemed to understand him (UCLA 1957b, pp. E4–E5). Before Erlangen, he had planned to publish something like *From the Chaos to Reality* almost immediately; it was not intended to be a definitive solution, but a suggestive sketch. As he had explained to Heinrich Scholz,

Perhaps you can already recognise, despite its totally unfinished state, the outlines of the building it is to become. I want to add that the sketch sounds more dogmatic than it's really intended to be; a subsequent execution would have to make clear that completely different systems are feasible, and that this is really just an example, inspired by the urge to get beyond programmatic generalities and to show, for once, what a system [like this] might itself actually look like. (ASP 1922b, p. 1)

But he found from the uncomprehending response at Erlangen that he would have to explain his project (though intended only as a sketch or example) much more thoroughly than he had in *From the Chaos to Reality*. This no doubt accounts for the proliferation of references to other authors in the final *Aufbau*, as well as its bulk, resulting from the effort to put everything in the terms of several different 'languages' (1928a, §95, pp. 133–4). The book's respectful attitude toward the philosophical tradition should not be seen, though, as deceptive; it indicates a more complex ambivalence than has been generally understood. On the one hand, as we saw, Carnap (like his Vienna Circle contemporaries) saw his proselytisation for a 'scientific philosophy' as a political duty, of involvement in the general culture and of helping to shape a rational *Gemeinschaftsgestalt*. On the other hand, he was not by nature very doctrinaire, and his personal style was always very much that of the mediator, as the vignette from Erlangen exemplifies. His impulse, in discussions where participants were talking past each other, was to find a common framework in which their positions could be located and dispassionately compared. This conciliatory impulse, though, was to some degree in tension with his new-found political duty to proselytise for a doctrine. The two tendencies could work together, as when the doctrine could be furthered by showing its commensurability with others – hence the *Aufbau*. But they could also be at odds, as in polemical documents like the pamphlets *Wissenschaftliche Weltauffassung*, *Scheinprobleme in der Philosophie*, or *Philosophy and Logical Syntax*. But these are the documents that have shaped the popular view of the Vienna Circle, and given it a reputation for partisan intolerance and simplistic vituperation that does scant justice to the complexity of its real views, and the degree of heated intramural controversy.

Apart from this tension between conciliation and confrontation as *tactics*, though, there was a tension in what Carnap actually thought, i.e. in his *personal* attitude toward the philosophical tradition. On the one hand there was once again a sense of duty toward promotion of the doctrine. But on the other there was a genuine personal interest, quite highly developed, in questions of values and the larger life context or *Lebensgefühl*, as one would naturally expect of someone from a family so immersed in *Bildung*, and of someone who had been so deeply involved in the German Youth Movement. It was not Carnap's intent, as the very expression *Lebensgefühl* might indicate, to trivialise these questions. This ambivalence is evident in the 1922 letter to Scholz already quoted from, where Carnap is discussing the possibility of taking an academic job. He could certainly become a private lecturer (*Privatdozent*), he says, but what then?

I am not a philosopher and don't really believe that a faculty would offer me a chair in philosophy. *The present discipline of philosophy* combines very heterogeneous subjects, after all. I see two main parts, in particular: 1) ethics, aesthetics, philosophy of religion, metaphysics; one might say: philosophy of culture and nature, or the science of life- and world-conceptions. 2) according to the traditional terminology: logic and epistemology. According to my conception the name 'philosophy' ought to be reserved for the first part alone, while the particular areas of the second part should be released into [the status of] specialised disciplines. (ASP 1922b, p. 2)

Of these, Carnap goes on, he could put up with teaching (2) but not (1); having to teach (1) in order to have an academic job related to (2) would not be worth the sacrifice of research time. This is not, he stresses, from lack of *interest* in (1), i.e. in 'philosophy proper', but he doesn't feel professionally qualified in that field:

Although I have a lively interest in it, and have made myself familiar with its questions and attempted solutions through books, lectures, seminars, and a number of conversations with friends – but [this was] always just from personal interest, from a desire for personal self-improvement, not as a productive researcher or a reproductive teacher. (ASP 1922b, p. 2)

Now it is of course possible that Carnap is here being respectful of Scholz's known philosophical views, and being careful not to put off a potential patron and supporter. But what he reports is no more than the literal truth; not only had he invested considerable time in thinking and talking about such questions, but he continued to do so, even through the whole 'partisan' Vienna period – during which, among other things, he surprised people with his knowledge of Heidegger (Friedman 2000, p. 8), and spent several weeks in Davos at the 'Europäische Hochschultage' in February and March 1929 to witness the confrontation between Cassirer and Heidegger (Friedman 2000, Chapter 1).

After the Erlangen conference, Carnap went to Mexico for several months with his wife and children, to visit his wife's parents, who had emigrated from Germany many years before. (It was their house near Freiburg in which Carnap and family lived from 1918 to 1926.) His father-in-law was very pessimistic about the future of Germany:

He emigrated in early youth, and although he still clings with faithful love to his old homeland, he now thinks very pessimistically about the state of things there and is often in complete despair. He thinks that through economic misfortune the mental life of Germany will also decline more and more, and that especially the institutions that serve cultural life are headed for extinction or a quite wretched existence. (ASP 1923d, p. 1r)

Though the USA made a favourable impression on him,[17] Carnap says he has decided against emigration, for the time being. He sees his own role at the theoretical level, not the level of worldly politics, even in the creation of institutions or new fields of scientific philosophy (ASP 1923c, p. 1r). And for theoretical work, for the particular contribution he sees himself able to make to his own ideal of a *Gemeinschaftsgestalt*, Germany still seems best: 'Although I, too, see the situation sombrely enough, I still believe more strongly in the vitality of the life of the mind among the German people, and thus also in the will and strength to maintain cultural institutions even in the most calamitous of economic bad times' (ASP 1923d, p. 1r).

He had found his task. Not only did he organise the Erlangen conference (at which further conferences were planned), but he initiated discussions with Reichenbach, Scholz, and several others (including, while he was briefly in New York, with a number of Americans) for the publication of a new journal of scientific philosophy. When publishers dragged their feet, Carnap seriously considered starting a publishing firm with his own money (a small inheritance in 1924) to spread the word (ASP/HR 1924a). Though the Vienna Circle came into existence before Carnap joined it, it can be said without exaggeration that if he had not found it ready-made, he would have invented it for himself. The whole panoply of Vienna Circle activity – conferences, manifestos, journals, pamphlets, academic teaching and popular dissemination and everything in between – came into being in Carnap's mind when he found his task after reading Russell's book in the winter of 1921–2.

---

[17] 'Mexico would certainly not be the right soil into which to transplant myself. I have the impression of the United States, on the other hand (of course this is only from a brief, two-week stay), that it promises a more fruitful future in terms of the life of the mind than one generally thinks here, and might thus not be a barren soil. The people [*Volk*] has a character that is in every respect youthful; of course it is often immature, but it is also innocent, and seems to be looking out for tasks that are worthy of it, that will attract its untapped energy and then automatically push aside the lust for money' (ASP 1923d, p. iv). Time will tell.

CHAPTER 6

Rational reconstruction

Russell's *Our Knowledge of the External World* gave Carnap the key to his construction of a 'total system of all concepts'. But other ramifications of this new beginning were less easily accommodated. One of the most important was to find an appropriate conception of the meta-perspective within which to locate the newly reconceived *Aufbau* project. It was during this period, between 1922 and his departure for Vienna in 1926, that Carnap arrived at the new conception of 'rational reconstruction'. This programme gave the *Encyclopédiste* and positivist project of conceptual replacement a much more precise and vivid form than Comte or Ostwald had been able to give it. The main improvement over these previous versions was that Carnap applied to this task the Leibnizian idea (in Frege's form) of unifying knowledge *deductively*. Any particular proposed replacement of a folk concept, then, would exhibit the place of that concept within the entire system of knowledge. This meant that any such proposal could be articulated and discussed much more precisely than had ever been envisaged before; rational reconstruction could, in principle, be just as precise and scientific as scientific discourse itself. However, it took some years for Carnap to work this idea out. He had found his task in 1922, but much remained to be done.

THE TASK AND ITS COMPONENTS

Carnap's task, his new calling, actually consisted of *two* main subtasks. The new disciplines that should free themselves from philosophy (as psychology had done a few decades previously), he explains in a letter to Scholz, are 'the (scientific) study of science [*Wissenschaftslehre*]' and 'the study of orders or structures [*Ordnungslehre*]':

Just as psychology, not so long ago, made itself independent, what should now follow are: *the study of science* [*Wissenschaftslehre*] (my examples are the essays 'Der Raum' and 'The Task of Physics') and *the study of structures* [*Ordnungslehre*] (examples: 'Guide to the Theory of Relations' [an early draft of the *Abriß der Logistik*], 'Three-dimensionality of Space and Causality', 'From the Chaos to Reality' – 'Structural Theory of the Object of Knowledge [*Strukturtheorie des Erkenntnisgegenstandes*]'). Especially the latter, as a formal science [*Formwissenschaft*], is much closer to mathematics than to philosophy, especially now that mathematics begins to grasp that its object isn't quantity and space but certain structural configurations [*Ordnungsgefüge*] that can be applied to, among other things, relations of quantity and space. (ASP 1922b, pp. 1v–2r)

Given that these disciplines are still in their infancy, Carnap conceded that it might be wise not to separate them completely just yet: 'The work on them, different as they are from each other, can be combined in the same person' (ASP 1922b, p. 2r). But he left little doubt which of the specialties he himself most wanted to focus on: the Russell-inspired task of constructing a 'structural theory of the object of knowledge' is 'a task . . . that I find very attractive' (ASP 1922b, p. 1r). This was the subject (and proto-discipline) on which Carnap was in the process, as he wrote those words, of organising the two conferences at Erlangen (above, Chapter 3, pp. 156–8). And: 'Such a structural theory seems to me the sort of answer to the category problem we should be seeking today [*die heute zu fordernde Antwort auf das Kategorienproblem*], and a theory of relations built for this purpose to be its most valuable tool' (ASP 1922b, 1r–1v).[1] The turning point of 1922 had not, then, meant the abandonment of his original Leibnizian vision of a categorial *calculus philosophicus* or a *System der Wissenschaft*.

The vehicle for this vision was now the 'study of structures [*Ordnungslehre*]', which underlay his new idea for a 'structural theory of the object of knowledge [*Strukturtheorie des Erkenntnisgegenstandes*]' and thus for his 'total system of all concepts'. He formulated this idea adumbrating the relations between theory and 'reality' in two theses:

Theses. I. The sense [*Sinn*] of every scientific statement consists in this: that a particular formal structure is ascribed to a particular piece of reality [*Wirklichkeitsstück*].

II. An object within reality [*Ding der Wirklichkeit*] is identified and includable [*erfaßbar*] within a scientific statement only when its [conceptual] neighbourhood [*Gebiet*] is put in correspondence with a constellation of a particular structure

---

[1] He probably had in mind the apparatus of 'quasi-analysis' which he was in the process of working out formally as he wrote that letter; an informal sketch had been presented in *From the Chaos to Reality*. The (unpublished) typescript 'Die Quasizerlegung' (ASP 1923a) in which this apparatus is presented and formalised is dated January 1923.

('structural reconstruction') and it is itself put in correspondence with a particular element of this constellation. (ASP 1922d, p. c1[r])

He acknowledges that these two theses seem mutually circular; each refers to the other. His tentative solution to the apparent circularity is to suggest a structural criterion for the whole of knowledge, in which the later *Aufbau* idea of 'purely structural description' (as exemplified in the railway map example of §14) is already evident:

The circularity that appears to reside in the mutual reference of these two theses to each other is to be solved as follows: science, insofar as it treats of reality, initially has the task of putting every sphere of reality [*Wirklichkeitssphäre*] into correspondence with a sufficiently differentiated constellation, i.e. one in which no two members are structurally similar when the corresponding elements of reality are not identical. When that is the case for all elements of a sector of reality, then the demands of the two theses are met and thus the first task of science, the identification of its objects, achieved. (ASP 1922d, p. cl[r])

Despite their unclarities these passages represent perhaps the first reasonably explicit statement of the 'rational reconstruction' (here called 'structural reconstruction') programme. And 'in place of the Kantian dictum that wants to restrict science to the mathematically quantitative', Carnap suggests: 'every science is a science only insofar as the study of structures [*Strukturlehre*] is contained in it' (ASP 1922d, p. a2).

What is missing, but is now thrust into the spotlight by the prominence given the notion of 'structure', is an account of what 'structure' *itself*, or a particular structure, could mean. If the meaning or 'sense' of a scientific statement resides in its assignment to a place within a 'structure', then it becomes a matter of some importance to determine the status and meaning of 'structure' – given Carnap's logicism, the status and meaning of the principles of logic. The available accounts, those of the Marburg school, of Frege, Russell, Brouwer, Hilbert, and Poincaré, all suffered from certain obvious shortcomings. What these accounts had in common was that they stopped the inquiry at a certain point; they just asserted that certain principles had meaning and were true, without giving any good reasons to think so.

But this was a question that remained open for several years, and did not get a satisfactory answer until Carnap moved to Vienna in 1926 and read the *Tractatus* more carefully. Until then, his conception of meta-discourse remained vague. Still, in the different parts of the new task that Carnap describes to Scholz in his letter, we can already distinguish the main features of the later Carnap's articulation of meta-theory. Within *Wissenschaftslehre* we can discern what one might call a 'clarification' (or perhaps 'schemati-sation') project, of so describing *existing* empirical science as to reveal its logical structure, or impose one on it, especially with a view to under-standing how it can be subject to empirical scrutiny. And within applied *Ordnungslehre* a 'constructive' project can be discerned, that begins with elementary observational components (initially specified phenomenologi-cally) and arrives at a structure of knowledge from scratch, independently of any concepts assumed within existing science, though obviously with existing science in mind as the target of reconstruction. Rational recon-struction was conceived, in the two Erlangen theses, as contributing most directly to this constructive project, and specifically as providing a logical representation or picture of the target area of knowledge, one in which each component of the knowledge in question corresponds to a deductive struc-ture, and all the inferential links are clearly displayed. Once such a structure exists, then it can also be applied as a standard for *Wissenschaftslehre*.

Wissenschaftslehre and *Ordnungslehre* are in practice fundamentally dif-ferent processes or tasks; the difference is related to that between what Reichenbach (1938, pp. 7–8) later called the 'context of discovery' and 'con-text of justification' or more broadly the 'descriptive' and the 'critical' tasks of epistemology. If a substantial amount of accepted knowledge already exists, then to propose a new framework for knowledge in general, two subtasks may be distinguished: that of developing the new framework from the ground up, and that of rearticulating or re-expressing existing knowledge (or whatever subset is to be regarded as legitimate) in terms commensurable with those of the new framework. This 'clarification' project is of course more closely involved with the practicalities of a going concern, an exist-ing enterprise. It naturally adopts the terms of art within that enterprise, and takes its methods as given. It attempts to discern within those existing practices a logical structure that will then make it possible to *place* the con-cepts of science within the *new* framework being proposed, so as to draw correspondences between concepts of existing science and certain nodes or substructures within the proposed framework.

'The formation of a concept consists in setting up a law for the use of a sign', Carnap writes (1926, p. 4), and this can result either from stipulation or from the evolution of 'language use [*Sprachgebrauch*]'. The 'clarifica-tion' task is essentially one of *discerning* the *use* of a 'law about the use of a sign' within an existing *Sprachgebrauch*. This 'clarification' project thus belongs largely to what Carnap would later call descriptive semantics, which he regarded as part of pragmatics – while the 'constructive' project, the

specification of the new framework with a particular application or interpretation in mind, corresponds (in terms of its purpose at the time, within
Carnap's larger project) more to the later category of (pure) semantics. But
both the 'clarificative' and 'constructive' projects have a role in the pragmatic programme of rational reconstruction. The 'clarification' component
corresponds, in Carnap's later terminology, to the preliminary 'clarification'
step of explication, in which agreement is reached on a rough specification
of the *explicandum*. And the 'constructive' component corresponds to the
rational reconstruction (later explication) itself, the proposal of a precise
explicatum.

Although the governing meta-logic remained unclear, Carnap began after
1922 to give logic a more privileged or canonical place. He later recalled,
of this period, 'When I considered a concept or a proposition occurring
in a scientific or philosophical discussion, I thought that I understood
it clearly only if I felt that I could express it, if I wanted to, in symbolic
language' (1963, p. 11). Expressibility in symbolic notation became not just a
touchstone for his own understanding, but a criterion for acceptability. The
symbolic expression became not just perspicuous but *canonical*. This also
applied to the *Wissenschaft* of philosophy itself: 'It is characteristic of this
method that apart from the basic concepts [*Grundbegriffe*] no "constants"
(in the sense of symbolic logic) are employed other than those of logic' (ASP
1922d, p. c2). And over the following years the meta-logic gradually becomes
clearer. Sometime during 1924 Carnap realised that the phenomenological
specification of the given was incompatible with the logical construction
from that point on. The two approaches were in competition with each
other – he found himself guilty of having 'inferred entities' at the basis of
his system that could be (and therefore should be, by Russell's principle)
'logically constructed'. This displacement of phenomenology by logic had
the momentous effect of levelling the distinction between primary and
secondary worlds. The primary world lost its role as a 'foundation' for
optional secondary worlds; the 'fiction' of the 'original chaos' was now
abandoned, leaving only the subsequent fictions of causality and substance
used to build the scientific secondary world. As a result, the fit between the
'clarificative' and 'constructive' projects becomes completely seamless. The
sentences representing the most basic sense impressions and those stating
the most abstract laws of physics are extensionally equivalent; the difference
between them is only one of language. The most unequivocal expression of
this optimism is Carnap's booklet *Physical Concept Formation* (*Physikalische
Begriffsbildung*) (1926).

On his arrival in Vienna that same year, Carnap found an answer to his question about the status and meaning of logic, in the *Tractatus*.[2] As we will see in Chapter 7, although this answer solved one problem, it raised another; it once again broke apart the 'clarificative' and 'constructive' components of Carnap's 1926 conception. The 'constructive' component became central, and the 'clarificative' project went into temporary eclipse. Carnap never accepted this unsatisfactory situation as final. He worked throughout his entire Vienna period to put the two pieces together again (Chapter 8), but only found a way of doing this after he dramatically threw off the Wittgensteinian yoke in early 1931 (Chapter 9). In the following section we review the trajectory of the 'constructive' project from its pre-Wittgensteinian origins to 1930. Then we consider the pre-Wittgensteinian conception of the 'clarificative' project, in which the two projects are conceived as fitting seamlessly into a single system.

THE EVOLUTION OF THE *AUFBAU* SYSTEM, 1922–1930

From some time in 1924, the aspects of the system that had begun under the auspices of phenomenology were transformed either into empirical statements about the workings of the sensory organs or into explicit statements of meta-logic, later called rules of 'logical syntax'.[3] Carnap's notes on a later conversation with Feigl (UCLA 1930a) shed some light on this. The conversation arose from a remark of Waismann's to the effect that 'the laws of nature are rules of syntax'. While this seemed to Carnap largely consistent with his own view that the laws of nature are 'operational rules for the constitution of the physical world', it also raised the problem that if these are seen as rules of 'syntax', then any sentence inconsistent with them would be nonsense, 'and that is not after all in accordance with our conception' (UCLA 1930a, p. 1). So two levels of operational rules are to be distinguished, those of first level (*Operationsvorschriften erster Stufe*), which

---

[2] According to his own report Carnap read the *Tractatus* on its first appearance in 1921 (in Ostwald's *Annalen der Natur- und Kulturphilosophie*), but 'at that time I did not make the great effort required to come to a clear understanding of the often obscure formulations' (1963, p. 24). It was only when he arrived in Vienna in 1926 that, along with the rest of the Circle, he read the book carefully and absorbed its ideas.

[3] The expression 'logical syntax' was common within the early Vienna Circle. It was taken from the *Tractatus*, where it means something like 'logical grammar', or 'the facts about the physical order of signs on a page that enable them to symbolize' (Proops 2001b), but Wittgenstein seems not to have thought that these rules could be made explicit; they could only 'show themselves', but not be spelled out. The Vienna Circle, by contrast, *assumed* their explicit specifiability, and also assumed that we humans (or we logicians) could *decide* on them; indeed, a good part of the discussions of the Vienna Circle revolved around the question what these constitutive rules *should be*.

include laws of nature as well as metric and dimensional conventions, and those of second level, which govern the observation language (since we are still essentially within the *Aufbau* system, the vocabulary is autopsychological, not physicalistic).[4] A sentence is not to be regarded as meaningless, then, if it contradicts our present laws of physics, but only if it violates the operational rules of second level, i.e. the syntactic rules laid down for the observation language (which in turn rest on the 'phenomenal syntax' by which we interpret the outputs of our sensory apparatus). Carnap recognises, of course, that this test is not practically applicable at present.[5]

However that may be, a question remains regarding the status of the 'phenomenal syntax'. The laws of physics themselves are empirical, once the operational rules of second level have been fixed. But what of the 'phenomenal syntax' on which *those* rules must in turn be based? Here Carnap compared 'our' Vienna Circle position with that of the phenomenologists:

We want to regard it [the phenomenal syntax] as empirical, but the *phenomenologists* want to regard it as a priori, or at least as knowable from a single instance, hence not empirical in the usual sense. But in reality there is only a gradual, if of course a rather large, difference between the empiricity [*Empirizität*] of the physical syntax and that of the phenomenal syntax. The difference is only this: it happens relatively frequently that we have new experiences of the kind that induce us to change the *physical* syntax (i.e. the laws of nature); specifically to change them according to the second-order operational rules, by means of which the physical syntax is stipulated as being dependent on phenomenal processes. But it seldom happens that we have new experiences of the kind that induce us to change the phenomenal syntax. That sort of thing happens e.g. if you go blind or when someone born blind is operated upon; one could also imagine the appearance of new senses whose field and qualitative space had a particular number of dimensions, or a change in the

---

[4] 'While the first-order operational rules are chosen to accommodate a particular experience ([a particular] phenomenal process), the second-order operational rules hold generally, for arbitrary phenomenal processes, but under the condition of a definite syntax of the phenomenal language (which includes, for instance: two-dimensionality of the visual field, three-dimensionality of the colour space, etc.). The second-order operational rules determine how the first-order operational rules are to be constructed, depending on the content of the phenomenal process [*je nach dem Inhalt des phänomenalen Ablaufs*]' (UCLA 1930a).

[5] 'The practical execution of the investigation is of course made more difficult by the fact that the second-order operational rules haven't been identified yet. They are constantly being applied in the construction of physics, but implicitly, without being mentioned. It would be an important job to identify them. Their justification would have to be a priori, at least in the sense of showing that with arbitrarily assumed phenomenal processes (always assuming our phenomenal syntax) other (second-order) operational rules wouldn't result in a simpler physics' (UCLA 1930a, pp. 1–2). This passage shows how interested Carnap was, even some years after the publication of the *Aufbau*, in a detailed *psychological* foundation for the laws of physics – which not only recalls Helmholtz, once again, but also makes very clear why Carnap would naturally have been interested in Husserl's effort to make explicit something like a 'phenomenal syntax'.

number of dimensions of the field or qualitative space e.g. of our visual sense. It isn't clear yet whether a given phenomenal process uniquely determines a particular syntax and phenomenal language or leaves a certain leeway . . . The mistake of the phenomenologists consists in regarding this gradual difference as a difference in principle. To be precise we would have to check every day whether the visual field was three-dimensional, the colour field three-dimensional, etc.; in practice, of course, we don't need to do this, since experience teaches us that in this respect changes occur very rarely. (UCLA 1930a, p. 2)

If one wanted to make the phenomenal syntax fully variable, Carnap went on, one could even think in terms of a *third* level of operational rules, prescribing how the second-level rules are to be set up for any possible phenomenal syntax (UCLA 1930a, p. 3).[6]

This conversation represented a kind of endpoint in the development of the *Aufbau* idea from 1922, in which the *Aufbau* itself was only one intermediate phase. At this endpoint in 1930, the earlier, partly phenomenological view of 1922 had in principle been completely resolved into empirical sentences on the one hand, rules of Wittgensteinian 'logical syntax' on the other. But Wittgenstein himself was not the only influence (perhaps not even the most important one) pushing Carnap toward such a 'Wittgensteinian' endpoint. Carnap's conception of the *Aufbau* project had begun to change much earlier. By January of 1925, when he had given a talk on the project at the University of Vienna, the starting point of *From the Chaos to Reality* had already been abandoned. The fiction of the original chaos had been dropped, along with the distinction between a fixed primary world that could be regarded as foundational and the many optional secondary worlds of 'reality'. So phenomenological discernment had no job to do any more; no pre-existing structure (arising, say, from a distinction between 'live' impressions and 'dead' ideas) needed to be discerned in an antecedent 'chaos'. The construction proceeded without such an introductory step. Indeed, the *elimination of subjectivity* had become a top priority for Carnap at this point, as we can see from the three 'theses' Carnap started the talk with. The first two are familiar from 1922 ('unity of the object realm [*des Gegenstandsbereiches*]' and 'methodological solipsism'), but the third was new – 'overcoming subjectivity: transition from material to structure' (ASP 1925a, 1925b). *This* is the context in which we find the idea – now explicitly brought to bear on the system *basis* – of the 'possibility of designation by purely structural statements'. The idea of a 'structural designation' had been there in 1922, as we saw, but it had then been assumed

---

[6] This foreshadows his later proposal regarding the empirical basis in his paper responding to Neurath, 'On protocol sentences' (1932e); see below, pp. 253–6.

that phenomenological discernment could *identify* the 'structures' within the 'material' of perception, *before* 'structural designation' goes to work on it. The phenomenological exercise of stripping away, in imagination, all 'externally imposed' structure from a fictive 'original chaos' (and then imaginatively discerning in that undifferentiated mental content two distinguishable 'aspects' of experience) was to be *followed by* further, structural characterisation of objects *in terms* of this phenomenologically provided basis. Now, in 1925, the idea of 'purely structural designation', which had been there from the beginning, was applied more comprehensively and systematically.

The *Aufbau* is in some respects a transitional work, still haunted by traces of the 1922 position, and not yet completely integrated into the Wittgensteinian Vienna Circle position of the 1930 conversation with Feigl. The very presence of Vaihinger's language of 'fictions', as one of four ways to represent the constitution system, suggests this. Another indication noted by commentators is the tension between an explicitly phenomenological starting point for determining the basis and the adherence to 'purely structural description'. On the one hand Carnap said that 'at the beginning of the system, experiences are simply to be taken as they present themselves', bracketing anything that may be taken as referring to 'real' objects outside the experience, in the manner of Husserl (1928a, §64, p. 86). But he had also claimed programmatically that 'all scientific statements are structural statements', and illustrated what he meant by a 'purely structural description' with his metaphor of the railway map (§14). This unresolved dissonance leads, it is said, to the famous difficulty of the 'founded' relation in §§153–5, where the question is faced how to eliminate the informally or phenomenologically supplied basic relation in favour of something *purely* 'structural'. We will return to this problem below.

Another dissonance often commented on is that between the programmatic stress on explicit definition and its evident violation in §126, at the ascent from two to three dimensions. This step in the *Aufbau* is a vestige of the earlier transition from a 'primary' world of pure perception, constructed by explicit definition from the chaotic given (phenomenologically reconstructed), to various possible 'secondary worlds' of 'reality', constructed by maximising spatial and temporal continuity subject to various constraints. This break in the mode of construction occurs exactly at the same point in the *Aufbau* construction as it does in *From the Chaos to Reality* – at the point where qualities (colours) are attributed to space-time points. It seems obvious that this must be an undigested survival from the earlier conception that even Carnap himself (in his introduction to the 1961 edition) recognised as inconsistent with the book's ostensible programme. And the maximands in §126 are suspiciously reminiscent of the 'tendencies' Carnap explicitly presents in 1922 as versions of Kant's categories of substance and cause. Indeed, the latter pair make an appearance in the *Aufbau* itself, in the same role – not in the section explicitly devoted to a *different* 'explication' of categories (as the basic relations, in §83), but in a later section (§135) that once again discusses the extension of a local, subjectively available realm to a global, objective world. The impression is reinforced that these are unprocessed vestiges of the earlier view.

But contrary to all these appearances, the published *Aufbau* is in fact, I will argue, very largely a consistent statement of the later, Vienna Circle view. Vaihinger's language of 'fictions' and the phenomenological motivation of the basis are explicitly presented as informal circumlocutions (as merely one of four 'languages' in which the constitution system can be represented, §95). They are ways of helping those approaching the subject from other standpoints to see what Carnap is getting at; they are not the canonical expression of what is being said – that is conveyed in the symbolic construction. Apparent survivals from earlier views often reveal themselves, on closer inspection, as subtle *reconstructions* of the earlier view, or even what Carnap would later call explications. This can be well illustrated by the notorious example just mentioned, the transition in §126 from the perceptual to the known world.

First, it should be noted that the idea of a fixed 'primary world' of completely unprocessed perception is entirely banished from the *Aufbau*. It not only plays no foundational role, as it had residually done in *From the Chaos to Reality*, but is completely absent. The 'fiction' of an undifferentiated chaos has been jettisoned, as well as the phenomenological exercise of discerning structure within it that extends this featureless chaos to a 'primary world' with a temporal dimension. That these changes were quite deliberate is evident from occasional retrospective comments about his earlier papers. In §124, for instance, where Carnap considers the construction of three-dimensional physical space from two-dimensional perceptual space, he cites his 1924 paper 'Three-dimensionality of Space and Causality' along with the works of others, and says:

The cited investigations are important because they (unlike other systems) *do* actually recognise the significance of the problem of the transition from the two-dimensional to the three-dimensional order, and try to solve it. But they are in error (even my own [i.e. 'Three-dimensionality of Space and Causality']) in their conception that the two-dimensionality of the visual field has to be regarded as ultimately given [*ursprünglich*]. In our constitution theory we have recognised that we must regard the two-dimensional order to be every bit as derived as the three-dimensional one, and that it thus presents a problem of its constitution . . . (1928a, §124, p. 164; PT p. 193)

In retrospect he sees the phenomenological discernment of the two-dimensionality of immediate perception – argued for at length in the 1924 paper, with separate consideration of each sense modality – as an over-reliance on intuition, substituting ad hoc imaginative reconstruction for more systematic and controlled empirical observation or logical derivation. And indeed, the two-dimensional visual field *is* constructed in the *Aufbau* (in §89 and §117, with alternative approaches considered in §92); it is not taken as given.[7]

The problem to be solved at §126 is a different one, then, from the analogous problem in 1922. We are not progressing from an unordered, two-dimensional 'primary world' to a three-dimensional 'secondary world' of 'reality' at this step. The step from two to three dimensions (§§124–5) is now entirely a mathematical one,[8] it lacks its former significance. And what occurs at §126 is just the projection of colours onto the world-points of mathematical space-time. There is no longer a *given* that is endowed with 'reality' at this point, but a logical construction to which a concrete instantiation is assigned.

---

[7] Another, perhaps more obvious, illustration that the 'primary world' of the early 1920s has been eliminated is in Carnap's *Aufbau* treatment of the three kinds of space from *Der Raum* (see also ASP 1928a, 1929e). *Formal space* remains more or less as it was in 1921; it is the subject of 'purely mathematical *abstract geometry*, which does not deal with space in any proper sense of this word, but with certain multidimensional order-configurations [*Ordnungsgefügen*]' (1928a, §107, p. 149; PT p. 177). It is constituted from logic directly, as in *Der Raum*. *Physical space*, on the other hand, is presented quite differently from its 1921 treatment. It is constituted as the first step in the construction of physical objects from autopsychological ones; this is the step from two to *n* dimensions. 'Abstract space' is assumed for this step, and physical space is *defined directly* on its basis; the construction of physical space by-passes the autopsychological altogether, which only enters in the next step, the assignment of colours and other (autopsychologically constituted) qualities to the world-points of physical space (the interpretation of configurations among them as 'geometrical' is retrospective, from the vantage point of a higher level in the constitution system; (1928a, §128, p. 170). The whole of physics is then constructed on the basis of these assignments of qualities to world-points (1928a, §136, pp. 180–2). The *intuitive space* of *Der Raum* has disappeared; there are only abstract (mathematical) space and physical space. 'Qualitative spatiality' has been expunged: 'In the constitution system the peculiar quality of spatiality, though such an essential feature of the external world in experience, makes no appearance *as* a quality, any more than other qualities do: colours, pitches, feelings, etc. For the constitution system concerns itself only with the structural, which in the case of space means only with the formal features of this configuration. But nothing knowable, i.e. conceptually capturable, is thereby lost to the constitution system. For the non-structural cannot, according to the thesis of the constitution theory, be the object of a scientific statement' (1928a, §125, p. 166; PT p. 195).
[8] It seems likely, though there is no mention of it in the *Aufbau*, that Carnap was inspired here by the mathematician Karl Menger (a member of the Vienna Circle), whose work in dimension theory was published during the mid-1920s, and is cited in the *Abriß der Logistik* (1929), p. 77 (I am grateful to Michael Friedman for drawing this citation to my attention).

However, there is nonetheless an analogy between these two transitions. In both cases, speaking informally, there is a transition from a *perceptual* world, whose structure is shared by all beings with the main features of human sensory equipment, to a *known* world, a (proto-)scientific world, underdetermined by the perceptual world. In both cases it is acknowledged that there is no *unique* constitution of the known from the perceptual. The results of this constitution will depend, rather, on the context in which, and purpose for which, it is undertaken, and the relative priority given to different possible optimands. In Kantian terms, this is where the intuitions meet the categories.[9] But within this common description of the two analogous transitions, there is a fundamental difference between them. Not only has the role of 'fictions' been reduced to a minimum in the later version, but those retained have been made part of a single system. The specification of what is given has been reduced to a schematic skeleton, and made (in principle) independent of intuitive or subjective considerations. What was supplied by phenomenological discernment previously is now constructed explicitly. So this transition no longer constitutes an objective world from subjective experience. Objectivity results now, rather, from the mutual agreement of subjective constructions over a certain range (§148).[10]

---

[9] It might be asked here why, in that case, Carnap ever thought that this transition (from a perceptual to a known world) could be reconstructed entirely by means of explicit definitions. In 1922, although Russell's 'principle of abstraction' inspired the first draft of the system (Chapter 5, pp. 147–8), it was *not* regarded as the only principle of construction. This requirement was an artefact of Carnap's acceptance of Wittgenstein's meaning criterion after 1926, in which all meaningful statements are truth functions of atomic sentences. As we will see below (Chapter 7), Carnap never thought universal laws or classical mathematics were meaningless. For him this was, rather, an unresolved issue within the framework of the *Tractatus* that had somehow to be addressed. As one step toward this (below, Chapter 7, pp. 191–6), he thought he had discovered a way of converting implicit into explicit definitions. In Carnap's later remarks in his 1961 introduction to the *Aufbau*, he says that he had gone beyond explicit definition 'without clearly being aware of it', though it had of course been necessary, he adds, as we have realised since then that the reduction of higher to lower concepts is not always possible by explicit definition. His breach of explicit definition at §126ff. is thus positioned in these late remarks (1961, pp. XIII–XIV) as a half-conscious anticipation of his later development in 'Testability and Meaning' and 'The Methodological Character of Theoretical Concepts'.

[10] Alan Richardson has suggested that Carnap provides 'not one, but two . . . distinct solutions to the problem of the objectivity of knowledge' during this period (Richardson 1998, p. 29), which he associates with 'significant philosophical tensions' between the *Aufbau* project and the 'methodology of critical conventionalism' he discerns in *Physical Concept Formation* (Richardson 1998, p. 182). The two distinct accounts of objectivity Richardson sees in the *Aufbau* are (1) Carnap 'constructs a notion of objectivity within the system of scientific concepts itself via the construction of the intersubjective world of science'; and (2) Carnap 'endorses the project of pure logical structure . . . through his notion of a "purely structural definite description"' (Richardson 1998, p. 29). Richardson's (1) more aptly describes Carnap's 1922 effort to rescue 'chaotic' subjectivity from its isolation, and to connect it by (a minimal system of) 'fictive' links with an 'objective' world. And (2), as we have seen, *succeeded* that earlier conception. The two were not simultaneous, as Richardson suggests. What Carnap means by 'objectivity', in the *Aufbau*, is just intersubjectivity (§2, p. 3; §16, pp. 20–21; §66,

Here Carnap contrasts his 1928 procedure not with his own previous self (since *From the Chaos to Reality* was never published), but with that of his Kantian friend (and Buchenbach neighbour, while the *Aufbau* was being written) Broder Christiansen. In contrast to certain other conceptions, such as Christiansen's, Carnap writes in §148, '*intersubjectivisation does not depend here* [in the *Aufbau*] *on a fiction*':

> The constitution system employs information given by other people only for constitutional purposes, first for the constitutional rounding out of the physical world, then also for the constitution of the heteropsychological. But these constitutions do not consist in the hypothetical inference to, or fictive invocation of, something non-given [*in der hypothetischen Erschließung oder fiktiven Ansetzung eines Nicht-Gegebenen*], but rather in a reorganisation of the given [*einer Umordnung des Gegebenen*] ... Metaphysical claims about the objects constituted by this reorganisation are not made, within the constitution system. (1928a, §148, pp. 199–200; PT p. 229)

It would appear then that the 'fictions' regarding the form of the given that still pervaded the 1922 system had, both programmatically and in fact, been largely eliminated by 1928. What are called 'fictions' in the *Aufbau* are now purely for convenience of presentation (§95).

But what about the categorical 'tendencies' that were to *guide* the construction of the known 'reality' from the perceived 'primary world'? Carnap was unsure how to reconstruct the Kantian idea of 'category'. In §83 he considers various possibilities, taking his departure from the idea of 'category' as a 'form taken by the synthesis of the manifold of experience to the unity of the object' (though he immediately points out that this is 'not a definition'). Now that the constitution system has provided more precise concepts than the traditional tables of categories, he says, what corresponds in our new system to this idea of a category? In the discussion (§26) of the form of the total system, four different senses of the system 'form' are discussed: as determined by the basis, by the form of hierarchy (*Stufenform*), by the form of object (*Gegenstandsform*), and by the system form itself (what gets reduced to what). As the choice of basis determines or tightly constrains the form of object and of system, Carnap says, these

pp. 90–1) – with the implication that the intersubjective is also unambiguous (*eindeutig*) (e.g. §136, p. 181). And the problem of achieving 'objective' (i.e. intersubjective) science despite a 'subjective' basis (i.e. an autopsychological one), though obviously *descended* from the problem of finding a transition from the purely phenomenal 'primary world' of 1922 to one of the (objective) 'secondary worlds' erected on its basis, is now a purely technical problem internal to the constitution system. The earlier conception of the task had been left behind by 1928; Carnap now thought even the subjective 'primary' world (or much of it) had to be reconstructed logically, as he no longer thought it could be relied on to reveal the necessary *Eindeutigkeit* to intuitive, phenomenological discernment.

three are not independent choices. He briefly considers the possibility that one might regard the form of hierarchy (*Stufenform*) as corresponding to the term 'category' (this would make *class* and *relation* the two categories).[11] But since the 'manifold of experience' in the constitution system consists of the basic elements, he thinks it better to take the basic relations – which also fix or constrain the object and system forms – as corresponding to categories. This is illustrated by the 1925 form of the constitution system (ASP 1925a, 1925b), whose five basic relations can be seen as corresponding, Carnap says, to the traditional categories of equality, similarity, intensity, spatiality, and temporality. In the present system, he says, it seems these may in fact be reducible in turn to a single basic relation ('Er', recollection of similarity), which would mean that '*the number of* (genuine) *categories is very small, perhaps there is only a single category*'. This, it seems to Carnap, is revealed by the greater power of modern logic; the over-complexity and over-crowdedness of traditional '*tables of categories* from Aristotle to Driesch' is due to 'the inadequacy of the tools they employed' (§156, p. 210; PT p. 243).

The older conception of 'category' from 1922 is not mentioned at all in §83, even as a rejected possibility. But it is still present in other passages of the *Aufbau* – this is just what gives the impression that it is a vestige from the earlier system. This impression is no less misleading, though, than the impression that §126 is a vestige of the transition from 'primary' to 'secondary' world. Carnap had begun the project with Vaihinger's idea of a category as a pragmatic principle or 'fiction' in mind (as the 'tendencies' of substance and cause that guide the construction of 'secondary' worlds from the 'chaos'). What seems to have occurred is that some time around 1925–6,[12] it no longer seemed right to include such *pragmatic* principles as his equivalents to the Kantian or Aristotelian 'categories' within the system of *cognitive* 'fictions'. When logic pushed aside phenomenological discernment of 'structure', it also exiled pragmatic principles from the realm of the cognitive (which might be understood here as a kind of explication of Kant's 'understanding [*Verstand*]', as opposed to a wider system of cognitive *and* pragmatic principles, which could be seen as corresponding to Kant's 'reason [*Vernunft*]'). In the *Aufbau* itself, though, it seems Carnap was not quite sure *how* to classify (or what status to give) these formerly categorical 'fictions', now practical principles. So it is hardly surprising that the parallel with the traditional categories of substance and cause is still occasionally suggested, even though their status has now changed. In §135, for instance,

---

[11] Klein (2004) considers this sense of 'category' in Carnap.

[12] The Vienna talk Carnap gave in January 1925 is still entitled 'Thoughts on the Category Problem: Prolegomena to a Constitution Theory' (ASP 1925a).

the visual world constructed in the previous sections is extended by means of the other senses to obtain the 'perceptual world [*Wahrnehmungswelt*]'. But, Carnap remarks, this extension is intuitively rather different when it is undertaken temporally (requiring a principle of induction or temporal extrapolation) from when it is undertaken spatially (requiring a kind of Machian 'principle of continuity'): 'In a certain sense the first kind of application of *ascription by analogy* can be regarded as an application of a *causality postulate*, the second as an application of a *substance postulate*'. But when these traditional categories are translated into the terms of the constitution system, they seem more like special cases of the same underlying principle: '*the two categories of causality and substantiality amount to application of the same analogy constitution along different coordinate* axes' (1928a, §135, p. 180; PT p. 208). There is no attempt to carry out this 'structural' reduction of the categories of cause and substance in any detail, but the general strategy is reasonably clear; the guiding principles of the attribution of qualities to physical space-time positions are to be expressed as formal variants of a single principle.

What this principle might be is hardly explored, except in a remarkable passage in §105, which discusses 'the problem of deducing the constitution rules [*der Deduktion der Konstitutionsregeln*]'. General constitution rules of the kind he has listed in the previous section might be deducible, Carnap speculates, from some single principle (as hinted in §135), on the analogy of a 'world formula' (of the kind imagined by Laplace[13]) from which all the laws of physics might be deducible. 'In the present case, as in that one, the highest principle is not known, but in the first instance provides rather a goal or direction for research, a goal whose attainability is not even assured' (1928a, §105, p. 146; PT pp. 165–6). This in itself is remarkable enough, as there is no indication how such a 'highest principle [*oberstes Prinzip*]' might relate to the principles of logic or the cognitive realm more generally. But Carnap goes further:

If the highest principle of construction were already known, a further task would consist in determining how it can be understood as necessarily resulting from the *point* of knowledge, or more precisely, *from the contribution of knowing to the more*

---

[13] Laplace's idea that an omniscient spirit could predict every event, with a comprehensive 'world formula', if it knew the position of every particle at some initial time, is of course rooted in the mechanical hypothesis. It had become the subject of widespread discussion after Emil Dubois-Reymond's (1872) argument that if all knowledge is of mechanical processes (which he assumed), then there are ineluctable limits to our knowledge; there is, as he said, an *ignorabimus* beyond which we cannot penetrate. Carnap knew, of course, that the mechanical assumptions could no longer be upheld, but as Howard Stein has pointed out to me, Gustav Mie had proposed a 'world function' for the post-mechanical 'field-theoretic ideal of unity', as Hilbert suggested it be called (Hilbert 1924, pp. 258–60), and Carnap may also have had this in mind in 1928.

comprehensive context of human life purposes [*für den umfassenderen Zweckzusammenhang des Lebens*], that the shaping of experiences into objects occurs precisely in the way it is represented to do in the constitution system, in the way it is given expression by the general constitution rules, and finally in the way it is summed up most concentratedly in the highest constitution principle. (1928a, §105, p. 146; PT p. 166)

Envisaged here, it seems, is not so much an ultimate *foundation* of knowledge construction in the overall purpose-context of life, but a dialectical interplay between them, as the purposes of human beings are of course constrained and shaped by their knowledge (cf. also ASP 1929d). Implicitly, at least, this prefigures the later Carnap; the difference lies in his almost Leibnizian (perhaps also Fregean and Marburg-derived) confidence, during this earlier period, in the powers of human reason to arrive at a *single* or a *unique* 'highest construction principle' on the model of Laplace's 'world-formula'. It is not surprising, therefore, to find evidence in this very passage that the practical orientation at the heart of his architectonic also looks *back* to the Leibnizian dream of a comprehensive system of categories:

This *teleological problem of knowledge-shaping* can in the present state of our knowledge at best be approached piecemeal, not as a whole. Such piecemeal approaches might include, for instance, the tendencies of substantialisation and causation that become important at the higher levels of the constitution system. (1928a §105, p. 146; PT p. 166)

It would appear, then, that even in their original 1922 conception these categorical 'tendencies' of substance and cause may have been envisaged as grounded – like, presumably, other 'conscious principles of the science of science' (such as the 'principle of maximal simplicity') – in something like an overall purpose-context of human life.

The pragmatic criterion for language choice at the level of the metatheory, which seems like such a radical innovation in Carnap's thought in the early 1930s, is clearly prefigured here, though of course not in a context of language pluralism. In any case this passage indicates that although any thought of a meta-perspective had certainly been pushed far into the background during the later 1920s, under the influence of Wittgenstein's sharp demarcation between cognitive meaning and the unsayable, it had not disappeared completely. (We will see in the next chapter how Carnap attempted to accommodate meta-logic within the Wittgensteinian single-language corset.) And the pragmatic tendency of the *Aufbau* did not go entirely undetected; Philipp Frank saw it right away. As he wrote later:

When I read [the *Aufbau*] it reminded me strongly of William James's pragmatic requirement, that the meaning of any statement is given by its 'cash value', that is, by what it means as a direction for human behavior. I wrote immediately to Carnap, 'what you advocate is pragmatism'. (Frank 1949, p. 33)

Like the other apparent vestiges of earlier ideas, then, the allusion to Carnap's earlier conception of 'category', in §105 and elsewhere, in fact points forward rather than backward – in this case to Carnap's much later conception, in which both 'theoretical investigations' *and* 'practical deliberations and decisions' bear on the choice of 'categorial concepts' (see below, Chapter 10, p. 265).

The *Aufbau* programme, exemplifying the 'constructive' component of rational reconstruction, had travelled a long distance from its origins in 1922. It had begun as a way of attaining an objective 'reality' from the chaotic and subjective 'primary world' of pure sensation, by using logic as a bootstrapping device to transmit phenomenal content from raw experience to theoretical statements. By 1928, it had evolved into something quite different, and went on developing into the early 1930s, as we will see in more detail in Chapters 7 and 8. The Wittgensteinian influence after 1926 did not change the direction of this development, but reinforced an existing process.

SCHEMATISING PHYSICS

In 1925–6, just as he was writing the *Aufbau*, Carnap also wrote *Physical Concept Formation*, in which the relation between physical concepts and observation is approached rather differently. There is no attempt, in this book, to found physical (or ordinary) knowledge on a phenomenal basis; but it is taken completely for granted that this is possible. 'Things and their qualities [*Dinge und Dingeigenschaften*]' are assumed from the start without comment; we perceive qualities of objects – colour, hardness, temperature, cohesion, elasticity, solubility, weight, etc. Some of these are perceived directly and spontaneously, others are revealed only in response to an action on our part, e.g. bending or dropping an object, stirring a substance into water to discover whether it is soluble, plucking a string to find its pitch, etc. This is a superficial distinction, though, as the spontaneously revealed qualities are elicited in response to certain conditions as well, only that we do not have to bring these about ourselves; the white light that is a condition for a certain surface to appear red is ordinarily provided for us by the sun, and so on. 'So every statement about a quality of an object says how it reacts to certain conditions or requirements [*Beanspruchungen*]', he says; '*A quality of a thing* [*Dingeigenschaft*] *is a mode of reacting* [*Reaktionsweise*]' (1926, p. 7). It is thus properly represented by a conditional.

To advance from this first, elementary step to the construction of stable qualities, we already go beyond anything we can perceive; we state a new conditional to the effect that when a certain body is irradiated with white light, it reflects red light. The original conditional stated that if a certain condition was met at time *t*, a certain quality was revealed in a particular object at *t*; the new conditional puts a universal quantifier over all times *t* in front of the original conditional; it states that *whenever* those conditions are met, that quality is revealed. So already at this level we meet the peculiarity of physical statements '*that they claim more than what has been* observed, in fact more than could ever be observed, *so they claim more than one may justifiably claim* [*als man rechtmäßigerweise behaupten darf*]' (1926, p. 8). Induction has no logical justification, and the axiom underlying it, 'Under the same conditions the same thing happens [*Unter gleichen Bedingungen geschieht Gleiches*]' is irrefutable by experience, as the same conditions are never met twice. Even if all observed conditions are the same, the time coordinate is different, and unobserved conditions can be hypothesised to be different (1926, p. 9). So if we drop this axiom, we must admit that 'because of the inexhaustibility of possible conditions, all physical statements (as well as all inductive statements of other sciences) may only be granted probability, not absolute validity' (1926, p. 9). The further steps, to the more abstract concepts of physics, follow this same hypothetical, inductive path, with the terms of the conditionals becoming classes of objects, and universal quantifiers put in front of them quantifying over these and other variables within the conditionals.

Though framed in very different terms from the *Aufbau*, the construction here is not at odds with it, but complementary; a fundamental *epistemological* construction, from the ground up, is taken for granted in the background.[14] This illustrates how the epistemological construction (the 'constructive' project), and the schematisation of the abstract statements of physics (the 'clarification' project), are conceived as separate, though complementary, tasks. In the context of the 'clarification' project, the fundamental thesis that 'all scientific statements are structural statements' is simply asserted unargued; the entire system of physics is presented as completely

---

[14] This is not to say that the possibility of a physical basis for the constitution system, as mooted in the published *Aufbau* (§59), would have been excluded as a possibility during this earlier period. However, it should be pointed out that even in the *Aufbau* the choice of physical basis was taken to violate the *epistemological* order (§59).

transparent from top to bottom. All the most abstract concepts, expressed in physics as sets of or relations among 14-tuples of numbers, are not just consistent with, but *identical* with, simply different ways of referring to, the perceptual facts expressed by the most elementary observation conditionals ('this rose is red'). Statements containing these abstract concepts are still about the observed world, Carnap says in *Physical Concept Formation*, 'as the qualities are not ignored when they are treated quantitatively, but just named in a particular way, by means of numbers' (1926, p. 47).

One of the basic pragmatic or methodological decisions facing a system of knowledge – one actually faced by physics in the eighteenth century, and by other sciences since then – is that regarding the degree to which it is to employ theoretical concepts, concepts not fully reducible to the given because they go beyond any possible number of observations, as we have seen in the case of permanent qualities of ordinary physical objects. Nearly all thinkers have been willing to countenance ordinary physical objects as legitimate constructs, but disagreement has generally begun soon after that step. The introduction of *quantitative* concepts into a field has almost invariably occasioned controversy, and usually faced hostility or rejection from some quarters. We saw in Chapter 3 that for Carnap the classic articulation of this debate was Goethe's attack on Newton in the *Theory of Colours*; this example reappears, for the same illustrative purpose, in *Physical Concept Formation*. Indeed it also reappears in the *Aufbau* itself. Carnap stresses that there is no right and wrong about this question (in his later terms, it is a practical question of language choice):

It is not obvious from the start that physics, if it wants to construct a domain of thoroughgoing law-governedness, has to eliminate the qualities and put bare numbers in their place. The opposing view (which was represented by Goethe against Newton, for instance, in the polemical section of his *Theory of Colours*) advocates that one remain in the domain of sense qualities themselves and ascertain the patterns of regularity that hold among them. That would amount to discovering the regularities within the domain that we have called the perceptual world. Laws of the kind exemplified by physical laws do not, of course, obtain there. One can demonstrate, though, that regularities must obtain nonetheless, if the constitution of the law-governed physical world is to be possible at all – but regularities of a much more complicated form than the physical ones. (1928a §136, p. 181; PT p. 209)

Nonetheless, for a number of practical reasons (of which Carnap lists and defends three in *Physical Concept Formation*, pp. 51–2), physics and most other natural sciences have taken the path of adopting the quantitative method. Without this decision, Carnap maintains, they could not have got much beyond Goethe himself and his qualitatively oriented conception of physical science:

> If physics had not followed Newton, as it actually did, but Goethe, it could certainly have taken a few steps beyond the correct insights of Goethe himself, but would soon have arrived at a barrier and would have had to give up the most extensive and important parts of today's physical knowledge. (1926, p. 52)

Above all, though, the sciences could not, using qualitative methods alone, have developed into the vast, unified systems of knowledge we have today:

> Above all the most important result of the development of physics in the last century could not have been achieved by taking this path: the more and more concentrated gathering of the parts of physics into a unified theory. In a Goethean, i.e. perceptual-qualitative treatment of physics, it falls apart into a series of subdisciplines that correspond to the different senses. Though certain relations can be traced among these parts, it is only Newtonian, quantitative treatment that can submerge the subdisciplines in a melting pot. (1926, p. 52)

The methodological decision in favour of quantitative method, once taken, requires a number of further decisions. No given, intrinsically appropriate, quantitative language fits automatically or uniquely with some range of natural phenomena; to make a quantitative language capable of representing some aspect of some process or phenomenon in nature, we must reach agreement on certain conventional rules regarding its applicability. Without such rules even the most elementary concepts of physics, e.g. that of a physical magnitude, have no meaning:

> It has sometimes been thought that a physical magnitude (e.g. time) has a sense [*Sinn*] in and for itself, quite independently of how it is to be measured; and that the question how to measure it is a second, separate question. Against that view it has to be stressed that the sense of every physical magnitude consists in the ascription of certain numbers to certain physical objects. Until it is decided how this ascription is to occur, the magnitude itself is indeterminate and statements about it are meaningless. (1926, p. 21)

To define a physical magnitude, five things must be agreed on: (1) we must determine when two values of the magnitude in question are to be regarded as 'the same value'; (2) we must define an ordering on the set of values and a positive direction; (3) we must define equality of 'distance', or difference between two values, and thus a metric or scale of measurement; (4) we must call some point on the scale 'zero'; (5) we must define a unit on the scale.[15] Obvious as these may appear, Carnap notes that the first of these

---

[15] These also occur in Chapter 6 (pp. 62–9) of *Philosophical Foundations of Physics* (1966), in a somewhat different order and with more discussion.

parameters was only defined unambiguously for the measurement of time, in modern physics, with the arrival of Einstein's theory of relativity (1926, pp. 21–2).

The pre-Wittgensteinian innocence of *Physical Concept Formation* harbours no doubts about the availability and transparency of theoretical statements. 'This abstract conception of the system of physics', Carnap says retrospectively about this little book, 'was later elaborated in my work on the theoretical language' (1963, p. 16). He was not yet troubled by doubts about the feasibility of integrating axiomatic systems into a logicist structure. No shadow of suspicion hovers over the formation of abstract concepts, or clouds the ultimate prospect that the 'clarificative' and 'constructive' components of rational reconstruction could be completed and harmoniously fit together. Such doubts arose only after 1926.

APPLICATIONS

The rational reconstruction programme was, as we have seen (esp. Chapters 1 and 5 above), the particular form taken by Carnap's quasi-utopian response to the Great War. In Vienna, he found a number of others with similar motivations. The basic philosophical ideas of the programme were in place by early 1922, before Carnap had read the *Tractatus*. And although the *Aufbau* system underwent many changes before its publication, it could still play the central 'political' role that Carnap had envisaged for a 'system of knowledge' in 1918 – the role, that is, of transforming the culture in accordance with an optimal 'form of community [*Gemeinschaftsgestalt*]' and coordinating human efforts 'to remove them from chaotic arbitrariness and subordinate them to goal-oriented reason'. The mission of the Vienna Circle (and its public arm, the Verein Ernst Mach) are described in very similar terms to those in which Carnap had spelled out his 'political' programme for philosophy in 1918 (Chapter 1, pp. 62–3).

The Vienna Circle believes . . . that it is fulfilling a demand of the times. It is urgent that we shape the tools of thought for everyday use, not only for the everyday use of the academic, but for everyone who is participating in any way in the conscious shaping of life [*der bewußten Lebensgestaltung*]. The intensity of life that is visible in the efforts to achieve a rational reorganization of the social and economic order also pervades the movement supporting a scientific world-conception. (Hahn *et al.* 1929, p. 86; PT p. 305)

An example of this culturally ambitious or, in a broad sense, 'political' application of Carnap's constitution system was a 'gemeinverständlicher

Vortrag' held in the Verein Ernst Mach in June 1929, entitled *Von Gott und Seele*. His subject is not just God and the soul, but all the entities whose existence is claimed in traditional systems of belief, and he tells a dialectical story of the historical interactions between 'poetic imagination' and 'critical intellect'. He explains that the existential claims of the imagination are very hard for the intellect to refute, because no number of counter-instances suffices to eliminate an existence claim: 'So it's no wonder that in myths, sagas, and legends numerous existential claims occur that have held up against all challenges for a long time' (ASP 1929c, p. 8). But even in antiquity, the 'critical intellect' made a discovery that enabled it to put severe limits on such claims: 'That is the discovery of *one* [single] *comprehensive space*. All things are in space: any two things are always spatially related to each other. So there is also a path from me to any [given] thing.' This meant that claims could now be subjected to a simple test: '*Every thing is accessible*. If someone now claims that a thing of a particular kind exists, I can demand of him that he show me the path from me to the claimed thing' (ASP 1929c, p. 8). The first response of imagination is to locate its favourite objects in remote or inaccessible places.[16] But this stops working as humankind explores more of the earth and the universe. 'Where does imagination escape to now? It goes straight for a really radical option: it evacuates its creations into the non-spatial, the "trans-spatial"' (ASP 1929c, p. 10). This is a good ruse because we quite legitimately refer to things that are not physical objects, and thus not locatable in space: 'And that is also how it is with our feelings, mental images, thoughts; everything in the so-called mental or spiritual [category] is non-spatial. Hence the escape of imagination into the *realm of spirits* in order not to be subject to the question [about location in] space by prosecuting reason.' So that is where the existence claims now shifted to.

With the *concept of God* this same transformation was undertaken. The Greek god Zeus lived on [Mount] Olympus. But he wasn't safe there; Olympus was after all climbable, even if no Greek had attempted the climb. And before the mountain was actually climbed, the putative God was removed from space into the realm of the spirits. God was regarded now as a *spiritual being without a body*. (ASP 1929c, p. 11)

---

[16] 'The intellect wants, by means of the spatial system, which encompasses all [corporeal] things, to test all existential claims. But imagination prefers not to expose its works to this test; it embarks on a remarkable flight, in several stages, from the prosecuting intellect. First it escapes into *distant places*, as hard as possible to reach. When the intellect asks the way to those mythical creatures, saga and fairy tale answer: the islands of the blessed lie out there beyond the pillars of Hercules; the goblins are hidden deep in the mountains; Zeus lives high up on Olympus; God sits on his heavenly throne above the clouds or above the firmament (ASP 1929c, p. 9).

This was not enough, though, because even if it was claimed that, unlike other beings with feelings and thoughts, gods and spirits are immaterial, 'it was unconsciously recognised after all, it seems, that something isn't quite right with that sort of claim, that there is at least something rather odd, something problematic about it'. Thus imagination arrived at 'the realm of "ideas"'; theology became metaphysics. 'Here the concept of God no longer has anything physical or anything physically rooted about it. It is removed into a completely non-spatial realm. The flight from the grasp of critical reason with its spatial system appears to have been completely successful' (ASP 1929c, pp. 11–12).

But all is not lost; 'critical intellect' has developed an answer – Carnap's own 'total system of all concepts', the comprehensive conceptual system (*Begriffssystem*) of the *Aufbau*; 'now a system is discovered that comprehends not just [corporeal] things, but everything thinkable, all concepts, whether thing-like or not [*dinglich oder nicht-dinglich*]'. It is the natural successor and generalisation, in the dialectical drama Carnap is telling, of physically all-encompassing space:

In space all things have spatial relations to each other, and there has to be a path of access from me to each thing. In the same way, on the basis of the concept-system, an all-comprehending conceptual space, so to speak, all concepts have relations to each other (in this case logical, conceptual relations). And here there has to be a connecting path to each concept from the contents of my experience, e.g. from my perceptions. Everything of which one can speak has to be traceable back to things experienced by me. All knowledge I can have relates either to my own feelings, mental images, thoughts, etc. or can be derived from my perceptions . . . (ASP 1929c, p. 12)

The central role of the constitution system in the Vienna Circle's pro-gramme of rational reconstruction in the service of 'the scientific world-conception [*wissenschaftliche Weltauffassung*]' is evident also in the mani-festo of that name. After its characterisation of the Vienna Circle as positivist on the one hand ('there is only empirical knowledge [*Erfahrungserkenntnis*], which rests on the immediately given') and, on the other, as 'characterised by the application of a particular method, i.e. *logical analysis*', the consti-tution system is adduced as the meeting place of these two basic features, and as the central constructive project:

We strive in our scientific work to reach the goal of unified science, by application of logical analysis to empirical content. As the meaning of every statement of science must be specifiable as a reduction to statements about the given, so the meaning of every concept . . . must be specifiable by stepwise reduction to other concepts, down to the concepts of the lowest level, which pertain to the given itself. Once such an analysis is carried through for all concepts, they are placed thereby into a reduction system, a 'constitution system'. Investigations that have the goal of such a constitution system, called '*constitution theory*', are thus the frame in which logical analysis is applied by the scientific world-conception [*wissenschaftliche Weltauffassung*]. (Hahn *et al* 1929, pp. 90–1; PT p. 309)

But this entire wide-ranging application of the *Aufbau* system, as well as the wider, 'political' role envisaged for it, had meanwhile, since about the time of Carnap's 1926 arrival in Vienna, been placed within a new logico-philosophical context. It was now articulated within the Wittgensteinian conception of meaning, which had effectively disposed of the question how to understand 'structure' and the nature and source of non-empirical knowledge. The cost, as we shall see, was that the smooth fit between the 'constructive' (*Aufbau*) component of rational reconstruction and its 'clarification' component had come undone. And putting these parts together again would be Carnap's first order of business after the *Aufbau* manuscript was off to the printer.

CHAPTER 7

The impact of Wittgenstein

The programme of rational reconstruction set out in 1922–3 had given great prominence to a notion of 'structure' that remained somewhat enigmatic. And though 'structure' itself was purely logical or analytic, its application instance in the 'constructive' project of the *Aufbau* sought to capture the component of knowledge that Helmholtz and Poincaré had said was all we ultimately could know about the world: 'What science can attain to is not the things themselves but only the relations among the things; apart from these relations there is no knowable reality' (Poincaré 1904, p. XIII). Carnap, as we saw, had taken this further, and built his project of rational reconstruction on the idea that 'every science is a science only insofar as the study of structures [*Strukturlehre*] is contained in it' (above, p. 163). Did this make our knowledge of 'structure' itself a form of synthetic knowledge? And finally, even if 'structure' *was* purely logical, where did the principles of *logic* come from? All Carnap's great role models in logic had answered this last question by gesturing toward a special source of knowledge, different from the empirical – the principles of logic were synthetic a priori, or traceable to a 'logical source of knowledge' that gives us our ability to grasp 'thoughts' residing in a 'third realm' distinct from the first realm of physical objects and the second realm of subjective consciousness.

As we saw, Carnap came increasingly to eschew the idea of grounding knowledge on any sort of intuition. Even in *Der Raum*, his Kantianism had been minimal; though synthetic a priori, the geometry of intuitive space had been a fact about the human perspective, not about the extra-human world. And though phenomenological discernment had still played a role in the identification of the basis, in the 1922 version of the constitution system, by 1925 Carnap had set the goal of 'overcoming subjectivity: transition from material to structure'.

The problem Carnap was therefore left with, about the nature and cognitive source of 'structure', was solved, in his view, by Wittgenstein. The principles of logic were artefacts of representation. They did not have a special source of meaning or source of knowledge; they were true simply by virtue of rearranging other true statements. Their truth piggy-backed on the truth of simple empirical or observation statements. So there was only *one* source of knowledge about the world.

This solution was very important for Carnap. But Wittgenstein *over-solved* the problem, so to speak. He threw out the baby with the bathwater. For Wittgenstein, no meta-discourse or meta-perspective was possible at all; there was no stepping outside one's language. The 'logical syntax' of the language (Chapter 6 above, footnote 3) could only 'reveal itself', it could not be articulated *in* language. Though deeply influenced by Frege, Russell, *and* Wittgenstein, Carnap never accepted this idea that we are trapped within our language, incapable of looking at it from outside. As we will see later in this chapter, he took Wittgenstein's arguments about the impossibility of referring to the expressions of a language *in* that language very seriously, but he was never entirely convinced, and in any case tried to develop a meta-logic within that constraint.

He never doubted, even during his most Wittgensteinian phase, that the 'logical syntax' of the language was subject to conscious human amendment and decision. This seems to have been the common position of the Vienna Circle. Though respectful and in some cases even reverent toward Wittgenstein, none of them ever took very seriously the idea that a particular form of logic, or some minimal fragment of it, is forced on us simply by the nature of representation. In the *Aufbau* Carnap had taken the legitimacy of *pragmatic* meta-discourse for granted (we saw an example in Chapter 6), with ample scope for deciding on the 'logical syntax' of the object language – principles of logic and the procedures of knowledge. But Wittgenstein's conception had cast pragmatic discourse into a kind of limbo; it was on the wrong side of the rigid demarcation between meaningful language and the unsayable. What remained open was the question whether such pragmatic discourse could also be, or could have a descriptive component that is, substantive (or 'cognitive' in later terms), i.e. whether a *Wissenschaftslogik* is possible (as Carnap might have put it a few years later) consisting of meta-sentences about a language (e.g. a potential language of *Wissenschaft*) that have meaning in the same sense, and by the same standards, as that language itself.

WITTGENSTEIN'S IMPORTANCE TO THE VIENNA CIRCLE

When Carnap moved to Vienna in 1926, he found the Circle studying the *Tractatus* line by line. 'Wittgenstein's book exerted a strong influence upon our Circle', Carnap later wrote; 'we learned much by our discussions of the book, and accepted many views as far as we could assimilate them to our basic conceptions' (1963, p. 24). 'The thinking of our Circle was strongly influenced by Wittgenstein's ideas, first because of our common reading of the *Tractatus* and later by virtue of Waismann's systematic exposition of certain conceptions of Wittgenstein's on the basis of his talks with him' (1963, p. 28). Carnap included himself in these statements: 'For me personally, Wittgenstein was perhaps the philosopher who, besides Russell and Frege, had the greatest influence on my thinking' (1963, p. 25).

In the Vienna Circle's view, Wittgenstein had solved the old Platonic problem of the cognitive status of mathematics, which had been a basic obstacle to any form of empiricism. 'It really does seem on first sight', Hans Hahn said, 'as if the very existence of mathematics must mean the failure of pure empiricism – as if we had in mathematics a knowledge about the world that doesn't come from experience, as if we had a priori knowledge. And this evident difficulty for empiricism is so obvious that anyone who wants to hold a consistent empiricism has to face this difficulty' (Hahn 1929, pp. 55–6). Wittgenstein had solved this problem. Of course he was not an empiricist, so it had not been part of his agenda to solve this basic problem for empiricism. But that did not make his solution any less important for the Circle.

The key idea was the picture theory of meaning. Language is a medium for representing the world by isomorphically corresponding to the arrangement of its elements, i.e. giving a 'logical picture'. Atomic sentences picture atomic facts, and all other (meaningful) sentences are truth-functional concatenations of atomic sentences. Though Wittgenstein adopted Frege's and Russell's all-encompassing conception of logic as universally applicable and inescapable, he rejected the view that the logical laws were laws *of something* in the world out there (something like the most general laws of nature, or the laws of thought). For Wittgenstein, logical laws were not laws *of* something; they were just an artefact or by-product of isomorphic representation. Certain concatenations of propositions come out true (or false) regardless of what facts hold; these are 'tautologous' (or contradictory) and empty. They say nothing whatever about the world. The Vienna Circle thought this idea of critical importance:

If one wants to regard logic – as this has in fact been done – as the study of the most general qualities of objects, as the study of objects in general [*überhaupt*], then empiricism would in fact be confronted here with an impassable hurdle. In reality, though, logic says nothing whatever about objects. Logic is not something that is to be found in the world. Logic only arises, rather, when – by means of a symbolism – we *speak about the world* . . . The sentences of logic say nothing about the world. (Hahn 1929, pp. 56–7; PT p. 40)

And since all this applies not only to mathematics generally, but to Carnap's more specific problems regarding 'structure', for him, too, the picture theory was Wittgenstein's essential contribution:

> The most important insight I gained from his work was the conception that the truth of logical statements is based only on their logical structure and on the meaning of the terms. Logical statements are true under all conceivable circumstances; thus their truth is independent of contingent facts of the world. On the other hand, it follows that these statements do not say anything about the world and thus have no factual content. (1963, p. 25)

Of course the Vienna Circle did not simply accept Wittgenstein's view as a whole, but only 'as far as we could assimilate them to our basic conceptions'. And the Circle's conception of language was quite different from Wittgenstein's, which was curiously detached from any actual use, everyday or theoretical. It was an abstract account of language in extreme generality that was completely untroubled by any actual applications. As Michael Dummett puts it, 'The *Tractatus* is a pure essay in the theory of meaning, from which every trace of epistemological or psychological consideration has been purged as thoroughly as the house is purged of leaven before the Passover' (Dummett 1981, p. 679). But it was not just unattached to any roots in sensory cognition or everyday application; it also remained curiously isolated from the abstract languages of pure and applied mathematics, which (in the Vienna Circle's interpretation, at least) it fell short of being able to account for or reconstruct. As a 'pure essay in the theory of meaning' it floated freely *between* the ground of sensory knowledge and the higher reaches of mathematical and scientific abstraction.

So to get the *Tractatus* to do what they wanted it to do – to reconcile mathematics with empiricism – the Circle had to make some modifications. They had to extend the *Tractatus* conception of language in both directions, both 'downward' to observation reports and 'upward' to mathematics. Their 'downward' extension gave the *Tractatus* view an epistemological and positivistic interpretation, taking Wittgenstein's 'atomic sentences' to be elementary observation sentences. The 'upward' extension amounted to combining the *Tractatus* with logicism, so that the empty and tautological status Wittgenstein gave logic was thereby transmitted to all of mathematics. This view was neither that of the first-generation logicists nor of Wittgenstein; it might be called 'tautologicism'.[1] Naturally, the Vienna

---

[1] Steve Awodey's term.

Circle did not distinguish their doubly extended version of the *Tractatus* view from Wittgenstein's own; to them it was a single and interlocking complex of ideas.

Wittgenstein's conception of meaning became the basis, more generally, for the Vienna Circle's conception of *reason*. Frege and Russell had developed a precise rational reconstruction of reason, but, the Vienna Circle thought, had not correctly diagnosed its precise role in human knowledge. What Wittgenstein had now shown was that logical transformations of sentences into other sentences are *tautological* – the same information is conveyed by the premises as by the conclusion. 'So the tautologies are *empty of content*, they say nothing' (1930a, p. 23). Frege's and Russell's explication of reason, then, together with Wittgenstein's diagnosis of that explication, meant that the difficulties faced by previous forms of empiricism had been overcome.[2] No attempt to achieve genuine knowledge by reason alone, on this view, could be successful, as Carnap put it:

As all sentences of logic are tautological and empty of content, nothing can be deduced from them about what reality must be like and cannot be like. The justification for every metaphysics based on logic, like the large-format one put forward by *Hegel*, is thus taken away. (1930a, p. 23)

This is a recurring motif in Vienna Circle writings at this time. In the programmatic pamphlet *Wissenschaftliche Weltauffassung*, for instance, metaphysics is found to suffer from two fundamental mistakes. The first is its uncritical use of the categories and the surface grammar of ordinary language – its reification of verbal illusions, embedded in everyday categories, that disappear upon analysis. The second 'fundamental mistake of metaphysics' is the 'conception that *thought* could either lead to knowledge by itself, without using any sort of empirical content, or that it could at least by deduction arrive at new contents from given facts'. This, they say, we now know is impossible:

Logical investigation leads to the result that all thinking, all deduction consists in nothing else but the transition from sentences to other sentences that contain nothing that was not already in the first ones (tautological transformation). So it is not possible to develop a metaphysics from 'pure thought'. (Hahn *et al.* 1929, p. 89; PT, p. 308)

Wittgenstein's conception still caused two serious problems for the Vienna Circle, however, despite his importance to them and their upward and

---

[2] '*Empiricism*, the conception that there is no synthetic a priori knowledge, always encountered its greatest difficulty in the interpretation of mathematics, which even *Mill* had not been able to overcome' (1930a, p. 23).

downward extensions of his conception of logic. First, there was what one might call the 'elucidation problem'. This was, once again, the problem of being trapped within the language. In Wittgenstein, this diagnosis of our predicament results from considerations about self-reference, essentially stemming from Russell, applied back to the very sentences that state or spell out the conception of language and representation (the picture theory and so on). But Russell's worries about impredicativity and the dangers of allowing a general sentence to fall within its own scope take on a new character within the picture theory. If language indeed has the isomorphic representational character claimed in the picture theory, the question inevitably arises how the 'elucidatory' sentences stating that theory (which are of course also in language), qualify as meaningful: Are they themselves pictures of facts, or are they tautological? Wittgenstein had, notoriously, answered this question by 'throwing away the ladder' and declaring his own sentences, in the *Tractatus*, to be nonsense. But the question also preoccupied the Circle. In one of their discussions, for instance,

Gödel asked how the discussion about logical questions could be justified, as it involves the utterance not of any meaningful sentences but only of elucidations [*Erläuterungen*]. This raises the question how admissible elucidations are to be demarcated from metaphysical pseudo-sentences. (ASP 1931d; Stadler 1997, p. 288; PT p. 254)

This brings down to bare bones a central question facing the Vienna Circle during this period: What protected its critique of traditional philosophy from *itself*? What was the status of the sentences in which this critique itself was stated?[3]

The other problem for the Vienna Circle resulted from their own 'upward' extension of the *Tractatus*, their 'tautologicism'. By tautologicism, all of mathematics (and thus theoretical science) is conceived as possessing the truth-functional character of meaningful language that the picture theory gives to logic. But it did not look to the Circle as if the logic of the *Tractatus* could be extended to allow for unbounded quantification, while still retaining the truth-functionally specified characterisation of logical

---

[3] Despite the Circle's (and especially Carnap's) intense preoccupation with this question in 1930–1, 'Is the verification principle itself verifiable?' soon emerged as an all-purpose one-line *refutation* of logical empiricism. It is quite inappropriate in any case to attribute a simple-minded 'verification principle' to the Vienna Circle. But the ignorant question survived undeterred, e.g. in Hilary Putnam: 'An obvious rejoinder [to the verification principle] was to say that the logical positivist criterion of significance was *self-refuting*: for the criterion itself is neither (a) "analytic" . . . nor (b) empirically testable. Strangely enough this criticism had very little impact on the logical positivists . . . I believe that the neglect of this particular philosophical gambit was a great mistake; that the gambit is not only correct, but contains a deep lesson' (Putnam 1981, p. 106).

truth. And this left it insufficient for expressing even a fragment of actually existing theoretical science. One might call this the 'finitism problem'.

On the surface, the *Tractatus* would seem to require finitism. First we have 'The proposition is a truth function of the elementary propositions' (5), then 'Every proposition is the result of truth operations with elementary propositions' (5.3), and then a few lines down 'All truth functions are results of a finite number of truth operations on the elementary propositions' (5.32). Was it unreasonable for the Circle to think this required finitism? Wittgenstein said nothing to contradict this in his talks with them (Waismann 1967, e.g. p. 188). The consensus in current *Tractatus* scholarship (e.g. Ricketts 1996) is that unbounded quantifiers are to be included under the heading of 'truth operations', making the issue one about the exclusion of higher-order or impredicative logic. The Vienna Circle, however, did not have the benefit of this view, and saw no alternative to taking Wittgenstein literally. Carnap himself, in any case, became a strict finitist during this period (see below, pp. 205–7).

The Circle's 'downward' extension of the *Tractatus* took 'elementary proposition' to mean something like 'observation protocol', as indeed Wittgenstein himself seems to have done at least sometimes during this period; in a conversation of 1930–1 he says that 'object' in the *Tractatus* is 'used for such things as a colour, a point in visual space, etc.' (Wittgenstein 1980, p. 120). Now if a scientific theory is a *truth function* of observation sentences, then it *can* only be a statement about a *finite* number of instances, not a universal law. This was why the picture theory, combined with the Circle's empiricism, made theoretical science as ordinarily conceived impossible.

This was especially difficult for Carnap to accept because it broke apart the 'clarificative' and 'constructive' components of his rational reconstruction programme. He had only just reconciled them (Chapter 6, pp. 177–81). But now, the 'theoretical language' needed in science was again put beyond the scope of any possible construction from below. So Carnap's task was clear: without the upward and downward extensions to the *Tractatus* system, rational reconstruction was doomed.

AXIOMATICS

In the *Aufbau*, Carnap had stipulated – in accordance with Wittgensteinian requirements – that all concepts were to be constituted by explicit definition, even concepts that subsequently figure in axiom systems (1928a, §2, p. 2). But he realised that, quite apart from the various fields of science, even some quite fundamental concepts of arithmetic and set theory might only be attainable axiomatically.[4] It thus became a fundamental challenge to develop a language in which axiomatically (or 'implicitly') defined concepts could be made clear and unambiguous (*eindeutig*). Moritz Schlick had made axiomatically defined concepts central to his view of scientific theory in his *General Theory of Knowledge* (1918, p. 35), but had also recognised that there was an unbridgeable gap between such concepts and anything observable. Carnap began to confront this problem in a 1927 paper that contrasts 'proper [*eigentliche*]', i.e. explicitly defined, concepts with 'improper [*uneigentliche*]' concepts, those defined implicitly by axiom systems:

> Logically, the implicitly defined concepts differ so radically from proper concepts that one may well have doubts about even calling them 'concepts' at all. We will retain this name, however, in view of common usage, especially within mathematics . . . [where] one talks as if one were dealing with concepts – 'point', 'line', 'between', etc. – that meet all the requirements of a legitimate concept. Since this is not the case, we will limit our terminological concession to usage by calling implicitly defined concepts '*improper concepts*'. (1927, pp. 366–7)

On the surface, it would appear that in this paper, Carnap faithfully follows Frege's denial, in his controversy with Hilbert, that 'improper' concepts can be applied unambiguously to objects. As Frege had said, a set of axioms can define a *second-order* concept explicitly, though of course this is a different concept and cannot be used in place of one defined implicitly by those same axioms (1927, p. 368). Like Frege, Carnap stresses that the implicitly defined concepts are not constants, as explicitly defined concepts are, but *variables* that range over many different possible models, both formal and empirical (1927, pp. 370–2). Carnap recognises, of course, that this property is precisely what makes such concepts useful in science; their deductive development 'is a means of producing empty theories to be kept in reserve for later use' (1927, p. 373). But this raises the epistemological problem of how they can ever come to be applied to the world we experience:

> Empirical concepts are constituted step by step in the systematic construction [*Aufbau*] of our world-knowledge. Each empirical concept, as a component of this structure, has a direct connection to reality. In contrast, the improper concepts hang in the air, so to speak, awaiting instructions. They are introduced by an axiom system, but that system does not relate directly to anything real. The axioms of this system and the theorems deduced in it do not properly form a theory (as they are not actually *about* anything in particular), but rather just a theory-schema, an empty framework for possible theories. (1927, p. 372)

---

[4] The following discussion draws on Awodey and Carus (2001), Sections I and II.

There are actually two aspects to this problem of disambiguation or *Eindeutigkeit*. First, how are we to tell whether a particular object before us actually falls under a given concept? As Carnap recognised, this is an instance of Frege's problem of defining a concept so that we know whether Julius Caesar, for instance, falls under it:

It belongs to the essence of a proper concept that for every object we can in principle decide whether it falls under that concept or not; and for sufficiently well known objects the decision can be carried out in practice as well. For the empirical concept horse, for instance, and any visible object we can unambiguously [*eindeutig*] decide – insofar as the concept has sufficiently sharp boundaries and the object is sufficiently well known – whether the object satisfies the concept, i.e. whether or not it is a horse. But for an improper concept the question whether a particular object falls under it is not decidable and thus has no sense. (1927, p. 367)

And second, conversely, how are we to tell whether a concept picks out a unique collection of objects? Implicitly defined concepts may be ambiguous because they leave open the possibility that, as Carnap puts it, '*the principle of excluded middle does not hold*' (1927, p. 364), i.e. we cannot establish either *p* or not-*p* for every atomic sentence *p* containing the concept.

Once he had settled down in Vienna and assimilated the Wittgensteinian doctrine, it became Carnap's top priority to address this problem. He devoted the bulk of his time from 1927 through early 1930 on a major treatise, entitled *Investigations in General Axiomatics* (*Untersuchungen zur allgemeinen Axiomatik*) in which he addressed these problems.[5] The approach is to convert implicit definitions into explicit ones by requiring axiomatic systems to be set up within a 'foundation discipline [*Grunddisziplin*]' of 'absolute' or explicitly defined concepts. He does not go into the question how the *Grunddisziplin* acquires this 'absolute' status.[6] But its function is clear:

Consequences can be drawn from a specified AS [axiom system] only if general rules of inference are given as well. So every treatment and appraisal of an AS assumes a logic, and indeed a contentful logic [*eine inhaltliche Logik*], i.e. a system of sentences that are not just combinations of signs, but have a particular meaning.

[5] That he was also implicitly addressing the 'elucidation problem' (above, p. 190) is indicated by the fact that he sometimes calls this project his 'Metalogik' (though a course he gave on the subject in 1928 was officially called 'Philosophical Foundations of Arithmetic', one student who attended it, Kurt Gödel, remembered it as 'Carnap's lectures on metalogic', and credited it with inspiring his interest in the completeness of axiom systems (Wang 1987, p. 17).

[6] In a crossed-out passage (ASP 1927a, p. 6), he says that if one accepts Russellian logicism, one could simply call the *Grunddisziplin* 'logic'. But he does not attempt to justify this further here, and says it is merely a terminological issue, as he wants to make the *Investigations* as neutral as possible among philosophical standpoints.

For otherwise it wouldn't put us in a position to act [*handeln*]; and deduction is action, for it means: constructing collocations of signs [*Zeichenzusammenstellungen*] by fixed rules from other collocations of signs.

In contrast to logical signs, the '*basic signs*', the signs of the '*basic concepts* [*Grundbegriffe*]' of an AS, have no definite meaning. For that is just the essential character of an AS – that it is not tied down to a particular area of application, that it deals not with objects determinate in themselves but with something indeterminate that gets its only determination through the axiom system. From this it emerges that the system of logical sentences we required to be in place prior to everything axiomatic cannot itself be an AS in the sense intended here. (ASP 1927a, p. 4)

Setting up a 'foundation discipline' with such a *non*-axiomatic system of logical (and arithmetic and set-theoretic) sentences gives a basis of meaning for all the mathematical signs in any axiom system expressed within it. This is essential for giving a purely mathematical axiom system a definite meaning.

An axiom system like the one Carnap himself had been working on in the early 1920s (on spacetime kinematics) – one that involved 'empirical concepts [*Realbegriffe*]' – could be given a meaning more straightforwardly, by substituting an explicitly defined concept for each implicitly defined basic concept the system, an empirically constituted one 'for which it can be shown that it has the formal character (*formale Beschaffenheit*)[7] of the improper concept given by the AS in question', and assigning this empirical concept to the improper concept as a value to a variable:

Through the contact between the empirical concept and the axioms (the former satisfying the latter), a connection is created, by a single stroke, with the whole of the theory-schema resting on the axiom system. The blood of empirical reality streams in through the point of connection and flows into the most ramified capillaries of the hitherto empty schema, which is thereby transformed into a genuine theory. (1927, p. 373)

For purely mathematical or theoretical axiom systems, for which this route was not available, Carnap had another strategy to remedy the *Eindeutigkeit* problem, in both directions, even under Wittgensteinian conditions (in case a *Grunddisziplin* of the kind required could not be devised). The centrepiece of the first part of the *Investigations in General Axiomatics* was a theorem by means of which Carnap thought he could go some way

---

[7] The 'formal character' of an empirical concept is a matter of its constitution; the assignment therefore has a conventional element just as the 'identification of the objects of science' by means of a constitution system as a whole does (1928a, §179).

toward solving this problem. It states, in brief, that an axiom system is complete (*entscheidungsdefinit*) if and only if it is categorical (*monomorph*).[8] This solves the second aspect of the problem straightforwardly, by providing a criterion for acceptability of implicitly defined concepts: if we can show that a given axiom system is categorical (as Dedekind had shown his axioms for arithmetic to be), then we also know that it is complete, and the law of excluded middle holds for concepts implicitly defined by it.

This theorem (in the other direction) can also be applied to the first aspect of the problem, in a somewhat more roundabout way. First, Carnap says that although it is meaningless to say of any particular object that it falls or does not fall under an implicitly defined concept, it *does* make sense to say of an object that it belongs to a structure falling under the *second*-order concept explicitly defined by the axiom system, e.g. as an element in a progression (1927, p. 367). Without establishing such a context, the problem of *Eindeutigkeit* does not even make sense. What *does* make sense is the question whether a given system of first-order objects, equipped with suitable operations and relations, falls under the second-order concept defined by the axiom system (in modern terms, whether a structure of the right kind is a model of the axiom system) – i.e. the question what collections of first-order objects qualify as objects of such a second-order concept. This might be regarded as an application of Frege's 'context principle': 'the meaning of words is to be sought only in the context of sentences [*im Satzzusammenhang*], not in isolation' (Frege 1884, p. 10).

Indeed, Carnap goes on to explicate this use of the context principle more precisely, giving it a more positive turn and making the notion of a 'context' more concrete. Assuming we have added enough axioms to our theory to specify all the properties of its implicitly defined concepts – i.e. assuming it is (consistent and) complete – Carnap's theorem tells us that its collections of first-order objects all have the same 'structure' (all the models of the theory are isomorphic), so the implicit definition has given an unambiguous 'structural' characterisation of the objects falling under the concept it defines.[9] The context principle is thus explicated to mean

---

[8] A brief argument for the theorem is given in the 1927 paper (1927, pp. 364–5); the full proof is given in the manuscript of the *Untersuchungen* (ASP 1927a), now also published as Carnap 2000 (Carus 2001 comments on this edition, pp. 372–3). As stated above, the theorem sounds obviously false (as e.g. second-order Peano arithmetic fails, though categorical, to be complete), but in fact Carnap did not mean by this quite what we do since Gödel. For more details on the *Untersuchungen*, on the theorem mentioned here (called the *Gabelbarkeitssatz*), on a sense in which it turns out – surprisingly – to be true, and on its impact on Gödel, see Awodey and Carus (2001) and Goldfarb (2005).

[9] Note that this is a different sense of 'structure', though, from the Fregean–Russellian one prominent in the *Aufbau*, whereby 'all scientific statements are structural statements [*alle wissenschaftlichen Aussagen sind Strukturaussagen*]'.

that if we know the truth value of every sentence in which the names of the first-order objects occur, then we know all their possible uses – all the *logical* properties of the objects – and have thereby uniquely determined their meanings.[10]

These applications of Carnap's theorem do not entirely solve the problem of *Eindeutigkeit* in non-empirical axiomatic systems, but they are a first step.[11] The more fundamental approach relied on the availability of a *Grunddisziplin* that could ground such systems in 'absolute' concepts.

A NEW FOUNDATION OF LOGIC

Within the *Axiomatics* itself, there was no effort to work out a conception of logic that showed it to be compatible with Wittgensteinian requirements, nor had Carnap specified there how the *Grunddisziplin* acquired its fixed interpretation. These tasks Carnap attempted in a loose sketch he wrote down in Davos in April 1929, when he was attending the 'Europäische Hochschultage' where Heidegger and Cassirer debated the legacy of Kant (Friedman 2000). The sketch was headed, ambitiously, 'New Foundation of Logic [*Neue Grundlegung der Logik*]'.[12] Its main idea is to erect a Hilbertian axiomatic superstructure on a Wittgensteinian basis. The atomic sentences are pictures of elementary facts, as in the *Tractatus*. But other signs, not given a definite meaning in advance, may also be added and treated just like atomic sentences, as may 'inference rules' governing the transformation of given sentence forms into other sentence forms. All sentences containing the meaningless signs still have a definite meaning, Carnap argues, as they confine the total space of possibilities to certain rows of the truth-table of a complete truth-functional state-description of the world as envisaged by Wittgenstein.[13] The only requirement of a 'logic' so constructed – evidently

---

[10] Under the assumption that the *Grunddisziplin* defines the single language in which everything meaningful can be said.

[11] A remark on probability, in a different context, casts some light on Carnap's attitude to the issue at this time: 'Here we have a similar situation to that of the "improper concepts". But different in this respect: In *that* case (with the "basic concepts" of an AS) the concept is not unambiguously determined even when the AS is *complete*, but only with respect to a structure; at least all questions are then unambiguously answerable. In *this* case, on the other hand, the meaning of the concept is determined [*wird der Begriff seiner Bedeutung nach festgelegt*] by a *complete* AS' (UCLA 1929d).

[12] The following discussion of the 'New Foundation' draws in part on Awodey and Carus (2007), Section II.

[13] Carnap's belief that this approach could be made to work rested on his '*Basic idea* [*Grundgedanke*]', the idea of a '*proof that every well-formed formula is a truth function of the atomic sentences, so is meaningful in the sense that it affirms certain* (possibly none or all) *possible world-configurations*' (1929a, p. 18). The sketch of his strategy for proving this appears to involve arbitrarily large truth tables to represent, at the limit, complete Wittgensteinian state-descriptions.

intended as a preliminary sketch for building a *Grunddisziplin* – is that it not allow inference to any atomic sentence that is not already among the premises.[14]

Axiom systems of any desired kind may then be framed within such a 'logic', and all theorems resulting from them can likewise be said to have a definite meaning because they constrain the truth-table of the complete state-description of the world.[15] This is the case even if they contain signs for infinite sets. These, Carnap says, are licensed within his system, though not purely 'formalistically' as in Hilbert. They have a definite meaning, even if not a complete one:

If now, to introduce the infinite, one 'adjoins ideal propositions' (Hilbert), i.e. writes down formulas that have no contentful meaning, but permit us to derive the mathematics of the infinite, then we have once again been able to determine the meaning of the signs introduced as meaningless, by investigating for which logical constants the formulas would become tautologies. (UCLA 1929e, p. 62)

Unlike Hilbert, Carnap admits no purely formal, uninterpreted signs. Nonetheless, he calls his idea 'radical formalism'[16] because it allows not only logical inferences, but any sort of inference whatever, including laws of physics or other inferences usually considered empirical, to be employed as part of a 'system of logic' in this way. In fact, '*any* sort of non-empirical axioms could be used here', as he said at a Berlin lecture in late 1929, 'such as an "axiom of induction" or Kantian pure principles' (UCLA 1929a, p. 1).

---

[14] 'Among the sentences that can be proved on the basis of a logic from certain atomic sentences (some true, some false), there can under certain circumstances be sentences, again, that contain no "logical" signs any more but only the signs that occur in atomic sentences. If the form of the proved sentence is such that it is not a "meaningful sentence" (in the above-discussed sense of meaning), then it is still an improper sentence; otherwise we have "*returned to an atomic sentence*". If this atomic sentence does not appear among those that were used to prove it, we speak of a "metaphysical derivation". If this is possible with a logic, we call it a "metaphysical logic"; if it can be shown for a logic that this cannot occur, it is a "metaphysics-free logic"' (ASP 1929a, p. 5).

[15] Though there is no explicit provision for the quantifiers, Carnap may have intended to develop them axiomatically on the model of Hilbert and Ackermann (1928, pp. 22–3 and 53–4), where the quantifiers are introduced by 'formal axioms', which are distinguished from the 'inhaltliche' (material, contentful) rules of inference, for both the propositional and the predicate calculus. The 'New Foundation' uses exactly these same terms.

[16] 'Formalism says: We want to introduce certain signs and formulas without giving their meaning, to make mathematics a uniform, complete system. We now extend that to a "*radical formalism*": it is permitted to add to those sentences ("atomic sentences") that express the most basic knowledge: (1) arbitrary formulas that are to be treated exactly like atomic sentences; they consist completely or partially of new signs; (2) arbitrary contentful transformation rules [*inhaltliche Umformungsregeln*] ("rules of inference") . . . It is to be shown here that nonetheless every formula that can arise from this has a definite meaning, as it is either a tautology . . . or a meaningful proposition, i.e. a truth function of the atomic sentences. Hence *despite radical formalism the demand for meaningfulness is fulfilled!*' (ASP 1929a, p. 1).

All axioms are at the same level; they are all tautological in the sense that they don't themselves say anything about the world; they are merely rules for rephrasing the content given in the atomic sentences. This was the main idea of another lecture he held a year later in Warsaw, entitled 'The tautological character of inference'. His shorthand notes for it begin: '*Thesis*: All inference is tautological; the conclusion means no more than the premises; only linguistic transformation', and he immediately clarifies that he means '"*inference*" not just in the formal-logical sense, but all (justified) scientific inference procedures' (ASP 1930h, p. 1). There is thus really just a '*single rule of inference* for science: One may transform a sentence as much as one likes, as long as its range [*Spielraum*]¹⁷ remains the same or is expanded. We need *no logical axioms*; they follow from this rule: e.g. p⊃pvq' (ASP 1930h, p. 2).¹⁸

The 'radical formalism' of the 'New Foundation' also turns out, on closer inspection, to have a direct application to the main outstanding problems at the heart of the *Aufbau*, and we may suspect that this motivation was at least equally behind the idea. On the basis of 'radical formalism', Carnap introduces a distinction here that would have great significance in his later work. This is the distinction between 'analytic' equivalences and merely 'empirical' ones. An equivalence is 'analytic' if it is necessary, i.e. based on a constitutive axiom – a law of logic or physics, part of the *system* of what was once called 'fictions' and what Carnap now called 'principles of syntax' (Chapter 6 above, footnote 3). An equivalence is 'empirical' if it is a merely extensional equivalence, without also being true by virtue of a principle or law that defines the system. Thus the ultimate fate of all remaining unmotivated or unconnected 'fictions', whose status had been uncertain since 1922, was to become principles of 'logical syntax', i.e. constitutive principles of the language.

This distinction between 'analytic' and 'empirical' equivalences does not appear in Carnap's published writings of this period. It is set out, however, in Eino Kaila's book *Logical Neo-Positivism: A Critical Study* (*Der logische Neupositivismus: Eine kritische Studie*), which appeared in 1930. Focused

---

¹⁷ 'Spielraum' ('range') is the complement of 'Gehalt' ('content'); as he explains earlier in these same lecture notes, 'We say: two sentences have the "*same content*" if in every possible case (i.e. in every consistent specification of the given, i.e. the premises) they have the same truth value. We say: the content of *s* is *contained* in that of *t* (if there is no case in which *s* is true and *t* false) if the *range* [*Spielraum*] that *t* leaves reality is *contained* in that left by *s*' (ASP 1930h, p. 2).

¹⁸ Note that in the 'New Foundation of Logic' a distinction is made between the finitary connectives among 'proper [*eigentliche*]' atomic sentences, defined by their truth tables (such as, in particular, '⊃'), and axiomatic 'contentful transformation rules [*inhaltliche Umformungsregeln*]' that can all be represented by '→' (ASP 1930h, p. 17). In the document quoted from here, it seems that this distinction may not have been maintained.

almost solely on the *Aufbau*, this was probably the first book-length critique of the Vienna Circle. It was based not only on a close reading of Carnap's text but also on Kaila's visit to Vienna during 1929, when he had personal contact with a number of Circle members, including Carnap. The 'principle of analytic equivalence [*Prinzip der analytischen Äquivalenz*]' occupies a large part of the exposition at the beginning of the book. Kaila notes:

> The distinction between 'analytic' and 'non-analytic' equivalences does not yet appear in the *Aufbau*; there all generally [i.e. extensionally] equivalent propositional functions are declared equivalent. But as this leads to some rather serious consequences [*einigermaßen bedenkliche Konsequenzen*], Carnap has modified his doctrine in the above sense. These later developments, which are still unpublished, are known to me from personal and epistolary communications of Herr Carnap. They are referred to here with his friendly permission. (Kaila 1930, p. 18; PT pp. 7–8)

What were these 'rather serious consequences' that Carnap himself acknowledged had led him to revise his position? The most obvious is perhaps the difficulty of defining theoretical, or indeed any general, concepts (defined over arbitrarily large or infinite sets) as extensionally equivalent to a construction from observational concepts (necessarily defined over a finite set of observations). The best known case, that of the transition from the two-dimensional observational world to the space-time world of physics, is (notoriously) by-passed in the *Aufbau* as discussed above (Chapter 6, pp. 169–72). But the same problem arises throughout. The equivalence of 'visual field' and the coordination of five quality-classes, regarded as merely extensional, depends on a particular selection of observations to constitute the quality-classes in question. In fact Carnap had obviously intended[19]

---

[19] As he later (1961, p. XXI) conceded: 'One could get the impression that for the reconstruction of a given concept A by concept B it is sufficient that B have the same extension as A. Actually, a stronger requirement must be fulfilled: the co-extensiveness of A and B must not be accidental, but necessary, i.e. it must rest either on the basis of logical rules or on the basis of natural laws' (1961, p. XIV). This condition had in fact to a large degree already been accommodated by Carnap in the *Aufbau* by his half-acknowledged requirement that, as we saw in Chapter 6 (pp. 166–77) above, the definitions, though not intended to reflect the nature of phenomenal experience exhaustively, should be empirically true of (the 'structure' of) that experience. Carnap points this out as well in his later preface: 'This condition is not mentioned in my book. But it was my intention to formulate the reconstruction in such a way that the co-extensiveness holds for any person (provided he has normal senses and that circumstances are not 'particularly unfavourable', §70 and 72), and hence is independent of the accidental selection of his observations and the course of his wanderings through the world. Hence the definitions of my system (to the extent they are not to be disregarded as erroneous) fulfil the cited conditions. For instance, the characterisation of the visual sense by the dimension number 5 rests upon the biological and psychological laws that say that the visual sense is the only sense of every (normal, not colour-blind) person, in which the order of qualities has five dimensions' (1961, p. XV).

this equivalence to hold more generally; the definition of the visual field as the sensory class that is five-dimensional relied implicitly on an empirical claim whose scope is general over the (arbitrarily large) class of possible observations it is defined on.

But what is the *'principle'* of analytic equivalence', and how was it to address this problem? Kaila is less than clear about this. An analytic equivalence, he says, is more than just an extensional equivalence. It asserts that two propositional functions have the same meaning, in Wittgenstein's sense:

So it is to be noted that identity of the meaning of equivalent propositional functions results from the 'thesis of extensionality' only when the equivalence is *analytic*. If the concepts concerned can be *split up* into already defined conceptual elements, then identity of meaning does not result. (Kaila 1930, p. 17; PT, p. 7)

Thus the equivalence 'for all x, x is a featherless biped iff x is a rational animal' is merely empirical, Kaila says, since the propositional functions 'is a featherless biped' and 'is a rational animal' can each be analyzed further (as the intersections between the classes 'featherless' and 'bipedal', 'rational' and 'animal', respectively). In the *Aufbau*, Kaila says (as quoted above), 'all generally [i.e. extensionally] equivalent propositional functions are declared to be equivalent', but now Carnap has determined that the construction must proceed only using *analytic* equivalences. But again, what is the 'principle' of analytic equivalence?[20]

Carnap clarifies this in a letter responding to Kaila's book: An equivalence is analytic only if it *defines* an equivalence, on the basis of the principles that constitute the language system in which it is used.[21] He writes:

The distinguishing feature of an analytic equivalence consists not in the condition that ψ be definable only by its equivalence with φ (this is sufficient, but not

---

[20] Kaila's own expression of this 'principle' seems circular: '*Analytically equivalent concepts have the same meaning*'. In elucidation of this he goes on: 'In case it is claimed that two analytically equivalent concepts could after all have a different "content", a different "sense", or that one "thinks of" them differently, it has to be answered that any such difference is scientifically meaningless since it *cannot* – by definition – *be expressed*' (Kaila 1930, p. 18; PT, p. 7).

[21] The concept of 'analytic equivalence' is introduced in the 'New Foundation' as follows: 'If p →q and q→p are provable, then p and q are called "*equivalent* (to each other)". If p→q and q→p are provable, and as logical sentences, then p and q are "*analytically equivalent*" . . . If p→q and q→p are provable, but not as logical sentences, only with the help of the atomic sentences, then p and q are called "*empirically equivalent*"' (ASP 1929a, p. 7). 'Logical sentences' are simply those that result from the application of contentful transformation rules, the 'proven sentences of a logic, for whose derivation no atomic sentences have been used' (ASP 1929a, p. 6). So if p and q are 'analytically equivalent', their mutual implication can be proved without the use of atomic sentences, i.e. by contentful transformation rules and 'improper' axioms alone.

necessary), but rather in the condition that the equivalence rests only on the definitions of ψ and φ, not on empirical sentences. (CK 1930a)[22]

How does this address the problems of the *Aufbau*? In a lecture 'On the constitution of the non-given [*Über die Konstitution des Nicht-Gegebenen*]' that he gave at Reichenbach's seminar in Berlin (October 1929), Carnap indicated where he saw the difference between his position of just a year before, as described in *Scheinprobleme* (which he now rejects) and his current one:

> *Empirically* equivalent concepts (functions) need not have the same meaning... But *analytically equivalent* concepts and propositions do. Put differently: If two propositions P and Q are to have different meanings, a form of the world [*Weltgestalt*] (a form of the given) must be *thinkable* in which one holds and not the other. This is the *decisive argument against every form of realism*! (and not the popular slogan of 'verifiability' . . . (now please do your best to forget my pamphlet [*Scheinprobleme in der Philosophie*]!)). (UCLA 1929a, p. 2)

The 'principle of analytic equivalence' applied then, in particular, to the specification of the given itself; the given was to be specified by 'rules of phenomenal syntax' in the sense we saw Carnap discussing with Feigl above (Chapter 6, pp. 166–8). Carnap's point in Berlin was that the given should be specified so as to make the meaning of any sentence referring to it unambiguous, i.e. so that it was impossible, using the 'rules of phenomenal syntax' (in conjunction with all other axioms of the logical, physical, methodological system), to specify the given in two different ways such that any sentences equivalent under one specification were not equivalent under a different one. Hence Carnap's remark here that the 'principle of analytic equivalence' was a more conclusive argument against realism than any form of verifiability (which could still be read into the *Scheinprobleme*).[23]

The 'principle of analytic equivalence' also appears to solve another (acknowledged) problem with the *Aufbau*, the ambiguity created in the higher levels of the construction by the inadequacy of explicit definition

---

[22] Carnap's letters to Kaila were rescued from Kaila's widow after his death (who followed Kaila's orders to burn his correspondence) by G.H. von Wright. However, these letters do not appear in the catalogue of von Wright's papers in Helsinki. Fortunately, Prof. Juha Manninen (Universities of Oulu and Helsinki) had borrowed these letters from von Wright and photocopied them. He very kindly made an additional copy for me, and they have been very useful in reconstructing this phase in Carnap's development, beyond the passages actually quoted here and in Chapter 8. The originals would appear to be lost.

[23] Reichenbach objected, according to Carnap's notes: 'It's all perfectly fine, if you admit that all sentences are either true or false; but that is an error'. Carnap responded: 'I don't need "true" and "false"; I simply note that in the formalistic process certain formulas are recognised by the physicist, others are rejected; that's enough for my argument' (UCLA 1929a, p. 3).

(as exhibited especially in §126 and discussed above, Chapter 6, pp. 169–72). The requirement that every step in the construction employ only 'analytic equivalences', rather than merely empirical ones, guarantees that each constituted object or concept just is, by definition, no more and no less than what it is constituted to be in the system. There is a problem here, of course, that Carnap would have had to face if he had continued on this path for more than a year or two: some of the 'rules of logical syntax' by virtue of which the non-explicitly defined concepts are constituted take the form – at least in the *Aufbau* version, and no alternative was suggested by Carnap – of optimands, features of the system to be maximised or minimised subject to a number of constraints. This means, as Carnap himself recognised (Chapter 6, pp. 175–7), that these 'rules' are ultimately, at some level, *practical* principles rather than cognitive ones. To include them among the 'rules of syntax' constitutive of the logico-physico-methodological system would therefore contradict the Wittgensteinian denial that normative statements have cognitive meaning. But the strategy was never, it seems, pursued far enough for that question even to arise.

Apart from these immediate applications to the *Aufbau* system, though, Carnap's principal motivation in the 'New Foundation' was clearly the attempt to force some version of a 'theoretical language' into the *Tractatus* corset, using Hilbert's axiomatic method as a framework. The *rules* laid down in axiom systems were to be the 'analytical' framework that defined what was *necessary* within a given system; they are the basis of the concept of 'analytic equivalence'. This role given to constitutive rules of language clearly prefigures the *Logical Syntax* and subsequent developments. So does the 'radical formalism' of the 'New Foundation', by which *all* such rules are treated as rules of inference, i.e. as rules for transforming groups of atomic sentences into extensionally equivalent ones – whether they are rules of the kind usually considered 'mathematical' or of the kind usually called 'empirical'. This foreshadows the later idea (1934, §51) of using 'P-rules' as well as 'L-rules' as possible transformation rules constitutive of a language. Together, these ideas had already moved some distance toward where Carnap would emerge in early 1931 (Chapter 9 below). But he was still attempting to account for the 'theoretical language' *within* the constraints of Wittgenstein's picture theory, and this was bound to fail, as we see in more detail in the next section. But for all its inconclusiveness and ultimate unworkability, the 'New Foundation' indicates how Carnap was attempting to extend a truth-functional, finitary, 'molecular' language[24] to something usable for mathematics and science. The cash value of a

---

[24] This is what Carnap called it retrospectively in 'Testability and Meaning'; see pp. 205–7 below.

'theoretical language' that was only an axiomatic, 'improper' adjunct to the atomic sentences and their truth functions was to be found in them and only in them, very much in Wittgenstein's spirit:

The sentence of mathematics expresses no thought. In life it is never the mathematical sentence we need. We use the mathematical sentence *only* to derive sentences that do not belong to mathematics from other sentences that also do not belong to mathematics. (Wittgenstein 1922, 6.21–6.211)

Not only the 'constructive' project but the entire project of rational reconstruction seems to be something quite different now from what it was in 1922. It had begun by constructing objective 'secondary worlds' of reality from the materials of the subjective chaos. Part of the *goal*, then, had been to construct the concepts constituting those 'secondary worlds' from more elementary materials. Now those very concepts have become a possible *starting point* of the construction; axioms containing them have been (potentially) used to *define* the language. As we saw in Chapter 6 (pp. 166–77), the shift from substantive or material 'fictions' and phenomenological discernment to linguistic rules put a definitive end to 'fictions' of the *material* or contentful kind that had originally guided the construction. But we seem to have ended up with just a new version of Vaihinger's undisciplined proliferation of 'fictions', in a new, linguistic guise. Principles of science, of inference, of method – of any kind! – have become 'rules of syntax'. Where did this leave empiricism?

In his development from 1922 to 1930, each solution that Carnap adopted to the problems facing him at each stage solved that immediate problem – but also brought with it problems, some not immediately apparent, that then required a new solution. At no point during this period did Carnap reach an equilibrium, an overall position that solved all the outstanding problems. Though he remained optimistic that he could ultimately extricate himself from the endless tangle of difficulties the 1922 breakthrough had brought with it, by 1930 it was becoming clear that the whole programme of rational reconstruction was running aground (the next Chapter looks at this crisis in more detail). Nowhere was this more apparent than in the wreckage of the former 'clarification' project, which the acceptance of Wittgenstein's picture theory had cast adrift.

THE ECLIPSE OF THE THEORETICAL LANGUAGE

Under the tyranny of the requirement that all meaningful sentences be truth functions of atomic sentences, the 'clarification' component of rational reconstruction had more or less been suspended. On occasion we are told in quite radical terms that scientific laws really are *nothing but* a restatement of the observational evidence we have for them. To the Bauhaus at Dessau in October 1929, Carnap said 'With the particular facts *everything is said* [*ist eigentlich alles gesagt*] that can be known' (ASP 1929f, p. 2). Apparent scientific laws and scientific concepts, he maintained, are just abbreviations for groups of facts observed in the past:

'At this point there is a *gravitational* pull of such and such a magnitude in such and such a direction' means 'In this region every object[25] experiences an acceleration in this direction and magnitude'. Thus the concept of 'gravity' is reduced to concepts of the observable thing-world [which is in turn reducible to elementary experiences]. Every statement about gravity can be translated into a sentence about the movement of bodies; there is therefore (for science) no 'gravity' that produces this movement in addition to the movements themselves. 'Gravity' is just a linguistic abbreviation. (ASP 1929f, pp. 1–2)

And scientific predictions only apparently refer to the future; really they are just summaries of already observed experiences recorded in atomic observation sentences (ASP 1930h, p. 2). To the objection 'But we *mean* something different!' Carnap responds with a distinction between (theoretical) 'content' and 'psychological content'; the subjective, imaginative, or emotional associations of words are irrelevant to their actual theoretical content. The 'representation function [*Darstellungsfunktion*]' of language is to be sharply distinguished from its 'rhetorical function [*Wirkungsfunktion*]' (cf. Kaila 1930, p. 15). The representation function is all there is to meaning; all else is merely 'accompanying mental images [*Begleitvorstellungen*]'.[26] And under the rubric of 'rhetorical function' Carnap includes not only what Frege had called 'colouring [*Färbung*]', but also what he had called 'Sinn'. In a note to himself in November 1929, Carnap considers the case of an equivalence between a physical law P and a truth-functional state-description (conjunction or alternation of atomic sentences) f, to which P is – as every physical law, in Carnap's view at this time, must be – fully reducible (and

---

[25] Michael Friedman (personal communication) objects that the use of a universal quantifier here is inconsistent with Carnap's proclaimed finitism. Carnap would have responded, I imagine, that he intends this expression to quantify over a restricted, indeed a finite domain. 'Every object in this region' would include only those objects ('in the observable thing-world') that we can observe and whose accelerations we can measure and record. Things would get more complicated, of course, if we took liquids and gases into account, but the number of *observations* (and observation sentences) would still be finite.

[26] This term already appears in the *Scheinprobleme*, where the 'core' of an experience is distinguished from its 'peripheral part', and correspondingly, the 'theoretical meaning' of a sentence is distinguished from its mere 'accompanying mental images [*Begleitvorstellungen*]' (1928b, pp. 31–3). But the more radical view discussed here is not present there yet.

'analytically equivalent'). Under the heading 'sense and meaning [*Sinn und Bedeutung*]', he writes:

> The senses of f and P are of course different; but the difference lies merely in the accompanying mental images [*Begleitvorstellungen*]. Proof: If they had a different meaning, that is, if one had in mind: P does say f, but it goes beyond that; then there would have to be a (perhaps unknown) q such that P = f & q, where q is not derivable from f, logically independent. It would have to be possible for f to be true and q false, so P also false. But this case is certainly excluded: if f is true, then *necessarily* P is true. Not just empirically![27] So it can't have more theoretical content, either. That is precisely the criterion. (UCLA 1929c, p. 1)

The extensionality thesis had already been in the *Aufbau*, and the '*logical* value [*logischer Wert*]' of a statement is sharply distinguished from its '*knowledge* value [*Erkenntniswert*]' (1928a, e.g. §95), and only the former is relevant for the constitutional system. But now 'logical value' is further narrowed down to those components of extensional meaning that derive directly from the *rules* setting up the basic 'logical' system (in the broad sense of the 'New Foundation').

Carnap later acknowledged that he had accepted a 'molecular language' (a language containing no unrestricted quantifiers) for science during this period. Though this issue is low-profile in the *Aufbau* itself[28] and is not considered in his autobiography (even in its longer, original version), he discusses it in 'Testability and Meaning' (§23) at some length. 'Such a language', he writes there, 'fulfils the requirements of confirmability and testability in its most radical form. Hence we understand the fact that certain epistemologists, especially positivists, propose or demand a molecular language as the language of science.' On the other hand, there are disadvantages:

> In a molecular language unrestricted universality cannot be expressed. Therefore, if such a language is chosen, we have to face the problem of how to deal with the physical laws. There seem to be in the main two possible ways. A law may be expressed in the form of a molecular sentence, namely a restricted universal sentence or a conjunction, concerning those instances of the law which have been observed so far. On the other hand a law may be taken, not as a sentence, but as a rule of inference according to which one molecular sentence (e.g. a prediction

---

[27] This use of 'necessary' ('analytic' in his new sense as opposed to 'merely empirical') is due to Carnap's definition of physical laws, at this time, as 'operation rules [*Operationsvorschriften*]', i.e. as 'inference rules [*Schlußregel*]' (of the kind he would later call 'P-rules'). Note that what Carnap has in effect done in this passage is to prove that P is identical to the set of its instances by *defining* it as equivalent to f!

[28] The only explicit reference to it that I know of occurs near the end of the main text of §180. I am grateful to Michael Friedman for pointing this passage out to me.

about a future event) can be inferred from other ones (e.g. sentences about observed events). Each of these ways has actually been followed, as we shall see. (1936–7, p. 18).

As examples of the 'first way' Carnap cites Russell's *Our Knowledge of the External World*, Lecture IV (though neither his quotations from Russell nor the tendency of Russell's text can unambiguously be interpreted this way) and Mach (without references). The 'second way' Carnap attributes to Schlick and Ramsey, who both appear to derive their views from Wittgenstein. 'I too accepted a molecular language', he says, referring to the *Aufbau* (somewhat vaguely, without a specific citation), and then expanding on this in a way that does not correspond to anything made explicit in that book:

According to the positivistic principle of testability in its most radical form, I restricted the atomic sentences to sentences about actual experiences. The laws of physics as well as all predictions were interpreted as records of present and (remembered) past experiences, namely those experiences from which the law or the prediction is usually said to be inferred by induction. (1936–7, p. 19)

'Thus', he continues, 'I followed the first of the two ways mentioned above; the physical laws also were interpreted as molecular sentences.' This is true, as we saw in the above quotations from his Bauhaus lectures and other manuscripts. But what he does not mention in 'Testability and Meaning' is that he *also* followed the 'second way', that of Wittgenstein and Ramsey; this is the view spelled out in the 'radical formalism' of the 'New Foundation' as well as the 1930 lecture 'The Tautological Character of Inference' (above, p. 198). Indeed, he appears to have held both views simultaneously, in different contexts. The 'first way' was relevant in the 'clarification' context, where the issue was the empirical content of physics, and its reducibility to observational evidence, while the 'second way' came to the fore within the context of the 'construction' project, when the status of inductive *inference* was the issue, and Carnap wanted to assimilate it to truth-functional inference to ensure its acceptability within Wittgensteinian constraints. His later distinction between these two ways, in 'Testability and Meaning', indicates his subsequent realisation that these two contexts had to be squared with each other.[29] In 1929–30, it seems, though he may have been uneasy about the fit between these two contexts (see below, Chapter 8), he had not yet made the problem explicit, and the resulting ambiguity led

---

[29] It is unclear exactly when Carnap abandoned the 'molecular' conception of theories. The first draft of *Logical Syntax* (1931–2) still appears to have contained a version of it (ASP 1932d, 1933b).

him into traps such as the argument about '*Sinn und Bedeutung*' quoted above (p. 205).

The Wittgensteinian position Carnap was considering in the 'New Foundation' is an odd, transitional mixture, then, looking both backward and forward. Despite the strong commitment to a radically 'molecular' and finitist, truth-functional conception of the cash value of theoretical statements, we can also see the *Syntax* appearing over the horizon. The reliance on constitutive rules of language is not only an attempt to obtain a meta-language by stealth; it also indicates that – although the object language itself retains its fixed interpretation in terms of atomic sentences – the trend toward defining languages by syntactic (ultimately semantic) rules was already under way. But in 1930, Carnap was feeling his way in the dark; he did not yet know what he was under way toward. Meanwhile, the rational reconstruction programme was reaching a crisis.

CHAPTER 8

The crisis of rational reconstruction, 1929–1930

Thanks to Neurath's efforts and other factors, the Vienna Circle had achieved a considerable notoriety by 1930. For Neurath himself, this had been largely a political matter – the desire to oppose irrationalist and anti-scientific intellectual movements at a fundamental level. He (rightly) saw these movements – which were very popular with students – as broadly sympathetic to the authoritarian fascism that was gaining ground throughout Europe. He was, of course, too late; time ran out too quickly for a long-term strategy aimed at intellectual influences to have much effect. But the strategy was reasonable, and given the dimensions of the threat, Carnap was willing to support it as a matter of civic duty, though his own time-horizons were much longer. His own understanding of 'politics', as we saw at the end of Chapter 1, comprised not just what is usually meant by that word, or the social activities of education and scientific research, but also the provision of fundamental conceptual frameworks for human discourse.

The Vienna Circle itself realised that its programmatic rhetoric exceeded what could be rigorously argued. Its members harboured various degrees of hope about the realisability of the promises made, but everyone (except perhaps, sometimes, Neurath himself) was aware that the basis for the programme was under construction, and might not be constructible at all in the form of its present design (ca. 1930). The gaps in the *Aufbau* construction were acknowledged, not least by its author. Logicism was incomplete, and had at best only a rather wobbly answer to the challenges from Brouwer and Hilbert. And the Circle's radical, Wittgenstein-inspired positivism was clearly problematic – at very least left a good deal of work to be done – as a plausible account of physics and natural science in general.

In the course of 1929 and 1930 the outlook worsened. The meta-mathematical approach of the Hilbert school, further developed within the ambit of the Circle itself by Tarski and Gödel, was at odds with

Wittgenstein's exclusion of meta-linguistic statements. And some of the results of the new meta-mathematics, notably Gödel's incompleteness theorems, began to undermine the very foundation of the whole edifice – the Wittgensteinian theory of meaning and logic. In addition, critiques of the *Aufbau* by Kaila and Reichenbach cast doubt on the feasibility of the positivistic conception of physics. These problems on all fronts forced Carnap to think of a radically different basis for rational reconstruction, which will be the subject of Chapter 9. Meanwhile, though, the bold claims asserted by the Vienna Circle rang increasingly hollow.

THE CONSTITUTION OF THE 'NON-GIVEN'

Kaila's book *Logical Neo-Positivism* (*Der logische Neupositivismus*) (above, Chapter 7, pp. 198–201), while sympathetic to many aspects of the *Aufbau*, was also severely critical. Its criticisms fell into two main categories: first, largely phenomenological or psychological critiques of Carnap's constitutional definitions; second, claims to the effect that the *practice* of science requires assumptions that Carnap either denied or could not account for. The first category took up most space; Kaila devoted the first five pages of his critique, for instance, to the claim (reminiscent of Brouwer) that the ordering of a relation depends on the subjective directionality of experienced time, and that therefore Carnap's attempt to define *any* relation extensionally must fail. When this claim was discussed in the Vienna Circle in December 1929 (proof copies of Kaila's book had evidently already circulated among Circle members), it actually caused some consternation (though Carnap attempted a counter-argument) until Gödel explained the Kuratowski definition of ordered pair (ASP1930i; Stadler 1997, pp. 276–7; PT 242–3).

The following two sections of Kaila's critique were entitled, respectively, 'Is experiential time [*die Erlebniszeit*] constitutable quasi-analytically?' and 'Is perceptual space [*der Wahrnehmungsraum*] constitutable quasi-analytically?' Kaila claimed that the 'purely structural' constitution of objective reality began *too far down*, at too low a level. The meagre autopsychological basis Carnap had used was unsuitable for the construction of physical objects and scientific concepts without the provision of more qualitative, *non*-structural components. The main line of argument was again phenomenological; for the extensional and quasi-analytical method to be feasible, a certain heterogeneity of the elements upon which it operates must already be present, or it will have no starting point.[1] Carnap, as we saw, had *begun* in 1922 with exactly this sort of approach; his present standpoint had resulted from a gradual, step-by-step learning process. On these questions, Kaila could be regarded as not having quite caught up, and Carnap had only to recapitulate his own recent development to respond (1930d).

Kaila's other line of criticism, based on the *practice* of science, was less easily dismissed. Here, too, some of the arguments were based on misunderstandings. Kaila objected to the structural characterisation of the given, for instance, on the grounds that qualitative, subjectively given starting points are *in practice* indispensable to science (Kaila 1930, pp. 78–9). Carnap had never denied this, of course; the constitution system was not supposed to be an empirical *theory* of the perceptual origins of knowledge, but a rational reconstruction. It was intended to show *that* all objects of knowledge could in principle be identified and characterised structurally, on some minimal basis, not *how* that identification actually occurs.

Kaila's critique came much closer to the bone, though, when he gave instances where Carnap appeared to legislate to scientists that conceptual tools they make frequent use of were illegitimate and must be dropped. One example is what Kaila, following Reichenbach's recent handbook contribution 'Goals and Paths of Physical Knowledge [*Ziele und Wege der physikalischen Erkenntnis*]' (Reichenbach 1929), called the 'probability principle [*Wahrscheinlichkeitsprinzip*]', whereby our experience was regarded as a (representative) sample of some larger reality:

If . . . our perceptions are like sampling trials [probeartige Ausschnitte] from an n-dimensional real manifold [reellen Mannigfaltigkeit], what conclusions can be drawn about the non-given content of that manifold? This is just the question that empirical science is there to answer. (Kaila 1930, p. 81; PT p. 48)

The 'reality' of the 'n-dimensional real manifold' is *defined*, Kaila explained (here too following Reichenbach[2]), by the 'probability principle', the assumption that our experience is a (reliable or representative) sample of

---

[1] 'If this logical method of construction [*Aufbaumethode*] is used, it must not begin [at a point that is] *epistemologically too early*: at least those "*different cases*" already have to be there, whose presence is the condition for applying the extensional method in general and the quasi-analytic constitutional method in particular' (Kaila 1930, p. 71; PT, p. 42).

[2] Who argued (Reichenbach 1929, p. 26) that 'the concept of probability is not brought in by inferring transcendental things from perceptions, in the spirit of realism. It is not the existential assertion [*Existentialbehauptung*] that brings the probability concept into knowledge, but rather the assertion of any kind of law-governed pattern [*gesetzliche Verknüpfung*], regardless of whether it is among things or experiences. For that reason it would be meaningless [*Sinnlos*] to say that one could speak of transcendental things with a certain probability: the probability concept is not applicable to the existential axiom itself, as this axiom is not inferred by inductive means. The connection between the probability concept and the existential assertion is rather, a different one. If one takes [the relation between external things and sense-experiences] as an *identity*, in the spirit of positivism, then the

a larger population of possible experiences, and that we may draw probabilistic inferences from the sample to the population:

> The assumption of empirical science that our perceptions are like '*sampling trials*' means that probability inferences [*Wahrscheinlichkeitsschlüsse*] can be drawn from the given to the non-given; it means that the distributions observed in the given can be generalised to the non-given. (Kaila 1930, p. 81; PT p. 48)

And in *this* sense of 'reality', Kaila maintained, the assumption of an objective reality was indispensable to science. On this he again endorsed Reichenbach,[3] who after concluding (with Hume) that 'the probability inference cannot be justified [*der Wahrscheinlichkeitsschluß ist nicht begründbar*]' and is 'empirically not provable [*empirisch nicht beweisbar*]', but nonetheless 'indispensable for knowledge of nature' (see also Reichenbach 1925, pp. 168ff.), had decided (against Hume) to regard the 'probability principle' as a fundamental principle of logic.[4] Hume, says Reichenbach, had regarded it as a merely psychological, irrational habit, but this does not help us to understand the nature of our apparently reliable scientific knowledge.

We therefore proceed differently: we introduce the concept of probability as a basic logical principle [*als logischen Grundbegriff*], whose meaning we assume to be given axiomatically. We thus lay down the following axiomatic conditions:

1. It is meaningful and permissible [*sinnvoll und zulässig*] to infer something for all cases, with [a certain] probability, from a finite number of cases.
2. It is meaningful and permissible to draw a probable inference, from the probability of an event, about its frequency within a finite set of instances. (Reichenbach 1929, pp. 26–7)

---

existential assertion becomes identical to the probability assertion; i.e. the belief in the existence of things is identical with the belief in the axiom of probability [i.e. the above "probability principle"]. Here two metaphysical hypotheses are reduced to one, and this is perhaps the strongest argument in favour of positivism' (see also Reichenbach 1925, pp. 167ff.). However, Reichenbach in this paper had come down in the end on the side of realism (in the sense described in this quotation, the inference to things that are more than a sum of sense perceptions), and against positivism.

[3] Though he rejects (p. 83; PT p. 49) the characterisation of the 'probability inference [*Wahrscheinlichkeitsschluß*]' as 'metaphysical', which Reichenbach had not shied away from: 'The concept of probability is introduced into science by means of the *inductive inference*; for such a claim about future perceptions can only be made with probability. The inductive inference is therefore also called the *probability inference* . . . An extremely peculiar metaphysical assumption enters into knowledge with this inference' (Reichenbach 1929, p. 25).

[4] There is a certain parallel to Carnap's development here. Reichenbach had much earlier, in his doctoral dissertation, argued for the a priori status of the 'probability principle' (Reichenbach 1916, Chapter 3, 'Deduction of the Probability Principle'). The difference is that Carnap at the time of *his* dissertation, five years later, saw a priori principles as pragmatic 'fictions', in the style of Vaihinger (rather as Reichenbach later did in 1920, though he does not use Vaihinger's words), while Reichenbach, in his dissertation, regards a priori principles as generated (Marburg style) by synthesis of the intellect, referring explicitly to Cassirer (Reichenbach 1916, p. 54).

Kaila went further, and took Carnap's constitution system to task for failing to supply a criterion for distinguishing between the 'real manifold' in this Reichenbachian sense and the infinite number of 'ideal manifolds' that his purely structural description also referred to, without being able to distinguish the real one. Not only was a purely structural characterisation incapable of picking out the world we actually experience from other structurally equivalent worlds (as Carnap himself had pointed out in §154 of the *Aufbau*), but even if this problem could be solved, structural characterisation had not been the basis of physics as practised since Galileo, which rests, Kaila claimed, on a certain criterion by means of which 'the *physical method*, as it is in fact given, *distinguishes the real manifold in principle*' (Kaila 1930, p. 86; PT p. 50). This criterion was that '*The relations contained in the real manifold describe objects of the same logical type as the relata themselves*' (Kaila 1930, p. 84; PT p. 49). The difference between two line segments is itself a segment; the temporal distance between two durations is also a duration, and so on, while the difference between two qualities (e.g. two pitches, two colours) is not itself a quality. The constitution system, Kaila says, treats this difference as merely structural, while in fact it is a difference in principle. No quality can be measured, he says, until it is put in correspondence with spatio-temporal relations, and turned into a numerical relation (e.g. the measurement of a difference in pitch is converted into a numerical characterisation of the difference between two vibrating strings, i.e. into a length): 'Physically nothing can be observed other than the dependence of phenomena on spatio-temporal relations; nothing can be measured other than the spatio-temporal objects described by these relations' (Kaila 1930, p. 85). Carnap thus has to reinterpret the physical method to suit the constitution system, Kaila said, and this leads him to misrepresent it:

A re-interpretation along these lines is offered by Carnap in his booklet *Physical Concept Formation* . . . Carnap says (p. 16), in line with the received view, that all measurement goes back to measurement of spatial lengths. But this is not supposed in principle to privilege spatio-temporal relations among phenomena above other relations. For (pp. 47ff.) even if such a reduction were not possible, all perceptible qualities, insofar as they display law-governed behavior among themselves, must for that reason be measurable. Measurement is thus supposed to be nothing but (p. 61) a particular kind of naming, using numbers instead of word-names. Thus we could 'measure' pitches by setting the just discernible differences of pitch as equal, and numbering the pitches of this series in order. 'There is no quantitative and qualitative side of nature' (p. 59), i.e. the spatio-temporal order is not in principle distinguished vis-à-vis the ideal orders. (Kaila 1930, pp. 86–7; PT p. 51)

In *Physical Concept Formation* Carnap had, of course, still been assuming that theoretical descriptions could be completely and seamlessly cashed out in qualitative, subjective terms. As we saw (Chapter 6, pp. 177–81), he even stresses this intertranslatability of the qualitative basis of physics and the completely abstract system of 14-tuples, to refute the charge that physics 'eliminates the qualities'. Put together with the purely structural constitution system, Kaila argues, this leaves Carnap without a basis for a physics of the world we live in rather than some range of abstractly possible ones. Galileo, after all, had said that the book of nature was written in geometrical figures – meaning, Kaila maintained, that it consisted entirely of spatiotemporal relations, relations that hold in the space and time we inhabit, not Carnap's 'abstract space' of the *Aufbau*: 'If Galilei, Huygens, Newton etc. had thought constitution-theoretically, how could they have erected the magnificent structure of physics – which came into being, after all, by reading in that "geometrical" "book of nature" and leaving everything else aside as physically irrelevant?' (Kaila 1930, p. 87; PT, p. 51). However sceptically Carnap may have viewed Kaila's 'method of physics' and its criterion for observability, practical irrelevance to physics as an enterprise was not something he wanted to be accused of; this was, after all, precisely the charge Carnap had laid at the door not only of metaphysical *Naturphilosophen* in general, as we saw, but specifically of Goethe's qualitative method, for instance, when contrasting it with the quantitative methods physics did in fact adopt over Goethe's objections (Chapter 6, p. 179).

After some initial correspondence, Kaila came to visit in Vienna in the late spring and early summer of 1929. Carnap spent much of November and December 1929 – as well as considerable time toward the end of 1930, after receiving a copy of Kaila's book – composing a response. Its working title was 'On the Constitution of the Non-Given [*Über die Konstitution des Nichtgegebenen*]' (echoing one of the Kaila passages quoted above) – which we have already met as the title of a talk he gave in Berlin (also in November 1929); the materials relating to this project, in his papers, refer to it as the 'Kaila-essay'. The issues in the foreground were those, not surprisingly, where Kaila makes common cause with Reichenbach – probability and induction. But these were to be used as an example of the larger point that the constitution theory, like science, employed *no* principles *whatever* that were not reducible to atomic sentences. Carnap summarises his plan, in a note to himself, as follows:

Perhaps *motivation* [*Aufgabestellung*] like this: Against the thesis of constitution theory the objection that one has to add extensions [*man müsse Ergänzungen*] *vornehmen*]; as this occurs even within science itself, transcending [*Transzendieren*] is permissible in metaphysics as well. Answer: no transcending occurs in science, despite a solipsistic basis; therefore scientific knowledge is consistent with the solipsistic thesis, but metaphysics not permissible.

First of all discussion of the logical form in which scientific derivation occurs. Then elucidation how introduction of the 'non-given' is just rearrangement [*Umordnung*], not introduction of anything new. Finally application to the most important case of seemingly new introduction: inductive inference [*Induktionsschluß*]. (UCLA 1930b, p. 2)

One obstacle to addressing the issue of inductive or statistical inference was that Carnap had not developed an account of probability consistent with the constitution system. As he wrote Kaila in a letter of early 1929:

You are right to say that the constitution theory should pay more attention to the inductive method of empirical science [*der Wirklichkeitswissenschaft*], and that to do this, it would have to give an account of the logical character of the concept of *probability*. I'm clear about the 'that', not about the 'how'. It seems to me, though, that I would seek an approach to the probability concept in a different direction from the one in your logic of probability.[5] I think that the concept of probability has to be interpreted in a positivist way so that probability inferences become just as analytic (tautological) as other (syllogistic) inferences. I have not so far paid much attention to the probability concept (I admit that this is a shortcoming), so I am not in a position to say anything very definite. A first attempt at interpretation (in all brevity, taking the simplest case) is given on the enclosed page.[6] (CK 1929a[7])

This was a period of great controversy and change in the theory of probability, and many different proposals were in the air (von Plato 1994). Carnap was, as we see here, in agreement with the purely logical conception of probability suggested by Wittgenstein and further developed by Waismann (1930), as far as it went, but this idea was, so far, not much more than a sketch, and had not been worked out nearly as fully as the frequency interpretations put forward by von Mises or Reichenbach. Richard von Mises, one of the leading figures in the development of mathematical statistics before Kolmogorov (von Plato 1994, Chapter 6), had also developed, even before the new developments of the 1920s in quantum physics, a general philosophical account of statistical inference (von Mises 1928) whereby causal relations in the explanation of nature were essentially to be displaced

---

[5] Carnap refers here to Kaila's (1926) book *Die Prinzipien der Wahrscheinlichkeitslogik*.
[6] This would appear to have been the table referred to on pp. 215–16 below.
[7] I am grateful to Prof. Juha Manninen for providing me a copy of this letter; see footnote 22 in Chapter 7 above.

by purely statistical ones, 'behind' which, Mises thought, we cannot ulti-mately go. Probability, then, could meaningfully be applied only to large populations (to a 'collective' [*Kollektiv*]) – not to sentences, and not to single events. Reichenbach (1929, 1930) disagreed with this radically pos-itivist philosophical interpretation. He sought rather to replace ordinary two-valued logic for empirical sentences by a probabilistic logic in which empirical sentences are not true or false but always probably true to some degree. Only the sentences of pure mathematics could be true or false (have probability 1 or 0); an empirical sentence has a probability depending on observations relevant to it.

In contrast to these theories, Carnap wanted, like Waismann (and like his own much later theory), to regard probability statements as purely logical relations among sentences; they were simply a way of expressing the logical 'degree of freedom [*Spielraum*]' given by some set of sentences (e.g. observation-recording sentences) to another sentence (e.g. a physical theory). So an inductive inference, for Carnap at this time, was simply a way of restating the evidence already available, and nothing *new* emerged from it. Provided the relation of evidence to theory could be regarded as a purely logical one, it did not matter how the probability axioms were stated, and Carnap did not think he needed a full development of the theory to be able to maintain his position against those of Kaila or Reichenbach. As he put it in a note he wrote to himself in November 1929:

Probability. According to the above [the passage immediately preceding this, on '*Sinn und Bedeutung*', is quoted above, p. 205], probability is surely reducible to some logical form [*sicherlich auf die logische Form zurückführbar*]. One might object: Fine, but how? I say: If someone gives me a correct introduction of the concept of probability, i.e. a formulation of the addition rule [*des Eins-Axioms*], I will show him that the statements licensed by it are just truth functions of the premises. As a logician I don't here need to show anything further. The epistemologist of physics is welcome to offer the right formulation.

Analogy: The pure mathematician says: $2 + 3 = 5$. If a physicist wants to contra-dict, he has to describe precisely the case where this does not seem to him correct.

Today there is not yet a correct formulation available. The following just as an example of what might be possible; in reality it would be much more compli-cated . . . How does this appear to intuition [*gefühlsmäßiger Befund*]? Well, that is precisely analogous to previous positivistic reductions . . . (UCLA 1929c, p. 1)

By 'the following', in the last paragraph, Carnap means a table he had compiled, illustrating the meaning of probable inference by analogy with inference to continued existence of an object when one's back is turned or inference to other minds.[8] (This seems also to have been the 'page' he had enclosed with the above-quoted letter to Kaila.) The main point of this table is to emphasise the transition from the 'old conception [*alte Auffassung*]' – whereby we 'know' something 'on the basis of observations' (about objects not presently observed or about other minds) – to the 'new conception [*neue Auffassung*]' whereby the *meaning* of the sentence arrived at by the 'inference [*Schluß*]' from observations is *exactly the same* as that of the conjoined observations themselves, and 'The point of using the expression [*die Zweckmäßigkeit der Ausdrucksweise*] *p* instead of *q* lies in the fact that by means of *p* useful accompanying mental images [*nützliche Begleitvorstellungen*] are stimulated [*angeregt*]'.[9]

We have already seen (Chapter 7, pp. 204–5) that Carnap distinguished sharply between the 'rhetorical function [*Wirkungsfunktion*]' and the 'representation function [*Darstellungsfunktion*]' of language, as Kaila had put it. He had also restricted the *meaning* of a physical statement (at least in some contexts; see Chapter 7, pp. 203–7) to the facts pictured (*dargestellt*) by them, i.e. to a finite number of observation sentences that support it. On the basis of these ideas, and the probability conception just mentioned, Carnap describes the intended thesis of his planned 'Kaila-essay' in three points:

Against metaphysics. By means of P = f [see above, Chapter 7, p. 205] *inductive metaphysics* also falls by the wayside. You can't derive anything that could go beyond what is already known. Examples.

Against realism. Also taken care of by means of P = f. Realism is basically therefore a variant on metaphysics, it too after all wants to derive something new. Perhaps

---

[8] Entitled 'Problem: What is the meaning of a *probability statement* about a future event? Elucidated by analogy to statements about the existence of an unseen object and about other minds' (UCLA 1928a).

[9] Referring to a distinction he had made in the *Scheinprobleme* (1928b, pp. 31–3), Carnap goes on to make this more precise: 'This idea can only be meant as an *object idea* [*Gegenstandsvorstellung*], not as a factual idea [*Sachverhaltsvorstellung*], as no true fact is simulated; if we regarded it as a factual idea and expressed it accordingly in a proposition, we would arrive at the false proposition r [(in the case of unobserved objects): "I see the book lying on the table"; (in the case of probability): "It will rain tomorrow"]. As these accompanying mental images may not be expressed by means of a proposition, one gives them (legitimate and practically useful) expression by the choice of language form p for the proposition q; the language form p stimulates the desired accompanying mental image, by coming close to the proposition r. It is distinguished from r, though, by a certain turn of phrase [e.g. (for the case of unobserved objects:) "The book is lying *unseen* on the table." etc.]' (UCLA 1928a). The psychologistic sound of this did not escape Carnap; in fact he classifies, in this table, the 'psychologistic interpretation' of the three different kinds of inferences it compares (i.e. 'The proposition p expresses a feeling of expectation') as a 'precursor to the positivistic reduction' (UCLA 1928a).

respond to Reichenbach's comparison of realist and positivist interpretations of a physical proposition.[10]

Against apriorism. Every a priori principle used in a derivation turns out to be a tautology, as we have shown that the result P says nothing more than the premises (cf. Reichenbach p. 40). (UCLA 1929c, p. 2)

Though Reichenbach had been willing (to Kaila's dismay) to describe the 'probability principle' as a 'metaphysical assumption', he had backed away, in the passage Carnap refers to here (Reichenbach 1929, pp. 40ff., 'The problem of the a priori') from classifying them as synthetic a priori.[11] Though the first and second points (*Against metaphysics* and *Against realism*) are evidently directed against Reichenbach, it seems the third was directed more against a position like that of Kaila, which holds that certain principles, such as the 'probability principle', are synthetic a priori (though Kaila did not use these words) in a *non*-Reichenbachian, *non*-conventional sense – 'that their validity does not derive from experience, but that they are correct independently of all experience' (Reichenbach 1929, p. 41).

Since Kaila was to be his main explicit target, the section on 'apriorism' in Carnap's draft was longer than the parts on 'inductive metaphysics' and 'realism'.[12] This section defined its subject as follows:

In the analysis of the sentences of science discussed earlier we distinguish, among the premises that are given for the justification of some scientific proposition, between empirical ones that reduce ultimately to the basic propositions, and non-empirical ones that we previously included under 'rules of inference'. The

[10] Discussed above (footnote 2).

[11] Here Reichenbach is consistent with his earlier position in *Relativity Theory and A Priori Knowledge* (Reichenbach 1920). Despite the crucial change in terminology after 1920, discussed by Friedman (1999, Chapter 3), here (in 1929) he once again appears to revert to his 1920 usage. There he had, on the one hand, rejected the a priori in one meaning ('*The concept of the a priori* undergoes a deep transformation through these considerations. Its one meaning, that an a priori proposition is to hold forever, independently of all experience, we can no longer uphold, after rejecting the Kantian analysis of reason' Reichenbach 1920, p. 74), but also *upheld* the a priori in a *different* meaning ('Its other meaning becomes all the more important: that the a priori principles constitute the world of experience in the first place. In fact there cannot be a single physical judgement going beyond the level of mere perception in the absence of certain assumptions about the representability of the object within a spacetime manifold and its functional context with other objects. But that does not license us to deduce that the form of these principles is determined in advance and is independent of experience.' Reichenbach 1920, p. 74) He calls these principles 'a priori' but also says they are not completely independent of experience, so this early conception seems to have been an implicitly dialectical one.

[12] Of the first draft, that is (November/December 1929), of which this section ('II. Der Apriorismus'; UCLA 1929e) is the only one to have survived; no parts of the second draft (late 1930), of which it seems thirty-five pages of shorthand were written, appear to survive except a 'Plan' later used as a rough table of contents (UCLA 1930b). The table of contents of the first draft (UCLA 1929f) shows it to have been about seventy-five pages (of shorthand) long.

non-empirical premises – the sentences that in an epistemological analysis (at any stage) are not reduced further, and do not give the contents of an experience (e.g. sense perceptions), thus do not belong to the *material* of experience – we will call '*a priori*' premises. 'Apriorism' we call the conception that there are synthetic, i.e. non-tautological a priori premises; more specifically, that such premises are to be met with in the actually practiced procedure of empirical science, and are also justified (or even indispensable). In contrast to that, '*empiricism*' will here be advocated, the conception that non-tautological a priori premises are not used in empirical science and indeed cannot be used there. (UCLA 1929e, p. 34)

In the text of this section, however (the only surviving part of the manuscript), despite this clear statement of intent, the actual practice of science received no further mention. The approach was, rather, entirely formal. Carnap first set up a logical language like that described in the 'New Foundation of Logic' (Chapter 7 above, pp. 196–203). Then he showed that the basic form of any possible non-empirical premise (one that introduces a new constant) can be regarded as giving a kind of implicit definition of the new constant: '*Result*. By laying down a sentence (to be regarded as a premise) Z, containing a new sign α, the *meaning* of α is (implicitly) *fixed*. With respect to this meaning Z is a *tautology*' (UCLA 1929e, p. 45).[13] Carnap then argued that all the different sentence forms a newly introduced non-empirical premise could have (e.g. it could be a variable, a function of individuals, a truth function of other sentences, a truth function of propositional functions, etc.) were reducible to that simplest form and thus also tautological (UCLA 1929e, pp. 49–50), and finally claimed that this list of possible forms was exhaustive, i.e. all possible consistent sentence forms were reducible to one of the given forms (UCLA 1929e, p. 40).

None of this gives us much insight how Carnap might actually have seen this to work 'in the actually practiced procedure of empirical science'. But other characterisations of the nature of theories during this time remain within the same strictly finitist, 'molecular' framework (that of the 'New Foundation'). His Bauhaus lecture on 'Der logische Aufbau der Welt' in

---

[13] The argument resulting in this conclusion makes evident that the kind of 'implicit' definition offered here is not of the axiomatic kind usually understood by this term, but a kind of contextual definition, of just the sort we saw Carnap employing above when discussing the 'analytic equivalence' of two sentences (Chapter 7, pp. 198–203). 'We begin by assuming that *only a single sign* occurs. Its way of occurring shows how the simplest sentence constructed using this sign, logical constants, and variables must look; we call it Y. We set up the truth table for the atomic sentences of Y. Then we see whether or not Y can be derived from Z in the various cases indicated by the rows of the table. The rows in which this is the case we connect by a disjunction, where each line is written as a conjunction; call this expression Y'. It reproduces the meaning of Y; for if Y is claimed, one of the chosen lines must be the case. The expression given, in which the new sign no longer occurs, we count as a definiens for Y; and that gives us a definition in use [*Gebrauchsdefinition*] of the new sign' (UCLA 1929e, p. 43).

October 1929 focused, for instance, mainly on the reductive aspect, i.e. on the distinction between cognitive meaning (*theoretischer Gehalt*) and subjective 'accompanying mental images [*Begleitvorstellungen*]', and emphasised that not only all peripheral connotations and associations belong to the latter, but all senses (intensions) as well. So all science referred only to the given; anything not entirely about the given was meaningless. Carnap again maintained (as we saw in Chapter 7), in another lecture, that a sentence that appears to be about 'gravity', for instance, really refers only to certain observation sentences; '. . . "gravity" is just a linguistic abbreviation' (ASP 1929g, pp. 1–2). We saw the wider uses of this position in 'On God and the Soul' (Chapter 6, pp. 181–4).

In another of the Bauhaus lectures, entitled 'The Task and Content of Science [*Aufgabe und Gehalt der Wissenschaft*]', Carnap also repeated the point that all meaning stems from 'particular facts [*einzelne Tatsachen*]' and nothing else. He also addressed here the question how we convey these facts by using language. '*No* language can genuinely reproduce qualities; *every* language gives merely a formal picture [*Abbildung*].' (Note how far Carnap has moved, under Wittgenstein's influence, in just three years since *Physical Concept Formation*.) And: 'The world is only *formally pictured* [*formal abgebildet*], its content is not reproduced! (i.e. certain equality or similarity relations among things are reproduced in sentences; not the essence of the things themselves)' (ASP 1929f, p. 1). On the other hand, as we also saw above: 'With the particular facts *everything is said* that can be known' (ASP 1929f, p. 2). Scientific laws are stated only for practical reasons, to be able to manage large numbers of facts economically, and to make predictions – though once again, Carnap insists that predictions are not in fact *about* the future; they are merely summaries of *past* observations.

He was caught in a fundamental dilemma (already alluded to in Chapter 7, pp. 203–7), of which another aspect here becomes visible. If the meaning of a law consists only of its already known instances, then no distinction is possible among the infinite number of laws consistent with any finite set of data points. The choice among these for our law of inference, as constitutive of the language, is entirely arbitrary. The distinction among them could only, within the view Carnap held, be a practical, heuristic one of which theory is more useful or fruitful (or perhaps simpler) – in any case a matter of what he had put beyond reach by classifying it as a merely rhetorical or practical function (*Wirkungsfunktion*) of language. Even the alternative of individuating theories by their senses or intensions had been blocked, as we saw (above, Chapter 7, pp. 204–5), by Carnap's explicit classification of sense as also part of the *Wirkungsfunktion*. An account of physics within this framework would thus have required a practical method of theory choice, an explicitly *pragmatic* conception of theories. But whatever ideas Carnap may have entertained on this front, they remained for now in the limbo to which Wittgenstein had consigned meta-discourse.

On the one hand, Carnap insisted that physical laws have *no* meaning beyond the particular experienced facts that fall under them. But on the other hand, scientific explanation was the subsumption of facts under a law. '"Explanation" in the scientific sense just means: *specification of a general statement* under which the fact falls', he said in one of the Bauhaus lectures (ASP 1929f, p. 3). But how is this relation of 'falling under', between a particular fact and a general theory, to be understood if the meaning of the general theory *just is* the conjunction of the facts that 'fall under' it? And conversely, what can we mean by a general theory? – Is the meaning of all the possible theories compatible with a finite list of observations to be regarded as identical?

That this dilemma bothered Carnap, and that he was groping for some way of accounting for scientific theories by taking the practical function (*Wirkungsfunktion*) of language more seriously, was hinted at in the short-hand notes for a lecture he contemplated, at one point in the summer of 1930, giving in Prague (perhaps his intended job talk there). This lecture outline was based almost entirely on ideas in Feigl's 1929 book *Theory and Experience in Physics* (*Theorie und Erfahrung in der Physik*).[14] Though Carnap did not give the talk in this form, it is suggestive that he should even have considered it. It also gives some clues how he might have tried to revive the 'clarification' project if he had not soon afterwards discarded the Wittgensteinian theory of meaning that had broken apart the two main components of rational reconstruction.

The notes scribbled for this Prague lecture *begin* with the relation between these two parts, in fact – he specifically addresses the difference between the 'psychological' and the 'physical' knowledge methods (*Erkenntnismethoden*). The psychological method is based on qualities, he says, on 'allocation into classes, topological order', while 'the step to physics occurs by

---

[14] Whether they were Feigl's or Carnap's ideas is not clear; they were in close touch during this period, conversed often, and Feigl acknowledges a debt to Carnap. Also, Carnap had originally agreed to write this volume (in the same series as *Physical Concept Formation*), signed a contract for it, and only suggested Feigl as a substitute when he ran out of time at the last moment; he may well have had some ideas for it that he passed on to Feigl. In his autobiography, Carnap mentions that Poincaré's and Duhem's influence 'on *my* philosophical thinking' (emphasis added) is evident 'in the two small companion volumes on physics by myself and by Feigl written when we were in Vienna' (1963, pp. 77–8).

the method of coincidence', i.e. with measurement.[15] One theme in Feigl's book he particularly stresses in this connection is the difference between 'Genesis and validity [*Gültigkeit*] of physical theories'. True, physical theories may often *arise* from a subjective belief in theoretical entities, or from deductive manipulation of initially empty axiom systems (which define their concepts implicitly), but their *Gültigkeit* can only be established on a limited, probabilistic basis (ASP 1929b). It seems he may, by this route, have been exploring the possibility of a new and more positive role for theories. To use his later jargon, he perhaps thought that although theories and their senses or other accompanying mental images (*Begleitvorstellungen*) lack *cognitive* meaning (pertaining to *Gültigkeit*), they might be regarded as having an essential practical or *heuristic* meaning (pertaining to *Genesis*). This is certainly the tendency of Feigl's text (Feigl 1929, esp. pp. 114–16). Like Feigl (1929, pp. 104–10), however, Carnap also includes a 'remark against conventionalism', which he portrays (with Dingler as the prime example) as greatly *over*emphasising the independence of theories from empirical fact, as well as exaggerating the role of regulative principles like simplicity: 'We always want to have the coordinative definitions as simple as possible; we accept complications in the axiom system. For the goal is not to make (seemingly) simple statements about the world. We want, rather, to talk about *reality* in the language of physical theory (against Dingler)' (ASP 1929b). Again, this is an argument that violates his official position of radical positivism; it employs a regulative ideal that is not expressible in the terms he officially regards as meaningful.[16]

THE COLLAPSE OF LOGICISM

In February 1930 Alfred Tarski came to Vienna for an extended visit that would play a key role in Carnap's development. Apart from Tarski's lectures, 'chiefly on meta-mathematics', Carnap recalls private discussions:

---

[15] It seems likely that Carnap is following Feigl's usage here (Feigl was Schlick's student) rather than referring specifically to Schlick's own version of the 'method of coincidences' (Schlick 1918, pp. 234ff.). Note also that the characterisation of the 'physical method' here is not dissimilar to Kaila's, as described above in this section.

[16] The apparent realism expressed in the quotation need not be taken too seriously. Any temptation to attribute it to Feigl's influence would be anachronistic, as in the book concerned, Feigl is very clear (e.g. pp. 134–5) that he uses the word 'reality [*Wirklichkeit*]' in a purely empirical, not in an ontological sense; he refers to the *Aufbau* and *Scheinprobleme* to indicate that ontological questions are pseudo-problems. It was only much later, in the USA, that Feigl began showing tendencies toward a more ambiguous realism.

Of special interest to me was his emphasis that certain concepts used in logical investigations, e.g. the consistency of axioms, the provability of a theorem in the deductive system, and the like, are to be expressed not in the language of the axioms (later called the object language), but in the meta-mathematical language (later called the meta-language). (1963, p. 30)

It was from these lectures and discussions, it seems, that Carnap derived the idea that it would be desirable to develop a precise meta-language in which discourse *about* the language of science could be framed. After Tarski's lecture to the Circle on the meta-mathematics of the propositional calculus, 'the question was raised whether meta-mathematics was of value also for philosophy'. And Carnap adds, 'I had gained the impression in my talks with Tarski that the formal theory of language was of great importance for the clarification of our philosophical problems'. The rest of the Circle (especially Schlick) were sceptical. After Tarski left, Carnap tried to make the new idea clear to his colleagues:

I tried to explain that it would be a great advantage for our philosophical discussions if a method were developed by which not only the analyzed object language, e.g., that of mathematics or physics, would be made exact, but also the philosophical meta-language used in the discussion. I pointed out that most of the puzzles, disagreements, and mutual misunderstandings in our discussions arose from the inexactness of the meta-language. (1963, p. 30)

Schlick's resistance was evidently motivated by the incompatibility of such an idea with Wittgenstein's strictures on meta-linguistic elucidations. Carnap had never entirely accepted those strictures, and in any case, he seems to have thought that the new meta-linguistic sentences could somehow ultimately be reduced to the single-language, Wittgensteinian, 'molecular' form (see below). In his autobiography, he does not even mention the immediate impact of these meetings on his own work – the *Axiomatics* project was abandoned.[17] We can date this event with some precision. A page of shorthand notes dated 22 February 1930 records a 'conversation with Tarski about categoricity [*Monomorphie*]'. Here Carnap recognises that 'nicht gabelbar' (essentially 'categorical') could not be defined in the basic system or 'foundation discipline [*Grunddisziplin*]' except under very specific assumptions. It was not clear at this point whether the meta-mathematical definitions and his old ones could be shown to be equivalent. But Tarski does seem to have convinced him that the meta-mathematical definition of 'decidable [*Entscheidungsdefinit*]', using 'or' in the meta-language rather than 'v' within the system (as in Carnap's previous definition), made 'decidable' a

---

[17] The next page, once again, draws on Awodey and Carus (2001).

clearly distinct notion from 'categorical [*monomorph*]' and 'nicht gabelbar' – 'since logic is not decidable' (ASP 1930a, p. 1). The last mention of the *Axiomatics* in Carnap's diary is on 24 February 1930, two days after this discussion note: 'Tarski visits me . . . talked about my *Axiomatics*. It seems correct, but certain concepts don't capture what is intended; they must be defined meta-mathematically rather than mathematically' (ASP 1930b).

But despite seeing the advantages of a precise meta-language for philosophy, and understanding Tarski's explanations, Carnap seems nonetheless to have gone on thinking there might be some way to avoid making these meta-mathematical definitions fundamental or ultimate. He still wanted to be able to interpret meta-mathematical concepts in some way as ultimately definable in terms of truth functions of atomic sentences. Though unlike Schlick he was happy to consider the idea of a precise meta-language, he continued to share Schlick's Wittgensteinian reluctance to regard *meaning* as constitutable any other way than as truth-functional reducibility to atomic sentences.

In the 'Discussion about the Foundations of Mathematics' in Königsberg later that year, Carnap put it very much like this following the symposium where he had presented the case for logicism (with Heyting speaking for intuitionism and von Neumann for formalism). Interestingly, he put his view forward as that of the *physicist*, opposed both to that of the *logician*, exemplified not only by Frege and Russell but also by Brouwer, and to that of the *mathematician*, exemplified by Hilbert. The logician, he said, makes the demand that 'every sign in the language . . . must have a definite, specifiable meaning', while the mathematician says, 'We feel no obligation to be held accountable for the meaning of mathematical signs; we demand the right to operate axiomatically in freedom, i.e. to set up axioms and operational specifications for a mathematical field and then to find the consequences formalistically' (Hahn *et al.* 1931, p. 141). Carnap saw his logicist standpoint – that of the physicist – as a way of reconciling these apparently incompatible views:

[Logicism] demands of the logico-mathematical system not only that it be consistent in itself, but that it be applicable in the field of empirical science. For it is the true purpose [*der eigentliche Sinn*] of this system to say how consequences can be deduced, i.e. which transformations of sentences are allowed. (Hahn *et al.* 1931, p. 141)

What he has in mind, though, is precisely the Wittgensteinian standard of 'applicable'. The logico-mathematical system is 'applicable' in this sense if it licenses truth-functional inference from atomic sentences to quantitative theoretical statements. Just as we demand of a deductive system, Carnap says, that it get us from 'All persons are mortal' and 'All Greeks are persons' to 'All Greeks are mortal' – a condition that all usable deductive systems meet – so we are justified in demanding that we be able to get from atomic sentences to quantitative statements. We want to be able to get from the sentence 'In this room are only the persons Hans and Peter' to the sentence 'In this room there are two persons'. Otherwise, Carnap says, we are unable to *apply* arithmetic to empirical matters. Frege–Russell logicism meets this requirement: 'With the Frege–Russell definition of number the required deduction is possible', while by Hilbert's axiomatic definition that is not so clear, though 'the exact form of the axiom system hasn't been given yet'. However, Carnap maintains, 'formalism can't get around giving operational rules for mathematical signs, i.e. rules that determine the use of these signs not only within mathematics but also in empirical science. And by this determination the meaning of all signs is then implicitly fixed' (Hahn *et al.* 1931, p. 142).

What he has in mind here is more explicit in a manuscript from November 1929. Here, using the same example as the following autumn in Königsberg, he says what kind of 'operational rules' or 'auxiliary premises [*Hilfsprämissen*]' he is thinking of:

For mathematics to be applicable to reality, which is the intent of the formalistic construction as well, there must occur formulas, among those by which the number-signs are introduced, that make it possible to infer an empirical statement containing numbers [*empirische Zahlaussage*] from empirical statements. For instance we need an auxiliary premise to be able to derive, from 'Fritz is now in this room' and 'Karl is now in this room' the sentence 'There are now *two* people in this room.' If we could not derive such a sentence, we would not be in a position to use number signs in the description of reality, as they certainly don't appear in the basic statements [*Grundaussagen*]; no application whatever of mathematics to reality would be possible. But if we introduce an auxiliary premise of the required kind, it will be tautological, as it is supposed to be valid independently of the empirically actual world configuration [*der empirisch vorliegenden Weltgestalt*]. But this determines the meaning of the sign 'two'. The axiom about 'two' (as lower bound) could have something like the following form:

$$(f\mathrm{x} \mathbin{\&} f\mathrm{y} \mathbin{\&} g\mathrm{x} \mathbin{\&} \neg\, g\mathrm{y}) \to 2_\mathrm{m}(f)$$

(The use of *g* is needed here to express the fact that x and y are distinct.) It is easy to obtain a definition of '2' from this that is closely related to that proposed by Frege and Russell.

If the numbers are defined, and also their combination [*Verknüpfung*] (e.g. addition by considering the disjunction between two mutually exclusive properties), then the formulas of finite arithmetic follow as tautologies. (UCLA 1929e, pp. 61–2)

The 'auxiliary axiom' for the applicability of 'two' was proposed as a principle of *logic*; it was 'tautological, as it is supposed to be valid independently of the empirically given world configuration'. Since it was to be part of the rules defining the 'logic', in the sense of the 'New Foundation', anything defined on its basis was 'analytically equivalent' to its definiens. Hilbert would presumably have regarded such an axiom as pointless, or as merely putting the intuitions about 'discrete patterns' (that he thought underlay finitary meta-mathematics) into words.

What was Carnap's underlying motivation in proposing such an 'auxiliary axiom'? In the context of the Königsberg discussion, it seems clearly to be part of a conception of 'meaning' – the Wittgensteinian one – that would soon be abandoned. However, this is not the end of the story. The idea comes up in his autobiography, thirty years later, when he discusses this pre-*Syntax* period (when the influence of Hilbert became 'clearly visible'):

We were not satisfied with Hilbert's skepticism about the possibility of giving an interpretation to the total formal system of mathematics. Frege had already strongly emphasised that the foundation problems of mathematics can only be solved if we look not solely at pure mathematics but also at the use of mathematical concepts in factual sentences. He had found his explication of cardinal numbers by asking himself the question: What does 'five' mean in contexts like 'I have five fingers on my right hand'? Since Schlick and I came to philosophy from physics, we looked at mathematics always from the point of view of its application in empirical science. The idea occurred to me that from the point of view of this application there seemed to be a possibility of reconciling the conflict between logicism and formalism. Suppose that mathematics is first constructed as a purely formal system in Hilbert's way, and that rules are then added for the application of the mathematical symbols and sentences in physics, and for the use of mathematical theorems for deductions within the language of physics. Then, it seemed to me, these latter rules must implicitly give an interpretation of mathematics. I was convinced that this latter interpretation would essentially agree with the logicist interpretation of Frege and Russell. (1963, p. 48)

Had he, in intervening decades, had some other idea for the kinds of 'auxiliary premises' or 'application rules' this idea was to employ? Had the idea become something else in his mind? It is not clear how he means this, as no other trace of the 'principle of analytic equivalence' (or 'New Foundation of Logic') phase of 1929–30 is referred to in his autobiography. It seems likely that the memory he had retained of this episode was sufficiently neutral with respect to the wider, Wittgensteinian background, and sufficiently separable from it, that he assimilated 'auxiliary premises' to something like his later 'correspondence rules'. And this is interesting because in both these cases, the use of 'correspondence rules' in a mathematical question of this kind indicates an openness to the Hilbertian, axiomatic, structuralist approach to mathematics – along the lines of Bourbaki – that he was officially opposing, at Königsberg and during the entire period before 1931. Even after that, he retained a strong preference – within a wider pluralistic environment – for languages built from the ground up, i.e. for a 'constructivist' or 'genetic'[18] conception, perhaps from a residual attachment to Frege's logicism. But his overriding priority was to find an account of mathematics that would portray it as not having any content of its own, not contributing anything to the factual knowledge it transforms. Though he had his own rooted bottom-up prejudices how such an account should go, he signalled (in passages such as the above) that he was also open to other approaches, should technical expedience favour them in the end (Awodey 2007).

Meanwhile, at the 1930 Königsberg conference, though, Carnap evidently combined this idea with a continuing hope that Hilbert's and Tarski's meta-mathematical 'method of bifurcation [*Methode der Zweiteilung*]' could still be reduced in principle to a single language of truth functions of atomic sentences. And the programme he spells out for this still seems to rely on the hope, despite his conversations with Tarski in February, and despite his abandonment of the *Axiomatics*, that the *Gabelbarkeitssatz* might still hold in some form:

My supposition . . . is that this logical analysis of the formalistic system will have the following result (if this supposition turns out to hold, then despite the formalist method of construction, logicism would be justified and the opposition between the two approaches would be overcome):

1. For every mathematical sign one or more *interpretations* are found, and in fact purely logical interpretations.
2. If the axiom system is consistent, then upon replacing each mathematical sign by its logical interpretation (or any one of its various interpretations), every *mathematical formula* becomes a *tautology* (a generally valid sentence).
3. If the axiom system is complete (in Hilbert's sense: no non-derivable formula can be added without contradiction), then the interpretation is unique [*eindeutig*]; every sign has exactly one interpretation, and with that the formalist construction is transformed into a logicist one. (1930, pp. 143–4)

---

[18] Hilbert's (1917) term.

The last point appears to rely specifically on the theorem that every complete axiom system is also categorical (the *Gabelbarkeitssatz*, in one direction); and Carnap seems to have thought that his 'auxiliary premises' could then transform a categorical axiom system into a unique one. At the same meeting in Königsberg, of course, Gödel had mentioned his theorem – which Carnap had already heard about, though probably not completely understood – that (using *'Zweiteilung'*) had shown the *Gabelbarkeitssatz* to be false. At the session where Gödel referred to his theorem – Carnap was probably in the audience – he makes clear that he had its destructive consequences for Carnap's *Axiomatics* in mind (Gödel 1930; Awodey and Carus 2001, p. 164; Goldfarb 2005).

By the time of the Königsberg conference, Carnap had scarcely absorbed the full implications of Gödel's shocking theorem. Insofar as he had considered its implications, it appears from his diary entries during this period that his attention was focused on the consequences of the theorem not for logicism but for Hilbert's programme. The very first entry in which Carnap mentions Gödel's discovery indicates that Gödel himself already saw that the second theorem was implied: 'difficulty of the consistency proof' (ASP 1930g). Certainly this was the most obvious and spectacular destructive consequence of the theorems, and the one that most riveted the attention of the mathematical world.

But the consequences for logicism (especially in the form of the Vienna Circle's 'tautologicism') must very soon have become evident to Carnap, possibly even before Königsberg, though he would no longer have had time to revise his contributions to the 'foundations' debate in the time available. Even with the attempt to turn implicit definitions into explicit ones along the lines of the *Axiomatics*, and even if the 'New Foundation of Logic' or the addition of 'auxiliary premises' had succeeded in reducing all mathematical statements into truth-functions of atomic sentences, there were nonetheless true sentences of arithmetic that could not be proved. Gödel's result showed that Carnap's axiomatic efforts had, in a sense, been irrelevant to the problems he had been trying to solve. By late 1930, once Carnap had had time to consider and absorb this, the implications were clear. And at that point, he no longer hesitated. The tension between the Wittgensteinian and Hilbertian approaches was resolved in favour of the latter.

But meanwhile, with the foundation for rational reconstruction crumbling, the original agreement within the Circle about the kind of structure to erect on that foundation also began to fray. The Circle began to split into a 'right wing' (Schlick and Waismann, who clung to the Wittgensteinian view, and were increasingly influenced by Wittgenstein personally) and a 'left wing' (headed by Neurath and Hahn). One of the central issues over which these sides disagreed was how to respond to Wittgenstein's issue of meta-linguistic elucidations. Carnap was sympathetic to the 'left wing', but as ever he played the mediator:

Carnap: the difference between Wittgenstein's and Neurath's position consists in the following: According to Wittgenstein there are propositions and then elucidations of propositions. The latter one could call improper propositions about sentences. They are the propositions that try to clarify the relation between propositions and the given. According to Neurath, there are no such propositions, they are superfluous. There are only protocol sentences and physical propositions. The so-called elucidations must either be transformable in a behaviorist sense into propositions about the behavior of the speaker or, if this is not possible, they belong not to science at all but to metaphysics. *Schlick*: The elucidations are not propositions, but actions. Perhaps it is possible to describe them in the behaviourist sense. *Carnap*: This would lead to very serious consequences. If there are only propositions and one can't explain the sense of sentences, but only makes statements about linguistic signs . . . then the whole problem of the picturing of the given [*Abbildung des Gegebenen*] by means of propositions disappears. (ASP1931d; Stadler 1997, p. 291; PT 256)

Carnap alludes, in this last sentence, to the new conception he had arrived at only a month before this meeting. This new conception not only gave him a way of acceding to Neurath's demand without losing the 'legitimate' elucidations needed to eliminate metaphysics; it also supplied a positive account of the status of science and mathematics. He was willing to face the 'serious consequences' this entailed – a complete overhaul of the conceptual platform on which the Vienna Circle's entire programme had rested since its inception as a movement.

CHAPTER 9

Liberation

On 21 January 1931 Carnap came down with a flu, and hardly slept that night. While tossing and turning, he had an idea how to escape the predicament described in the last two chapters. When he got up the next morning, he sat down and sketched an outline. The title he put down was '*Versuch einer Metalogik*' ('Attempt at a metalogic'). He calls it by the same name, then, that he had given his effort at a 'general axiomatics' a few years earlier (above, Chapter 7, note 5). In both cases, the allusion was to Hilbert's 'meta-mathematics'. But in the first case, as we saw, the object of the 'meta-logic' had been to *assimilate* Hilbert's meta-mathematics into the object language, i.e. into a logicist framework. So the 'meta-logic' of 1927–9 had not really been 'meta'. All the object languages within the scope of the *General Axiomatics* had been situated in a 'basic system', which defined a *single* language that *adumbrated* both metalanguage and object language. But now, in January 1931, the 'meta-logic' is genuine.

This was not simply a return, of course, to where he had been in 1926 or before; the Wittgensteinian captivity had left its mark, and the meta-logic that emerged in early 1931 was a chastened one. The requirement that meta-discourse remain internal to a single language system (of object language and a specific hierarchy of meta-languages) remained in force. And though for Carnap this new step was certainly a liberation, he remained within the Wittgensteinian ambit in one very important respect. Up to this point, he and the Vienna Circle had been struggling desperately to accommodate the possibility of elucidations, of a meta-discourse, within the domain of *empirical* meaning. What Carnap realised in his sleepless night was that this entire strategy – which was not working – could be dropped. There was another way sentences could be significant, in the Wittgensteinian view; there were the tautologies of logic. And this was Carnap's new strategy: the meta-discourse could become part of *logic* instead.

THE SYNTAX BREAKTHROUGH

The importance of this step is reflected in the uncharacteristically dramatic description Carnap gives of it in his autobiography:

After thinking about these problems for several years, the whole theory of language structure and its possible applications in philosophy came to me like a vision during a sleepless night in January 1931, when I was ill. On the following day, still in bed with a fever, I wrote down my ideas on forty-four pages under the title 'Attempt at a Metalogic'. These shorthand notes were the first version of my book *Logical Syntax of Language*. (1963, p. 53)

The actual 'Attempt at a Metalogic' (which has been partially preserved) does not, however, resemble the *Logical Syntax* in the least. Only against the background of the thought process reconstructed in the last two chapters can the significance of this document be deciphered.[1] In contrast to the 'New Foundation' (above, Chapter 7, pp. 196–203), Carnap now adopts the fully formal viewpoint of Hilbert, Gödel, and Tarski, according to which the logical language is a system of uninterpreted marks rather than meaningful signs. As he would put it in another manuscript a few weeks later:

In the calculus we 'calculate' with the signs, i.e. we carry out operations on the sign complexes according to certain rules, without regard to the *meaning* of the signs. We *can* certainly attend to the meanings of the signs, e.g. to a certain sentence in connection with 'p', or to the meaning of the word 'or' in connection with 'v', etc. The essential thing is that in the operation rules these meanings are not mentioned. (UCLA 1931e, p. 18)

In the 'New Foundation', the atomic sentences had been pictures of atomic facts, and this had given them their meaning. In the *Versuch*, an atomic sentence is a finite sequence of superscript dots, followed by the letter 'f' with a finite sequence of subscript dots, followed by a left parenthesis, followed by the letter 'a' with a finite sequence of subscript dots, followed by a right parenthesis, e.g.:

$$\overset{....}{f}_{..}(a_{..})$$

An atomic sentence was thus a certain finite string of finitely many basic marks (*Zeichen*), equivalence classes of certain two-dimensional arrangements of pencil or chalk traces, arranged in some order. The particular instances of a *Zeichen* were *physical* marks, at a particular location on the

---

[1] Of the original shorthand document, pp. 1–23 and 44 are preserved in UCLA 1931b. The present discussion overlaps in several places with my paper about it (with Steve Awodey) 'Carnap's Dream: Gödel, Wittgenstein, and *Logical Syntax*' (Awodey and Carus forthcoming).

blackboard or on a page, which represent the *Zeichen* of the calculus just as a geometrical diagram represents relations in pure, uninterpreted mathematical geometry.

In the 'New Foundation', a sentence is a tautology because of what it says, or not, about the world. In the *Versuch*, being a tautology is a property of a string of marks that is defined entirely in terms of its outer form – the type and order of the marks occurring in it. No use is made of the 'meaning' or 'designation' of the marks (*Zeichen*) in defining the central notions of truth-value assignment, consequence or tautology. 'The calculus-theory, in which we set up the rules and describe the operations, has the signs themselves, configured on paper, as its object' (UCLA 1931e, p. 18). Carnap even mentions that the undefined notion 'true' might be better to avoid entirely.[2]

This idea represented no technical innovation in logic; it was an application of Hilbert's axiomatic, meta-mathematical method, further developed by Gödel and Tarski. But Carnap's idea was precisely to *apply* this approach to the entirety of human knowledge. Since the rational reconstruction programme, during the Vienna years, had rested on Wittgenstein's basic account of the logical language framework in which all knowledge was to be expressed, the Hilbertian perspective of regarding language purely as a system of rules, without reference to anything outside itself, was indeed revolutionary. It gave Carnap a way of escaping the confinement of all possible knowledge within the absolute constraints imposed by a (naturally or metaphysically) fixed structure of our means of expression, and offered an alternative method for the unification and clarification of knowledge.

To avoid mortgaging the meta-logic to supposed 'necessities' of representation or assumptions about the world, Carnap hoped to dispense entirely with 'existential presuppositions'. Arithmetic was to be formulated without assuming any axioms; he envisaged in the *Versuch* that arithmetic could simply be read off from the syntax of the logical object language – as opposed to being expressed in that language.[3] Thus the numbers are not defined as higher-order concepts in the logicist style of Frege and Russell, but 'purely as figures' (*rein figurell*), on the basis of the dot sequences attached to the symbols. Arithmetical properties and statements then belong to the

---

[2] In the margin of p. 3 of the manuscript, Carnap has scrawled, 'Regarding the undefined concept "*true*". It is completely different from the other concepts of metalogic. Perhaps avoidable? [Perhaps] just define which atomic sentences are the "basis" of a sentence, and how (?).' A few weeks later, as we will see below, he is more definite: 'in metalogic we cannot work with the concepts of truth and falsehood' (UCLA 1931e, p. 26).

[3] An addition of 7 February 1931 to the manuscript says, 'the syntax of the rows of dots is arithmetic' (UCLA 1931b, p. 1).

meta-language. The commutativity of addition, for instance, was supposed to follow from the fact that n-many dots written to the left of m-many dots gives the same series of dots as writing them to the right of m-many dots. Mathematical induction *in the meta-language* is considered, but declared superfluous on the basis of a rather hasty proof that, on inspection, turns out to be circular (making implicit use of induction).

If arithmetic was to be formulated in the meta-language of logic, then analysis was to be formulated in its meta-meta-language; real numbers are properties or series of natural numbers, and their properties and statements about them, in turn, belong one level up. Carnap may have been guided, in this idea, by Russell's suggestion, in his introduction to the *Tractatus*, that one could escape from the Wittgensteinian impossibility of talking about language by using a hierarchy of languages:

> These difficulties suggest to my mind some such possibility as this: that every language has, as Mr. Wittgenstein says, a structure concerning which, *in the language*, nothing can be said, but that there may be another language dealing with the structure of the first language, and having itself a new structure, and that to this hierarchy of languages there may be no limit. (Russell 1922, p. 286)

Carnap had now, he thought, found a way of implementing this idea, and of applying it to achieve a hierarchy consisting of language, meta-language, meta-meta-language, and so on;[4] this must initially have seemed very compelling. It had seemed that he could get arithmetic 'for free' – without any specifically *arithmetic* assumptions. Had this worked, he would have achieved the logicist reduction of mathematics to logic without even having to build any tendentious presuppositions into the 'logic'.

Carnap says that not only 'the whole theory of language structure' came to him like a vision, but also 'its possible applications in philosophy'. The most important of these was the recovery of a substantive meta-discourse. He later recounted that 'the philosophical problems in which we were interested ended up with problems of the logical analysis of language', and since 'in our view the issue in philosophical problems concerned the language, not the world', the Circle thought that 'these problems should be formulated not in the object language but in the metalanguage'. It was therefore his '*chief motivation*' (my emphasis) for the 'development of the syntactical

---

[4] The *Versuch* ends with a summary in four points: '(1) The particular *natural numbers* occur as signs of *the language itself*. (2) The so-called "*properties of natural numbers*" are not proper properties, but syntactic (Wittgenstein: internal) ones, so are to be expressed in the *metalanguage*. (3) A particular *real number* is a property or sequence of natural numbers, so is also to be expressed in the *metalanguage*. (4) The *properties of real numbers* are not real properties, but syntactic properties (with respect to the syntax of the metalanguage), and thus *to be expressed in the meta-metalanguage*' (UCLA 1931b, p. 44).

method' to develop a 'suitable metalanguage' that would 'essentially contribute toward greater clarity in the formulation of philosophical problems
and greater fruitfulness in their discussions' (1963, p. 55). In the *Versuch*
itself, there is no hint of this or any other philosophical application. On
the contrary, the new meta-logical standpoint would, if anything, appear
on the surface to *undermine* the Vienna Circle's previous critique of metaphysics (based on the *Tractatus* theory of meaning). Carnap's excitement at
the new idea seems indeed to have derived at least partly from the prospect
it held out of a new and *entirely different* basis for that critique – one that
was no longer dependent on the success of Frege–Russell logicism or any
other foundational programme.

Meaning, in the sense of empirical content (the Vienna Circle's 'downward extension' of the *Tractatus*), could be dispensed with, in this new
conception, as a criterion for distinguishing between metaphysical and scientific statements. Instead, a 'suitable meta-language' would be created,
whose point would reside precisely in its complete *avoidance* of material
reference. Sentences in this standard language would have no empirical
content whatever; it would be an abstract system of content-free signs,
referring only to other systems of signs (especially to the language of science, in abstraction from its empirical content). Previously, the Vienna
Circle had attempted by hook or crook to give meta-linguistic elucidations some kind of *empirical* status. Now Carnap proposed the opposite:
empirical status was to be reserved *only* to the language of empirical science
itself. (How this empirical status was to be conferred on sentences in *that*
language was a problem Carnap bracketed, for now, but it soon issued in
the 'protocol sentence debate', and would continue to haunt him, in various forms, all his life.) The purely *formal* meta-language would henceforth
be the only vehicle for elucidations. This suggested a natural criterion to
distinguish legitimate from illegitimate elucidations: legitimate ones were
to be framed in a standard meta-language, and would not refer to any supposed extra-linguistic *objects*. So a legitimate elucidation had to be formal
in exactly the sense that an uninterpreted axiom system, e.g. of geometry,
is entirely formal. Otherwise it would necessarily be empirical, and thus be
the province of a special science, i.e. judgeable by the criteria of that special
science.

This is a radically different basis for the critique of metaphysics from the
picture theory, on which the Vienna Circle had relied in all its well-known
pronouncements (and is associated with to this day). Meaning was no longer
the issue. Atomic sentences, as pictures of atomic facts, no longer play any
role in distinguishing meaningful from meaningless sentences. The new

meta-logical or syntactic viewpoint is significant, as Eino Kaila agreed after discussion with Carnap a few months later, because of its 'elimination of verification by comparison with facts [*Ausschaltung der Verifikation durch Vergleich mit Sachverhalten*]' (ASP 1931m).

THE CANONICAL META-LANGUAGE

Carnap immediately threw himself into the task of developing the 'suitable meta-language', the canonical 'meta-logic' for what would soon be called the 'formal mode of speech'. But the framework of the *Versuch* turned out to be insufficient, and over the first half of 1931, it went through a number of modifications before it resembled anything like even Language I of the *Syntax* book published three years later.

Carnap worked at the *Versuch* for a week or two after the sleepless night, then took a step back and tried to put the new approach in perspective, so as to explain its place within an elementary exposition of logic and method (for a popular series Neurath was planning) tentatively entitled *Introduction to Scientific Philosophy* (UCLA 1930c, 1931a, 1931c). Its first part ('The Language of Science') was to be an overview of language, logic, and mathematics. (There was also to be a second part covering the empirical sciences, including psychology and social science, emphasising their unity.) This project was begun in earnest in late February (UCLA 1931d) and, by 11 March, Carnap had written 115 pages of 'The Language of Science' in shorthand (UCLA 1931h).

The general goal of this project was to make plausible in the simplest terms that all of logic – all reasoning – could be represented purely formally. Elementary propositional logic is first introduced using truth tables to define the connectives, the notions of 'range' and 'content' (as well as 'sameness of content'), logical consequence, and the concepts of tautology and contradiction. Then there is an abrupt change of gear:

Now we shall go on to revisit this entire train of thought in a different form, this time with the help of the '*calculus*', of calculation with logical formulas. We must learn this method as it is an exact and indispensable tool for applications . . . In a sense, we have two languages before us here. The first consists of the 'logical formulas', sign-complexes in which the signs 'p', 'q', . . . , '∼', 'v' are concatenated in a certain way. In the second language, which we are now considering, we pay no attention to the meaning [*Sinn*] of the logical formulas; we do not distinguish, as in the first language, whether p is true or false. In this second language, the so-called *metalogical language*, we form '*metalogical*' concepts with which to describe the formulas of the first language as figural complexes. (UCLA 1931e, pp. 17–18)

The particular challenge that most preoccupied Carnap was to reinterpret the 'content' of a sentence in purely formal terms. In the first part of 'The Language of Science', he had introduced the 'content' of a sentence, along Wittgensteinian lines, as the set of rows of its truth table a sentence excludes (the 'range' – the complement of 'content' – was thus the set of rows in which the sentence is true). The problem of finding a formal equivalent for this pair of concepts merged therefore into the larger problem of defining 'tautology' in purely formal terms, since a tautology, true in *all* rows of its truth table, has *no* content. And of course 'one of the principal tasks of metalogic is to stipulate [*festzusetzen*] whether a formula is a tautology'. But this in turn raised the very problem Gödel had addressed in his just-published incompleteness paper; provability from the axioms was no longer an adequate criterion for tautologous-ness. A stronger alternative had to be found – something that could still count as 'formal', i.e. be solely an artefact of rules, but not rely on truth (since 'in metalogic we cannot work with the concepts of truth and falsehood', UCLA 1931e, p. 26). This was to be a stronger sort of logical truth than provability in a formal system, but was still to be determined strictly in terms of the formal character of the symbols.

A chess analogy[5] may help clarify what Carnap needed here. Think of the starting position of the pieces on a chessboard as the axioms, the permitted moves as the rules of inference, and a sequence of moves ending in checkmate as a proof of a theorem. But now observe that there are configurations of pieces on the board that constitute checkmate, but cannot be reached from the starting position by any sequence of permitted rules. Such a configuration represents an analytic sentence that has no proof. In this way, it should be possible, Carnap thought, to define 'analytic sentence' entirely formally, in accordance with all the same rules of inference as 'provable sentence', and yet still give a wider scope to 'analytic' than to 'provable'. Analyticity could thus play the role that the Wittgensteinian conception of tautology had played in the earlier Vienna Circle conception – indeed a weightier role, as it now also functioned effectively as the concept of truth in the meta-language.

'Tautology' could be defined formally for propositional logic simply by setting up a correspondence with the truth-table schema. But 'for the later parts of the calculus (functional calculus, construction of arithmetic) a different procedure, the axiomatic one, is indispensable' (UCLA 1931e, p. 26). It is not clear how Carnap envisaged the axiomatic construction of

---

[5] Due to Steve Awodey.

arithmetic at this point, except that he evidently wanted to steer clear of any axiomatisation that could fall afoul of Gödel incompleteness. He set about attempting to define 'content' and 'tautology' in purely combinatorial terms, without explicitly invoking any axioms of arithmetic. The idea of arbitrarily long truth tables over complete state-descriptions, from the 'New Foundation of Logic', was revived, and translated into a formal equivalent (UCLA 1931g, pp. 41–59).

Still working in the framework of this plan for an *Introduction to Scientific Philosophy* (UCLA 1931g, 1931i), Carnap began on 25 March to write a new section on 'Mathematics as a Part of Syntax' (UCLA 1931k).[6] A week or two later, he realised that the section on mathematics was getting disproportionately long and complicated (UCLA 1931l, 1931m). So it now became an independent project that he referred to as 'Foundation [*Grundlegung*] of Mathematics' (UCLA 1931m, 1931n). He started over several times (UCLA 1931o); on 11 April he considered Skolem's primitive recursive arithmetic as the framework for the object language (UCLA 1931p). And on 15 April, he started again, now under the title 'Logic, Metalogic, and Mathematics' (UCLA 1931q). A few days later, his diary records a conversation with Gödel, about 'my attempt at a logic without existential presuppositions'. The real numbers, he realises, will not be attainable with such a starting point. Gödel suggests 'Brouwer's method' (ASP 1931i).

In the following days, sometime between 21 April and 7 May, there was a change of direction. Up to then, as the conversation with Gödel indicates, Carnap had persisted in the original January attempt to dispense entirely with existential presuppositions. This had been the surest way of guaranteeing that the new strategy left no hostages to fate, and depended on nothing but linguistic conventions. But in late April, the difficulty of constructing the real numbers seems to have convinced him that there was no way to get arithmetic for free; he would have to introduce certain assumptions into the meta-language after all. These could still be regarded as conventions, not 'existential' in the sense that they assume something about the world or about the nature of representation. But they did leave a hostage to fate: if they should turn out to have questionable consequences, could substitutes be found that lacked those consequences but did the required work? Carnap therefore tried to keep the assumptions to the barest minimum by opting for Skolem's primitive recursive arithmetic. Language I was now recognisably in sight.

[6] He also, that same day, wrote a section of the *Introduction to Scientific Philosophy* itself entitled 'The Tautological Character of Inference' (UCLA 1931j); it is not entirely clear how the two were to be related.

On 7 May, at a meeting of the Circle, he announced that he would soon be giving an exposition of his new meta-logic, in which he would show that it is possible to speak about language, even 'in a certain sense' in the same language (ASP 1931k; Stadler 1997, p. 304; PT p. 269). This can only mean that by then he had at least tentatively decided on an axiomatic arithmetic, enabling him to arithmetise the syntactic meta-language, Gödel style. How seriously he took this idea as the framework for the canonical meta-language itself, at this point, is not clear; the first notes we have of a system resembling the one he actually presented to the Vienna Circle in June are from late May, and the first notes of an arithmetised meta-logic are from 17 June, the day before he presented it to the Circle (UCLA 1931r)!

The three lectures to the Vienna Circle on meta-logic, in June 1931, were recorded (somewhat elliptically) by Rose Rand (ASP 1931l; Stadler 1997, pp. 314–29; PT pp. 279–94), together with a further discussion in the following meeting on 2 July (ASP 1931n; Stadler 1997, pp. 330–4; PT pp. 294–9). The first two lectures (except some brief concluding remarks in the second) essentially recapitulate the idea of the *Versuch*. Carnap begins by mentioning two motivations for his work on meta-logic: '(1) what changes to the Russellian language will be useful? (2) The form of the metalogic: are there sentences about sentences, what meaning [*Sinn*] do they have, are they empirical sentences or tautologies, does a hierarchy of languages arise?' (ASP 1931l; Stadler 1997, p. 314; PT p. 279). The problems of logicism evidently loomed large, but so did the problem of meta-discourse. 'What is the purpose of introducing these signs?' Carnap asks, after his initial exposition. To answer this question, after reminding his audience that 'In a metalogical sentence about a formula we can't write down that formula itself, but only its metalogical description', he gives an example of a meta-logical sentence asserting that a string of characters in German script is an elementary disjunction formula.

Now is this sentence analytic, empirical, or synthetic a priori? Hilbert's view is that it is synthetic a priori, on the basis of pure intuition. This view perhaps came about because the formula and its description were not distinguished clearly enough. The metalogical sentence I cited is in fact analytic, for the metalogical definition of the concept 'elementary disjunction' yields the result that a formula with a certain description is an elementary disjunction. The sentence identifying the formula on the board here as an elementary disjunction, on the other hand, is an empirical sentence. (ASP 1931l; Stadler 1997, pp. 316–17; PT pp. 281–2)

The problem of elucidations, then, had been definitively solved, and the meaning relation had (for now) been eliminated. At the end of the 2 July discussion, an exasperated outside visitor asked, 'So are we allowed to speak about language now or not?' and Carnap responded 'If what you mean by language is signs, sounds, chalk marks, etc. then you can talk about language, but you can't talk about "meaning"' (ASP 1931l; Stadler 1997, p. 334; PT p. 299). Nor was there any need to, any more.

At the end of the second lecture, Carnap indicated that the approach outlined up to that point ran into a serious obstacle: the concept of 'provability' (as distinct from 'proof') could not actually be expressed with the tools he has provided so far (those of the *Versuch*). He proposed therefore to arithmetise syntax; expressions could then be referred to by their Gödel numbers, rather than by spatiotemporal coordinates of physical objects (ASP 1931l; Stadler 1997, pp. 324–5; PT pp. 289–90).[7] This afforded a generality over instances lacking in the previous approach; in an arithmetised syntax, asserting the provability of a sentence does not require that an actual proof be exhibited with that sentence as its final line; the claim is only that a number with certain properties exists (1934a, §19, pp. 50–1). This step greatly increases the scope and power of the syntactical method: 'The difference between arithmetised metalogic and the metalogic portrayed so far is this: arithmetised metalogic treats not the empirically available configurations, but all possible configurations. Our previous metalogic is the descriptive theory of certain given configurations, it is the geography of language forms, while the arithmetised metalogic is the geometry of language forms' (ASP 1931l; Stadler 1997, p. 325; PT p. 290).

In the third lecture, Carnap briefly explained how this arithmetisation was to work, and how he intended to extend its application beyond arithmetic to all of empirical knowledge (see the next section below). In the discussion following this lecture, the new criterion for excluding metaphysics was already in operation. 'All the questions of syntax that we discuss here in the Circle can be treated' using the new meta-logic, he says. 'Even the assertion that certain sentences, e.g. those of Heidegger, are meaningless, can be expressed precisely [*exakt*] by a metalogical sentence' (ASP 1931l; Stadler 1997, p. 329; PT p. 294).

So Carnap's retreat from his initial hope, in January, of dispensing altogether with 'existential presuppositions', and opting for an axiomatised arithmetic, had brought several important advantages. First, the introduction of an axiomatic arithmetic, however simple, into the meta-language, meant that the universe of discourse could change from named objects

---

7 This raises the question why Carnap still needed 'descriptive syntax', whose sole purpose in the *Syntax* book (§§24–5) appears to be referring to expressions without invoking meaning. The answer is to be sought in the evolution of Carnap's physicalism, the subject of the next section below.

to *numbered* positions (in any desired 'space'). Second, arithmetisation brought a greater scope and generality that allowed e.g. concepts like 'provability' to be expressed in the meta-language. Finally, arithmetisation collapsed the meta-language (and the rest of the hierarchy) into the object language, thus bringing Carnap back to a single language after all. In answer to the question, after the third lecture, 'So are we to draw the inference that there is only a *single* language?' Carnap replied 'Well, there are sentences of very different form . . . , but all of them, even the metalogical ones, are in a *single* language'. And this went for the entire hierarchy; when Neurath asks, 'Is the metalogic of the metalogic expressible in the original language?' Carnap answered 'Yes, one can set things up that way' (ASP 1931l; Stadler 1997, p. 329; PT p. 294).

By mid-1931, then, six months after the 'vision' of the sleepless night, Carnap was well on the way to a canonical meta-language that would solve all the problems besetting the programme of rational reconstruction and yet completely avoid meaning and reference. But they would return, as we shall see, to haunt him very soon.

PHYSICALISM

The confluence of syntax and physicalism in mid-1931

During the first half of 1931, it seems, the new meta-logical thought process had little or no impact on Carnap's *epistemological* view of scientific theories and their empirical content. Although from the viewpoint of the meta-language atomic sentences were regarded as purely formal, within the scientific object language they still possessed, in Carnap's view, a kind of automatic or intrinsic interpretation by virtue of reporting simple observations. This interpretation gave them their empirical content, which they transmitted by truth-functional concatenation to theoretical sentences; at this level, the picture theory remained in force. In late March 1931, more than two months after the breakthrough on the sleepless night, Carnap was still writing that 'every sentence is a truth-function of atomic sentences' (UCLA 1931j, p. 111). What he meant was 'every sentence of the scientific object language'. Also untouched, for now, was the particular form of the ostensibly truth-functional constitution of knowledge from observation in the *Aufbau*. In March 1931, he still maintained at a Vienna Circle meeting that 'The standpoint of methodological solipsism remains the only possible one for me' (ASP 1931h; Stadler 1997, p. 298; PT p. 263). Though the idea of giving empirical content to the elucidatory meta-language had been abandoned, this was no reason to abandon the *Aufbau* account of empirical concepts itself.

But this would soon begin to change. Quite apart from all the other influences and preoccupations we have discussed here, Carnap's thought had, since about 1928, been undergoing yet another kind of transformation, this one due largely, it seems, to Neurath. But it is not as straightforwardly characterised as that provenance might suggest. Responding to Neurath's (1928) review of the *Aufbau*, Carnap had written (in October 1928):

What is especially significant for me is of course what you say in the way of pointing toward extensions and further work. In the course of my deliberations it has now become clearer and clearer to me that the two points you mention here, and which you had previously brought home to me more comprehensively and emphatically, really are among the most important of those one might consider in this connection – and the first is perhaps the most important of all, i.e. the point that a logic, a method of concept formation, must be set up that takes into account the fact that what we have before us is always a mixture of crystals and dirt. It must, in other words, be one that specifies what demands are to be made of scientific concepts and statements while the 'ideal language' is not available. And secondly, that it is important to deal with historical and sociological problems. Of course the two are connected, as there is naturally going to be more dirt in sociology than in physics. I now seriously intend to approach the first task, though not immediately by way of writing something, rather by way of thinking about it; a few ideas in this direction are already beginning to form . . . (ASP 1928c, p. 1)

The first result of this new commitment had been the larger applications of the *Aufbau* we saw in the 1929 lecture 'Von Gott und Seele' (Chapter 6 above), also reflected in the manifesto pamphlet *Wissenschaftliche Weltauffassung*, published the same year, which Carnap and Neurath wrote jointly with Hans Hahn. Carnap participated fully in the efforts to disseminate the Vienna Circle's programme more widely; he even went on a week-long trip to Dessau to give four lectures at the Bauhaus. But these had still been applications of the 'ideal language', albeit to broader and 'dirtier' realms. (The engagement with Reichenbach and Kaila described in Chapter 8 above can be seen in the same light.) It was not until May of 1930 that Carnap turned explicitly to the 'dirty' subject of psychology (in which he had long had a special interest) with a lecture at Karl Bühler's psychological colloquium entitled 'Psychology in the Framework of Unified Science' (ASP 1930f).[8] The main emphasis of this talk, as in a more general lecture to the Ernst

---

[8] This would appear to be a (pre-syntactic) first draft of the 1932 paper 'Psychology in Physical Language'; ASP/RR 1930a is a very rough typescript from (Rose Rand's?) shorthand notes on this talk (or a similar one).

Mach Society the week before (ASP 1930e), and a more politically oriented one to Helene Bauer's socialist workshop (ASP 1930c), was the endorsement of the *physical language* as superior to the phenomenal language for the practical conduct of science.

How are we to understand this? It would appear that these are the first steps in a development that would continue well into Carnap's American period, and has sometimes been seen as a more 'pragmatic' reorientation. Carnap's 'physicalism' during these years has certainly been discussed as a doctrine, and compared with Neurath's version of the doctrine (e.g. Uebel 1992a, 1992b). But neither at this time nor later was Carnap ever very concerned with the doctrinal details (this may account for his apparent willingness to sweep doctrinal differences between himself and Neurath under the rug, as Uebel notes). It seems to have been more of a shift of attitude or priorities, as Carnap retrospectively emphasised: 'In our discussions Neurath, in particular, urged the development toward a physicalistic attitude. I say deliberately "attitude" and not "belief" because it was a practical question of preference, not a theoretical question of truth' (1963, p. 51). But wherein did this attitude consist?

When I suggested that we should not discuss the theses of idealism and materialism but rather the problem of the choice of a language, Neurath accepted this point but tried to turn my weapon against me. The choice of a language form is a practical decision, he argued, just as the choice of a route for a railroad or that of a constitution for a government. He emphasized that all practical decisions are interconnected and should therefore be made from the point of view of a general goal. The decisive criterion would be how well a certain language form, or a railroad, or a constitution, could be expected to serve the community which intended to use it. His emphasis on the interdependence of all decisions, including those in the theoretical fields, and his warning against isolating the deliberation of any practical question, even that of the choice of a language form, made a strong impression upon my own thinking . . . (1963, p. 51)

This goes well beyond the shift in emphasis from 'crystals' toward 'dirt'; Carnap here seems to be projecting his later pluralism onto his initial, pre-syntactic shift toward the physical language in 1930. This shift was evidently associated in his mind with the entire reorientation that followed, and it seems reasonable to suppose that his subsequent embrace of linguistic pluralism (see next section below, and Chapter 10) was at least partly conditioned by Neurath's 'emphasis on the interdependence of all decisions . . . and his warning against isolating the deliberation of any practical question', and that the process of reorienting his thought in this direction began some time before the 'syntax' breakthrough of January 1931 that would eventually supply the context for the first doctrinal formulation of this pluralism.

This change reflects a recalibration in Carnap's view of philosophy and its role that accompanied the transition from the rational reconstruction programme of the 1920s to the later ideal of explication. Before this change, his conception of philosophy had been somewhat out of phase with his basic convictions – his utopian voluntarism and his commitment to a high-level, conceptual 'politics' of the kind we saw in Chapter 1. Philosophy had served this programme, but had also still been the effort to see things whole, to understand, to gain insight; this was still the role of philosophy in the *Tractatus*, as the Vienna Circle saw it. What 'physicalism' seems to have stood for in Carnap's mind was the subsumption of this traditional role within a new task of actively shaping and building the world, rather than just passively understanding it – not in the sense of Marx's eleventh thesis on Feuerbach (Marx would have regarded language frameworks as superstructure), but very much in that interventionist spirit. Physicalism signalled Carnap's view of philosophy as a *Möglichkeitswissenschaft*, a 'science of possibilities' in the sense of Musil (see the final paragraph of Chapter 1 above). Philosophy became a *constructive* enterprise, an engineering task. The emphasis shifted from understanding the world as it *is* to conceiving and exploring possibilities of how it *might be*, what we might turn it into. This did not mean abandoning the previous conception of philosophy as an 'enterprise of understanding' (Stein 2004) so much as subordinating that conception to the new engineering view. Understanding *became* at least partly a matter of appraising and devising practical consequences. The traditional philosophical project of gaining insight found its proper context within the larger programme of designing the world to our specifications – not just through physical technology but also, especially, through conceptual technology, the linguistic frameworks that mediate the knowledge we use to shape our individual and social lives. There is certainly an analogy to Kant here, and probably a continuity with respect to *both* the 'primacy of the practical' *and* the strong emphasis on the a priori. But for Kant this had meant founding a new discipline, transcendental philosophy, to *rescue* metaphysics by putting it on a diet. For Carnap, in contrast, the whole idea of metaphysics, and philosophy in the traditional sense, was henceforth 'opium for the educated' (ASP 1934a), and a top priority for its constructive successor discipline was *liberation* from the weight of the past.[9]

---

[9] On this theme see the final section ('Reason and the Weight of the Past') of Carus (2004). On the analogy to Kant, see Friedman (2007) and Richardson (2007).

Commentators have noted the absence of a doctrinal commitment on Carnap's part during this period, and his unwillingness to follow Neurath's more decided and specific views.[10] Carnap still insisted, as he had in the *Aufbau*, that a phenomenal basis was preferable to a physical one for epistemological purposes. In none of the May 1930 talks was the relation between these two parallel languages discussed; they were both 'total languages', each appropriate to its purpose. The advantages of the physical language were stressed, without any corresponding discussion of the disadvantages of the phenomenal language. What emerged was essentially the view that the phenomenal language was more fundamental and precise from the viewpoint of the pure understander as outside observer, for the epistemologist who deals in 'crystals'. But the physical language was more appropriate for the committed participant observer who deals in 'dirt'.

Not all members of the Vienna Circle were happy with this shift. For Schlick and Waismann, who remained in regular contact with Wittgenstein, philosophy was to remain more crystalline, and stand apart from the dirty worlds of knowledge and practice. Hahn, Neurath, and Carnap, on the other hand, understood in their different ways that the wider resistance to the Vienna Circle's ideas was not purely cognitive but involved values as well. They thought philosophy could not stand apart from the embeddedness of its objects – knowledge, science, the logic of science – in the practical world. The well-known split into the 'right' and 'left' wings of the Circle during this period involved much more than the details of the protocol sentence debate or the first signs of Wittgenstein's later philosophy. It reflected two quite different conceptions of how to continue the philosophical tradition in the modern world. For the 'right wing' (if not for Wittgenstein himself) philosophy was still conceived very much in the German academic tradition descended from Kant, German idealism, and the successive generations of neo-Kantians and phenomenologists. Though they differed in doctrine, Schlick and Waismann did not see the point and role of philosophy much differently from Natorp, Cassirer, Rickert, or Husserl. Carnap and the 'left wing' were feeling their way to a new conception adequate both to the state of our knowledge – the *Entzauberung* of the natural and social worlds – and the democratic realities of knowledge-driven, technology-dependent societies. The 'enterprise of understanding' became a branch of engineering.

---

[10] Such as those put forward in a note Neurath wrote in May 1930, headed 'Einheitlichkeit der Gegenstände aller Wissenschaften' (ASP 1930d), which Carnap had used as the basis for a discussion with Paul Lazarsfeld and also for his talk at Bühler's seminar mentioned above; see also Uebel (1992a, 1992b).

But this retrospective diagnosis was hardly explicit at the time. When first proposed in 1930–1, 'physicalism' sounded very much like a new doctrine. Neurath took the initiative. Carnap was receptive, but also wanted to build bridges. He was open to Neurath's new *attitude*, that is, but wanted to be sure that the goals of the *Aufbau* were not lost from sight. This bridge-building effort continued in the spring of 1931; it seems not, as we saw, to have been affected by the syntax breakthrough in January. Just before that event, in early January, Carnap had given a talk on the philosophy of the Vienna Circle in Munich, in which the physical language is given pride of place, just as in the May 1930 talks. But again the phenomenal language was invoked as a parallel language, and as more suitable for epistemology. The relation between the two languages was still not discussed (ASP 1931a, 1931b; also 1931c). In early March, Hahn and Carnap joined Neurath for a 'Discussion of Physicalism' which seems to have been the first time Neurath advanced his more radical view of eliminating the phenomenal language entirely (ASP 1931e). But the following day in the Circle, Carnap again tried to mediate (ASP 1931f). Though endorsing certain theses of 'physicalism', especially the role of the physical language as the universal language of science (because of its intersubjectivity), he still maintained that 'the sentences of the physical language only become verifiable by translating them into the phenomenal language' (ASP 1931g; Stadler 1997, p. 293; PT p. 258). In early May, finally, Carnap and Neurath had another discussion in which they tried to characterise the relation between the two languages more precisely. We can distinguish at least five events, Carnap wrote after this meeting: (a) the thing sensed, e.g. a tree; (b) the retinal impression of the tree; (c) the corresponding trace of that impression in the visual processing part of the brain; (d) the corresponding intent, in the linguistic centres of the brain, to impart a report of that impression; and (e) the utterance corresponding to that intent. Whether we regard (e) as an indicator only for (a), skipping the intervening steps, or also for all or any of those (and further) intervening steps also, is a matter of convention, he writes, and will vary according to our purposes. And we can observe empirically that there is a correspondence between these five steps as viewed from a subjective point of view and the same steps viewed as a physical causal chain (ASP 1931j). Carnap was clearly on the way to the pragmatic view of the observation language that later found its context within the new pluralism of 'On Protocol Sentences' (1932e).

The incorporation of an axiomatic arithmetic into the object language, in late May or June 1931, and the consequent unification of object language and meta-language by arithmetisation, put this tentative physicalism in a new light and gave it much greater leverage. For the physicalist object language now also made the meta-language physicalist; there could be a single *universal* language, and that language could be the language of physics. It would have an observational part – that would still be the *Elementarerlebnisse* of the *Aufbau* and their quasi-analysis, up through the steps resulting in colours and other qualities. Its theoretical part would then result in the four-dimensional space-time manifold onto which these qualities could be projected, just as in §126 of the *Aufbau*.

The first result of this confluence, and indeed the only published document of this early, single-language syntax phase, was the paper 'The Physical Language as a Universal Language of Science' (1932b).[11] Here physicalism and the 'syntax' revolution of the sleepless night fused into a single doctrine. After three pages of introductory discussion about the idea that all objects and facts are of a single kind, we are told that these expressions are a concession to the customary 'material' (*inhaltliche*) way of speaking. The 'correct' way, Carnap says, speaks of words rather than 'objects' and sentences rather than 'facts', for a philosophical investigation is an analysis of *language*. In a footnote he indicates that a comprehensive, strictly formal theory of language forms, a 'metalogic', will soon be forthcoming, and will justify the 'thesis of metalogic' here invoked, that 'meaningful' (*sinnvolle*) philosophical sentences are the meta-logical ones, i.e. those that speak only of the form of language (1932b, p. 435; PT p. 38). And yet here again we find that the phenomenal language is proposed as essential for epistemological purposes, for 'verification'. It was only in the discussion arising from this paper that Carnap made the abrupt transition, later in 1932, to the pluralism about the observation language that signalled yet another revolution in his thought, which will be the subject of Chapter 10.

Physicalism and the problem of reference

With the original 'syntax' breakthrough of 21 January, the problem of meaning had been pushed *down* a level, from the meta-level of *Wissenschaftslogik* down to the object level of empirical sentences. And even there, at the empirical level, it seems Carnap had originally hoped to dispose of meaning altogether with his purely formal definition of 'content' as consequence class.[12] By June, this hope had evidently faded, so the problem remained how to accommodate the meaning relation where it *was* still required, at

---

[11] There are many *un*published documents, e.g. ASP 1932a.
[12] There is still a vestige of this in 'Die physikalische Sprache', where Carnap mentions that not only criterial definitions but even ostensive definition could be regarded as intra-linguistic; 'elephant', for instance, criterially defined as an animal with certain characteristics, might be ostensively defined as 'an animal of the kind present at a certain space-time location' (1932b, pp. 435–6; PT p. 39).

the empirical level, i.e. how to characterise the relation between a sentence and the observational fact it reports or depicts. This problem, at least in this general form, was bracketed at the time, though it soon emerged as the main focus of contention in the 'protocol sentence debate'.

A special case of this broader problem had been of more immediate concern to Carnap even in January, however, and could not be put on hold: how to characterise the relation between a syntactic sentence and its particular, physical (written or auditory) *instances* within the framework of the syntactic meta-language. A solution to this problem is needed to define the sense in which a meta-language is 'about' an object language. It is also needed for the practical task of distinguishing syntactical sentences from arbitrary non-referring strings (lack of reference obviously is not sufficient *by itself* to qualify a sentence as meta-linguistic).

The relation between a *Zeichen* and its instances had originally been conceived, in January, as given by the relation between pure and descriptive syntax, on the model of abstract and physical geometry. Descriptive syntax had mapped a sign onto an equivalence class of physical traces, just as abstract geometry mapped mathematical relations onto physical spatial configurations. But when Carnap had moved on to an arithmetised syntax, expressions could now be referred to by their Gödel numbers. Why, then, did Carnap still need descriptive syntax to refer to expressions on the page or blackboard, as set out in the *Logical Syntax*, §§18–19 and §§24–5? The answer is that the shift to arithmetised syntax coincided, in June 1931, with the confluence of physicalism and the new syntax idea. As we saw above, it had only been in June, and possibly the day before the second lecture, that Carnap had decided in favour of arithmetisation. The third lecture, a week later, began by showing how the meta-logic corresponded with his (and Neurath's) proposal for the physical language:

A singular metalogical sentence says that a row of signs of a particular kind is located at a certain place. More important than these are the metalogical conditional sentences. A *formula* is a one-dimensional row of discrete objects of different kinds, i.e. a configuration of the kind we can describe in our language. The metalogical concepts of the different kinds correspond to the qualities of the physical language. (ASP 1931l; Stadler 1997, p. 325; PT p. 290)

No sooner, then, had he achieved a way of referring to expressions without the apparatus of descriptive syntax than he inflicted on himself the need to refer to token *instances* of expressions physicalistically. He now needed a way of cashing out such reference in *physical* terms, on the analogy of the correspondence between mathematical geometry and the description of empirical regularities in physical laws using physical geometry. It was essential now that meaning, the relation between physical signs (chalk marks, utterances) and the formulas they refer to, be entirely specifiable in physical terms, so that the linguistic objects around us can be regarded as physical objects. The obscurities in the *Tractatus* surrounding the question how a mere 'sign' becomes a 'symbol' had to be eliminated without remainder. A formula could be referred to by its Gödel number, but it was still necessary to specify in physical terms how a particular token instance of it (*this* one, on the blackboard in front of us) instantiates the formula.[13] 'Gödel can make do with arithmetised concepts', Carnap said in the third lecture,

as he is only concerned with arithmetic. But since we want to describe the physical configurations, i.e. combinations of signs, we also need these empirical concepts. As we are only describing these physical configurations, rows of linguistic signs, we can express the metalogic in our ordinary language, and indeed in such a way that it doesn't contradict the views of Wittgenstein. This is not a matter of sentences about sentences, but of singular as well as conditional sentences about physical configurations. (ASP 1931l; Stadler 1997, p. 327; PT p. 292)

This elimination of meaning, or its reduction to a physical relation, was an artefact, as we will see in more detail in Chapter 10 (pp. 256–63), of Carnap's continued adherence to an *internal* conception of meta-discourse (and thus of explication or rational reconstruction).

Before moving on to the next steps in Carnap's development, it is worth pausing to point out that the analogy to pure and physical geometry employed here, both before and after the move to physicalism, has given rise to significant misunderstandings. Carnap is not blameless; his own formulations, in the *Syntax* and even much later, are somewhat misleading. In the *Introduction to Semantics*, for instance, we find:

Both in semantics and in syntax, the relation between the descriptive and the pure field is perfectly analogous to the relation between pure or mathematical geometry, which is a part of mathematics and hence analytic, and physical geometry, which is a part of physics, and hence empirical. (1942, p. 12)

But it is not 'perfectly analogous' at all, and this has misled many interpreters.[14] There is certainly an analogy; the logical relationship is in both

---

[13] It is clear from the exposition of descriptive syntax in §§ 24–5 of the *Syntax* (1934a, pp. 66–73; PT pp. 76–82) that this is the point of it, as also from the first illustrative example ('A sentence of descriptive syntax can e.g. say that a linguistic expression of a certain form is to be found at a certain location'), as well as the subsequent examples in the comparative tables of §25 (e.g. 'At position a of this book there is a sign that consists of two horizontal bars').

[14] Such as Wilfrid Sellars; see Carus (2004), p. 336. In his reply to Sellars, Carnap shows himself, despite the quoted passage from *Introduction to Semantics* and others like it, to be perfectly aware

cases (geometry and semantics) that of theory to model. But the *purposes* for which the theory is developed are different in the two cases. In geometry, only empirically interpreted theories are put forward as theories to explain and account for phenomena. In syntax and semantics, empirically interpreted theories may also be put forward, in the same way, to account for the empirical phenomena (the observed expressions) of a *used* language. Quite separately from (and irrelevantly to) this, however, pure semantic or syntactic theories (with or without empirical models) may be put forward as *explications* of vague concepts in ordinary language, such as the logical words that indicate connections among segments of everyday speech that could by some behavioural standard be classed as 'deductive'. An empirically interpreted semantic theory may succeed or fail as an empirical hypothesis, but this has no bearing on its corresponding purely logical theory as a candidate for *explicating* such vague concepts of ordinary language. So while in the geometry case there is only one practically relevant relation between theory and model, in the semantics case there are two quite different (and only tangentially related) ones.[15]

The divergence is in practice even greater than this might suggest. As Carnap was well aware (and often repeated), ordinary used languages are logically very complex – too complex, as a rule, even to be amenable to straightforward codification.[16] Thus an interpreted semantic theory put forward as an empirical hypothesis to explain certain linguistic behaviour would be quite different (much more complex) than one proposed, in engineering mode, as an explication. The first would, in fact, be something very like Chomsky's generative grammars and the many variants on them proposed in the past decades, while the second takes the form of relatively simple axiom systems, like those of set theory or arithmetic. The chances of the *same pure semantic theory* occurring in both these contexts are in practice nil. Far from being 'perfectly analogous', then, the cases of geometry and semantics are utterly different.

---

of the distinction spelled out in the above paragraph; indeed he makes it himself, in response to Sellars's misunderstanding (Carus 2004, pp. 332–8). More recently, Thomas Ricketts (2004a, p. 261) has been similarly misled.

[15] One might defend Carnap's formulation by considering that pure geometry is also applied 'empirically' to 'possible worlds' that approximate the real one (e.g. the application of Euclidean geometry to the real world), and thus fails, in such cases, as an empirical hypothesis; on the other hand, for a proposed explication to be usable and applicable, it must have *some* resemblance to the vague concepts it is to replace. So the distinction between the two uses I suggest above is not entirely clear-cut. (I am grateful to Howard Stein for pointing this out to me.) Carnap's way of stating the analogy, however, and claiming it to be 'perfect' without considering such subtleties, indicates that he momentarily lost the distinction between these uses from sight altogether.

[16] As Carnap says, e.g., in his reply to Bar-Hillel (1963, p. 941); see also the extended example in *Die Aufgabe der Wissenschaftslogik* (1934c), pp. 8–9.

Some writers, however, have taken the geometry analogy at face value. The purpose of Carnap's *Wissenschaftslogik*, in this view – both in its original, syntactic form and its later semantic continuation – was not to change our language but to account for its behaviour empirically, just as in geometry one tries to account empirically for certain features of our environment.[17] Now it is true that, at the time he was writing *Logical Syntax*, Carnap often spoke this way. The voluntarist element central to his thought from his student days, somewhat constricted during the Vienna years, re-emerged with the principle of tolerance (below, Chapter 10), opening up the 'boundless ocean of free possibilities'. But Carnap had not yet developed a way of making explicit the voluntarist shaping of concepts and language or 'conceptual engineering' that would later become so important. Still, he did make clear even in the *Syntax* itself that one way a syntactic sentence could be understood was not as a claim or assertion about all languages or some particular existing language, but as applying to *proposed* languages – 'a language (not previously specified) being proposed as the language of science (or of a part of science)' or even 'a language (not previously specified) of which the construction and investigation is being proposed, independently of the question whether it is to serve as a language of science' (1934a, §78, p. 226; PT p. 299). Soon afterwards, he explicitly emphasised that *Wissenschaftslogik* was a matter of constructive proposals rather than assertions (1934b). And 'the task of *Wissenschaftslogik*' was, he wrote in a pamphlet on this very question, to be an *instrument* for the construction of a unified science, specifically for bridging the gap between natural and human sciences maintained by German idealism (1934c, pp. 15–19, 26–7). In 'Testability and Meaning', the practical orientation of *Wissenschaftslogik* was again made explicit:

> . . . we must above all distinguish between two main kinds of questions about meaningfulness; to the first kind belong the questions referring to a historically given language-system, to the second kind those referring to a language-system which is yet to be constructed. These two kinds of questions have an entirely different character. A question of the first kind is a theoretical one; it asks what is the actual state of affairs; and the answer is either true or false. The second question is a practical one; it asks how we shall proceed; and the answer is not an assertion but a proposal or decision . . . There is no question of right or wrong, but only a practical question of convenience or inconvenience of a system form, i.e. of its suitability for certain purposes. (1936–7, pp. 3–4)

[17] Following this line of thought, Ricketts (2004a, pp. 260–3) saddles himself with the problem of coordinating the 'speech habits of a community' with a calculus to determine what it could mean for one of Carnap's proposed languages to be 'adopted in practice'. Sellars made this same mistake, in somewhat different words (Carus 2004, pp. 324–6, 331–2). This is discussed further in Chapter 11 (pp. 273–84) below.

And, of course, the 'principle of empiricism' itself was reformulated here as 'not in the form of an assertion . . . but rather in the form of a proposal or requirement' – as a proposed *constraint* on the language of science (1936–7, p. 33; see also Ricketts 1994).

Even where he did fall back, during the mid-1930s, into the terminology of regarding *Wissenschaftslogik* as a descriptive, empirical enterprise rather than a voluntarist, engineering enterprise, this seems to be due more to the unavailability of other terms (e.g. 'pragmatics') than a reflection of what Carnap really intended. In 'Testability and Meaning', for instance, despite the above very clear statement, Carnap also calls Part III of the paper an 'empirical' analysis of confirmation and testing (following the 'logical' analysis of confirmation and testing in Part II): 'while the logical analysis belongs to an analytic theory of the formal, syntactical structure of language, here we will carry out an empirical analysis of the application of language' (1936, p. 454).[18] That this did not reflect what he intended is clear from a marked-up copy of 'Testability and Meaning' in his papers, evidently corrected at least a year after its original publication, in which Carnap crossed out 'empirical' in this section and changed it to 'pragmatic' (ASP 1938a).[19]

ANOTHER FIRST DRAFT UNDERMINED BY GÖDEL

In the autumn of 1931, after moving to Prague, Carnap sat down once again to put the new ideas into a systematic treatise, essentially the first draft of *Logical Syntax*. Here the canonical meta-language, now called the 'model language' (*Modellsprache*), is spelled out as essentially what would later be Language I. It was only in this manuscript that Carnap tried seriously to construct the definition of analyticity he had realised he needed since at least March. The table of contents (the only part of this draft that seems to have

---

[18] Ricketts adduces this usage in Part III as evidence for his interpretation (2004a, p. 263).

[19] Much later, in the Schilpp volume, caught between Bar-Hillel's charge that he paid insufficient attention to the logical analysis of natural languages and Beth's charge that his analyses of formal languages may be misunderstood as applying to natural languages, Carnap again clarifies that his engineering proposals are *not* applicable directly to natural language. The most he is willing to grant is that 'the following is possible: (1) an empirical description of the most important and most frequently used syntactical forms occurring in a natural language, which indications of their frequencies, but without any claim of completeness, or (2) the complete representation of the syntactical structure of a constructed language which is to some extent similar to the syntactical structure (e.g., order of words) of a part of a certain natural language. Work of the first kind has for a long time been carried out by linguists, and that of the second kind is sometimes done by logicians, though only to a very limited extent' (1963, p. 931). Under (2) Carnap describes almost exactly the conception of a 'grid' that Ricketts thinks is the relation Carnap *generally* intends between 'calculi' and 'languages'. If this were true, would Carnap not have taken this opportunity to point it out?

survived) lists the notion *analytic* alongside *synthetic* and *contradictory* under the heading 'IV.B. Theory of content of formulas' (corresponding roughly to IV.B(a) of *Logical Syntax*, which – in the English translation – gives the general definition of 'analytic'). This is followed in Section IV.C. by a discussion of soundness, consistency, and completeness, including sections on the 'antinomies' and 'the incompleteness of all formal systems' which appear to correspond closely to IV.B(c) of the (English) *Logical Syntax*, where the Gödel incompleteness of arithmetic is discussed (ASP 1932d).

It is not known exactly how analyticity was originally defined, but from the evidence available it is clear that the definition was defective. Gödel objected to its application to the 'extended model language'.[20] Furthermore, he points out, it will be *impossible* to give a correct definition of it in *any* meta-language that can be faithfully represented in the object language, e.g. by arithmetisation. This fact has since become known as Tarski's theorem on the indefinability of truth. Carnap's single language approach, it turned out, would not work after all.[21]

Although Carnap, with Gödel's assistance, developed a new definition of analyticity, in a meta-language, this definition no longer had the privileged status that one in the *same language* (had it been possible) could have claimed. And indeed there is no basis for singling out any particular meta-language as more 'suitable' or 'natural' for this purpose than any other. One option may be more *useful* than others, but there is no basis for privileging it as uniquely 'correct'. So the idea of a *canonical* meta-language, in which he had invested almost two years of intense work, now began to seem somewhat arbitrary. Once again, a brave new programme that had at first solved all the problems seemed to have run aground. And as before, only a radical shift of perspective could help.

---

[20] Just as in the June 1931 lectures to the Vienna Circle (see above, pp. 237–8) held just before Carnap embarked on composing the first draft, it seems that the 'model language' was regarded as the 'proper language [*eigentliche Sprache*]', while the full resources of classical mathematics could be developed by using the 'model language' as a meta-language for axiomatic formal systems, Hilbert-style; the model language together with these axiomatic extensions was then called the 'extended model language'.

[21] Gödel's objection to Carnap's original definition of analyticity is explained in a letter dated 11 September 1932 (Gödel 2003, pp. 346–8). Carnap had apparently tried to define the notion 'analytic sentence' inductively, using what we would now call a substitutional treatment of quantification. Gödel points out that this definition is circular, and makes a suggestion for a replacement. Carnap attempts to reconstruct Gödel's proposal, and asks for help in finding the right definition, especially since, as he says, everything else in his book depends on it (Gödel 2003, pp. 350–2). Judging from his note of a few days later, Carnap finally did work out the solution for himself. The key new idea here is that the meta-language of definition needs to be stronger than the language for which analyticity is to be defined (Gödel 2003, p. 354). In his reply, Gödel confirms that this is the idea, and remarks that one cannot give the definition of 'analytic' in the same language, otherwise 'contradictions will result'. For details on this exchange, see Goldfarb (2003) as well as Awodey and Carus (forthcoming).

CHAPTER 10

Tolerance

In October 1932, soon after the exchange with Gödel, Carnap's thought underwent yet another major revolution. It does not appear to have occurred all at once, in a blinding flash of insight, like its predecessor in January 1931. Carnap recorded no single inspiration or breakthrough moment; we do not even know exactly when the turning point came. It seems to have been less a single insight than a continuous process that had begun at least a few months before the correspondence with Gödel, which that exchange then pushed in the direction of a new and radical resolution. The governing idea of the new attitude was the 'principle of tolerance'. The shift toward physicalism, discussed in Chapter 9, may have helped this process along. In particular, the discussion of the empirical basis growing out of the 'protocol sentence debate' was the context in which the new doctrine of tolerance found its first expression.

THE PROTOCOL SENTENCE DEBATE IN 1932

Though Neurath had done much to inspire Carnap's turn to physicalism in 1930–31, he was unhappy with the paper on 'The Physical Language' because he saw vestiges of foundationalism in it. Also he felt himself unfairly anticipated as well as misrepresented. After an emotional correspondence with Carnap in early 1932, he sent a draft reply in May. Much of it, Carnap said, was unintelligible to him, but – as the co-editor of *Erkenntnis* (and as a friend) – he set to work on drastic revisions. The result was Neurath's well-known paper 'Protocol Sentences' (Neurath 1932), containing the proposal for a physicalistic, observer-indexed form of basic observation sentence, to counteract the danger of absolutising or hypostatising evidence reports. At about the same time, critiques of 'The Physical Language' (and of its pendant, 'Psychology in Physical Language') were sent to *Erkenntnis* by Edgar Zilsel and by the Gestalt psychologist Karl Duncker.

When he began to compose replies to these critiques, in the summer of 1932, Carnap had recently completed work on the *Metalogik* and sent it for review to Gödel and others. At that point he took for granted that the single-language strategy pursued there (and in 'The Physical Language'), resting on his first-draft definition of analyticity, would succeed. But now Neurath's critique raised the question: *which* single language? Was Carnap's proposal in 'The Physical Language' for compatibility between the physical and phenomenal languages, and their usefulness for different purposes, sustainable? Carnap began to write his reply as a response to these questions, and a defence of his position in 'The Physical Language'. This early part of the reply seems to have survived as section 1 of his paper 'On Protocol Sentences' (1932e).

Carnap then spent the later part of the summer in the Tyrolean Alps. In September, Feigl stopped by for several days with the young Karl Popper in tow, and the three went for extended walks in the mountains. The conversation turned to – what else? – protocol sentences, and Popper put forward his account of the 'relativity of basic statements', apparently more or less as later presented in §29–30 of *Logik der Forschung*:

Science does not rest upon solid bedrock. The bold structure of its theories rises, as it were, above a swamp. It is like a building erected on piles. The piles are driven down from above into the swamp, but not down to any natural or 'given' base; and if we stop driving the piles deeper, it is not because we have reached firm ground. We simply stop when we are satisfied that the piles are firm enough to carry the structure, at least for the time being. (Popper 1935, §30, pp. 75–6; PT p. 111)

This seems to have left a lasting impression on Carnap.[1] It fit very well with his own conception (put forward in a conversation with Neurath the year before; above, Chapter 9, p. 244), summarised in the section of 'On Protocol Sentences' where Popper's position is discussed. It gave precedence, in effect, to physicalist protocol sentences but did not exclude the possibility of phenomenalist ones as a last (or further) resort. And it reinforced Carnap's growing pragmatic tendency that we also saw manifested in his attraction to the physicalist attitude (cf. also ASP/RR 1932a).

It is curious and ironic that Popper, who thus appears to have played a role in moving Carnap one step closer to linguistic pluralism and the

---

[1] As late as the 1950s, when he was writing his autobiography, Carnap singles out Popper's work on 'protocol sentences' for praise, and goes so far as to say that Popper's ideas 'helped in clarifying and strengthening the physicalistic conception which I had developed together with Neurath' (1963, p. 32). Note also that Hempel quotes the above passage in his contribution to the Schilpp volume on Carnap (Hempel 1963, p. 702), associating it explicitly with the point that Carnap had endorsed in 'On Protocol Sentences' and continued to endorse later.

principle of tolerance, himself never grasped this doctrine. Despite his pluralism of observation languages, Popper seems not to have noticed, or not to have seen the point, of the generalised principle of tolerance as later expressed in the *Syntax* book,[2] despite the fact that one of its earliest applications was Carnap's defence of *Logik der Forschung* against Reichenbach's emphatically vituperative review in *Erkenntnis* – with the (by now characteristic) injunction that both Popper's and Reichenbach's ideas should be regarded as proposals for the design of the scientific language: 'It seems to me that what we have in this case (as in many questions of the logic of science, so-called epistemological questions) is not a true-false question, but rather a question of a decision or stipulation regarding the syntax of the scientific language to be built up' (1935b, p. 292). Each of them should propose their preferred rules; 'so it is a matter of two proposals, not two contradictory theses!' (1935b, p. 293). The implications of each proposal could then be worked out and compared.

Soon after this encounter with Feigl and Popper came the letter from Gödel (above, Chapter 9, pp. 250–1) that, apparently, catalyzed the radical redesign of the *Syntax* book. Carnap quickly realised, as he was considering how to solve the basic logical problems Gödel pointed out, that there was a deep analogy between the difficulties he faced in the design of the canonical meta-logic (the 'system language') and the difficulties in specifying the form of the observation language. In both cases, the issue could be regarded as one of designing or choosing a language, rather than of answering a substantive factual or mathematical question. It was a small step to extend this perspective to *all* meta-theoretical questions. It not only dovetailed very nicely with the 'metalogical' turn of January 1931;[3] it also, finally, brought Carnap's philosophical views into better harmony with his basic utopian and voluntarist convictions.

THE OPEN SEA OF FREE POSSIBILITIES

The first opportunity of articulating the new idea was the reply to Neurath, left half-finished in the early summer. Its new introductory paragraph now took a very different line: 'In my view the issue here is not between two

---

[2] Despite his remark that 'if ever a history of the rational philosophy of the earlier half of this century should be written, this book ought to have a place in it second to none' (Popper 1963, p. 203), the principle of tolerance itself – surely the most revolutionary aspect of the book – is never mentioned. Like many others, Popper was misled by Part V (probably written largely pre-tolerance; see pp. 261–3 below), with its near-exclusive emphasis on the 'formal mode of speech'.

[3] With some caveats to be discussed below, pp. 261–3.

conceptions that contradict each other, but rather between *two methods for constructing the language of science, which are both possible and justified* (1932e, p. 215; PT p. 457). Moreover:

Not only the question whether the protocol sentences are inside or outside the syntax language, but also the further question regarding their precise specification, is to be answered, it seems to me, not by an assertion, but by a stipulation [*Festsetzung*]. Though I earlier [in 'Die physikalische Sprache'] left this question open . . . I now think that the different answers are not contradictory. They are to be taken as proposals for stipulations [*Vorschläge zu Festsetzungen*]; the task is to investigate these different possible stipulations as to their consequences and assess their usefulness. (1932e, p. 216; PT p. 458)

His previously written response to Neurath's critique is retained, but now in a very different context, as the pragmatic defence of a *proposal*. And he is very much aware that this approach takes him even further away from the Vienna Circle's pre-1931 programme:

In all theories of knowledge to date there is a certain *absolutism*: in the realistic theories an absolutism of objects, in the idealistic ones (including phenomenology) an absolutism of the 'given', of 'experiences', of 'immediate phenomena [*unmittelbare Phänomene*]'. Even in positivism we find this residual idealistic absolutism; in the logical positivism of our circle – in the works on the logic of science (epistemology) published to date by Wittgenstein, Schlick, Carnap – it takes the subtler form of an absolutism of primitive propositions ('elementary propositions', 'atomic propositions'). (1932e, p. 228; PT p. 469)

In the *Logical Syntax*, this would be put forward as an explicit 'principle of tolerance', in the context not of epistemology, now, but of philosophies of mathematics, particularly intuitionism. Progress in logic had been severely hampered, Carnap said in his preface, by the timid notion that logic had to be 'correct', that the object was to find the one 'true' logic. The point of the *Syntax* book, he says in the preface, is to eliminate this notion, and to untie the ship of logic from its mooring to the prejudice of 'correctness'. 'Before us', he concludes enthusiastically, 'lies the open sea of free possibilities'. The principle of tolerance is expressed, in §§16–17, as the exhortation to state meta-theoretic or *wissenschaftslogische* proposals in precise terms, as explicit rules or definitions, within the formation or transformation rules of a precisely defined language or calculus. The voluntaristic implications of this *constructive* requirement are made explicit:

Once it is understood that all pro- and anti-intuitionist considerations are concerned with the form of a calculus, the question will no longer be asked in the form 'What *is* the case?' but rather 'How do we *want* to set this up in the language being constructed?' . . . And with that, the dogmatic frame of mind that often makes the discussion unfruitful is banished. (1934a, p. 42; PT pp. 46–7)

This 'dogmatic frame of mind' results, in Carnap's view, from the reliance on inherently vague philosophical *Erörterungen* – inconclusive, meandering discussions or considerations – rather than on precise statements of definitions and rules. He indicates how he has tried, in Language I of the *Syntax*, to capture the philosophical concerns (expressed in various gradations of finitism or constructivism) voiced by Brouwer, Kaufmann, Wittgenstein, and others. But, he points out, there is no way of telling whether he has expressed *precisely* what they have in mind, as they have not expressed their views as proposed precise definitions and rules, but only in terms of vague *Erörterungen* that leave many specific questions open, when one gets down to the brass tacks of constructing an actual language (1934a, p. 44). Or they impose normative restrictions and requirements. Carnap's most general statement of the principle of tolerance, therefore, addresses these tendencies directly, contrasting them with his own programme of precise and explicit rules:

Our attitude to demands of this kind may be stated generally by the *principle of tolerance: we do not want to impose restrictions but to state conventions . . . In logic there are no morals*. Everyone can construct his logic, i.e. his language form, however he wants. If he wants to discuss it with us, though, he will have to make precise how he wants to set things up. He has to give syntactic rules rather than philosophical considerations [*Erörterungen*]. (1934e, p. 45; PT pp. 51–2)

This sets the stage, at last, for the replacement of the rational reconstruction project by the successor project of explication.

THE FIRST ATTEMPT TO ARTICULATE A PROGRAMME OF EXPLICATION

In the *Logical Syntax*, the ideal of explication makes its first appearance. However, it takes a form that Carnap soon recognised as inadequate, and another decade would pass before the less restrictive form officially named 'explication' materialised.[4] In the *Syntax*, it is called 'translation' from the material into the formal mode of speech. Sentences stated in the material mode that can be given a formal equivalent are called 'pseudo-object sentences' (§74), or 'quasi-syntactical sentences' (§§63–4). Carnap gives reasonably precise definitions of 'translation' (§61) and 'interpretation' (§62),

---

[4] It first appears in the paper 'Two Concepts of Probability' (1945); the most detailed exposition is in Chapter 1 of *Logical Foundations of Probability* (Carnap 1950b).

relying on his definition of 'content' as (roughly) 'consequence class', and hence 'identity of content' as 'identity of consequence class'. This definition of 'translation' is then applied, in §64, to define translation from the material into the formal mode of speech. But at this step he encounters a fundamental obstacle, which he notices and acknowledges, but breezily waves aside. In fact, it undermines the central philosophical project of the *Syntax*, of 'translation' from the material into the formal mode of speech.

The obstacle is simple to describe. Carnap defines a translation from the material into the formal mode of speech as follows: a sentence Q('a') in a syntactic meta-language L_2 is a translation of a corresponding sentence P(a) in an object language L_1 (where 'a' is an object name) if and only if P(a) and Q('a') have the same content. Informally, he says, a sentence in L_1 is translatable if it attributes a property P to an object 'to which there corresponds a different, syntactic property that so to speak runs parallel with it, i.e. a property that holds of an object's designation when and only when P holds of the object' (1934a, §74, p. 213; PT p. 287). So the consequence classes of P(a) and Q('a') cannot be identical, as they are in different languages; they must rather in some sense be isomorphic. If L_1 and L_2 are different languages, any piecemeal translation thus presupposes a global translation of the entire language L_1 into L_2. So if L_1 and its translation into L_2 are not *already* perfectly well defined, we need to know *all* the consequences of every sentence in L_1 before we can proceed with translating any given expression – an infinitely vast and quite ill-defined undertaking.

Over a certain narrow range of object expressions, the proposal is perfectly coherent, and even quite plausible, e.g. Carnap's well-worn example 'Five is a number, not a thing', which he translates into the formal mode as '"Five" is a number word, not a thing word', assuming that the formation rules of the syntax language state unambiguous criteria for 'number word' and 'thing word'. But this translation also assumes that the *object language* concepts of 'number' and 'thing' are well defined. And what is the object language L_1 in this case? Carnap assumes a precise language of arithmetic. But what if it is the ordinary language of, say, primary school arithmetic teachers? It is, after all, the application of the 'translation' technique to ordinary and philosophical language that gives the exposition of Part V of the *Syntax* much of its interest. In that case, why should we assume that the two sentences have *exactly* the same content, i.e. the same implications in every context whatever? To reach that conclusion, we would have to idealise the object language, i.e. put it into a precise and completely unambiguous form. The particular idealisation of L_I that in this case would result in $Q('a')$ being a translation, in Carnap's sense, of $P(a)$ might well be agreed to by some or even most users of the informal language in question.

Where the assumption that object-language concepts are well defined becomes much less plausible is when the vaguer sentences of everyday language or traditional philosophy are to be translated into the formal mode. Here Carnap acknowledges that the object language is (usually) not one to which his definition of 'translation' even applies.[5] It is hardly surprising, then, that the 'translations' he nonetheless offers entangle him in flagrant contradictions. One of his arguments for the superiority of the formal mode to the material mode, for instance, turns on the impossibility of deriving certain undesirable or unwanted consequences from the formal-mode translations that *are* derivable from their corresponding material-mode sentences.[6] But if the material-mode sentence and its formal-mode 'translation' have different consequences, then by Carnap's own definition their 'content' differs, and the purported translation is *not* a translation in the sense he has himself defined.

This (and the many analogous problems with other 'translations' offered in Part V) might have been possible to get around by introducing something like a scale of 'degrees of translation', so that a formal-mode sentence might be an 'approximate translation' of a material-mode one, but Carnap attempts nothing of the sort. He admits that in many cases, an author has not made his intentions sufficiently clear, and one can only guess approximately at the meaning; 'one can at best conjecture that one has captured what the author meant more or less accurately, i.e. that one has given a translation that deviates less or more from one that the author himself would give from L_I into L_2' (§64, p. 183; PT p. 240). But he gives no hint of a metric or a criterion for deciding how 'far' a translation may diverge from its corresponding material-mode sentence without ceasing to be a translation.

Some of the translations Carnap offers are downright absurd. The most notorious is perhaps the material-mode sentence 'Yesterday's lecture was

---

[5] On the same page as the above definition, he says that 'the examples below . . . belong almost exclusively to ordinary language; they are thus not formulated with sufficient precision to permit the application of exact concepts' (§74, p. 213; PT p. 287). And later, when he offers translations of philosophical statements: 'As the original sentences are mostly ambiguous, a translation into the formal mode of speech cannot be specified unambiguously [*eindeutig*]. In fact it cannot even be claimed with certainty that the sentence involved is a pseudo-object sentence and thus in the material mode of speech. The present translations are therefore no more than informal suggestions.' The burden of supplying a more exact translation, he adds, is on those who would defend the philosophical theses mentioned (§79, p. 229; PT p. 302).

[6] Examples 12, 13, and 14 in §75, p. 217; PT pp. 290–1.

about Babylon', to be translated into the formal mode, Carnap suggests in all apparent seriousness, by 'The word "Babylon" occurred in yesterday's lecture.' Carnap might have reasoned that the ordinary-language word 'about' is extremely vague, and leaves a great deal of scope for interpretation, but even a moment's thought should have convinced him that no amount of stretching would make 'the text T is about X' always equivalent to 'the name of X occurs in T'.

The root of the problem is that pseudo-object sentences are actually intended, at bottom, as the later *explicanda*. They are the *unclear* concepts that require clarification, possibly followed by replacement, i.e. explication. So the definition Carnap offers in §74 of *Syntax* is hopelessly inadequate to the task, as it assumes that the concepts to be clarified are *already* clear. This is plainly at cross purposes with the stated intentions of the book, and especially of Part V, where translation from the material into the formal mode is offered as the principal tool for dissolving the philosophical confusions resulting from the expression of meta-theoretical discussions in the material mode of speech (§§78 and 80).

The technical implementation of Carnap's stated programme fails, then. This is partly to be blamed, no doubt, on the tensions introduced into the published *Syntax* by the abrupt change in its fundamental doctrine after much of it (including the more discursive 'philosophical' Part V) had already been written; this will be discussed below. But the main obstacle to a satisfactory account of explication was Carnap's continued attachment to the Wittgensteinian ideal of requiring philosophical or meta-scientific sentences to be *internal* (in his later terms) to the system into which they were to be reconstructed or explicated. Specifically, the language *in* which the translation is done (stated) is also the language (L_2) *into* which the translation is to be made (from L_1). In January 1931 he had switched, it is true, from judging meta-discourse by one cognitive standard to judging it by the other – from the standard for *Realwissenschaft* (empirical significance) to that for *Formalwissenschaft* (logical significance). But the standard was (again) still internal. Wittgensteinian scruples about the impossibility of stepping outside the language still prevented him from considering a meta-language for statement and discussion of the translation that was distinct from the target language for rational reconstruction (or explication). Carnap was still making the same mistake as he had made in the *Metalogik*, in other words, except that instead of trying to confine everything within a *single* language, he was trying to confine it within *two*. Despite his new pluralism, he seemed to indicate that we should choose *one particular* scientific object language, and *one particular* meta-language to be the target language for *all* explications; the idea of a canonical 'model language' has not yet been quite buried. Though the language was no longer fixed, and the meta-language was not fixed even relatively to a chosen object language, Carnap still clung to the notion that once a language was chosen, all significant discourse – including meta-discourse – must be confined to the framework thereby established. The principle of tolerance had not yet sunk in far enough to dissolve this residue.

Meanwhile, this residual Fregean-Wittgensteinian universalism prevented him from appreciating that translation from the material mode (by hypothesis vague and often misleading) to the (precise) formal mode must take place *outside* the language of either the material-mode object concept or the syntactic meta-language of that concept's formal-mode translation. It must be done, that is, in a meta-meta-language *distinct* from the meta-language, a meta-meta-language that has sufficient flexibility to refer to vague material mode expressions. And it must be preceded by a propaedeutic process of clarification, in which agreement is reached – pre-systematically, so to speak – on a better-defined subconcept of the ill-defined notion to be 'translated' or replaced. Translation from the material into the formal mode should have been recognised as inherently *external*, in other words, as it was by hypothesis not determinate within the (clearly stated) set of formation and transformation rules of the target language. But Carnap was not ready, in 1934, to acknowledge that *any* external discourse could be significant. This had to await the availability, within the meta-perspective, of a species of discourse (to be called 'pragmatics' by the late 1930s) in which practical considerations bearing on the choice of explications (or entire language systems) could be framed. When explication finally was advanced as the successor to rational reconstruction, in the mid-1940s, as we will see in the next chapter, Carnap acknowledged its external status.

Despite the gap between the *Syntax* programme and its technical implementation, and despite the lingering prejudice that only sentences internal to a chosen language framework could have meaning, the *spirit* of the later ideal of explication pervades the *Syntax* and associated publications. Though the mechanics are still somewhat muddled, the previous (rational reconstruction) programme of *replacement* (of pre-scientific concepts by precise ones) has now become a more open one. Despite his official adherence to an internal procedure of rational reconstruction, Carnap in fact acknowledges even in the *Syntax* that many translations are not claims but proposals, and emphasises the importance of specifying the language into which a translation is offered. Otherwise, he says, it is unclear whether a claim or a proposal is intended, and if the latter, it is not clear *what* proposal is being offered (§78, p. 226; PT p. 299).[7]

The transformation of philosophical doctrines into proposals regarding the form of language rests on the principle of tolerance. If there were a 'correct' language, then there could be no proposals, but only claims. Carnap's technical approach to translation from the material into the formal mode of speech, on the other hand, stems from the original syntax idea of January 1931, which was still a response to the Wittgensteinian problems of meaning that had preoccupied the Circle before that. So while the spirit of the new enterprise, epitomised in the principle of tolerance, was now in much better harmony with Carnap's voluntarist convictions, it was still yoked to an apparatus that had no hope of doing it justice.

TENSIONS WITHIN THE PUBLISHED *LOGICAL SYNTAX*

The quasi-Wittgensteinian view Carnap held before January 1931 could be called a 'meaning foundationalism' – the meanings of all sentences rest on the representation of atomic facts by atomic sentences. The sleepless night in January 1931 brought the replacement of this meaning foundationalism by an axiomatic approach to language as a whole, in which all workings of the language are exhaustively specified by explicit rules stated in a meta-language. In its original statement, this 'syntax' view completely excluded the possibility of 'meaning' – even in its informal sense of representational correspondence between configurations of linguistic objects and config-urations of objects in the world. There seemed no way of capturing any such correspondence in explicit formation or transformation rules for a lan-guage. Only a year after the *Syntax* book was published, though, Tarski's definition of truth suggested to Carnap that such correspondences could, after all, be captured in meta-linguistic rules. This amounted to defining a new notion of meaning 'from above', in contrast to the one built up 'from below' that Carnap rejected in January 1931. The rules specifying the language could now also specify an 'interpretation' rigorously, rather than regarding the rules as descriptive and determined by a more fundamental notion of meaning built up from atomic components.

In January 1931, then, the rejection of meaning foundationalism and its replacement by an axiomatic approach was all of a piece. But seen retrospectively from Carnap's later standpoint, this original syntax view

---

[7] See also ASP 1932b and 1933a, as well as 'On the Character of Philosophical Problems' (1934d, pp. 122–4).

could be regarded as having been composed of separable elements: (a) the requirement that a language be entirely specified by explicit rules; (b) the distinction between a language (a calculus, a purely syntactic symbol system) and its interpretation; and (c) the restriction of material reference to the scientific object language, while only calculi, in abstraction from any possible interpretation, were to be considered as possible *wissenschaftslogische* meta-languages. This last element was the basis for the philosophically most visible aspect of the book, the emphasis given to the formal mode of speech.

Components (a) and (b) are necessary pre-conditions for the tolerance idea. Without distinguishing language from content, there can be no alternatives at all. And they will not be clearly stated – unambiguously available for tolerant consideration – without the requirement that language be specified by explicit rules. These two retrospectively visible components survive as fundamental components of Carnap's semantic period. (It is rather misleading, then, to call them 'syntactic'.) Component (c), on the other hand, the overreaction against Wittgensteinian 'meaning' that accompanied the January 1931 insight, did not survive. In distinguishing between a language and its interpretation, Carnap's first (and, as we saw, understandable) response was to reject that imprecise notion of meaning entirely. But this restriction was loosened when he saw that interpretations could *also* be specified by explicit rules (governing satisfaction, designation, and truth).

So (a) and (b) were consistent with tolerance, while (c) was not. This tension is hard to detect in the published *Syntax* book because these incompatible doctrines occupy different sections, and are never brought into confrontation with each other. In the introduction, tolerance is highlighted. In the opening chapters and in the exposition of Language I, the formal mode and the rejection of meaning come to the fore, except in §§16–17, where tolerance is again in the spotlight. The exposition of Language II is largely neutral and technical, though in a few sections (e.g. §38) certain provisions (e.g. the elimination of classes) are implicitly defended as 'correct'. Part IV of the book, on general syntax, is dominated by tolerance. And in Part V, finally, on 'Philosophy and Syntax', the emphasis is almost entirely on the exclusion of meaning (the restriction to the 'formal mode of speech'); tolerance hardly makes an appearance. (It arrives, belatedly and somewhat timidly, toward the end in the discussion of rival conceptions of the 'foundations of mathematics'.) Since this last section was by far the most widely read, it captured the imagination of philosophers. The distinction between 'formal' and 'material' modes of speech, introduced in 'The

Physical Language', was discussed in more detail and applied to a wide range of philosophical problems. This distinction relied on the exclusion of meaning, and was thus incompatible with the principle of tolerance. The absence of any confrontation between tolerance and the rejection of meaning was not by design, but resulted straightforwardly from the order of composition;[8] Part V was largely written before the October 1932 turn to tolerance, while Part IV was written in 1933.[9]

AFTER *SYNTAX*

The principle of tolerance had been the late arrival in *Logical Syntax*. As we saw, it was no part of the book's conception or even its first draft. But in the end it won out over the other main component of the book, the formal mode of speech. In the *Introduction to Semantics* of 1942, Carnap included a section in which he discussed the 'modifications which the views explained in [*Logical Syntax*] have to undergo, especially in view of semantics' (1942, p. 246). The exclusive emphasis on syntax and the formal mode of speech was abandoned, and Carnap recognised that much of Part V would have to be reformulated. But 'the *principle of tolerance* . . . as explained in §17, is still maintained' (1942, p. 247). In 'Empiricism, Semantics, and Ontology' (1950a), finally, Carnap generalised what had been the 'formal mode of speech' to the realm of discourse 'internal' to a 'language framework'. On this basis he could then formulate his mature programme of explication (1950b, §§1–6), which recognised explication and language choice as practical questions residing *outside* any such chosen framework.

There is little evidence, published or unpublished, bearing on this important transition in Carnap's thought. It was a consequence of the adoption of tolerance, but this consequence had taken some time to emerge; it had not been immediately apparent. It is easy to see why not. Though Carnap had abandoned the idea that we cannot step outside language, this idea had in turn rested on a foundation that was not so easily dismantled. The sharp distinction between concepts and sentences internal to a system and those outside it had been one of the main lessons Carnap had learned from Frege,

---

[8] It is also true, however, that Carnap himself further aggravated the resulting misunderstandings by over-emphasising the 'syntax' dimension, the rejection of meaning, in popular expositions such as the strident *Philosophy and Logical Syntax* (1935a) where again tolerance makes only a token appearance (pp. 75–8).

[9] Carnap detailed the chronology of the book's composition when he sent off the typescript (ASP 1933b; also ASP 1932c).

and the application of this Fregean distinction to epistemology had been
the basis of the Vienna Circle's formulation of rational reconstruction, as
we saw in Chapter 6. It had made possible their characteristic approach
to the replacement of folk concepts in the context of a *deductive* system
of knowledge. Wittgensteinian considerations about the impossibility of
stepping outside language had then reinforced that sharp distinction even
further. But even when that further element had been dispensed with, it
was difficult now to backtrack from the sharp Fregean distinction between
internal and external, and make this dichotomy less absolute. It was hard
to *retain* the idea of a sharp distinction between internal and external for
constructed languages while allowing room for other systems (ordinary language) that *lacked* this sharp distinction. And only this concession would
make it possible, in the late 1930s, to regard ordinary language and formal
systems as mobile points along a continuum rather than as fixed diametrical
opposites.

This was especially difficult for Carnap because it made the distinction
between meaningful and meaningless questions or sentences less sharp than
it had previously seemed. 'External' could, under that previous dispensation, be largely regarded as co-extensive with 'meaningless'.[10] This was
certainly crisper and tidier than the later doctrine,[11] in which even *cognitive*
meaning is once again (as before 1926) a less sharply defined, more gradual concept, so that sufficiently clarified ordinary-language concepts could
now qualify as explicanda. The difficult thing was to retain the distinction
between internal and external, but to allow for a more gradual, dynamic,
piecemeal progress from ordinary language concepts to the explicata of our
scientific framework (1950b, §2; 1963, pp. 934–6).[12]

---

[10] Carnap continued to adhere to this increasingly inadequate usage, though eventually he conceded
that one might regard the normative or optative as a different sort of 'meaning component' (1963,
p. 1001).

[11] As Warren Goldfarb (1997) points out (pp. 63–5), though in stressing what was lost in moving from
the 'syntactic' to the semantic approach, he somewhat neglects the above-discussed shortcomings
of the former.

[12] It should be clear from the entire story told in this book that the characterisation of Carnap by
Thomas Mormann (2000, p. 36), endorsed by Wolters (2004, p. 37) is wide of the mark even for
the early Carnap, let alone the later: 'Carnap's worldview had a Cartesian air about it. He thought
in clear and distinct concepts and distinctions: Everything was either the one or the other: either
science or metaphysics; sentences were either analytic or synthetic; questions either external or
internal; judgements were either about facts or about values. He opposed nuances [*Zwischentöne*],
imponderables, and unanalysable transitions.' This of the perpetual bridge-builder who played
down differences and emphasised areas of agreement, of the practical-minded conceptual engineer
who sought to devise a continuous scale of confirmation for messy, empirical concepts, and of the
proponent of the unity of science who took a gradualist view of biological phenomena such as
consciousness!

As he progressed to this more subtle view, Carnap was of course still able to maintain that, taken at their traditional face value as questions about language-transcendent existence or substance, external questions sow confusion by masquerading as factual or theoretical sentences, and constrict inquiry by conveying the impression that there can be cognitively decidable questions – matters of fact – beyond the scope of science. But as he gradually retreated from the insistence that explication must be entirely internal (which as we saw had vitiated the first attempt to articulate an ideal of explication), Carnap was able to reframe external questions as *pragmatic* questions of language choice, practical choices among candidate explications. This has often been regarded as a dismissal of such questions, but actually, Carnap regarded them of the utmost importance; 'many problems concerning conceptual frameworks seem to me to belong to the most important problems of philosophy', he wrote a few years later, and added explicitly that he was thinking here 'both of theoretical investigations and of practical deliberations and decisions with respect to an acceptance or a change of frameworks, especially of the most general frameworks containing categorial concepts which are fundamental for the representation of all knowledge' (1963, p. 862).[13]

It was the principle of tolerance in this more general context of explication and conceptual engineering that set Carnap apart from the mainstream of analytic philosophy in the last decades of his life. It set him apart, especially, from Quine, whose influence from the early 1950s began to overshadow Carnap's. Quine had notoriously rejected explication altogether in 'Two Dogmas' (Quine 1951, p. 25). When he later, in *Word and Object*, embraced a version of it (Quine 1960, pp. 258ff.), he characteristically conflated explication with a particular linguistic proposal. Where Carnap – in view of the entire development sketched in this book – had come to *distinguish* his advocacy of the physicalist programme from his ideal of explication, subordinating the former to the latter, Quine ran them together again. He returned, in effect, to where Carnap had been before 1931, the rational reconstruction phase of the Vienna Circle. For Quine, as for that earlier programme, *'explication is elimination'* (Quine 1960, p. 260). As he illustrates with his example of the Wiener and Kuratowski definitions of the concept 'ordered pair', the initial problem 'is dissolved by showing how we can dispense with ordered pairs in any problematic sense in favour of certain clearer notions' (Quine 1960, p. 260). And so it is with all explications,

---

[13] Howard Stein has often (in conversation) emphasised the importance of this passage, as one of the few manifestations in print of a dimension that was much more obvious in Carnap as a teacher and in personal discussion.

for Quine; they replace useful but somehow defective or misleading concepts with more unambiguously *internal* ones. Explication was not, as it had become in Carnap's hands, an external matter; it remained entirely internal, Vienna Circle style.[14] For Quine it was an application of Occam's Razor, in the Russellian tradition. And thus the apparent pluralism of Quine's explication programme was skin deep. The Wiener and Kuratowski definitions of ordered pair are both internal to the same underlying logic and set theory, and both eliminate the explicandum in favour of a new concept definable solely within that framework. For Quine, this eliminative character was *required* of an explication. For Carnap, it was physicalistically desirable, but any replacement for an explicandum that could serve the core purposes agreed on by its users qualifies as an explication. It need not *also* meet further *philosophical* criteria, of the kind Quine insisted on.[15] Carnap, too, preferred that an explicatum be defined within a constructed or technical language (if possible one of those in standard use within the discipline in question). But this was much weaker than Quine's eliminative requirement; for Carnap it was only a desideratum, not a binding constraint;[16] this flexibility and scope was made possible by the new gradualism about cognitive meaning attained during the late 1930s.

Carnap never got very far in characterising the kind of external discourse in which 'theoretical investigations and practical deliberations and decisions with respect to an acceptance or a change of frameworks' would be carried on. He gave it a name, 'pragmatics', but remained vague about details. Quine, of course, for whom all questions were internal, rejected the whole idea outright; the supposed distinction between semantics and pragmatics was a 'pernicious error' (Quine 1987, p. 211). Even for Carnap, it remained a rather indistinct ideal. His formal predilections led him to hope that it could eventually be made a technical subject, but he was – by his standards – quite realistic about the prospects for this. When his student

---

[14] For Quine, rejection of external questions went beyond explication; for him there were no external questions, period. Semantic ascent was possible, but 'is only a momentary retreat from the world, for the utility of the truth-predicate is precisely the cancellation of linguistic reference' (quoted in the introduction, above, p. 25); so semantic ascent did not amount to the possibility of a genuine meta-perspective, as we have no choice but ultimately 'to acquiesce in the mother tongue'. Since the 'conceptual scheme' in which science and ordinary language were fused by definitional fiat (see the introduction, above, pp. 24–6) was not well defined, Quine did not encounter the same obstacles to 'internal' explication that we saw in Carnap's *Syntax* on pp. 256–61 above.

[15] As Michael Friedman (forthcoming) has diagnosed in Quine's version of empiricism, noting that this insistence seems to contradict Quine's otherwise thorough-going naturalism.

[16] 'The explicatum may belong to the ordinary language, although perhaps to a more exact part of it . . .The only essential requirement is that the explicatum be more precise than the explicandum; it is unimportant to which part of the language it belongs' (1963, p. 936).

R. M. Martin produced a technical apparatus for pragmatics (Martin 1959), Carnap wrote to Evert Beth, the editor of the series to which the book had been submitted, recommending it for publication but suggesting that it might have been best to clear the ground first with more preliminary clarifications, as agreement had not yet been reached even there.[17] He was right to be sceptical, of course, and subsequent investigation of concepts such as 'belief' – which he held to be a basic concept of pragmatics (1955, p. 250) – has revealed that they contain fundamental ambiguities that would need to be decided one way or another before proceeding with any sort of formalisation.[18]

So it is easy to take the sceptical, Quinean position that the whole idea was going nowhere. But this would be to overlook a dimension in which Carnap and Quine were largely in agreement, the importance of what Quine called 'naturalistic epistemology'. They classified this activity differently; for Quine it was simply part of science.[19] For Carnap, too, there was a purely descriptive, scientific element to it; this was part of what he called descriptive pragmatics – the descriptive study of human cognition in all its aspects as an essential basis for the practical task of conceptual engineering. It was essential for that task because the biological, physiological, psychological, linguistic, sociological, economic, and historical knowledge about our cognitive capacities and the development of our actual knowledge are the data we have at our disposal when we seek to construct languages and decide among explications. They define the existing possibility space within which we construct languages adequate to what we know already, and from which we can extrapolate to imagine new possibilities. This knowledge

---

[17] 'Since probably at the present time various authors would choose different concepts and different methods, it might at first be advisable to write a less technical treatise explaining the concepts, defining them informally in such a way as to indicate clearly how they would be defined in a formalised metalanguage without necessarily giving actually their formalised definition, studying alternative explications of the various concepts, etc. (What I have in mind is roughly analogous to Russell's preparatory discussions in his *Principles of Mathematics* before writing the *Principia* or my preliminary discussions in *Meaning and Necessity* in preparation for a not yet written treatise of a semantics of extensions and intensions in either an extensional or an intensional formalised metalanguage.)' (ASP 1958a).

[18] He would not, of course, have been the least surprised about the contradictions arising from the 'folk' concept of belief, as famously diagnosed by Kripke (1979). In all the discussion arising out of this and similar analyses, very few efforts at anything like what Carnap called *explication* have been undertaken; attention has focused more on the natural-language or 'folk' concepts themselves than on their systematic replacement by better concepts. Even where the latter has been attempted, e.g. by Stephen Stich (1983), the difficulties and unfamiliarity of the territory (essentially, the absence of a larger explanatory framework in which to locate such an explicatum) have, as in Stich's case, caused the bold proposal to be withdrawn (Stich 1996).

[19] See Richardson (forthcoming) on the fundamental differences between Quine's 'naturalism' and that of Dewey on the one hand, Carnap on the other.

has to explication a relation analogous to that of biological knowledge to medicine, or physical knowledge to structural engineering.

And naturalistic epistemology in this broad sense has made great strides since Carnap's death, on many different fronts. We know much more now about the processing involved in the various human sensory systems,[20] and can model higher-level capabilities like understanding language and written texts. One of the early protagonists of the cognitive revolution, Noam Chomsky, had used Carnap's own idea of regarding natural languages as systems of rules. This rule-based approach has been challenged by theories that modelled human processing on self-organising weighted networks (parallel or 'connectionist' processing).[21] Hybrids between these two approaches,[22] seeking to portray human thought as a dialectical interplay between the two poles of receptive processing and active shaping of a 'situation model' (Kintsch 1998), recapitulate a basic Kantian motif and are thus reminiscent of Helmholtz, who has justly been called the father of cognitive science (Gregory 1998).

The result of this work is a very different, more 'constructivist' understanding of human cognition even at the biological level. This is complemented and reinforced by Vygotskian theories of the interface between socially mediated knowledge and individual development (e.g. Wertsch 1985; Tomasello 1999). While the resulting picture is not incompatible with certain insights of the later Wittgenstein, philosophers have not really caught up with the new view of human cognition to emerge from this body of empirical work, or made much effort to come to terms with it.

The mention of Vygotsky will raise a further sceptical question in many readers' minds, though, about the possibility of a Carnapian pragmatics. What about the *social* dimension of a 'naturalised epistemology'? This would appear to be a more fundamental obstacle to Carnap's entire project. Though his ideal of explication leaves room for fundamental disagreements about the choice among categorial frameworks, he did not himself really take seriously any doubts about the rationality of the scientific enterprise. He did not in practice distinguish between that enterprise and the knowledge generated by it as an objective artefact. We have become habituated to this distinction in the wake of Kuhn's *Structure of Scientific Revolutions* and

---

[20] Due to such work as that of Marr (1982), Newcombe and Huttenlocher (2000), and many others.

[21] Carnap would have been pleased to note that his own attempt to attain qualities by quasi-analysis in the *Aufbau* rested on a concept of 'degree of similarity' which is much more elegantly and economically defined and implemented by weightings in a perceptual network.

[22] Such as those discussed, in different ways, by Nelson (1996), Kintsch (1998), and Tomasello (1999).

the more radical forms of scepticism developed since then. When Carnap (who was Kuhn's series editor) encountered this book, he embraced it enthusiastically. He saw Kuhn's efforts to apply empirical inquiry to the study of empirical inquiry as a practical enterprise akin to his own efforts to construct an inductive logic. Both served the end of improving organised inquiry as a practical tool in the service of human needs and aspirations (Reisch 1991).

He did not foresee the Pandora's Box that Kuhn's book would open. He could not have conceived of the situation that has now resulted, in which there is no agreement among historians and philosophers of science even on the most basic assumptions about the character of the enterprise.[23] But given that result, Carnap would have seen no reason to retract or modify his ideal of explication. Where positions are held so tenaciously and heels are so far dug in, only a pluralistic view that regards the different positions as proposals for the form of meta-language for the study of science could have any hope of bringing about whatever mutual understanding might still be possible. And he would have realised immediately that the pragmatics most urgently needed in this situation is not formal – that would be premature. What is needed now is not yet explication, in his terms, but clarification: convergence on mutually agreed *explicanda* (among some subset of discussion participants, at least). This suggests a programme for a clarificatory pragmatics consisting in a certain kind of conceptual history of the scientific enterprise, with special attention to episodes in which major changes of theoretical direction were undertaken. Such a history would be 'internal' to present science, in Carnap's sense.[24] It would view past science through the lens of present science. Not in the service of a 'whiggish' triumphalism, but rather with a view to using the best conceptual tools available to identify the precise content of past scientific controversies *in our own terms*,[25] assessing the strengths and weaknesses – with respect to evidence and technical tools available at the time – of the different viewpoints. (This involves no claim that present science is 'the truth', or that it is in every way superior to past science. It involves only the usual prudence we observe when addressing

[23] This situation is an aspect of the 'new politics of knowledge' discussed in Chapter 11, pp. 293–309 below.

[24] This is, of course, a narrower sense of 'internal' than that usually employed in the traditional distinction between internal and external history of science. Reasonable doubt has been cast on the possibility of any such distinction, but 'internal' history in the sense suggested here (which one might call 'strictly internal history' to emphasise the difference) is well defined.

[25] This assumes, of course, that the past concepts *can*, in fact, be translated into our terms. A believer in strong incommensurability might deny this possibility. But such a position would also have to accept that past observations are irrelevant to present theories, which in turn begins to sound rather arbitrary when it finds itself forced to address the question where 'past' ends and 'present' begins.

any practical question; present knowledge has to be our default reference point in the development of a pragmatics of theory choice or language choice just as it is in the choice of medical treatments or of flight safety arrangements.) Such investigations can provide us with the explicanda that *external* histories of science – sociology, psychology, economics, and anthropology of science – might then address in the service of (descriptive) pragmatics.

But even the sum of such internal and external histories does not yet suffice to yield what a Carnapian pragmatics actually requires to support the programme of explication, the external discourse in which 'theoretical investigations and practical deliberations and decisions with respect to an acceptance or a change of frameworks' are pursued. For this we need, rather, something that can shed light on the history of explication itself, or more concretely, the history of particular explications. It is only against the background of such histories that the *present* activity of explication can be properly informed about its limits and its possibilities. (Of course the past need not *determine* the future, but in fact the great explicators have all, like Newton himself, stood on the shoulders of giants.) In particular, what is needed are what one might call the *genealogies* of important scientific concepts and ideas, the sequence of their explications offered and used by the relevant knowledge communities. There is more to this than just the bare knowledge of the sequence; there is also the *understanding* of how it progressed and why, to which external histories may contribute but which they do not exhaust. When Richard Feynman set out to explain quantum electrodynamics to a general audience, he admitted that they would not understand it, but wanted them to listen anyway: 'You see, my physics students don't understand it, either. That is because *I* don't understand it. Nobody does' (Feynman 1985, p. 9). Understanding lags behind knowledge, it takes time to catch up. It takes time to *place* a given piece of news – new knowledge – within the world we live and act in, the rough-and-ready system of interlocking concepts we use to locate ourselves in that world. To be able to use our knowledge (and certainly to use it for the jobs of clarification and explication), we must understand it, to some degree. Intertwined with the 'enterprise of knowledge', over the course of its history, has been what Howard Stein (2004) calls an 'enterprise of understanding' that at least partly *consists* in constructing and explaining precisely those conceptual genealogies, sequences of explications, that provide present tasks of explication with their possibility space. This enterprise overlaps to some degree, of course, with the historical discipline of philosophy. The investigation of conceptual genealogies – which could therefore be justly called *philosophical history of science* – is perhaps the most important component of the 'naturalistic epistemology' that, I suggest, a present-day continuation of Carnapian descriptive pragmatics is developing in support of the normative ideal of explication.[26] How the latter might be envisaged more concretely, in this light, is touched on in the next chapter.

But before leaving this subject it must be said that, although Carnap welcomed Kuhn's book and was more than willing to countenance a social-scientific dimension in the history of science, his attitude toward the situation Kuhn and subsequent authors diagnosed was quite different from the present mainstream. The general tenor of 'science studies' since Kuhn has been to portray the scientific tradition as something quite different from its starry-eyed self-image. Rather than an open-minded, value-neutral, dispassionate, empirically oriented search for reliable knowledge, science is now often portrayed as prone to ideological distortion, systematically subservient to social elites and their agendas, and subject to the whims of dominant personalities and intellectual fashions. In the human and social sciences, it is (rightly) pointed out, the erstwhile race to emulate 'genuine' science by adopting a theoretical apparatus and quantitative measurement was often a cloak for less respectable agendas. To some degree all this is of course a necessary corrective to the mindless formulations of supposed 'scientific method', and uncritical portrayal of heroic science, in school textbooks and other popularisations. Carnap might well have agreed that a dose of cold, dispassionate, criticism of science from an outside perspective was desirable, especially in view of the enormous and increasing power wielded by scientific establishments.

But his attitude would have been quite different from the present mainstream in two fundamental respects: First, he would not have interpreted the results of 'science studies' as licensing any inductive conclusions about what science 'is'. And second, he would have seen the main utility of this work in pointing out *obstacles* that an optimal conceptual system should help to *overcome* (and he would have set to work on the engineering task of designing such a system). Carnap did, of course, have his own conception of science, but it did not derive from induction over a population of instances (which would in any case raise the problem of how to define the relevant population). Nor was it exhausted by positive formal criteria, such as that of having one or more theoretical languages (1939, 1956), or by constraints,

---

[26] Some of the best and earliest such work was, in fact, undertaken by Carnap's own student Howard Stein (e.g. 1958, 1967, 1990, 2002). Some outstanding recent examples are Tait (1997), Smith (2001, 2002a, 2002b); Awodey and Reck (2002); Zabell (2005); Friedman (2002, 2006); and DiSalle (2006).

such as that of empiricism. His conception derived from (as well as being presupposed by, and part of) his ideal of explication; it was an ideal, not a descriptive concept. And this ideal was inspired, as we have seen, by the great exemplars of explication, the giants on whose shoulders we all stand – not only the great scientists, but also the great conceptual engineers among the philosophers.[27]

---

[27] Among the latter, Carnap would have counted not only the figures who recur frequently in the past ten chapters (Kant, Frege, Russell, Wittgenstein), but also, in particular, Aristotle, Leibniz, Peirce, and Whitehead (1963, p. 862).

CHAPTER 11

The ideal of explication

We have traced the steps, over the past ten chapters, by which Carnap progressed from a position within the mainstream of scientific neo-Kantianism, strongly influenced – as that tradition was – by positivism, to the embrace of tolerance in 1932. The full application of the new principle was impeded for many years by lingering prejudices from earlier stages in his development. This delay, combined with Carnap's predilection for working on particular language projects rather than the architectonic of the overall ideal, meant that he never fully spelled out his ideal of explication as an account of reason, and it is left to those following in his footsteps to piece together the hints he left. Inevitably, we round out and supplement those fragments with new materials of our own, suiting his ideas to fit our very different environment. In keeping with the discussion of Carnapian pragmatics at the end of Chapter 10, the following sketch is placed in a naturalistic context. The ideal of explication is meant to be an ideal, not a descriptive theory, but to convey how it could be relevant to real life, it has to be given some social and historical texture.

To vindicate the approach of situating the development toward this ideal in a larger context, and to give some indication how it can indeed be employed as an ideal of reason in a broader sense, I will conclude, in the final section, by applying it in a more ill-structured and quite different context of discourse: the realm of political interaction in democratic societies.

EVOLVED AND CONSTRUCTED LANGUAGES

Faced with the Hegelian task of a 'history of reason', Carnap's point of departure would have been to distinguish sharply between two kinds of coding or representation systems, which we might call 'evolved' and 'constructed' systems (Carnap sometimes calls them 'informal' and 'formal' languages, or 'word-languages' and 'artificially constructed symbolic languages', or 'natural' and 'artificial' languages, among other pairs of terms). He took this fundamental distinction so entirely for granted that, despite its centrality to his thought, he never fully spelled out his view of it. He would undoubtedly, though, have endorsed the characterisation by a very different philosopher, Gaston Bachelard, who made a slogan of the *coupure épistemologique* (epistemological discontinuity or rupture) between scientific and everyday modes of thinking. Carnap would have agreed with Bachelard that we are autonomous and responsible beings (both individually and as a species) only insofar as we construct our conceptual frameworks self-consciously, rather than going complacently with the flow of our inherited concepts (Bachelard 1934, 1938).

But despite this *coupure épistemologique*, Carnap also, especially after the late 1930s, saw a continuity between the two kinds of system. Even in the *Syntax*, he regards evolved languages *as* calculi, i.e. *as* systems of formation and transformation rules. He included a large variety of signal and symbol systems under the heading of 'calculus', and saw no break anywhere along that broad spectrum, at which everything to one side was a 'calculus', leaving the rest to some other status. Nor is there any suggestion that a constructed calculus is to be taken as a map or grid constraining a more amorphous evolved language, such as that used by scientists.[1] The constructed languages are to be regarded, rather, as candidate vehicles for the construction of science as a unified theory, including a meta-language in which to construct and evaluate the syntax of the object language (later also its semantics and pragmatics).

To illustrate this continuity between evolved and constructed systems, in Carnap's spirit, one could cite the historical development of more precise and self-consciously constructed languages. In the beginning, at some point before the dawn of history, there were only evolved languages. But the first written records reveal that groups of specialists – legal, commercial, religious – had already developed partly formalised languages as tools of government, trade, or theological disputation. The development of ever more precise technical languages on this basis was very gradual.[2] And the literate population remained tiny. Still, even in antiquity the *coupure épistemologique* between the language of geometry and the evolved language of everyday life was essentially as radical as it is now. The difference was that – apart from the bold extrapolations of Plato and a few followers – the language of geometry had only very limited relevance to knowledge of

---

[1] This idea has been attributed to Carnap by Ricketts (2004a, 2004b).

[2] There were certainly revolutionary breakthroughs, such as the discovery of deductive geometry in ancient Greece. Even here, though, recent scholarship suggests that, however condensed in time, this development was also quite gradual and did not occur in a single revolutionary step (Netz 1999).

the world, and knowledge had limited importance to society. It was only in the seventeenth century, and especially with the publication of Newton's *Principia* in 1687, that it became more widely clear to educated people that the language of genuine knowledge was starkly different from the evolved language of everyday life. Only at that point did a scientific culture begin to form, and an international community of those acculturated in the new attitudes and fluent in the new languages. (The existence of such a community, however small and embattled, was the basis for the Enlightenment.)

This very gradual diachronic progression from evolved languages to constructed ones illustrates the continuity Carnap saw between them. The same wide spectrum of precision can also be observed *synchronically* across different usage contexts in present societies. Most everyday discourse still takes place in our relatively amorphous,[3] chaotically evolved vernacular. At the other extreme are the constructed languages used in the hard sciences and by computers. In between we find specialists using partially constructed languages of law, medicine, or accounting whose usage is much more tightly constrained than that of everyday language, but much looser than that of mathematical physics. Again, as in the diachronic illustration, there is no sharp boundary. There is a practical division of labour among those who study the different kinds of systems; as a rule, the study of evolved languages is an empirical discipline (linguistics), while the self-conscious creation of symbolic systems for pure and applied science is regarded as mathematical or formal. But there are many intermediate cases (e.g. music theory, which evolved over hundreds of years in response to musical practice, but has formal elements). So 'evolved' and 'constructed' are useful as comparative or relative concepts, to each other. One language can be more or less constructed than another, but there is no absolute scale of 'constructedness'.

From an empirical viewpoint, Carnap would of course have allowed that evolved and constructed languages *both* 'evolve'; biology treats cultural evolution (of which the evolution of constructed languages is a part) and physical evolution as interacting processes (e.g. Bonner 1983, Boyd and Richerson 1985). The two different processes operate at different speeds in different media. But this empirical viewpoint is compatible with an *ideal* viewpoint that places a positive value on the one kind of evolutionary process because of its role in liberating the human species (especially those human individuals who seek it out) from unreflective passivity in thought

---

[3] 'Amorphous' only in the sense that such contexts allow (relatively to constructed languages) more leeway in usage; they are not as tightly constrained by agreement among their users. For Carnap, though, they would still be regarded as rule systems. There is no passage in his writings suggesting that he would regard a used language as 'logically amorphous' in the sense Ricketts suggests.

and action. (To regard war or starvation as natural phenomena, from an empirical standpoint, does not prevent us from also adopting an ideal standpoint that envisages a world without these phenomena.) Evolved and constructed languages exist side by side, from the empirical viewpoint, and usually the interactions between them are marginal. From Carnap's ideal viewpoint, however, the liberation of human thought from passive complacency and the shackles of the past depends on the progressive replacement of evolved by constructed languages.[4] Not by wholesale replacement of an entire language; this is impossible. We have to stand on one part of the boat while we repair other parts of it on the open sea. And the two kinds of system are adapted to different purposes; neither can replace the other across the whole spectrum of its uses.[5]

Explication, then, is what relates these kinds of systems to each other. It aims less to *describe* their relation in social practice than to *raise* the degree of construction (or 'constructedness') in human languages – especially in those at the more constructed end of the spectrum (which are seen as gradually dragging the less constructed along behind them). In the *Syntax*, as we saw (Chapter 10, pp. 256–61 above), explication had been conceived as the replacement of an explicandum (a material-mode concept) by a concept framed in the formal mode of speech. But this had remained, as in rational reconstruction, an *internal* process of replacement. The later Carnap abandons this idea and recognises explication as external. Theory choice and language choice are acknowledged to be practical matters, so sentences pertaining to them no longer all have 'cognitive' meaning; some must rather have normative or 'optative' meaning.[6] The ideal of explication is itself external, then; it is (normative) pragmatics, though particular explications may belong to any part of science or any part of the meta-theory of science (syntax, semantics, pragmatics).

The ideal of explication is one of piecemeal upgrading; it starts *in medias res*, not from first principles. But how are we to conceive of this as taking place in the actual practice of science, as a social institution? This is where the picture sketched so far would begin to fall afoul of current scepticism

---

[4] 'I do not share the apparently widespread view that the vagueness and ambiguity of most words in everyday language do not much interfere with human communication. It is hard for me to understand how someone could really believe this, in view of the countless misunderstandings and failures to get something across that we observe daily. I would have thought that there could be no disagreement about the damage done by this vagueness' (ASP 1956a).

[5] Nor does this interaction take the form, suggested by Ricketts (2004a, pp. 260–3) of the wholesale *superimposition* of a constructed onto an evolved language, in which the constructed language would act as a grid or coordinate system for the evolved one (the correspondence relation between which and the evolved language would also have to be specified, in an appropriately constructed meta-language).

[6] See 1963, Section VI, 'Value Judgements', pp. 999–1016.

about the 'idealisations' of old-style philosophy of science. In fact, Carnap's picture is quite compatible with a more sociologistic, post-Wittgensteinian, post-Kuhnian view of scientific practice. Viewed as empirical phenomena, evolved and constructed languages can be regarded as residing in different social contexts. And from an ideal or engineering viewpoint they can be seen as having different functions, different uses in life. Either way, this fits well with the picture we find, say, in the opening passages of *Philosophical Investigations*, e.g. Sections 11 and 12, where Wittgenstein compares the heterogeneity of language uses to the different uses of various tools in a toolbox or the levers in the cabin of a steam locomotive; or Section 23, where he lists some of the different functions of different kinds of sentences. An 'evolved' language, then, would in Carnapian terms be the communicative medium for this vast heterogeneity of uses, while a 'constructed' language is purpose-built for a much narrower range of uses within the codification and search for systematic ('scientific') knowledge (1963, pp. 938–9) – which in turn has an enormous variety of social uses and entanglements. But these are again, from a Carnapian viewpoint, to be regarded as a matter for 'external' deliberation.[7]

On the one hand, in this picture, we participate in a rather chaotic *Lebenswelt* – immediate awareness embedded in the everyday life around us. It is ordered to some degree by categories of common sense local to a particular culture, perhaps also partly ordered by more precise concepts from constructed languages that have diffused into certain local common usages. This is the world in which we live and act, articulated and presented to us in evolved languages. On the other hand, the local cultures of certain subcommunities that specialise in a particular task – the systematic pursuit of knowledge (the 'sciences', however one might want to identify those) – have constructed various elaborate devices for this purpose, including communicative systems whose rules are, to varying degrees, consciously and deliberately made up and agreed on, and often continually renegotiated. Collectively, the subcommunities employing such systems use them to represent a provisional theory of the world, the most adequate they have been able to devise so far – adequate, for instance, to all the facts they collectively know. This theory is represented in constructed languages – ideally, in the long run, a single one, so as to exhibit the commensurability of all the parts of the theory and to enable us to bring these different

---

[7] Which would ordinarily begin in some dialect of an evolved language, though as we will see below, this is only the first step of a more intricate dialectic; some versions or dialects of the evolved language are more 'constructed' than others.

parts to bear on problems whose solution requires many different kinds of knowledge.[8]

The explicative interaction between evolved and constructed systems takes the form not of wholesale replacement or superimposition, for Carnap, but of piecemeal exchange within the context of a dynamic mutual feedback relation. From the engineering point of view, this of course raises problems of its own, one of which is the clear identification, within the language subject to explication, of the 'pieces' to be thus replaced piecemeal by explications framed in the terms of constructed languages. In the absence of sharp individuation of concepts, how can we clearly identify an explicandum? For Carnap, explication must be preceded by what he calls 'clarification', the largely *informal* task of establishing a mutual understanding about the identity of the explicandum before proceeding with its replacement. And though he did not underestimate this challenge, he thought it could be overcome, at a practical level:

There is a temptation to think that, since the explicandum cannot be given in exact terms anyway, it does not matter much how we formulate the problem. But this would be quite wrong. On the contrary, since even in the best case we cannot reach full exactness, we must, in order to prevent the discussion of the problem from becoming entirely futile, do all we can to make at least practically clear what is meant as the explicandum. What X means by a certain term in contexts of a certain kind is at least practically clear to Y if Y is able to predict correctly X's interpretation from most of the simple, ordinary cases of the use of the term in those contexts. It seems to me that, in raising problems of analysis or explication, philosophers very frequently violate this requirement. They ask questions like: 'What is causality?', 'What is life?', 'What is mind?', 'What is justice?', etc. Then they often immediately start to look for an answer without first examining the tacit assumption that the terms of the question are at least practically clear enough to serve as a basis for an investigation, for an analysis or explication. Even though the terms in question are unsystematic, inexact terms, there are means for reaching a relatively good mutual understanding as to their intended meaning. (1950b, p. 4)

---

[8] Carnap used an example of Neurath's (1932, p. 58) to illustrate this, that of a forest fire. 'A practical decision in the present moment may perhaps depend [on a prediction how soon the fire can be extinguished]. Then knowledge of many facts and laws of quite different kinds is relevant as a basis for our prediction . . . [not just biological and physical, but also sociological and economic facts and laws] . . . The same is true for very many cases of predictions both in everyday life and in science. In order to derive such predictions we need to combine sentences of different fields. If now the terms of the different branches of science were of fundamentally different character – as some philosophers believe – then we could not connect them logically and it would be impossible to come to a prediction. Therefore the *unity of the language* of science is the basis for the practical application of knowledge in our life' (ASP 1936a, pp. 22–3). A more obvious example, in our present context, might be environmental trade-offs, which involve not just physical, chemical, and biological, but also economic, sociological, and political knowledge.

But there is the further problem of how to characterise the relation between an explicandum, thus informally identified within an evolved language, and an explicatum precisely defined within a more constructed system. This relation *cannot itself be precise*. This is just the fundamental feature of explication, often misunderstood, that made the path to it so thorny for Carnap – and that sets it apart from both pre-1931 rational reconstruction and 'translation' into the formal mode of speech. In these programmes, the language supplying the replacements for informal usages were self-sufficient, so that the process of replacement was internal to those languages. Explication, in contrast, is a process external to the precise target language:

Since the datum is inexact, the problem itself is not stated in exact terms; and yet we are asked to give an exact solution. This is one of the puzzling peculiarities of explication. It follows that, if a solution for a problem of explication is proposed, we cannot decide in an exact way whether it is right or wrong. Strictly speaking, the question whether the solution is right or wrong makes no good sense because there is no clear-cut answer. The question should rather be whether the proposed solution is satisfactory, whether it is more satisfactory than another one, and the like. (1950b, p. 4)

(By 'right or wrong' Carnap means 'true or false'; by 'satisfactory' he means 'useful or helpful to the people in question'.) Moreover, the relation between explicandum and explicatum is not itself an *internal* question, at least not within the explicatum language, as Carnap's student Howard Stein pointed out:

The explicatum, as an exactly characterized concept, belongs to some formalized discourse – some 'framework'. The explicandum . . . belongs ipso facto to a mode of discourse outside that framework. Therefore *any* question about the relation of the explicatum to the explicandum is an 'external' question; this holds, in particular, of the question whether an explication is adequate – that is, whether the explicatum does in some appropriate sense fully represent, within the framework, the function performed (let us say) 'presystematically' by the explicandum. (Stein 1992, p. 280)

And such an external question is, for Carnap, as he often repeated, 'the practical problem whether or not to incorporate into the language the new linguistic forms' in question (1950a, p. 209). The mutual feedback relation between the two modes of discourse thus becomes strikingly evident: on the one hand, explications defined within constructed languages offer piecemeal *replacements* for evolved concepts in used languages. But on the other hand, the choice among alternative explications is a practical problem. It must be made in the context of action, which overlaps to some degree with the *Lebenswelt* in which the participants articulate the values and preferences that guide their choices. The *process* of choice can of course itself be formally represented within a decision theory or game theory or other formalism, but the values and preferences embodied in the utility functions that occur in the relevant interpretations of such formalisms must still be supplied from outside by the people making the choice. For Carnap, then, the context of action and the context of knowledge are not mutually interreducible. He would of course readily agree with Quine (who also acquiesces in an is-ought distinction; Quine 1974, pp. 49–52) that our values are just as much part of nature as our organisms or our social interactions or whatever else produces those values (Quine 1974, pp. 51–2), and that the theory of nature is thus also a (descriptive) theory of values. But this, he would point out, does not relieve us of the responsibility of choice, any more than a scientific understanding of the processes leading people to choose different jobs would relieve us of the need to make a living, or of the responsibility of deciding how to do it.

The question remains, however, how to locate this process, even from an ideal point of view, in a naturalistic (sociolinguistic or anthropological) setting. This is not a question Carnap considered, but he knew it was an essential part of a complete theory of scientific language; the logical structure of theories had somehow to be discernible in the practical enterprise. Scientists have no choice but to use evolved languages in their work, both when they discuss the constructed languages they use and in other, more practical tasks. But there is an important difference between the local dialect of a scientific profession and most other dialects in a society.[9] A scientific dialect is organised around, often explicitly subordinating itself to, the rules of one or more provisionally agreed-upon *regulative* constructed language systems. These systems may not always be adhered to in fact, but they are acknowledged to have normative force within the profession. Not all parts of practical life within a science are equally subject to these theoretical norms. At one extreme, graduate teaching in the regulative theory is very tightly constrained by the constructed language system. But this system may, at the other extreme, be only peripherally relevant to disputes about promotion, recruitment, or wider university politics. Such a professional dialect has two aspects, then. On the one hand, it overlaps with the evolved languages used outside science, the 'folk' categories of the surrounding *Lebenswelt*. On the other hand, it is also normatively guided by its regulative constructed-language systems. Empirically, this suspension or tug-of-war between two determinative influences may manifest itself as a continuum

---

[9] In practice there is, once again, a range of gradations. The legal and accounting professions, for instance, use technical languages that are influenced by various sciences, but also have many grey areas where traditional, inherited categories still hold sway.

between two poles, without any very clear boundaries in between.[10] But for analytical purposes we can roughly divide the dialect of a scientific community into three schematic parts or zones along that continuum: at one end, (1) the regulative constructed systems; at the other end, (3) the part that largely overlaps with 'folk' categories of everyday speech. Between them is (2) a grey area of interpolations within or extrapolations from the constructed-language system, or informal conventions required to apply it, or any number of informal, ad hoc, auxiliary constructions useful for bringing the constructed language to bear on desired problems.[11] Surveying the three zones in terms of the explication process, (1) is the realm of provisionally agreed explicata; (3) includes, among other things, the practical and normative (ethical, aesthetic, etc.) parts of language where there are no widely accepted explications at all; and (2) is the source of explicanda. It is here, in the shop talk of scientists, constrained by but not limited to the constructed languages that regulate their discipline, that informal, vague concepts, still partly embedded in the *Lebenswelt*, most urgently need to be clarified and explicated.[12]

---

[10] There would seem to be an obvious distinction between the informal talk surrounding the use of the regulative constructed language and its experimental applications, on the one hand, and the language used in the wider penumbra of issues not directly related to the regulative system, on the other. This is a practically indispensable distinction that can, at a practical level, be agreed on by most participants in most specific cases. But as with the equally indispensable distinction between theory and observation, it is extremely difficult to make precise. Nonetheless, in the real world of the scientific professions there is sufficiently broad agreement about which norms operate where that the professions are able to function as viable continuing enterprises.

[11] To see how coarse and oversimplified this three-part schema is, one need only reflect for a moment on how much is contained in 'zone (2)' as here described: experimental findings, data, facts, empirical generalisations, oral tradition and lore about the use of apparatus (Franklin 1986, 2002), about the importance and reliability of various facts and empirical generalisations, about statistics and other analytical tools (except insofar as they have a place within the regulative theory itself), and the use of computers for all these purposes; discussions about the relative significance of various results; the kinds of 'thick' causal concepts discussed in some of the recent literature on 'causation' (e.g. Cartwright 2004), and other 'folk' concepts of this kind (Norton 2003, forthcoming); the 'values of inquiry' cited by Kuhn (1977) and variously contested by others (e.g. Longino 1995); and much else. To put it briefly, one might say in Howard Stein's (2004) terms that while the 'enterprise of knowledge' is in zone (1), the 'enterprise of understanding' is in zone (2).

[12] Note that within zone (1), something like the use of a formal language as a grid or coordinate system for a used language, of the kind Ricketts suggests as the *overall* relation between the two kinds of system, may in fact operate. But that is only because, within this zone, the language defers to or *becomes* the constructed language. Whatever part of it is not completely identical with the constructed language is entirely subordinated to it, as a kind of user interface for beginning students or for those not yet fully at home in the use of the constructed language itself. When an instructor of introductory analysis uses the term 'first derivative', she may *use* it loosely, but ultimately there is no leeway, no 'amorphousness' of the kind Ricketts associates with used languages, in what she intends to convey. Still, it is true within this zone that, as Ricketts suggests, the superimposition of a calculus onto the used language gives the language a deductive force beyond what its resources *qua* used language could warrant.

The dialect of a scientific profession – or a somewhat idealised or standardised version of scientific language that integrates a number of scientific dialects – seems to be approximately what Neurath had in mind when he portrayed the language of the 'republic of scientists', the single encyclopaedic language, as a 'universal vernacular' (Neurath 1932, 1934). Though a biologist, for instance, may herself have only the vaguest knowledge of physics, the entire theory of quantum electrodynamics lurks behind her use of the word 'light'. She provisionally accepts that theory as normative for her scientific use of the word. The parts of zone (2) that are not discipline-specific, then, can plausibly be conceived as a shared scientific dialect in the late-Carnapian view being proposed here. As in Neurath's version, this language is not perfectly well defined. On the other hand, the above discussion enables us to be a little more precise about the kinds of indeterminacy and vagueness inherent in this language. Rather than assuming, as Neurath does (Cartwright *et al.* 1996, pp. 188ff.), that '*Ballungen*' – the remaining 'clots' of vagueness and indeterminacy – are to be expected anywhere at all within the 'universal vernacular', we can narrow down where they are most likely to appear. They are *least* likely to appear in zone (1), where the language, insofar as it is not the regulative system itself, essentially *defers* to that system, and where many terms may have no corresponding explicanda or informal equivalents at all. It would also be inappropriate to speak of *Ballungen* in zone (3), which is more like one gigantic *Ballung*, a huge tangle, and from the viewpoint of the regulative system, it is hardly worth identifying or localising particular *Ballungen* within it.[13] Such particular, localised, reasonably clear or clarifiable explicanda are to be found, rather, in zone (2). It is here that there are sufficient constraints on the use of terms to allow agreement on a clarification, the necessary preliminary to explication. Of course the explication of a term in this category (e.g. a new explication of the informal usage 'at the same time' in classical physics) can also feed back to a reorganisation or replacement of the regulative language system – zone (1) itself.

To apply constructed language systems to actual science, then, it is unnecessary for Carnap to think of evolved languages as behavioural *instances* of constructed languages.[14] How those systems are used in the practical

---

[13] For some disciplines, it may be worthwhile; a vague concept for which no directly *physical* explication is conceivable (at a given time within the discipline), which, therefore is not an explicandum within physics, may be a perfectly usable explicandum within economics or linguistics. Whether these are to be regarded as ultimately unifiable or as autonomous 'levels of explanation' is a completely separate question that need not be decided to make this distinction.

[14] Ricketts proposes to 'represent a change in an investigator's speech habits as the rejection of a hypothesis on the basis of contradictions between observation sentences logically implied by a theory

activities of a scientific discipline, including its empirical research, is a matter of their pragmatics (even for Carnap himself, though he thought of observation sentences as ultimately providing the interpretation of a theoretical language), and the choice of language belongs to this practical realm as well. The choice is made using (a local version of) the 'universal vernacular' of zone (2); Carnap accepted something like Neurath's view that this 'universal vernacular' was at any given time provisional; it was constantly upgrading itself by interaction with the various sectors of zone (1).

The regulative system in zone (1) can be regarded, in this late-Carnapian view, as the 'hard core' of a Kuhnian 'paradigm' or Lakatosian 'research programme'. That the existing regulative language system of a discipline is 'incommensurable' (in the Kuhnian sense) with some alternative system simply means that the two are not equivalent or intertranslatable.[15] This does not mean, though, that they are incapable of being compared. It just means that there is no way of comparing them directly *within* zone (1) itself.[16] They can share a zone (2) without sharing a zone (1); e.g. we can compare different explicata of the explicandum 'at the same time'. Within the larger context of the scientific dialect (or 'universal vernacular') as a whole, incorporating all three zones, there will in any reasonably developed science be resources within zone (2) that allow comparison of two constructed systems, and allow the consequences of choosing one or the other to be considered, insofar as they can be known or guessed at in advance. Among these resources is a body of experimental findings that any candidate system must be able, by appropriate 'schematisations' within the semantics of the language system, to account for.[17]

that includes the hypothesis and observation reports that appear in the investigator's protocol . . . the logical syntax of a calculus is imposed like a grid on an investigator's used language, on her speech habits. With this grid in place, we represent an investigator's acceptance and rejection of sentences as the epistemic evaluation of hypotheses. Without this grid, we simply have changes in speech dispositions' (2004a, p. 263). In the present account, experimentation, observation, recording of data, and much else (see footnote 11 above) belong to zone (2) of the scientific dialect, while Carnap intended his frameworks as systems for the unification of the regulative systems in zone (1). This does not mean that the activity or language within zone (2) cannot be studied, but that its meta-theory belongs mainly to the pragmatics, not the syntax or semantics, of the proposed language.

[15] Kuhn appears specifically to have had in mind a situation in which (some) syntactically equivalent sentences (in some sense) of the two calculi have different interpretations, because the designata of the *vocabulary* of the two semantical systems differ. But under the approach suggested here, they can be regarded as alternative explicata, in zone (1), of a single, informal explicandum in zone (2).

[16] Earman (1992, pp. 15–18) and Franklin (1986), among others, argue essentially this.

[17] Carnap, of course, thought of theories as interpreted by their observational consequences; the semantics of a theory was to be defined as deductively (or inductively) derivable from evidence reported in an observation sublanguage. As Stein (1992, 1994) has pointed out, no such comprehensive theory exists, and even if it ever did, the logical derivation of an observation would very likely be unmanageably complex. But he also suggests that Carnap could have dispensed with this approach; a body

Of course these elaborations, sketchy though they are, go far beyond anything Carnap actually said himself. But they are entirely consistent with what he *did* say, and they suggest a way of locating his ideal of explication within the kind of naturalistic epistemology he approved and encouraged (e.g. ASP 1950a, 1955b, 1966a). A characteristically Carnapian feature of this conception is the dynamic and 'dialectical' nature of the interplay between the theory (the 'regulative language system') of a discipline and its body of informal understandings (including informally – or 'physicalistically' – described experimental results). The body of informal understandings (zone (2) in the above discussion, embedded in a Neurathian 'universal vernacular') can be regarded as the 'zone of proximal development' for the cognitive progress of the species as a whole.[18] This is the target zone for explication, both theoretical and meta-theoretical. And since the concepts in this zone are by hypothesis vague and informal, there is no way of knowing in advance whether the explication of some particular concept will be theoretical, meta-theoretical, or both. Within the dialect of a scientific discipline, there is no need for a demarcation between 'science' and 'philosophy'.

OBJECTIONS

Many objections could be levelled against the Carnapian ideal of explication outlined above.[19] I will consider four, representing different, though sometimes overlapping, tendencies within current philosophy: (a) the

of accepted experimental results could instead be regarded as interpreted by appropriate 'schematisations' – structural equivalents to observation – within the theory that allow a potential observer to know practically how to derive future observations from (and accommodate past ones to) the theory (e.g. at what relative angle to expect two different light sources to appear in the night sky at a certain time) without requiring the theory itself to account for the entire process of observation. One could regard such 'schematisations' (as well as any apparatus of coordinating definitions, correspondence rules, and the like) as part of 'zone (1)' of the scientific dialect, or as part of the interface between zones (1) and (2).

18 To use an expression of L. S. Vygotsky's, one that seems peculiarly appropriate in this context; the 'zone of proximal development' in his framework contains the social and propositional content within learnable reach of an individual learner at a certain stage of her internal development. It is thus the interface, for Vygotsky, between socially available knowledge and individual cognition, i.e. the site of individual assimilation of that knowledge (Vygotsky 1978; Wertsch 1985; Frawley 1997). The scientifically influenced used language of scientists plays a similar role, within the Carnapian view being expounded here, for the learning process of society as a whole, explication being the social learning process whereby vague concepts become clearer.

19 Many objections have also been levelled at *other* aspects of Carnap's work. He offered a series of explications for the distinction between analytic and synthetic sentences, as well as for that between theoretical and observation statements, which are generally agreed to have been defective. These and other criticisms are not addressed here, though it is assumed throughout that the defects of the particular language engineering projects can be bracketed, and that the success or failure of the ideal of explication does not depend on anything material in those projects.

piecemeal identification and replacement of explicanda violates Frege's context principle; (b) the 'possibilities' among which there is a choice, in Carnap's view, are actually not well defined, so the supposed pluralism is hollow; (c) the scope of 'language' is too wide in Carnap's ideal, so that there is a danger that matters of scientific fact will be assimilated to the realm of mere convention. And finally, (d) the distinction between evolved and constructed languages cannot bear the weight Carnap's ideal puts on it, since constructed languages are embedded in evolved ones and we must remain within our evolved conceptual scheme while we construct new ones. Thus there can be no genuine alternatives to our evolved language, which we must fall back on in the end anyway.

The context principle

The meanings of concepts in both the target language and the explication language are fully determined only in the context of their uses in sentences. The meaning of a word is determined by *all of its possible uses* within its language (Tait 1986; Reck 1997). How, then, can we pluck an explicandum out of its context in an evolved language and replace it with an equally context-free explicatum? Worse, how can we replace an explicandum in one context with an explicatum in a different one? But this is not the later Carnap's conception. As we have seen, he gave up the precision in the replacement process he had sought in the *Syntax*. In his later view, the explicandum is, by hypothesis, *less* precise than the explicatum. Nor does he regard the meaning of the explicandum within its evolved-language context as a binding *constraint* on the explicatum meaning within its constructed-language context. The idea is rather to single out a few important uses of the explicandum – especially those of interest in the context of the problems the explication is undertaken to address – and to focus on those. Within the total semantic field of a particular concept occurring in a used language, explication focuses on a core subset.[20] This core, though, is not assumed to be somehow naturally given, or to be *discoverable*, independently identifiable, as a natural kind within the total semantic field; it is *solely* a provisional singling out of certain uses for the purpose of explication. It is relative to the specific purposes of those who are singling it out. The step of

---

[20] This core subset is to be conceived as more like a purpose-relative 'core domain [*Kernbereich*]' (distinguished from its 'Unbestimmtheitszone') of von Mises (1939), Chapter I, §3, Section 5 (pp. 97–9) than like the cognitive 'Core [*Kern*]' (as opposed to the rhetorical 'Nebenteil'), or the 'sufficient' (as opposed to 'dispensable') components of a concept in *Scheinprobleme* (1928b) §§2–3, which are presented as inherent or fixed.

clarification is simply the step of *agreeing* (among those interested) which of these uses are to belong to the explicatory core.

In the case of the more developed sciences, such explications will often, perhaps nearly always, be *motivated* by theoretical interests. They will be driven less by puzzlement about a concept in an evolved language than by the desire to extend a constructed language. In these cases, explicata within an established formal system will often be proposed that bear little resemblance to *any* pre-existing explicandum in an evolved language (Stein 1992, p. 281). But in less developed sciences, whose concepts are still largely embedded in informal usage and defined by it, explication will be driven more by the effort to make those evolved concepts more precise. There, no single system is accepted yet as the standard explicatum language (or as one of a small number of regulative languages), and explications are often highly controversial because any given decision concerns not just a particular extension of an already accepted theoretical language involved in defining a particular explicatum (with or without a corresponding explicandum), but fixes the entire language in which this and (potentially) *all future* explicata are to be embedded as a part.

The same contrary tendencies appear at the level of *meta*-theoretical explications, i.e. those more concerned with problems traditionally called 'philosophical' – which Carnap, putting the stress on the creative aspect of generating and trying out new explicata and new formal systems, called problems of 'conceptual engineering'. On the one hand, we have explications motivated mainly or exclusively by constructional, engineering interests; as in the developed sciences, these need not correspond to any particular explicandum in an evolved language. On the other hand, though, we have explications motivated by the desire to clarify and make precise a vague concept in zone 2 of the scientific vernacular that is of importance in the construction of a complete theory or meta-theory but has not yet found a secure place in any part of it. (An example of the latter, close to Carnap's heart in his later years, is the concept of probability.) Even more than in the case of less-developed sciences, such explications will be especially controversial, as there is not in general even a widespread practical agreement (e.g. within a particular profession), about the 'core uses' of the explicandum to be regarded as the basis for explication.

Piecemeal replacement of explicanda by explicata does not violate Frege's context principle, then, because the explicanda are assumed not to be well defined, and the focus of explication is only a provisional subset of its meaning established by practical agreement during the propaedeutic step of clarification. An explicatum, on the other hand, *is* assumed to be defined within the context of a formal language which, ideally (though perhaps not in every actual case), establishes its meaning under all possible *internal* uses, within the (constructed) explication language. In Carnap's view this is just what the important difference between explicandum and explicatum consists in: the one is vague and ill defined, while the other is more precise and *better* defined. The dynamic feedback process of explication makes the scientific vernacular as a whole more self-conscious and deliberate; fewer of its concepts are passively accepted from fashion cascades or folk wisdom.

The alternatives are not well defined, so Carnap's pluralism is hollow

As John Earman (1992, p. 13) puts it, 'Carnap assumes what needs to be proved', namely that the alternative languages Carnap says we can choose from '[have] been produced'. There is no genuine bazaar, Earman says, if the goods are not on the table, ready to take home and use. Even Carnap had admitted, after all, that his own heroic attempt to 'produce' a phenomenalistic language in the *Aufbau* had been a failure ('if, as he originally assumed, the reduction has to proceed by explicit definitions') – so why should we regard the phenomenalist language as a serious alternative to a materialist or physicalist language? And without genuine alternatives, isn't the pluralism a fake?[21]

First it should be said that although Carnap did admit that the *Aufbau* had been a failure by the standards he had set for himself at the time, he later dismissed those (Wittgensteinian) standards. Yes, he had gone beyond explicit definition, he said, but here he had been half-consciously anticipating the Vienna Circle's later liberalisation of empiricism and the abandonment of the verification principle (Chapter 6 above, e.g. footnote 9). And while his interests shifted from the *Aufbau* construction to other projects, and he no longer invested the hopes in an *Aufbau*-like construction he had expressed in 'Von Gott und Seele' (Chapter 6, pp. 181–4), he certainly did not give up on the idea! On the contrary, he indicated how he would approach the problem differently now (1961), and hinted that it would be part of a larger naturalistic epistemology.

The more fundamental question Earman raises is whether the alternative languages must be *available*, in the sense of fully worked out and ready to go, *in advance* of a choice among them. But this very statement of the

---

[21] Wesley Salmon (1994, p. 285) took this argument of Earman's to show that Carnap's supposed pluralism really amounts to a sort of closet realism, since no convincing alternatives have been forthcoming.

question immediately makes clear that there can be no straightforward yes or no answer. 'Fully worked out' is not clearly defined. If part of what we mean by it is 'demonstrably consistent', then of course we would deprive ourselves of classical mathematics and many other useful tools. The choice of a language is always provisional; we don't know what monsters may be lurking in the shadows and may pounce on us in the future, forcing us to abandon our choice and retreat to more secure ground. We only ever find such things out by making a choice and trying to make it work. On the other hand, Earman is clearly right that alternative languages must be regarded as promising enough candidates to begin with if we are going to entrust ourselves to them even provisionally.[22]

So not only is the answer a matter of degree rather than a yes or no, but it is a matter of inclinations or values as well as fact and theory. Whether we think of some alternative as 'sufficiently promising' to adopt it provisionally, or to take it into account as a possible candidate for adoption, depends at least partly on normative factors, as well as e.g. our tolerance for risk. And Carnap's adventurousness in this respect has been a constant theme in this book. We have encountered it in every phase of his career and in many different contexts; he clearly did not believe an option had *already* to be fully worked out to be taken seriously as a possible framework for some inquiry. His pluralism was not just a matter of philosophical conviction, after he found the right context for it after 1932; it was a value in itself. Like Musil, he wanted – just as in his youth (see Chapter 1) – to balance the 'sense of reality' with a 'sense of possibilities'; the strong utopian streak in him made the here-and-now, the down-to-earth, less important than what might be possible in the long term. And how is humanity to realise its endless possibilities, he thought, if we don't get started on envisaging them, exploring them, playing with them? Even if they are not immediately applicable, keeping them in mind gives us more perspective and greater freedom from the parochial here and now.

Carnap would, then, have thought Earman's question tendentiously posed. It is not a matter of 'relativism', or of glorifying theft over honest toil, to envisage possibilities other than those presently in use. The ideal of explication places the burden of proof not on the pluralist who wishes to envisage new possibilities, but on the *anti*-pluralist to demonstrate that some envisaged alternative is *not* possible. The *Aufbau* may not have 'produced' a phenomenalistic language ready for use, but does this show that

---

[22] Carnap emphasises that he regards 'acceptance' of a kind of entities or a linguistic framework as entirely pragmatic; it is essentially just the (provisional) decision to use it or explore it (1950a, pp. 213–15).

such a language is *impossible?* Certainly not,[23] and the human track record of predicting future cognitive achievements is notoriously poor.

Factual scientific questions assimilated to conventional ones

Quite separately from all this, Earman (1992, p. 14) worries that Carnap is 'obviously [on] a very slippery slope' when he considers 'such matters as whether time is finite or infinite and whether the world is deterministic' to be questions of language choice rather than questions of fact. The issue, Earman says, 'is whether determinism is a scientific claim to be argued over the way one argues over other deep scientific claims, none of which ever gets definitively settled by the dictates of experimental evidence', or whether determinism is defined (or not) into the language.

But Carnap does not claim to have an answer to this question – on the contrary, this is precisely the kind of question he wants to convince us *is* a question, i.e. that we have a *choice.* We have the option of accepting certain empirical claims, and allowing these to constrain or guide the construction of our language (1939, §12, pp. 26–9). We can then formulate determinism as a scientific claim in this language, and if we are lucky it is true or false. But if the choice of language does *not* (as Earman indeed hypothesises) ever get 'definitively settled by the dictates of experimental evidence', then we have the option of regarding the question at the meta-level, as an external question, a pragmatic choice among languages. At this level, wider considerations can be brought to bear than at the internal scientific level – such as considerations of the compatibility of determinism with areas of human empirical knowledge and practical endeavour that are not, in the first instance, included within the scope of the object language chosen for the physical sciences, in which the claim was originally stated.

Thus Carnap himself, for instance, in responding to Herbert Feigl's (1963) paper about physicalism, agrees with the substance of Feigl's position, but disagrees with Feigl's way of formulating mind–body identity as an empirical statement:

The identity statement . . . is a sentence of the object language; this may mislead the reader into believing that the controversy about the identity view concerns a question of fact. This impression may be further strengthened by Feigl's reference to certain facts as 'evidence' for the identity view. It seems preferable to me to

---

[23] Apart from the new possibilities offered by connectionism (above, Chapter 10, footnote 18), there are recent efforts to resurrect the *Aufbau,* avoiding criticisms such as Goodman's, by Hannes Leitgeb (2007, forthcoming).

formulate the question in the metalanguage, not as a factual question about the world, but as a question concerning the choice of a language form. Although we prefer a different language, we must admit that a dualistic language can be constructed and used without coming into conflict with either the laws of logic or with empirically known facts. However, in the dualistic language the identity statement mentioned above is false; the philosopher who uses this language is therefore justified in denying the statement. Those facts which Feigl proposes as evidence for the identity view are perhaps better regarded as reasons for preferring a monistic language. (1963, pp. 885–6)

For those with a taste for 'just the facts, ma'am', this procedure of kicking the problem upstairs seems like cheating. It exposes the discussion to considerations that are messier and less precise than the facts and procedures of natural science. This is presumably why Quine, for instance, sought to keep 'semantic ascent' securely anchored to the world (the object language of science) by means of the truth predicate, and to have no truck with pragmatics. Traditionally, philosophers have gone to the opposite extreme, regarding such questions that fail to be 'definitively settled by the dictates of experimental evidence'; they have often regarded them as 'metaphysical' questions to which modes of reasoning or argument can be applied that 'go beyond' or 'transcend' the reasoning used in science and mathematics, or that appeal to something more 'immediately accessible' to unprejudiced awareness than the abstractions of science. Carnap's approach goes to neither of these extremes, and avoids the conservatism shared by both. A vague, pre-systematic question can be explicated (replaced, made precise) as either internal or external to the scientific object language; there is no inherent, irrevocable, predetermined 'right' choice. There may be clear explications at both levels, and indeed both avenues can be pursued simultaneously. Or, if a problem is provisionally 'kicked upstairs' (a meta-scientific explication is chosen), it can later be kicked 'downstairs' again (reformulated as an internal, object-level question), if the growth of empirical knowledge makes that feasible.

Constructed languages are embedded in evolved languages

The final objection I will consider, and perhaps the most fundamental, is not that constructed languages are *in empirical fact* embedded in evolved languages, or developed *historically* from them by gradual degrees (both of which a Carnapian perspective can, as we saw, easily acknowledge). The objection is that whatever is represented or communicated in a constructed language is *in principle* parasitic on the subjective understanding mediated by evolved languages. Something must, in other words, always remain irreducibly tacit in the use of constructed languages, something supplied by the reliance of their human users on informal background understandings enmeshed with evolved languages. This objection takes many forms. Perhaps the best-known variety takes its starting point from the late Wittgenstein's considerations about the dependence of rule-following on implicit understandings that cannot be fully spelled out. But a similar conception was central to ordinary language philosophy in the Austin tradition, and echoes can be found in many later philosophers, such as Quine, who says that we must resign ourselves, in the end, to 'acquiescing in the mother tongue and taking its words at face value' (Quine 1969, p. 49).

It might be thought that Carnap himself shares a version of this view, as he takes entirely for granted that there is a common interpreted metalanguage in which people are able to communicate:

Since the metalanguage *ML* serves as a means of communication between author and reader or among participants in a discussion, I always presupposed, both in syntax and in semantics, that a fixed interpretation of *ML*, which is shared by all participants, is given. This interpretation is usually not formulated explicitly; but since *ML* uses English words, it is assumed that these words are understood in their ordinary senses. The necessity of this presupposition of a common shared metalanguage seems to me obvious . . . It seems to be obvious that, if two men wish to find out whether or not their views on certain objects agree, they must first of all use a common language to make sure that they are talking about the same objects. (1963, pp. 929–30)

But Carnap's 'presupposition of a common interpreted metalanguage' is not a 'profound parallel', as Ricketts suggests, to Quine's 'acquiescing in the mother tongue and taking its words at face value' (Ricketts 2004b, p. 199). There is certainly a parallel, but it is superficial rather than 'profound', since for Carnap there is no 'acquiescence'. The common interpreted metalanguage is merely a provisional starting point, not a resting place. Its concepts are to be taken, where possible, in their *explicated* senses, in the full knowledge that these assumed explications cannot be cashed out within the 'mother tongue' itself.[24] And its remaining un-explicated clots or *Ballungen* are not acquiesced in, but assumed ultimately to be in need of explication. Carnap does not, then, take the 'mother tongue' at 'face value'.

---

[24] As he indeed says explicitly, later in the reply to Beth quoted from above: 'It is of course not quite possible to use the ordinary language with a perfectly fixed interpretation, because of the inevitable vagueness and ambiguity of ordinary words. Nevertheless it is possible at least to approximate a fixed interpretation to a certain extent, e.g. by a suitable choice of less vague words and by suitable paraphrases' (1963, p. 930; cf. ASP 1955a). Such a tidied-up version of ordinary language corresponds to the 'universal vernacular' of 'zone (2)' in the discussion above, pp. 281–4.

While he acknowledges that in practice, constructed languages *are* embedded in evolved languages, he does not regard this as a conceptual, or even a practical, necessity (1963, pp. 933–40). Constructed languages clearly *are* able to function autonomously as instruments for the articulation of knowledge systems that are quite independent of their evolved meta-languages. And this new knowledge, as it begins to be understood, also feeds back into our informal meta-language (our 'zone (2)'). Explication seeks to facilitate and accelerate this process, to make our universal vernacular more effective, especially as an instrument for the deliberate shaping of life (*bewußte Lebensgestaltung*) – for undermining the passive acceptance of folk traditions, ideologies, and marketing messages by replacing them with consciously intended values and explicit theories. To be satisfied with Wittgenstein's diagnosis of the embeddedness of constructed languages, in this view, would be like telling Galileo there was no point in his new physics because it ran counter to folk intuition. The dramatic explosion of scientific knowledge over the past two centuries, along with the increasing acceptance and spread of science in (some) societies, made Carnap optimistic that radical change, and a fundamental overhaul of our conceptual apparatus, is indeed possible. Of course he would readily have admitted that the understanding of science is still largely quite superficial, and dominated by folk categories, but this would have seemed to him a practical challenge for enlightened parents and educators, not a reason to think that folk categories must ultimately be acquiesced in. While it is obviously a grave danger to human survival that unexamined folk categories dominate political life, this is a reason to work toward overcoming and replacing those categories, Carnap thought, not a reason for resignation.

CONCLUSION: PLURALISM AND THE INTEGRITY OF THE ENLIGHTENMENT

Behind some of these objections, especially the fourth, lies a deeper and more persistent, more widespread attitude that is harder to answer head-on, as it is not usually made explicit. If it were, it might be expressed as the suspicion that some, perhaps most, 'folk' categories (including those within a scientific vernacular) are indispensable – to human emotional and practical needs, to the progress of science, or to something else. While it may be *possible*, therefore, to explicate them progressively, the costs would exceed the benefits. Certain folk categories are so deeply embedded that we will never be able to dispense with them in practice, even if we know they are defective. There is, in this view, an ineluctable limit to any programme of Enlightenment. We can only escape from our inherited concepts to a certain point, and no further.

The appeal of this 'Enlightenment fatigue', long confined to conservatives and romantics, has broadened considerably in recent years. There is a growing sense that the world has changed beyond recognition, and that the formula of Enlightenment has lost its relevance. Of the many sources feeding this widely shared anxiety, two have special importance for intellectual life: the unmanageable proliferation of knowledge and the steady increase in pluralism. Neither is new; both already appear as central preoccupations in Musil's *Man without Qualities*. But both have continued to gather momentum in the seven or eight decades since he wrote.

Resignation before these relentless forces is widespread even among people who are well disposed to the idea of Enlightenment. The idea that we can liberate ourselves – achieve moral autonomy on the basis of intellectual autonomy – has come to seem charmingly old-fashioned. It is this weary sense of hopelessness before the inevitable that persuades so many readers that forceful articulations of Enlightenment fatigue, such as Richard Rorty's, must somehow be on the right track. Arguments have little weight against the inexorable march of history.

Nonetheless I will conclude this book by offering arguments against the idea that there are inherent limits to explication. Using the Carnapian tools described and developed in the pages above, I will seek to refute the suggestion that the modern trends of knowledge proliferation and of pluralism are grounds for despairing of the Enlightenment in its original form.

Pluralism and the new politics of knowledge

Knowledge proliferation and socio-political pluralism undermine the Enlightenment project in different but mutually reinforcing ways. Knowledge proliferation is perhaps the more invidious, especially at the level of the individual person seeking to orient herself and achieve a level of intellectual autonomy. It is not easy or frictionless to replace folk knowledge by better and more self-conscious knowledge. It takes time and effort. Mental resources must be devoted to systematic education and self-education, even to a more diffuse cultivation of self-awareness or a quest to be better informed. There is a cost; time and mental resources thus invested cannot be used on other things. And this cost grows in direct proportion to the scope and extent of explicated knowledge. The more knowledge there is, the less of it one can assimilate and use. This paradoxical situation, just by itself, seems to undermine the core idea of the entire philosophical tradition since Plato, and especially of the Enlightenment – the doctrine that knowledge sets us free. The very opposite has come to pass. When there is too much knowledge, we drown in it. We are forced to conform *more* rather than less to authority or to folk traditions.

At the social level, this is reflected in the widely lamented syndrome of 'specialisation' or, as it is usually called, '*over*-specialisation' (though what the optimal level of specialisation might be is rarely discussed). As more and more is known, more and more people are needed to be the expert carriers and appliers of this knowledge. But no one is left to mediate among the endlessly proliferating specialties, sub-specialties, and 'interdisciplinary' subjects that soon become new specialties of their own. There is no longer a place to go for the big picture, no one who can tell us which knowledge is relevant to which problems. The disciplines traditionally cast in this overview role – philosophy, literary studies, history – have seemed bent on becoming specialties themselves, and further splitting into sub-specialties. 'For high-flying thoughts', wrote Musil (1930, pp. 358–9; PT p. 389), 'we have created a kind of poultry farm we call philosophy, theology, or literature, where these thoughts can happily multiply beyond what anyone can encompass. Which is as it should be, for then no one needs to feel guilty any more about the impossibility of personally keeping track of it all.' There are far more experts among us than ever before, but no one to tell us what expert to consult when. So at the social level, too, greater knowledge effectively results in greater ignorance.

These perverse effects of knowledge proliferation are greatly amplified, however, in a context of social pluralism. The disintegration of a homogeneous, widely accepted 'educated culture', in its various national versions, has not made way for new or plural bases for enculturation. Nothing has stepped in to provide the coherence (or hierarchy of 'importance' assigned to various parts of knowledge) once provided by such a shared 'republic of letters' with its canon of texts or hierarchy of priorities. The individual growing up in present pluralistic societies is left adrift, at the mercy of momentary fashion or adolescent whim, with no compelling reason to become even half-literate in any *particular* republic of letters. Rather than a choice among *several* possible educated cultures to serve as a basis for coherence (to organize the vast seas of knowledge and set life priorities), as one might have expected in a pluralistic society, young people rarely have the option of choosing even *one* (Carus 2002).

At the social level, knowledge proliferation in a pluralistic context results in what has been called the 'new politics of knowledge' (Sanger 2006). This has many different aspects and symptoms. For years, it seemed like a tempest in an academic teapot, and was fought out, in the United States, under such headings as the 'science wars' or disputes about the 'canon' in various disciplines, the contents of 'Western Civ' courses, or the 'objectivity' of history. While clearly important within the university context, these battles had little evident bearing on the wider status or use of knowledge in society. They often, to varying degrees, reflected long-suppressed claims to equal status by social groups other than the traditional European-descended establishment, but this did not in itself involve a challenge to the importance of higher-quality, academically generated knowledge as such within the wider society. This is now beginning to change, under the levelling influence of the internet (though that is perhaps more symptom than cause). One striking indication of this influence is the discussion surrounding the 'open source' software movement that has resulted in such remarkable triumphs of spontaneous organisation as the Linux operating system. Applied to knowledge more generally, this idea has given rise, with astonishing speed and momentum, to – among many other projects – Wikipedia, which has become indispensable to journalists, students, and teachers worldwide despite being open to anyone who wishes to contribute, and its lack of any academic quality control or review process. As it has grown and thrived, the Wikipedia has attracted much attention. Among dedicated participants, it has given rise to a vibrant anti-authoritarian culture that celebrates the 'wisdom of crowds' (Surowiecki 2004) over the expertise of individuals, especially when such expertise is certified by, or derived from, an academic discipline. The ideology is above all anti-elitist, directed against socially recognised or licenced expertise. As Larry Sanger, a disillusioned co-founder of Wikipedia, puts it,

Wikipedia has become the flag around which a certain kind of internet partisan has rallied. These partisans are . . . high school and college students tired of being talked down to by their teachers, open source devotees, cranks resentful of professionals, privacy and free speech advocates, old-fashioned anarchists, and . . . epistemic collectivists who give often undue weight to the so-called wisdom of crowds. (Sanger 2006)

This ideology has obvious continuities, then, with traditional American anti-intellectualism, the know-nothing resistance to authority that refuses to recognise the right of anyone to dictate to the plain citizen what she should believe (Hofstedter 1963). This is a long-standing tradition, of course, and shows up most obviously in the many well-known oddities of American folk opinion, such as the surprisingly high incidence of personal encounters with extra-terrestrial aliens or the widespread rejection of

Darwin's theory of evolution. So in many ways the 'new politics of knowledge' is just the old politics of knowledge. But there is a difference. Perhaps because of the rapid success of undertakings such as Wikipedia, and the degree to which it in particular has become indispensable even to those who distrust it, the 'wisdom of crowds' ideology has gained wider credibility, reinforcing the idea, associated with academic anti-modernism, that there are no quality differences in knowledge. There is no 'better' knowledge or 'inferior' knowledge; any such quality judgement is simply the expression of an establishment ideology.

There can obviously be no Enlightenment where this is accepted. Individual or social life cannot be improved by better knowledge if there is no better knowledge. Could such an attitude ever prevail for long in our knowledge-driven society, where so much of the infrastructure of daily life depends on the recognition of highly technical knowledge as 'better' than available alternatives? This is an empirical question; popular ideologies are often in radical contradiction to obvious facts in a society. What seems indisputable, though, is that as knowledge-driven societies become more pluralistic, the 'new politics of knowledge' will play a larger and larger role – perhaps even, increasingly, as a more widely acknowledged framework for actual *political* debate. In the short term, meanwhile, the erosion of perceived quality differences in knowledge may already be having political consequences. With the rise of the internet as the main source of political information, for instance, and loss of influence by newspapers and other 'mainstream' media, it has become easier for governments to market their policies, and set the terms of such debate as there is, by well-positioned sound bites and selective disinformation. This degradation of the public sphere has lowered the level and sophistication of debate, has made it harder for critical voices to affect policy processes, and has returned more power into the hands of large, well-financed interest groups and incumbent governments (Lanier 2006). But if such examples make the integrity of the Enlightenment – the connection between knowledge and practice – seem obviously and urgently relevant, they still leave us with the fundamental problem at the core of the 'new politics of knowledge': Who decides? Who is to be in control of what is regarded as 'better' knowledge, if there is such a thing? Even if we think it is *obvious* that there is such a thing, how are these questions to be decided, in the absence of the authorities that have so evidently lost their once authoritative status?

Long before the problem acquired its present dimensions, there was a subculture within the Enlightenment that regarded this question as unanswerable, and was uncomfortable with the *Encyclopédiste* ambition of shaping life and society in accordance with improved knowledge replacing folk knowledge. This was the liberal tradition, particularly in England and its cultural offspring – the common-law anti-authoritarianism of the Levellers, Mandeville, Locke, and the American revolutionaries. Liberalism sought to distinguish between two kinds or levels of values: public or framework values, on the one hand, and private or *content* values on the other. The prevalence of certain framework values (such as free speech or impartial contract enforcement) was to ensure the plurality of content values (religious, educational, or cultural preferences). This distinction was not of course dreamt up in anticipation of the new politics of knowledge; it developed in the context of the first modern societies (England and the Netherlands) that tolerated religions other than the established one practised by the majority. It is neatly encapsulated in Voltaire's famous remark to the effect that 'I detest what you are saying, but will defend to the death your right to say it' – which still seems perverse and counter-intuitive to the vast majority of the world's population.

This two-level approach to values has coexisted peacefully, if often quarrelsomely, with the more constructivist, engineering-oriented social activism of the *Encyclopédiste* and positivist tradition. But now the inexorable pressures of knowledge proliferation and social pluralism, as just described, seem to be forcing these traditions apart. Liberalism and Enlightenment, it is widely thought, must go separate ways. This is argued not only by radical anti-Enlightenment liberals such as Rorty but even, for instance, by John Rawls, whose own ambitious attempt to articulate the liberal two-level approach brought him into direct confrontation with one of the leading representatives of old-fashioned Enlightenment rationalism, Jürgen Habermas. Their famous debate epitomises this fundamental trade-off between pluralism and reason forced on us by the new politics of knowledge.

The Rawls–Habermas debate and a fundamental trade-off

Habermas's heroic effort to rescue the integrity of the Enlightenment may well seem to be the last and only chance of reconciling reason with a form of liberalism – but the liberalism that results is not of the pluralistic, two-level Anglo-Saxon sort represented by Rawls,[25] who, especially in his later work (esp. Rawls 1996), sought to ground liberal principles of justice in

---

[25] It is pointless to attempt a summary of Rawls's complex and subtle theory as it evolved over three decades. I have tried to make the discussion here comprehensible on its own, without assuming a detailed knowledge of Rawls's writings, but of course it will mean more to someone who has at

purely political considerations, without recourse to any larger 'comprehensive' doctrine to justify them, e.g. from a moral or intellectual point of view. Habermas objected that it is impossible to isolate the political from the moral and intellectual as Rawls had proposed. Rawls – unlike Rorty – assumed that each individual or group in a society will in fact *have* a 'comprehensive' doctrine of some kind (a religion, or some such conception as the Enlightenment, relating knowledge to practical decisions), but he envisaged the possibility that these doctrines can co-exist peacefully by virtue of an 'overlapping consensus' among them, concerning the rules of justice agreed in a previous step (in his imagined 'original position'). This overlapping consensus ensures that the just society agreed in the first step is also stable. If the comprehensive doctrines are 'reasonable' ones (Rawls 1996, pp. 58–66), he argues, this is sufficient to guarantee an overlapping consensus. He distinguishes 'reasonable' in this sense from 'rational' in the sense of means-ends rationality (Rawls 1996, pp. 48–54).[26] The rules of justice are agreed behind a 'veil of ignorance' that prevents the participants from knowing what their station – or indeed, their identity – will be in the resulting society. These merely rational participants have no comprehensive doctrines and are thus not yet 'reasonable'. It is the rules emerging from this first step that spell out or indeed largely *define* the 'reasonable'. The overlapping consensus will result in the second step, Rawls claimed,[27] among all comprehensive doctrines that accept the framework values (are 'reasonable').

Habermas's critique focused on the abstractness – and normative blindness – of the first step, and the seemingly paradoxical absence in the first step of the reason applied in the second (Habermas 1995, pp. 111–19). He prefers a 'comprehensive doctrine', specifically his theory of communicative action (discussed above in the Introduction, pp. 26–31), which yields an account of reason as a set of procedural requirements on political deliberation so as to approximate an 'ideal speech community' in which all participants are uncoerced and, above all, disinterested participants – participants without any content values or other personal (non-universal) agendas at stake. The 'discourse ethics' governing this interaction then ensures that the norms of justice agreed on there are not just 'reasonable' but *valid*, i.e. *true* – by the same standard (historically agreed standards of adequacy within a

---

least some acquaintance with them. The most important texts for present purposes are the exchange between Habermas and Rawls in the *Journal of Philosophy* (1995) and Habermas's (1996) reply.

[26] Very roughly, the 'reasonable' is the realm of framework values, as discussed above, while the 'rational' is the realm of content values, which are regarded as supplying ends exogenous to the 'rationality' according to which those ends are then pursued.

[27] He does not give a precise definition of 'reasonable', and offers no game-theoretic or other form of proof for this result; the argument is informal throughout (Rawls 1996, pp. 133–72).

discourse community) that any knowledge can be true. Rawls's attempts to avoid questions of validity and truth, Habermas says, are unsuccessful (Habermas 1995, p. 131); the assumptions he builds both into his concept of 'political persons' and into his assumption of 'reasonableness' transcend the merely political, and inescapably raise just the larger moral and philosophical questions that Rawls seeks to bracket or exclude.

Rawls retorts that the 'reason' he employs is innocuous, and that it requires no metaphysical presuppositions of the sort Habermas accuses him of needing. His argument, he says, 'does not rely on a Platonic and Kantian reason, or if so, it does so in the same way Habermas does. No sensible view can possibly get by without the reasonable and rational as I use them' (Rawls 1995, p. 138). It is Habermas, rather, he says, whose comprehensive doctrine of communicative action has the ambition of adumbrating the full scope of 'Hegel's view of *Sittlichkeit*, an apparently metaphysical doctrine of ethical life . . . [within] the theory of communicative action with its procedural presuppositions of ideal discourse' (Rawls 1995, p. 136). In fact,

Habermas's own doctrine, I believe, is one of logic in the broad Hegelian sense: a philosophical analysis of the presuppositions of rational discourse (of theoretical and practical reason) which includes within itself all the allegedly substantial elements of religious and metaphysical doctrines. His logic is metaphysical in the following sense: it presents an account of what there is. (Rawls 1995, p. 137)

Habermas's goal, of course, had been to 'sublimate' all such metaphysical views as Hegel's into his *non*-metaphysical, purely 'procedural' account of communicative rationality. In doing so he had relied, as we saw in a different context (in the Introduction above), on 'the radically anti-Platonic insight that there is neither a higher nor a deeper reality to which we could appeal – we who find ourselves already situated in our linguistically structured forms of life' (Habermas 1992, quoted by Rawls 1995, p. 136).

This controversy is a classic expression of a trade-off that has faced the Enlightenment from its beginnings. Two fundamental values appear to be in conflict: pluralism and reason. If radical pluralism is accepted, then what 'absolute' reason can there be for the framework values that uphold this pluralism itself? Rawls (whose earlier *Theory of Justice* had not yet taken pluralism quite so seriously) attempts in his later work, with great ingenuity, to build a fundamental pluralism of values into a coherent system of political order. As long as they meet the minimal standards imposed by the 'reasonable', he says, different value systems can not only agree on principles of justice, but can co-exist in a free and equal society. Habermas doubts this; instead he seeks to develop a single *true* conception of reason that can justify pluralism – up to a point – but that requires no metaphysical justification, only the acceptance of the 'linguistically structured forms of life' in which we 'find ourselves already situated'. Rawls focuses on pluralism and tries to finesse reason; Habermas focuses on reason and lets pluralism fall where it may.

Nor does this seem to be just a problem of theory. On the contrary, this trade-off is one of the central political issues today, one that bedevils present attempts at free and equal co-existence in multi-cultural, pluralistic societies. The most obvious and visible tension is that between the attempt to define *framework* values for such societies – culture-neutral rules that can serve as a level playing field in the interactions among its multiple cultures – and the fact, or at least the appearance, that such framework rules, when articulated, do in fact embody or privilege the *content* values of *one particular* culture within the society at the expense of competing content values.[28] There seems to be no universally accepted, culture-neutral conception of 'reason' that could be appealed to in formulating such framework principles. The challenge to liberal societies in recent years could not be more visible; it is in the news every day.

The Rawls–Habermas debate, then, exhibits this fundamental trade-off between pluralism and reason, liberalism and Enlightenment, in a very clear light. So stark is the predicament, in fact, that it is tempting to conclude there is no escape – no way of reconciling these fundamental values of the original Enlightenment. But here is where the Carnapian ideal of explication can help. Rawls and Habermas share many assumptions that a Carnapian perspective allows us to dispense with. One is their unquestioning acceptance of the ordinary natural language in which we find ourselves situated (our 'linguistically structured forms of life') as the canonical and ineluctable medium for all discourse, supplying us with the conceptual structure of a 'reason common to all humans' (Habermas 1995, p. 110). But (quite apart from the arguments throughout this book against passive acceptance of folk categories) the 'new politics of knowledge' and the social trends driving it – knowledge proliferation and social pluralism – give this assumption the lie. Why should we believe in a 'reason common to all humans' in the face of such overwhelming contrary evidence?

---

[28] Historically, of course, this is clearly the case. The best-known sets of supposedly neutral rules embodying supposedly neutral framework values *did*, in fact, arise in a particular concrete historical situation in northwest Europe and in the context of particular events there (such as the Dutch Revolt, the English Civil War, the Glorious Revolution), and have often been interpreted as the expression of a nascent bourgeoisie (e.g. Wilson 1984, de Vries 1976, Coleman 1977).

How the ideal of explication can reconcile pluralism and reason

If there is to be a 'reason common to all humans' – or even a reason that can function as a level playing field for a particular negotiation or a (possibly open-ended) series of interactions – then, in the Carnapian view, we have to *build* it. The historical experience of constructing forms of discourse to frame institutions that embody a practice of reason shows how extremely difficult and complex this is. The practice of reason develops first. Terms acquire increasingly precise meanings in a context where they are being used and applied. Only later does self-conscious reflection make it possible to extrapolate from that experience and make the rules of reasoning themselves subject to conscious choice. A paradigmatic example is the history of the development of scientific reasoning. It took over two millennia for the reasoning employed by the ancient mathematicians, first discussed by Aristotle, to be made explicit by Frege and Dedekind. Reasoning from (or on the basis of) observational evidence, also discussed in antiquity, has still not been articulated in such canonical form, despite its centrality to the scientific enterprise.

The analytical devices of Rawls and Habermas for arriving at rules of justice are akin to the after-the-fact meta-reflection that Frege's reconstruction of mathematical reasoning represents in the history of scientific reasoning. These systems are designed to arrive at highly abstract and general rules – so abstract that they are difficult to recognise in particular pieces of legislation or judicial decisions, and may often be interpreted differently when applied to concrete cases. The Rawls and Habermas frameworks are to everyday political and judicial interaction what inductive logic, in its various forms, is to the practice of empirical science. Indeed, they explicitly share the scientific or meta-scientific ambition of articulating those more abstract and general principles so as to apply them *beyond* the societies they are modelled on, i.e. to give humankind a tool to guide its institution-building in the future.

It seems quite perverse, given this ambition, that Rawls and Habermas, in constructing their otherwise highly abstract meta-frameworks, should specifically *eschew* scientific reasoning as the basis for the procedures they envisage. Instead they seek to reach further back or down into recesses of human nature that are supposedly universal and do not depend on a specific enculturation in the scientific outlook. Scientific reasoning is disqualified and marginalised as merely 'instrumental' or as pertaining to the merely 'rational' pursuit of content values, rather than being integrated into a conception of universal reason, as in Kant. The fear is evidently that to mortgage a purportedly *universal* framework to the special concerns of a particular subculture would be to make it unacceptable to other subcultures, especially those whose values lead them to reject scientific reasoning in certain respects.

The Carnapian approach, however, is *fundamentally* pluralistic. At the Rawlsian or Habermasian level of utopian abstraction, it would certainly admit scientific reasoning as central and indispensable – but it would also invite all participants to specify their *own* rules of (scientific) reasoning. For Carnap, remember, there is no 'true' account of what scientific reasoning 'is'. Our knowledge must be accommodated, but how we articulate it – what it 'means', how we are to understand it – is not prescribed by the knowledge itself. As intimated above, knowledge and understanding are not mutually exclusive; certain problems can plausibly be located at either the object level or the meta-level. Carnap's ideal was pragmatic to the core:

The acceptance or rejection of abstract linguistic forms, just as the acceptance or rejection of any other linguistic forms in any branch of science, will finally be decided by their efficiency as instruments, the ratio of the results achieved to the amount and complexity of the efforts required. To decree dogmatic prohibitions of certain linguistic forms instead of testing them by their success or failure in practical use, is worse than futile; it is positively harmful because it may obstruct scientific progress. The history of science shows examples of such prohibitions based on prejudices deriving from religious, mythological, metaphysical, or other irrational sources, which slowed up the developments for shorter or longer periods of time. Let us learn from the lessons of history. Let us grant to those who work in any special field of investigation the freedom to use any form of expression which seems useful to them; the work in the field will sooner or later lead to the elimination of those forms which have no useful function. *Let us be cautious in making assertions and critical in examining them, but tolerant in permitting linguistic forms.* (1950a, p. 221)

In the utopian task of formulating guiding principles for institution-building, undertaken in different ways by Rawls and Habermas, the Carnapian ideal would thus envisage the same degree of *bewußte Lebensgestaltung* (conscious shaping of life) in the 'linguistic forms' employed as in the highly abstract results of the envisaged procedures. This constructive emphasis, within the context of a fundamental pluralism, is what gives the Carnapian ideal the potential of overcoming the trade-off so vividly exhibited by the debate between Rawls and Habermas. And unlike either of them, moreover, it also offers a way of addressing the 'new politics of knowledge'. In the Introduction to this book, following a suggestion of Richard Jeffrey, I portrayed the Carnapian model of explication as a kind of 'convention' in which all concerned could come together to agree, uncoerced, on constitutive language rules. This would be a *different* sort of ideal convention from those imagined by Rawls or Habermas, a convention of free and equal citizens to decide *not* on the fundamental principles of justice (and then a constitution to embody those principles), but – in the first instance – to clarify what the abstract concepts in question actually *mean* (in practice) to the participants and then, on the basis of such clarifications, to negotiate explicata (establish meanings) that can lay the groundwork for a practice recognisable to all concerned as instantiating those abstract concepts.

The ambition would not initially be the construction of a 'reason common to all humans' (that might be an ideal, long-term goal) but a form of discourse that makes communication possible within some specific context where a mutual need for institution-building is acknowledged. The model for this convention would be the (idealised) social process of explication as described in Part I of this chapter. How do we get from individual (content-value-specific) languages to a common language for civic interaction? We proceed just as scientists do when setting up a language for some specific cognitive purpose. We bootstrap: we make ourselves understood to each other however we can, and from those tentative footholds we agree on rules of communicative interaction so that we can make ourselves *better* and more clearly understood for the purpose agreed on. What is that purpose? That, too, must be negotiated, in an analogy to the clarification phase; the scope of the concepts we define is not there to be found; it is our responsibility to decide. (Both Rawls and Habermas believe they can justify more specific ideas about the purposes at stake in their respective ideal negotiations; the Carnapian conception suggested here leaves the purpose(s) open.) The essential advantage of this Carnapian approach is that it does not require content values and framework values to be articulated in the *same* language; the framework language is negotiated *separately*, as a communicative tool optimised for a specific purpose.

This may seem rather abstract and utopian, but in fact it is exactly what happens in actual confrontations among groups or nations with different values (when they do not descend into violence). We do not rely on a supposedly pre-existing 'reason common to all humans', we *create* new conceptual frameworks to bridge the differences. Of course these efforts to bridge differences often break down; violent and atavistic impulses still tend to carry the day, as they have throughout human history. Ideals of reason are, in a sense, irrelevant to such early stages in the moral history of our species. It is an empirical matter to find out under exactly what conditions more advanced stages, allowing scope for aspirations of justice and benevolence, can play a role in human civic intercourse, but certainly a minimum of material civilisation and of available knowledge seem critical. In any case, once the conditions have been met where institution-building is preferred to violence, new legal and conceptual frameworks are created. And when that begins to happen, it is not a fixed pattern of reason imposed by human nature that we draw on, but human ingenuity in creating *new* frameworks to meet unfamiliar challenges. In the past few generations, for instance, our species has created, for the first time in its history, the foundations for an international political system, including an international financial system and the beginnings of an international rule of law, especially among certain subgroups of nations such as the European Union. Within some pluralistic countries radically new institutions have begun to ensure the full participation in society of previously excluded people. These are new inventions, they had to be made up as we went along – they did not attempt to follow some imagined pattern of a supposedly pre-existing 'reason common to all humans'. On the contrary, they would probably have been regarded as *contrary* to reason among most inhabitants of nineteenth-century Europe or the USA. When we go about designing and negotiating an international framework for the rationing and trading of carbon emission rights the system will be judged by results – the pricing of the cost of emissions into everyday goods and services and the consequent reduction in emissions – not by its correspondence to some supposedly pre-existing universal human reason.

The suggested Carnapian perspective (and the scenario of a piecemeal, step-by-step 'language-engineering convention') can also remedy certain features of the Rawls and Habermas systems that many commentators have balked at. A language-engineering convention, for instance, does not require the 'veil of ignorance' in which Rawls hides the individual identities of the participants in his 'original position' (modelled on the 'state of nature' in Hobbes and Locke). What could it mean to imagine ourselves as participating in a debate about the rules of justice in abstraction from anything that actually roots us in a particular society? In a Carnapian 'language-engineering convention', we can imagine ourselves participating as human beings of flesh and blood – the people we actually are, rather than some abstraction in a hypothetical state of nature. We can also imagine it proceeding step by step, in real time, rather than having to fix a meta-framework outside history, so to speak, in abstraction from the actual practice in which the concepts to be clarified and explicated have meanings. It can be conceived as a continuous, dialectical process, in which a language is built piece by piece over a long period. This can apply even to the central question of what follows from what; as in the actual history of logic, mathematics, probability, and inductive practice, it can evolve piecemeal over many years. The participants *devise* a conception of reason in the course of their discussions, as their repeated interactions reveal to each other what they actually *mean*, in practice, by the concepts they use. Above all they reveal what statements or claims are licensed by which other statements. In the course of these mutual observations, they can, if they desire to, converge on agreements about which meanings and inference rules to adopt. When that occurs, at least some parties to such an agreement, and perhaps all of them, have – for that context and purpose – adopted meanings and inference rules that are 'artificial' for them, i.e. that differ from the ones they began with. So the account of reason is *explicitly agreed on* rather than just assumed from ordinary language.

In contrast to Habermas's scenario of an 'ideal speech situation', the Carnapian 'language-engineering convention', once again, does not require us to be disinterested – to abstract from our concrete interests and values. The concepts devised must nevertheless embody an adequate practical reason, for we *engineer* them precisely to serve as tools for social and political interaction. But at the same time we know and admit that we *are* 'interested parties' to any debate about the language to be chosen, with strong content values of our own. There is no need, in the language-engineering approach, to make a fundamental distinction between the 'rational' and the 'reasonable' as both Rawls and Habermas require. Some such pair of concepts may, certainly, be regarded as distinct, and the participants to the convention may agree to distinguish them in the language they arrive at. But the language-engineering approach does not *require* such a distinction,[29] as both Rawls and Habermas do, to permit the emergence of the fundamental norms of justice.

The Carnapian ideal does nothing to mitigate the lofty abstractness of the Rawlsian or Habermasian meta-perspective on social life, but its relative modesty perhaps makes the abstract perspective less difficult to apply to concrete situations. In their celebrated controversy, Rawls and Habermas – each the author of an extremely ambitious and intricate system of thought – vie with each other for the honour of being the more modest (Habermas 1995, p. 131; Rawls 1995, pp. 137–8). Rawls thinks himself more modest than Habermas because Habermas puts forward a 'comprehensive doctrine', while Rawls's own system restricts its ambitions to the merely political sphere. Habermas thinks himself more modest because his theory

---

[29] Which is in any case hard to impose on ordinary language, or to discern there unambiguously; see Carus 2004, pp. 342–3.

is merely procedural rather than substantive. While Rawls claims he can anticipate the *results* of his imagined negotiation in the original position and subsequent steps, Habermas leaves more such outcomes to the actual participants in real-life negotiations. The Carnapian ideal is modest in Habermas's sense, but much more so. It does not claim to know even what procedural norms should govern the process of building a language for the articulation of framework values. And it does not specify a scope; the negotiation toward a common language can be as ambitious or as narrow as the purposes (left open) of the participants require.

But how can the suggested Carnapian resolution of the Rawls–Habermas debate address the fundamental question posed by the 'new politics of knowledge': Who is to decide what counts as good and not-so-good knowledge? In pluralistic societies, as discussed above, it seems likely that a tentative answer to this question will increasingly be a precondition for any kind of substantive politics at all. Any debate – about the rules for the organisation, company, neighbourhood playground, society, nation, or international system – will increasingly be *preceded* by an at least implicit agreement about which language to use, and by a more self-conscious *shaping* of such languages. As socio-political pluralism takes hold, it becomes less and less realistic to *assume* a common language among the parties. It will become more and more necessary to make agreement on a common language a condition for any substantive policy dialogue within a pluralistic society. In any case, it already is foolhardy, and is becoming more so every day, to trust *ex ante* in the existence of such a language. It is becoming increasingly urgent that we face this; we cannot assume such a language, a 'reason common to all humans', we have to *invent* it. We have no choice but to engage in collaborative language engineering to negotiate the abysses among different groups of humans.

This is where the Carnapian perspective differs fundamentally from those of Rawls and Habermas; they insist – with Kant and Rousseau – that any system of political order be rooted in some common substratum of untutored universal human nature, in a 'manifest image',[30] while the Carnapian ideal regards human institutions (including languages) as the products of human constructive ingenuity, no less than science, technology, and other human tools. We *make* them, they are not out there to be found or revealed. What reason is there to think that natural languages could in fact behave in accordance with anything like Habermas's discourse

---

[30] Carus (2004) discusses this notion of Wilfrid Sellars critically, and suggests how a version of it that escapes these criticisms can be recovered within the Carnapian ideal.

ethics? To lay down conditions for disinterested discourse is ipso facto to require a certain degree of constructedness. There is only one language that functions approximately as Habermas's discourse ethics for communicative reason prescribes[31] – the scientific ('universal') vernacular, which is, as we saw, partly constructed. Here we have a language that is used in common by a world-wide community of participants in a matter of intense joint involvement. These participants have many different priorities and pre-occupations. They live their personal lives in many different cultures with mutually inconsistent content values. And yet they are able to communicate in a common, artificially created and constantly renegotiated vernacular, enabling them to co-operate productively in the creation and application of new knowledge. The public language of politics agreed, or successively negotiated, in a 'language-engineering' scenario would be of a similar kind. Indeed, the language used in actual political debate *has* traditionally been such a partly constructed language; it has been structurally shaped by the more obviously constructed (or partly constructed) language of the law, which in turn becomes increasingly precise as it takes statistical, biological, economic, and other specialised languages on board. It seems likely that this trend will continue; as discussed above, the 'new politics of knowledge' will force the language in which politics itself is conducted to be an ever more self-conscious, artificial, negotiated one, since the uncritical acceptance of a default language will increasingly be seen as a concession to unwarranted authority.

So what is the answer? Whose knowledge is 'better' and whose is less good? The Enlightenment has traditionally claimed that there are *impersonal procedures* that can effectively determine what makes a given piece of knowledge 'better' (in a more or less precisely specifiable way) than another. Opposing this answer were not only liberal sceptics such as Locke, but also those who claimed that such procedures (in some versions: any *possible* such procedures) merely express or exemplify a particular partisan interest, and should be accorded no special privilege on that account. And indeed, it has proven much more difficult than anyone had ever imagined to specify any such procedures (as the failure of Carnap's own lifelong efforts eloquently testifies). The Enlightenment's heavy reliance on them is clearly no longer tenable in its original form. The original Enlightenment, though ethically and politically pluralistic, was *intellectually* not pluralistic. It really did think that natural science – including social science, in its view – would, progressively, find the true answers. Science, it thought, would provide

---

[31] As Michael Friedman (2001, pp. 53–6) has indeed suggested.

the replacement, once and for all, for the lore of the church and other traditional institutions, thereby providing *authoritative* knowledge, in an authoritative (encyclopaedic) language, in the ideal future.

We can all admit that this ideal has been discredited. But the Carnapian ideal can correct this failure by building in a radical pluralism at the very heart of the Enlightenment project. The answer to the question 'who decides?' is *not* that there *exist* some putative impersonal adjudicatory procedures out there (even if only procedural ones, with substantive questions left open for future negotiation). The Carnapian answer, rather, is on two levels, resolving the dissonance between liberalism and Enlightenment. At the framework level, we decide *collectively* on purpose-built languages of mutual interaction, as briefly sketched above (not necessarily a single language for all contexts). At this level, it is true, we have to compromise; we have to arrive at languages everyone else can live with, too. But there is more to life than politics. The language of politics is the language for the negotiation of *framework* values. But at the *content* level we decide *individually* (or in collaboration with those who share our content values). For everything other than politics, we are free to adopt whatever language we like. At the content level, we can invent our own language, or our own dialect of some language (e.g. of the universal vernacular), suited to the particular concerns we want to articulate. This is true even at the boundary, always under negotiation, between content and framework values. And yet the remodelled, pluralistic Enlightenment is not merely pluralistic; it is also constructive. It retains its intimate connection with the 'universal vernacular'. Its post-Carnapian programme is not only to improve the universal vernacular, but to turn the public language of politics and civic deliberation *into* the largest feasible subset of that universal vernacular, by education, political action, popularisation, and all available forms of non-coercive persuasion.

This extremely compressed sketch of a Carnapian approach to the 'new politics of knowledge' and to the Rawls–Habermas debate obviously raises many fundamental issues that cannot be addressed adequately in the space available here.[32] The sketch is intended merely to illustrate, rather, how the Carnapian ideal, freed from the inappropriately narrow context it has long been confined to, can prove fruitful well beyond 'philosophy of science' as it has evolved over the past half-century. The purpose of the book has been to place this Carnapian ideal back into the broader context from which it emerged, and the sketch provided here of its possible application to the

---

[32] Some of the immediately relevant ones are addressed in my (forthcoming) paper 'On Carnap's Logic of Normative Statements'.

arena of political and social deliberation aims to show how it can plausibly be regarded as the basis for a *Bildungsideal* appropriate to modernity of the kind that Carnap set out to construct in the 1920s.[33]

It also conveys, I hope, that the Carnapian ideal is a more open-ended conception of reason than that of Kant (let alone Rawls or Habermas). This ideal does not claim to know what reason *is*. It imposes a minimal constraint – any larger conception of reason must accommodate our knowledge; it cannot be obviously inconsistent with what we know. But our knowledge is so limited, compared to the vastness of our ignorance, that this is a very loose constraint. It is much too early in the history of systematic human cognition to make pronouncements about the ultimate nature of reason. We are in our cognitive infancy. And from Carnap's point of view, we are needlessly prolonging our infancy. Sixty years after he first set his sights on the open sea of free possibilities, it still lies before us, all but unexplored. We have been extremely timid, clinging to the shoreline, hardly daring to venture out of sight of land. The warm, familiar, safe harbour of habit and tradition appeals to us as much as it ever did to our ancestors. It is time we ventured forth again in the pioneering spirit of the original Enlightenment, emboldened by Carnap's example.

---

[33] I owe Michael Friedman the idea of using the Rawls-Habermas debate as an illuminating context to bring out this dimension of Carnap's ideal.

Bibliography

I CITED ARCHIVAL SOURCES

(A) ARCHIVES OF SCIENTIFIC PHILOSOPHY, HILLMAN LIBRARY, UNIVERSITY OF PITTSBURGH, CARNAP PAPERS (ASP)

1908a [081-47-06] 'Tagebuch' (shorthand), February 1908.

1911a [081-47-05] 'Religion und Kirche: Mein Vortrag in der Freiburger Freischar, vermutlich 1911' (shorthand, with many corrections).

1914a [081-36-01] Notes on Poincaré's *Wissenschaft und Hypothese* (Poincaré 1904); (shorthand), 1914.

1916a [089-74-01] Letter to Eduard Le Seur (longhand copy by Carnap's sister Agnes), March 1916.

1916b [028-09-06] 'Ausweis: Das Eiserne Kreuz II. Klasse' (certificate), 24 September 1916.

1917a [081-48-02] Letter to Wilhelm Flitner, copied out in shorthand by Carnap, 13 April 1917.

1917b [089-74-08] 'Über den Austritt aus der Kirche: Bemerkungen zu Mutters Aufzeichnungen vom 30.3.17' (shorthand), 10 August 1917.

1918a [028-09-04] 'Mitgliedsbuch [of the USPD]' (certificate), 1 August 1918.

1918b [110-01-01] Inaugural issue of *Politische Rundbriefe*, 5 October 1918. Carnap's contribution 'Völkerbund – Staatenbund' begins on p. 4 of this issue.

1918c [110-01-04] *Politischer Rundbrief* of 23 October 1918. Continuation of Carnap's essay on pp. 15–16 of this issue.

1918d [089-72-04] 'Deutschlands Niederlage: Sinnloses Schicksal oder Schuld?' (typed), 29 October 1918.

1919a [111-D-60] Carnap's annotated copy of Frege's *Grundlagen der Arithmetik*.

1919b [110-01-28] *Politischer Rundbrief* of 1 April 1919. Recommendation of G. Landauer's book *Revolution und Sozialismus*, p. 124.

1920a [081-39-03] 'Begriffsschrift bei Whitehead und Russell' (shorthand notes on *Principia Mathematica*), June 1920.

1920b [081-06-01] 'Axiomatik der Raum-Zeit Welt' (handwritten outline), June 1920.

1920c [081-05-04] 'Skelett der Erkenntnistheorie' (shorthand), August 1920.

1920d [081-47-01] Circular Letter to Sera Friends (typed, carbon), 7 November 1920.

1921a [081-05-06] 'Analyse des Weltbildes' (shorthand), 27 April 1921.

1921b [081-39-02] Notes on Russell's *Foundations of Geometry*, 28 April 1921.

1921c   [110-05-07] First draft of 'Die Aufgabe der Physik' (1923), when still intended as 'Briefwechsel' with Hugo Dingler (carbon), begun 21 July 1921, finished 6 August 1921.

1921d   [081-05-05] 'Über die Analyse von Erlebnissen' (shorthand), 11 September 1921.

1921e   [102-68-34] Letter to Bertrand Russell (typed, carbon), 17 November 1921.

1921f   [081-48-04] Letter to Wilhelm Flitner (typed, carbon), 10 December 1921.

1921g   [081-28-01] Notes on Frege's two 1903 papers 'Über die Grundlagen der Geometrie' (shorthand), 1921.

1922a   [081-05-01] 'Vom Chaos zur Wirklichkeit' (typed, with handwritten corrections), July 1922.

1922b   [102-72-10] Letter to Heinrich Scholz (typed, carbon), Berlin, 11 October 1922.

1922c   [091-17-11a, b] (a) 'Aufforderung zur Teilnahme an Besprechungen über Beziehungslehre'; (b) 'Aufforderung zur Teilnahme an Besprechungen über den Aufbau der Wirklichkeit (Strukturtheorie der Erkenntnis' (typed, carbon), November 1922.

1922d   [091-17-12] Three positions papers on: (a) Beziehungslehre und Strukturlehre; (b) Ansätze zur Charakterisierung von Strukturen (with Bernhard Merten); (c) Aufbau der Wirklichkeit (Strukturtheorie des Erkenntnisgegenstandes) (carbons); late 1922.

1923a   [081-04-01] 'Die Quasizerlegung' (typed, carbon), 27 December 1922 to 25 January 1923.

1923b   [091-17-02] 'Zweites Rundschreiben über die Erlanger Tagung' (longhand, stencil copy), 19 February 1923.

1923c   [102-72-08] Letter to Heinrich Scholz (typed, carbon), Kiel, 2 March 1923

1923d   [102-72-09] Letter to Heinrich Scholz (typed, carbon), Mexico, 13 August 1923.

1924a   [081-02-07] 'Topologie der Raum-Zeit Welt' (typed), 1924.

1925a   [081-05-03] 'Gedanken zum Kategorienproblem. Prolegomena zu einer Konstitutionstheorie (Vortrag Wien)' (shorthand), 21 January 1925.

1925b   [081-05-02] 'Entwurf einer Konstitutionstheorie der Erkenntnisgegenstände' (typed), first sketch, 17 December 1924; this version typed, 28 January 1925.

1926a   [081-05-07] 'Thesen zur Konstitutionstheorie (Vortrag Wien, 29.6. und 3.7.26)' (typed), before 29 June 1926.

1926b   [110-07-16A] 'Die logischen Grundlagen der physikalischen Methode [vielleicht besser "des physikalischen Systems"] (Vortrag Prag)' (shorthand), 11 December 1926.

1927a   [080-34-03/4] 'Untersuchungen zur allgemeinen Axiomatik', [Part I]; now published as Carnap 2000; begun in 1927, worked on through 1928 and 1929 (though during these later years most effort went into Part II, while the present part was circulating among colleagues).

1928a   [110-09-15/16] 'Übung: Ausgewählte Fragen zu den philosophischen Grundlagen der Geometrie (für Fortgeschrittene)' and 'Gegen die Apriorität der Dreidimensionalität' (shorthand), 12 November 1928.

1928b   [102-68-24] Letter to Bertrand Russell (typed, carbon), 11 August 1928.

1928c   [029-16-01] Letter to Neurath (typed, carbon), Zuoz (Engadin), 7 October 1928.

1929a   [089-64-01] 'Neue Grundlegung der Logik' (shorthand), Davos, 27 March 1929.

1929b   [110-07-32] 'Die Stellung der Physik im Aufbau der Erkenntnis: Feigls Vorschlag für meinen Vortrag (Prag) – nicht gehalten' (shorthand), 30 June 1929.

1929c   [089-63-01] 'Von Gott und Seele: Scheinfragen in Metaphysik und Theologie' (typed), lecture held at Ernst Mach Verein in June 1929. Now published as Carnap (2004).

1929d   [110-07-49] 'Wissenschaft und Leben', first lecture at the Dessau Bauhaus (shorthand), written 1 October 1929, given 15 October 1929.

1929e   [110-07-48] 'Die vierdimensionale Raum-Zeit-Welt der modernen Physik', second lecture at Dessau Bauhaus (shorthand), written 7 October 1929, given 18 October 1929.

1929f   [110-07-47] 'Aufgabe und Gehalt der Wissenschaft', third lecture at Dessau Bauhaus (shorthand), 9 October 1929.

1929g   [110-07-45] 'Der logische Aufbau der Welt', fourth lecture at Dessau Bauhaus (shorthand), 10 October 1929.

1929i   [085-66-01/2] 'Die Entwicklung der theoretischen Philosophie seit Descartes', lecture course, first given in Vienna, summer semester 1929 (shorthand).

1929j   [110-09-07] 'Einführung in die Philosophie', lecture course, first held in Vienna, winter semester 1929–30 (shorthand).

1930a   [090-15-03] 'Gespräch mit Tarski über Monomorphie' (shorthand), 22 February 1930.

1930b   [025-73-04] Diary entry of 24 February 1930.

1930c   [110-07-39] 'Die materialistische Basis der Wissenschaft (Referat in der sozialistischen Arbeitsgemeinschaft [Helene Bauer])' (shorthand), 24 April 1930.

1930d   [029-17-06] 'Einheitlichkeit der Gegenstände aller Wissenschaften' (typed), by Neurath, May 1930.

1930e   [110-07-29] 'Einheitswissenschaft auf physikalischer Basis (Mach-Verein)', 20 May 1930.

1930f   [110-07-40] 'Die Psychologie im Rahmen der Einheitswissenschaft (Referat in Bühlers psychologischem Kolloquium)' (shorthand), 28 May 1930.

1930g   [025-73-04] Diary entry of 26 August 1930.

1930h   [110-07-35] 'Der tautologische Charakter des Schließens (Warschau)' (shorthand), 20 November 1930.

1930i   [081-07-06] Minutes of Vienna Circle meeting on 11 December 1930 (typed), taken by Rose Rand; now published in Stadler 1997, pp. 276–278; PT pp. 242–4.

1931a   [110-07-24] 'Die Philosophie des Wiener Kreises' (shorthand), 10 January 1931.

1931b   [081-03-05] 'Die Philosophie des Wiener Kreises: Vortrag in München, Kant-Gesellschaft' (typed from Ina's stenographic notes at the lecture), 10 January 1931.

1931c   [110-07-36] 'Erläuterung einiger philosophischer Ausdrücke', lecture to the socialist students of Ottakring (shorthand), 30 January 1931.

1931d   [081-07-11] Minutes of Vienna Circle meeting on 26 February 1931 (typed), taken by Rose Rand; now published in Stadler 1997, pp. 288–92; PT pp. 254–8.

1931e   [029-17-03] 'Neurath: Besprechung über Physikalismus am 4. März 1931' (typed, carbon), with discussion contributions by Hans Hahn.

1931f   [110-07-13] 'Physikalismus (Schlick-Zirkel)' (shorthand), 5 March 1931.

1931g   [081-07-12] Minutes of Vienna Circle meeting on 5 March 1931 (typed), taken by Rose Rand; now published in Stadler 1997, pp. 292–7; PT pp. 258–62.

1931h   [081-07-13] Minutes of Vienna Circle meeting on 12 March 1931 (typed), taken by Rose Rand; now published in Stadler 1997, pp. 297–302; PT pp. 263–7.

1931i   [025-73-05] Diary entry of 21 April 1931.

1931j   [029-17-02] 'Zur phänomenalen Sprache (in Anknüpfung an das Gespräch mit Neurath, 1.5.)' (shorthand), 2 May 1931.

1931k   [081-07-14] Minutes of Vienna Circle meeting on 7 May 1931 (typed), taken by Rose Rand; now published in Stadler 1997, pp. 302–5; PT pp. 267–9.

1931l   [081-07-17, 18,19] Carnap's 'Referate über Metalogik'; Minutes of Vienna Circle meetings on 11, 18, and 25 June 1931 (typed), taken by Rose Rand; now published in Stadler 1997, pp. 314–29; PT pp. 279–94.

1931m   [025-73-05] Diary entry of 26 June 1931.

1931n   [081-07-20] Discussion of Carnap's 'Referate über Metalogik'; Minutes of Vienna Circle meeting on 2 July 1931 (typed), taken by Rose Rand; now published in Stadler 1997, pp. 330–4; PT pp. 294–9.

1932a   [110-07-23] 'Die Syntax als Grundlage der wissenschaftlichen Philosophie: Referat in Reichenbachs Kolloquium, Berlin' (shorthand), written 1 July 1932, given 4 July 1932.

1932b   [110-07-26] 'Über den Charakter der philosophischen Probleme', lecture in Copenhagen (shorthand), 2 and 7 November 1932.

1932c   [110-04-09] 'Niederschrift des Konzepts des ersten MS "Metalogik" (das später getippt worden ist)', 14 December 1933.

1932d   [110-04-07] Table of Contents of *Metalogik* (first draft of *Logical Syntax*), put together from several different versions (typed, with handwritten corrections and remarks, including some by Neurath).

1933a   [110-04-02] 'Über den Charakter der philosophischen Probleme', German original of the article (1934d) published only in an English translation, 24–5 June 1933.

1933b   [110-04-08/9] 'Arbeit am neuen MS "Syntax" (1933, für den Druck)' (shorthand), 14 December 1933.

1933c   [029-03-06] Letter to Neurath (carbon), 23 December 1933.

1934a   [110-08-17] 'Philosophie – Opium für die Gebildeten', lecture to the Freidenkerbund in Brünn (shorthand), 26 March 1934, given 5 April 1934.

1934b   [085-66-02] 'Die naturphilosophische Strömungen der Gegenwart', lecture course, first held in Prague, summer semester 1934 (shorthand).

1935a   [102-70-10] Letter to Schlick (typed), 4 December 1935.

1936a   [081-03-02] 'The Unity of Science: Lecture at the Colloquium (Ch. Morris), Chicago, 11 February 1936' (typed).

1938a   [110-02-09] Annotated copy of 'Testability and Meaning' (longhand annotations).

1940a   [091-18-07] 'In Frankreich 1916–17' (shorthand), 8 June 1940.

1950a [085-74-01] 'Für das psycholog. meeting Urbana [Prof. Miller]' (shorthand), 1 January 1950.

1954a [086-06-02] 'Remarks on Physicalism and Related Topics (Discussion with Wilfried Sellars)' (typed), December 1954.

1955a [091-27-02] Summary of E. V. Beth's paper for Schilpp volume, with comments (shorthand), 19 August 1955.

1955b [089-48-04] 'Über psychologische Begriffe' (shorthand), 22 December 1955.

1956a [091-26-01] Summary of Y. Bar-Hillel's paper for Schilpp volume, with appended page of same date, with material not included in Carnap's reply (shorthand), 23 February 1956.

1957a [082-07-01] 'How Can Induction Be Justified?' (typed), April 1957.

1958a [088-05-05] Letter to E. V. Beth (typed carbon), 6 April 1958.

1962a [027-06-29] Letter from Feigl to Carnap (typed), 2 May 1962.

1963a [III-G-121] Carnap's annotated copy of the Schilpp volume (longhand and shorthand annotations).

1966a [089-48-03] 'On the basis of the mind–body dualism' (shorthand), 26 March 1966.

1966b [091-17-01] 'R. C. Vorlesungen (als Student) Univ. Jena/Freiburg SS 1910—SS 1914; WS 1918—SS 1919' (longhand), 25 April 1966.

1966b [III-B-39] Carnap's annotated copy of the Suhrkamp reissue (1966) of *Scheinprobleme in der Philosophie*, with an afterword by Günther Patzig, pp. 85–136 (shorthand annotations).

(B) ARCHIVES OF SCIENTIFIC PHILOSOPHY, HILLMAN LIBRARY, UNIVERSITY OF PITTSBURGH, RAND PAPERS (ASP/RR)

1928a [10-15-09] 'Briefwechsel Carnap-Gomperz' (very rough and imperfect typescript), no date.

1930a [12-02-01] 'Carnap Aufsatz' (very rough and imperfect typescript with some handwritten corrections), no date.

1932a [10-15-10] 'Carnap-Schlick-Waismann-Hahn: Über Protokollsätze' (rough typescript), no date.

1933a [10-15-14] 'Neurath zu Carnaps Kritik an der Übersetzungsarbeit' (typed, carbon), no date.

(C) STAATS- UND UNIVERSITÄTSBIBLIOTHEK HAMBURG, NACHLASS- UND AUTOGRAPHENSAMMLUNG, WILHELM FLITNER PAPERS, WITH SOME PHOTOCOPIES AVAILABLE AT ARCHIVES OF SCIENTIFIC PHILOSOPHY (ASP/WF)

1916a [WF12] Letter to Flitner, from the front ('Schützengraben'), 3 July 1916.

1916b [WF13] Letter to Flitner, 'Im Quartier', 8 July 1916.

1916c [WF18] Letter to Flitner, Jena, 29 August 1916.

1916d [WF19] Letter to Flitner, 'Im Quartier', 8 September 1916.

(D) ARCHIVES OF SCIENTIFIC PHILOSOPHY, HILLMAN LIBRARY,
UNIVERSITY OF PITTSBURGH, REICHENBACH PAPERS (ASP/HR)

1924a   [016-28-06] Letter to Reichenbach, Buchenbach, 10 May 1924.

(E) HUGO-DINGLER ARCHIV, HOFBIBLIOTHEK ASCHAFFENBURG,
WITH SOME PHOTOCOPIES AVAILABLE AT THE ARCHIVES OF
SCIENTIFIC PHILOSOPHY, HILLMAN LIBRARY, UNIVERSITY OF
PITTSBURGH (ASP/HD)

1920a   [HD 02] Letter to Dingler, Buchenbach, 14 November 1920.
1921a   [HD08] Review of Dingler's *Grundlagen der Physik* (Dingler 1919) in *Münchner Neue Nachrichten*, 26 July 1921.

(F) CARNAP-KAILA CORRESPONDENCE IN THE POSSESSION OF
PROF. JUHA MANNINEN, UNIVERSITY OF HELSINKI (CK)

1929a   Letter to Kaila, 28 January 1929.
1930a   Letter to Kaila, 12 December 1930.

(G) YOUNG RESEARCH LIBRARY, UNIVERSITY OF CALIFORNIA
AT LOS ANGELES, SPECIAL COLLECTIONS DEPARTMENT,
MANUSCRIPT COLLECTION NO. 1029, RUDOLF CARNAP
PAPERS (UCLA)

1919a   [Box 5, CM19, items 1 and 2] 'Fachwissenschaftliche Hausarbeit zur Prüfung fur das Lehramt an höheren Schulen. *Aufgabe*: Es sind die bisherigen Ergebnisse der Theorie über die Anregung, insbesondere die stoßweise Anregung von Schwingungen zusammenzustellen und kritisch zu besprechen' (typed, carbon), after May 1919.
1920a   [Box 3, CM12, only item] 'Welche philosophische Bedeutung hat das Problem der Grundlegung der Geometrie? Prüfungsarbeit für Prof. Bauch, Jena, Lehramtsprüfung' (typed, very faded carbon; includes fold-out chart at end, 'System der logischen und mathematischen Wissenschaften'), March 1920.
1928a   [Box 4, CM13, item 5 'Welchen Sinn hat die Wahrscheinlichkeitsaussage über ein künftiges Ereignis? [zu. S. 26]' (typed table), 20 November [1928]. This table appears to have been enclosed in a letter to Kaila of 28 January 1929.
1929a   [Box 4, CM13, item 3] 'Über die Konstitution des Nicht-Gegebenen (für Vortrag Berlin)' (shorthand), 6 October 1929.
1929b   [Box 3, CM10, item 4, first loose sheet] 'Ordnung der Metaphysiker, nach dem Grade der Schlimmheit' (shorthand), Dessau, 21 October 1929.
1929c   [Box 4, CM13, item 9] 'Konstitution des Nicht-Gegebenen: Weiter' (shorthand), 8 November 1929.
1929d   [Box 4, CM13, item 10] 'Wahrscheinlichkeit' (shorthand), 17 November 1929.

1929e [Box 4, CM13, item 4] 'Über die Konstitution des Nicht-Gegebenen: II. Der Apriorismus' (shorthand), pages numbered 34–62, first page dated 12 November 1929.

1929f [Box 4, CM13, item 2] 'Über die Konstitution des Nicht-Gegebenen' (shorthand table of contents extending through p. 72), 19 November 1929.

1930a [Box 4, CM13, item 7] 'Über die Naturgesetze als Operationsvorschriften (Konstitutionsregeln) [Gespräch mit Feigl]', 2 August 1930.

1930b [Box 4, CM13, item 1] 'Plan für Kaila-Aufsatz: Über die Erkenntnis des sog. "Nicht-Gegebenen"' (shorthand), 2 November 1930; also an outline headed 'Kaila-Aufsatz' on a separate sheet dated 29 October 1930.

1930c [Box 3, CM10, loose sheet] 'Einführung in die wissenschaftliche Philosophie: [alter] Plan' (shorthand), 18 November 1930.

1931a [Box 3, CM10, loose sheets] 'Einführung in die wissenschaftliche Philosophie. Einleitung: Überlieferte Philosophie und wissenschaftliche Philosophie' (shorthand), Mösern, 1 January 1931.

1931b [Box 4, CM14, item 1] 'Versuch einer Metalogik [22.1.31 im Bett geschrieben. In der schlaflosen Nacht vorher ausgedacht (Halsentzündung).]' (shorthand); begun 22 January 1931, continued 30 January 1931, with later annotations.

1931c [Box 3, CM10, loose sheets] 'Einführung in die wissenschaftliche Philosophie' (typed outline in two parts, 'Die Sprache der Wissenschaft' and 'Die Grundlagen der Wissenschaften') [Annotation: 'Auf Neuraths Vorschlag anstelle meines geplanten Buches "Einführung in die wissenschaftliche Philosophie" zwei kleine Bände für seine geplante Sammlung'], 24 February 1931.

1931d [Box 3, CM10, item 7] 'Band I: Die Sprache der Wissenschaft. I. Formale Untersuchung der Sprache' (first chapter of book manuscript, pp. 1–16, shorthand), 25 February 1931.

1931e [Box 3, CM10, item 8] '2. Der Kalkül' (pp. 17–29, shorthand).

1931f [Box 3, CM10, item 9] 'Inhaltliche Richtigkeit und Vollständigkeit des Satzkalküls' (pp. 30–40, shorthand).

1931g [Box 3, CM10, item 10] '3. Spielraum und Gehalt' [later annotation: 'vom März 1931'] (pp. 41a-64, shorthand).

1931h [Box 3, CM10, loose sheets] 'MS "Einführung" Inhaltsverzeichnis. Band I: Die Sprache der Wissenschaft. Eine Einführung in die Logik' (shorthand), 11 March 1931.

1931i [Box 3, CM10, item 11] 'Satzfunktionen (Logik der Begriffe)' (pp. 65–87, shorthand), 14 March 1931.

1931j [Box 3, CM10, item 13 'Der tautologische Charakter des Schließens' (pp. 107–15, shorthand), 25 March 1931.

1931k [Box 3, CM11, item 2] 'B. Grundlegung der Mathematik. Oder: Die Mathematik als Teil der Syntax. I. Arithmetik.' [later annotation: 'zum MS: "Die Sprache der Wissenschaft"'] (pp. 1–18, shorthand), 25 March 1931.

1931l [Box 3, CM11, item 3] 'Die reellen Zahlen' (pp. 19–33, shorthand), 2 April 1931.

1931m [Box 3, CM11, loose sheet] 'B. Grundlegung der Mathematik (oder: Die Mathematik als Teil der Syntax)' (shorthand table of contents up to p. 48), 4 April 1931.

1931n   [Box 3, CM11, item 5] 'Von hier an neuer Aufbau!' (pp. 18–32, shorthand), 6 April 1931.

1931o   [Box C, CM11, loose sheet] 'Plan: Grundlegung der Mathematik' (shorthand outline), 8 April 1931.

1931p   [Box 3, CM11, item 11] 'Neue Fassung des Zahlenkalküls, im Anschluß an Skolem' (separately paginated, pp. 1–17, shorthand), 11 April 1931.

1931q   [Box 4, CM14, item 4, loose sheet] 'Logik, Metalogik und Mathematik' [annotation: 'Dies ist der Grundentwurf für das MS. Unter Verwertung dieses Rahmens, aber mit der inhaltlichen Durchführung des neuen Entwurfs vom 27. 5. ist das MS auszuarbeiten!], 15 April 1931 [later annotation: 'einige Blätter (Anfangsblätter verschiedener Anfangsteile oder MSe), die die Entwicklung zeigen, die zur "logischen Syntax" geführt hat'].

1931r   [Box 4, CM14, item 4, loose sheets] Three sheets appended to 1931q: 'I. Metalogik. Neuer Entwurf: Stellenzahlen anstatt Dingnamen!' (shorthand), 27 May 1931; 'II. Axiomatisierung der Metalogik (neu formuliert 15. 6. 31) (früher: 29.5.)' (shorthand); 'III. Arithmetisierung der Metalogik (in Anlehnung an Gödel)' (shorthand), 17 June 1931.

1956a   [Box 6, CMS2, sections 1–11] Shorthand originals (in German) of Part II of Carnap's autobiography (April–June 1956).

1956b   [Box 6, CMS1, sections 1–13] Shorthand originals (in German) of Part I of Carnap's autobiography (July–November 1956).

1957a   [Box 2, CM3, first two folders (marked 'M-A3' and 'M-A4' in blue crayon), sections 2–11] Original English version, dictated by Carnap (using UCLA 1956a and 1956b) and typed by Ina, with many marked deletions and revisions in longhand, as well as shorthand interpolations and added sheets. M-A3 (183 pp.) is Part I of the autobiography, M-A4 (179 pp.) is Part II. Divided into lettered sections, A through V (pagination is by section); 1957–8.

1957b   [Box 2, CM3, second folder (marked 'M-A5'), 58 loose pages] Pages removed from 1957a that were to be omitted from published version (1963) in their entirety; pagination continuous with 1957a, in the same lettered sections; 1957.

II PUBLISHED WORKS AND SECONDARY LITERATURE CITED

d'Alembert, J. L. (1751) *Preliminary Discourse to the Encyclopedia of Diderot*, trans. by R. N. Schwab (Chicago: University of Chicago Press, 1995).

Ash, M. G. (1998) *Gestalt Psychology in German Culture 1890–1967: Holism and the Quest for Objectivity* (Cambridge: Cambridge University Press).

Aufmuth, U. (1979) *Die deutsche Wandervogelbewegung unter soziologischem Aspekt* (Göttingen: Vandenhoek und Ruprecht).

Awodey, S. and A. W. Carus (2001) 'Carnap, Completeness, and Categoricity: The *Gabelbarkeitssatz* of 1928', *Erkenntnis* 54, pp. 145–72.

Awodey, S. and A. W. Carus (2003) 'Carnap vs. Gödel on Syntax and Tolerance', in P. Parrini, W. C. Salmon, and M. H. Salmon, eds., *Logical Empiricism:*

Historical and Contemporary Perspectives (Pittsburgh: University of Pittsburgh Press), pp. 57–64.

Awodey, S. and A. W. Carus (2004) 'How Carnap Could Have Replied to Gödel', in Awodey and Klein (2004), pp. 199–220.

Awodey, S. and A. W. Carus (2007) 'The Turning Point: Philosophy of Mathematics in Logical Empiricism from the *Tractatus* to *Logical Syntax*', in A. Richardson and T. Uebel, eds., *The Cambridge Companion to Logical Empiricism* (Cambridge: Cambridge University Press), pp. 165–92.

Awodey, S. and A. W. Carus (forthcoming) 'Carnap's Dream: Gödel, Wittgenstein, and *Logical Syntax*', in *Synthese*.

Awodey, S. and C. Klein, eds. (2004) *Carnap Brought Home: The View from Jena* (LaSalle, IL: Open Court).

Awodey, S. and E. Reck (2002) 'Completeness and Categoricity. Part I: Nineteenth-century Axiomatics to Twentieth-Century Metalogic', *History and Philosophy of Logic* 23, pp. 1–30.

Ayer, A. J. (1937) 'Verification and Experience', *Proceedings of the Aristotelian Society* 37, pp. 137–56.

Ayer, A. J. (1982) *Philosophy in the Twentieth Century* (New York: Random House).

Bachelard, G. (1934) *Le Nouvel Esprit scientifique* (Paris: Alcan).

Bachelard, G. (1938) *La Formation de l'esprit scientifique: Contribution à une psychanalyse de la connaissance objective* (Paris: Vrin).

Baker, K. M. (1975) *Condorcet: From Natural Philosophy to Social Mathematics* (Chicago: University of Chicago Press).

Banks, E. C. (2005) 'Kant, Herbart, and Riemann', *Kant-Studien* 96, pp. 208–34.

Bauch, B. (1911) *Studien zur Philosophie der exakten Wissenschaften* (Heidelberg: Winter).

Beaney, M. (1996) *Frege: Making Sense* (London: Duckworth).

Beaney, M. (2004) 'Carnap's Conception of Explication: From Frege to Husserl?' in Awodey and Klein (2004), pp. 117–50.

Beeck, K.-H. (1975) *Friedrich Wilhelm Dörpfeld: Anpassung im Zwiespalt* (Neuwied: Luchterhand).

Bereiter, C. and M. Scardamalia (1993) *Surpassing Ourselves: An Inquiry into the Nature and Implications of Expertise* (LaSalle, IL: Open Court).

Berlin, I. (1973) 'J. L. Austin and the Early Beginnings of Oxford Philosophy', repr. in *Personal Impressions*, 2nd edn (London: Pimlico, 1998), pp. 130–45.

Beth, E. W. (1963) 'Carnap's Views on the Advantages of Constructed Systems over Natural Languages in the Philosophy of Science', in Schilpp (1963), pp. 469–502.

Bias-Engels, S. (1988) *Zwischen Wandervogel und Wissenschaft: Zur Geschichte von Jugendbewegung und Studentenschaft 1896–1920* (Cologne: Verlag Wissenschaft und Politik).

Bird, G. H. (1995) 'Carnap and Quine: Internal and External Questions', *Erkenntnis* 42, pp. 41–64.

Bird, G. H. (2006) *The Revolutionary Kant: A Commentary on the Critique of Pure Reason* (LaSalle, IL: Open Court).

Blakeslee, S. (2003) 'Moved by Thought', *The New York Times*, Science Pages, (13 October 2003).

Blaug, M. (1980) *The Methodology of Economics, or How Economists Explain* (Cambridge: Cambridge University Press).

Bloor, D. (1976) *Knowledge and Social Imagery* (London: Routledge and Kegan Paul).

Bloor, D. (1996) *Wittgenstein, Rules, and Institutions* (London: Routledge).

Bohnert, H. G. (1975a) 'Homage to Rudolf Carnap, 10', in J. Hintikka, ed., *Rudolf Carnap, Logical Empiricist* (Dordrecht: Reidel), pp. XXXI–XLIV.

Bohnert, H. G. (1975b) 'Carnap's Logicism', in J. Hintikka, ed., *Rudolf Carnap, Logical Empiricist* (Dordrecht: Reidel), pp. 183–216.

Boltzmann, L. (1896) 'Ein Wort der Mathematik an die Energetik', *Annalen der Physik und Chemie* 57, pp. 39–71.

Bonner, J. T. (1983) *The Evolution of Culture in Animals* (Princeton: Princeton University Press).

Boyd, R. and P. J. Richerson (1985) *Culture and the Evolutionary Process* (Chicago: University of Chicago Press).

Brandom, R. B. (1994) *Making It Explicit: Reasoning, Representing, and Discursive Commitment* (Cambridge, MA: Harvard University Press).

Brandom, R. B. (1999) *Articulating Reasons: An Introduction to Inferentialism* (Cambridge, MA: Harvard University Press).

Bruford, W. H. (1975) *The German Tradition of Self-Cultivation: Bildung from Humboldt to Thomas Mann* (Cambridge: Cambridge University Press).

Burge, T. (1992) 'Philosophy of Language and Mind: 1950–1990', *Philosophical Review* 101, pp. 3–52.

Burling, R. (2006) *The Talking Ape: How Language Evolved* (Oxford: Oxford University Press).

Carnap, R. (1922) *Der Raum: Ein Beitrag zur Wissenschaftslehre*, Kant-Studien Ergänzungshefte, Nr. 56 (Berlin: Reuther & Reichard).

Carnap, R. (1923) 'Über die Aufgabe der Physik und die Anwendung des Grundsatzes der Einfachstheit', *Kant-Studien* 28, pp. 90–107.

Carnap, R. (1924) 'Dreidimensionalität des Raumes und Kausalität: Eine Untersuchung über den logischen Zusammenhang zweier Fiktionen', *Annalen der Philosophie und philosophischen Kritik* 4, pp. 105–30.

Carnap, R. (1926) *Physikalische Begriffsbildung* (Karlsruhe: Braun).

Carnap, R. (1927) 'Eigentliche und uneigentliche Begriffe', *Symposion* 1, pp. 355–74.

Carnap, R. (1928a) *Der logische Aufbau der Welt* (Berlin: Weltkreis).

Carnap, R. (1928b) *Scheinprobleme in der Philosophie* (Berlin: Weltkreis).

Carnap, R. (1929) *Abriß der Logistik, mit besonderer Berücksichtigung der Relationstheorie und ihrer Anwendungen* (Vienna: Springer).

Carnap, R. (1930a) 'Die alte und die neue Logik', *Erkenntnis* 1, pp. 12–26.

Carnap, R. (1930b) Review of Kaufmann (1930), *Deutsche Literaturzeitung* 51, cols. 1674–8.

Carnap, R. (1930c) 'Bericht über Untersuchungen zur allgemeinen Axiomatik', *Erkenntnis* 1, pp. 303–7.

Carnap, R. (1930d) Review of Kaila (1930), *Erkenntnis* 2, pp. 75–7.

Carnap, R. (1931) 'Die logizistische Grundlegung der Mathematik', *Erkenntnis* 2, pp. 91–105.

Carnap, R. (1932a) 'Überwindung der Metaphysik durch logische Analyse der Sprache', *Erkenntnis* 2, pp. 219–41.

Carnap, R. (1932b) 'Die physikalische Sprache als Universalsprache der Wissenschaft', *Erkenntnis* 2, pp. 432–65, trans. M. Black as *Unity of Science* (London: Routledge, 1934).

Carnap, R. (1932c) 'Psychologie in physikalischer Sprache', *Erkenntnis* 3, pp. 107–42.

Carnap, R. (1932d) 'Erwiderung auf die vorstehenden Aufsätze von E. Zilsel und K. Duncker', *Erkenntnis* 3, pp. 177–88.

Carnap, R. (1932e) 'Über Protokollsätze', *Erkenntnis* 3, pp. 215–28; trans. R. Creath and R. Nollan as 'On Protocol Sentences', *Nous* 21 (1987), pp. 457–70.

Carnap, R. (1934a) *Logische Syntax der Sprache* (Vienna: Springer), trans. Amethe Smeaton as *The Logical Syntax of Language* (London: Routledge, 1937).

Carnap, R. (1934b) 'Theoretische Fragen und praktische Entscheidungen', *Natur und Geist* 2, pp. 257–60.

Carnap, R. (1934c) *Die Aufgabe der Wissenschaftslogik* (Vienna: Gerold), trans. H. Kaal as 'The Task of the Logic of Science', in B. McGuinness, ed., *Unified Science: The Vienna Circle Monograph Series* (Dordrecht: Reidel, 1987), pp. 46–66.

Carnap, R. (1934d) 'On the Character of Philosophical Problems', *Philosophy of Science* 1, pp. 5–19; German original 'Über den Charakter philosophischer Probleme' published in R. Carnap, *Scheinprobleme in der Philosophie und andere metaphysikkritische Schriften*, ed. T. Mormann (Hamburg: Meiner, 2004), pp. 111–27.

Carnap, R. (1935a) *Philosophy and Logical Syntax* (London: Routledge).

Carnap, R. (1935b) Review of Popper (1935), *Erkenntnis* 5, pp. 290–4.

Carnap, R. (1936) 'Wahrheit und Bewährung', in *Actes du Congrès international de philosophie scientifique, Sorbonne, Paris 1935, fasc. 4. Unité de la science* (Paris: Hermann), pp. 18–23.

Carnap, R. (1936–7) 'Testability and Meaning', *Philosophy of Science* 3, pp. 419–71 and 4, pp. 1–40.

Carnap, R. (1939) *Foundations of Logic and Mathematics* (Chicago: University of Chicago Press).

Carnap, R. (1942) *Introduction to Semantics* (Cambridge, MA: Harvard University Press).

Carnap, R. (1945) 'The Two Concepts of Probability', *Philosophy and Phenomenological Research* 5, pp. 513–32.

Carnap, R. (1950a) 'Empiricism, Semantics, and Ontology', repr. in his *Meaning and Necessity*, 2nd edn (Chicago: University of Chicago Press, 1956), pp. 205–21.

Carnap, R. (1950b) *Logical Foundations of Probability* (Chicago: University of Chicago Press).

Carnap, R. (1955) 'On Some Concepts of Pragmatics', *Philosophical Studies* 6 (1955), pp. 89–91, repr. in *Meaning and Necessity*, 2nd edn (Chicago: University of Chicago Press, 1956), pp. 249–51.

Carnap, R. (1956) 'The Methodological Character of Theoretical Concepts', in H. Feigl and M. Scriven, eds., *The Foundations of Science and the Concepts of Psychology and Psychoanalysis* (Minneapolis: University of Minnesota Press), pp. 38–76.

Carnap, R. (1961) 'Vorwort zur Zweiten Auflage', in Carnap (1928), 2nd edn (Hamburg: Meiner), pp. X–XV.

Carnap, R. (1963) 'Carnap's Intellectual Autobiography' and 'The Philosopher Replies', in Schilpp (1963), pp. 3–84, 859–1013.

Carnap, R. (1966) *Philosophical Foundations of Physics: An Introduction to the Philosophy of Science* (New York: Basic Books).

Carnap, R. (1968) 'Inductive Logic and Inductive Intuition', in I. Lakatos, ed., *The Problem of Inductive Logic* (Amsterdam: North Holland).

Carnap, R. (2000) *Untersuchungen zur allgemeinen Axiomatik*, ed. T. Bonk and J. Mosterin (Darmstadt: Wissenschaftliche Buchgesellschaft).

Cartwright, N. (2004) 'Causation: One Word, Many Things', *Philosophy of Science* 71, pp. 805–19.

Cartwright, N., J. Cat, L. Fleck, and T. E. Uebel (1996) *Otto Neurath: Philosophy between Science and Politics* (Cambridge: Cambridge University Press).

Carus, A. W. (1999) 'Carnap, Syntax, and Truth', in J. Peregrin, ed., *Truth and its Nature (If Any)* (Dordrecht: Kluwer), pp. 15–35.

Carus, A. W. (2001) 'The Philosopher without Qualities', review article of T. Mormann (1999) and R. Carnap (2000), in M. Heidelberger and F. Stadler, eds., *History of Philosophy and Science* (Dordrecht: Kluwer), pp. 369–77.

Carus, A. W. (2002) 'Moral Expertise', in B. Smith, ed., *Liberal Education in a Knowledge Society* (Chicago and LaSalle, IL: Open Court), pp. 175–222.

Carus, A. W. (2004) 'Sellars, Carnap, and the Logical Space of Reasons', in Awodey and Klein (2004), pp. 313–52.

Carus, A. W. (forthcoming) 'On Carnap's Logic of Normative Statements'.

Carus, A. W. and S. C. Ogilvie (forthcoming) 'Turning Qualitative into Quantitative Evidence: A Well-Used Method Made Explicit', *Economic History Review* (longer version available online as Cambridge Working Paper in Economics 0512, Faculty of Economics and Politics, University of Cambridge).

Cassirer, E. (1907) 'Kant und die moderne Mathematik', *Kant-Studien* 12, pp. 1–49.

Cassirer, E. (1910) *Substanzbegriff und Funktionsbegriff: Untersuchungen über die Grundfragen der Erkenntniskritik* (Darmstadt: Wissenschaftliche Buchgesellschaft, 1994), trans. W. C. and M. C. Swabey as *Substance and Function and Einstein's Theory of Relativity* (LaSalle, IL: Open Court, 1923).

Cassirer, E. (1912) 'Hermann Cohen und die Erneuerung der Kantischen Philosophie', *Kant-Studien* 17, pp. 252–73.

Cassirer, E. (1922) *Das Erkenntnisproblem in der Philosophie und Wissenschaft der neueren Zeit*, vol. 2, 3rd edn (repr. Darmstadt: Wissenschaftliche Buchgesellschaft 1994).

Cassirer, E. (1927) 'Erkenntnistheorie nebst den Grenzfragen der Logik und Denkpsychologie', repr. in E. Cassirer, *Erkenntnis, Begriff, Kultur* (Hamburg: Meiner, 1993) pp. 77–154.

Cassirer, E. (1929) 'Formen und Formwandlungen des philosophischen Wahrheitsbegriffs', inaugural lecture at the University of Hamburg on 7 November 1929, repr. in E. Cassirer, *Geist und Leben: Schriften zu den Lebensordnungen von Natur und Kunst, Geschichte und Sprache* (Leipzig: Reclam, 1993) pp. 193–217.

Ceynowa, K. (1993) *Zwischen Pragmatismus und Fiktionalismus: Hans Vaihingers 'Philosophie des Als Ob'* (Würzburg: Königshausen & Neumann).

Coffa, A. (1991) *The Semantic Tradition from Kant to Carnap: To the Vienna Station* (Cambridge: Cambridge University Press).

Cohen, H. (1871) *Kants Theorie der Erfahrung* (Berlin: Dümmler).

Cohen, H. (1885) *Kants Theorie der Erfahrung*, 2nd edn (Berlin: Dümmler).

Coleman, D. C. (1977) *The Economy of England, 1450–1750* (Oxford: Oxford University Press).

Comte, A. (1822) *Plan des travaux scientifiques nécessaires pour réorganiser la société*, trans. ed. W. Ostwald as *Entwurf der wissenschaftlichen Arbeiten, welche für eine Reorganisation der Gesellschaft erforderlich sind* (Leipzig: Unesma, 1914).

Creath, R. (1996) 'The Unity of Science: Carnap, Neurath, and Beyond', in Galison and Stump (1996).

Dahms, H.-J. (1994) *Positivismusstreit: Die Auseinandersetzungen der Frankfurter Schule mit dem logischen Positivismus, dem amerikanischen Pragmatismus und dem kritischen Realismus* (Frankfurt am Main: Suhrkamp).

Dahms, H.-J. (2004) '*Neue Sachlichkeit* in the Architecture and Philosophy of the 1920s', in Awodey and Klein (2004), pp. 353–72.

Danto, A. (1995) 'The Decline and Fall of the Analytical Philosophy of History', in F. A. Ankersmit and H. Kellner, eds., *A New Philosophy of History* (Chicago: University of Chicago Press), pp. 71–85.

Dedekind, R. (1887) *Was sind und was sollen die Zahlen?* (Braunschweig: Vieweg).

Deltete, R. (1999) 'Helm and Boltzmann: Energetics at the Lübeck Naturforscherversammlung', *Synthese* 119, pp. 45–68.

Denker, A., ed. (2002) M. Heidegger and H. Rickert, *Briefe 1912–1933 and andere Dokumente* (Frankfurt am Main: Klostermann).

Dingler, H. (1919) *Die Grundlagen der Physik: Synthetische Prinzipien der mathematischen Naturphilosophie* (Berlin and Leipzig: Vereinigung wissenschaftlicher Verleger).

DiSalle, R. (1992) 'Helmholtz's Empiricist Philosophy of Mathematics: Between Laws of Perception and Laws of Nature', in D. Cahan, ed., *Hermann von Helmholtz and the Foundations of Nineteenth-Century Science* (Berkeley and Los Angeles: University of California Press), pp. 461–97.

DiSalle, R. (2006) *Understanding Space-Time: The Philosophical Development of Physics from Newton to Einstein* (Cambridge: Cambridge University Press).

Dörpfeld, F. W. (1963) *Ausgewählte pädagogische Schriften*, ed. Albert Reble (Paderborn: Schöningh).

Dray, W. (2000) 'Explanation in History', in J. H. Fetzer, ed., *Science, Explanation, and Rationality: The Philosophy of C. G. Hempel* (Oxford: Oxford University Press), pp. 217–42.

Driesch, H. (1913) *Die Logik als Aufgabe* (Tübingen: Mohr-Siebeck).

Dubois-Reymond, E. (1872) 'Über die Grenzen des Naturerkennens', repr. in *Reden von Emil Dubois-Reymond*, 2nd edn (Leipzig: Veit, 1912), vol. 1, pp. 441–72.

Dubois-Reymond, E. (1880) 'Die sieben Welträtsel', repr. in *Reden von Emil Dubois-Reymond*, 2nd edn (Leipzig: Veit, 1912), vol. 2, pp. 65–98.

Dummett, M. (1963) 'Realism', repr. in *Truth and other Enigmas* (London: Duckworth, 1978), pp. 145–65.

Dummett, M. (1973) 'The Significance of Quine's Indeterminacy Thesis', repr. in *Truth and other Enigmas* (London: Duckworth, 1978), pp. 375–416.

Dummett, M. (1981) *Frege: Philosophy of Language*, 2nd edn (London: Duckworth).

Dummett, M. (1991) *Frege: Philosophy of Mathematics* (London: Duckworth).

Dummett, M. (1993) 'Realism and Anti-Realism', in *The Seas of Language* (Oxford: Oxford University Press), pp. 462–78.

Dupré, J. (1993) *The Disorder of Things: Metaphysical Foundations of the Disunity of Science* (Cambridge, MA: Harvard University Press).

Earman, J. (1992) 'Carnap, Kuhn, and the Philosophy of Scientific Methodology', in P. Horwich, ed., *World Changes: Thomas Kuhn and the Nature of Science* (Cambridge, MA: MIT Press), pp. 9–36.

Ebbs, G. (1997) *Rule-Following and Realism* (Cambridge, MA: Harvard University Press).

Einstein, A. (1916) 'Die Grundlage der allgemeinen Relativitätstheorie', *Annalen der Physik* 49, pp. 769–822.

Einstein, A. (1921) *Geometrie und Erfahrung* (Berlin: Springer).

Eisler, R. (1910) *Geschichte des Monismus* (Leipzig: Kröner).

Elias, N. (1939) *Über den Prozess der Zivilisation: Soziogenetische und phylogenetische Untersuchungen* (repr. Frankfurt am Main: Suhrkamp, 1997).

Elias, N. (1989) *Studien über die Deutschen: Machtkämpfe und Habitusentwicklung im 19. und 20. Jahrhundert* (Frankfurt am Main: Suhrkamp).

Erdmann, B. (1921) *Die Philosophischen Grundlagen von Helmholtz' Wahrnehmungstheorie* (Berlin: Verlag Akademie der Wissenschaften).

Ewald, O. (1912) 'Die deutsche Philosophie im Jahre 1911', *Kant-Studien* 17, pp. 382–420.

Feigl, H. (1929) *Theorie und Erfahrung in der Physik* (Karlsruhe: Braun).

Feigl, H. (1943) 'Logical Empiricism', in D. D. Runes, ed., *Twentieth-Century Philosophy* (New York: Philosophical Library), repr. in H. Feigl and W. Sellars, eds., *Readings in Philosophical Analysis* (New York: Appleton-Century-Crofts, 1949), pp. 3–26.

Feigl, H. (1963) 'Physicalism, Unity of Science, and the Foundations of Psychology', in Schilpp (1963), pp. 227–68.

Feynman, R. (1985) *QED: The Strange Theory of Light and Matter* (Princeton: Princeton University Press).

Flitner, A. and J. Wittig, eds. (2000) *Optik – Technik – Soziale Kultur: Siegfried Czapski, Weggefährte und Nachfolger Ernst Abbes* (Rudolstadt: Hain).

Flitner, W. (1986) *Erinnerungen, 1889–1945* (Paderborn: Schoeningh).

Frank, P. (1907) 'Kausalgesetz und Erfahrung', *Annalen der Naturphilosophie* 6, pp. 443–50.

Frank, P. (1949) *Modern Science and Its Philosophy* (Cambridge, MA: Harvard University Press).

Franklin, A. (1986) *The Neglect of Experiment* (Cambridge: Cambridge University Press).

Franklin, A. (2002) *Selectivity and Discord: Two Problems of Experiment* (Pittsburgh: University of Pittsburgh Press).

Frawley, W. (1997) *Vygotsky and Cognitive Science: Language and the Unification of the Social and Computational Mind* (Cambridge, MA: Harvard University Press).

Frege, G. (1879) *Begriffsschrift; Eine der arithmetischen nachgebildete Formelsprache des reinen Denkens* (Halle: Nebert), repr. in G. Frege *Begriffsschrift und andere Aufsätze* (Hildesheim: Olms, 1964).

Frege, G. (1881) 'Booles rechnende Logik und die Begriffsschrift', in G. Frege, *Nachgelassene Schriften*, ed. H. Hermes, F. Kambartel, and F. Kaulbach (Hamburg: Felix Meiner, 1969).

Frege, G. (1882) 'Über die wissenschaftliche Berechtigung einer Begriffsschrift', *Zeitschrift für Philosophie und philosophische Kritik* 81, repr. in G. Frege, *Begriffsschrift und andere Aufsätze* (Hildesheim: Olms, 1964).

Frege, G. (1884) *Die Grundlagen der Arithmetik: Eine logisch-mathematische Untersuchung über den Begriff der Zahl*, repr. 1986 (Hamburg: Meiner), pp. 9–52.

Frege, G. (1918) 'Der Gedanke', repr. in G. Frege, *Logische Untersuchungen*, ed. G. Patzig (Göttingen: Vandenhoek und Ruprecht, 1966), pp. 30–53.

Frege, G. (1924/5) 'Erkenntnisquellen der Mathematik und der mathematischen Naturwissenschaften', in G. Frege, *Nachgelassene Schriften*, ed. H. Hermes, F. Kambartel, and F. Kaulbach (Hamburg: Felix Meiner, 1969), pp. 286–94.

Friedman, M. (1992) *Kant and the Exact Sciences* (Cambridge, MA: Harvard University Press).

Friedman, M. (1996) 'Exorcising the Philosophical Tradition: Comments on John McDowell's *Mind and World*', *Philosophical Review* 105, pp. 427–67.

Friedman, M. (1997) 'Helmholtz's *Zeichentheorie* and Schlick's *Allgemeine Erkenntnislehre*: Early Logical Empiricism and its Nineteenth-Century Background', *Philosophical Topics* 25, pp. 19–50.

Friedman, M. (1999) *Reconsidering Logical Positivism* (Cambridge: Cambridge University Press).

Friedman, M. (2000) *A Parting of the Ways: Carnap, Cassirer, Heidegger* (LaSalle, IL: Open Court).

Friedman, M. (2001) *Dynamics of Reason: The 1999 Kant Lectures at Stanford University* (Palo Alto, CA: CSLI Publications).

Friedman, M. (2002) 'Geometry as a Branch of Physics: Background and Context for Einstein's "Geometry and Experience"', in D. Malament, ed., *Reading*

Natural Philosophy: Essays in the History and Philosophy of Science and Mathematics (LaSalle, IL: Open Court), pp. 193–229.

Friedman, M. (2003) 'Kuhn and Logical Empiricism', in T. Nickels, ed., *Thomas Kuhn* (Cambridge: Cambridge University Press), pp. 19–44.

Friedman, M. (2006) 'Kant – *Naturphilosophie* – Electromagnetism', in M. Friedman and A. Nordman, eds., *The Kantian Legacy in Nineteenth-Century Science* (Cambridge, MA: MIT Press), pp. 51–79.

Friedman, M. (2007) 'The *Aufbau* and the Rejection of Metaphysics', in R. Creath and M. Friedman, eds. *The Cambridge Companion to Carnap* (Cambridge: Cambridge University Press).

Friedman, M. (forthcoming) 'Carnap and Quine: Twentieth-Century Echoes of Kant and Hume', Howard Stein Lecture at the University of Chicago (2006). To be published in *Philosophical Topics*.

Gabriel, G. (2001) 'Existenz- und Zahlaussage: Herbart und Frege', in A. Hoeschen and L. Schneider, eds., *Herbarts Kultursystem: Perspektiven der Transdisziplinarität im 19. Jahrhundert* (Würzburg: Königshausen & Neumann), pp. 149–62, trans. Erich Reck as 'Existential and Number Statements: Herbart and Frege', in M. Beaney and E. Reck, eds., *Gottlob Frege: Critical Assessment of Leading Philosophers*, vol. 1 (London: Routledge, 2005), pp. 109–23.

Gabriel, G. (2004) 'Introduction: Carnap Brought Home', in Awodey and Klein (2004), pp. 1–21.

Galilei, G. (1644) *The Assayer*, in S. Drake, ed., *Discoveries and Opinions of Galileo* (New York: Doubleday, 1957).

Galison, P. (1996) 'Constructing Modernism: The Cultural Location of *Aufbau*', in R. N. Giere and A. W. Richardson, eds., *Origins of Logical Empiricism* (Minneapolis: University of Minnesota Press), pp. 17–44.

Galison, P. and D. J. Stump, eds. (1996) *The Disunity of Science: Boundaries, Contexts, and Power* (Stanford, CA: Stanford University Press).

Gay, P. (1968) *Weimar Culture: The Outsider as Insider* (London: Penguin).

Geach, P. (1983) 'Wittgenstein's Operator *N*', *Analysis* 41, pp. 573–89.

Giere, R. N. (1999) *Science Without Laws* (Chicago: University of Chicago Press).

Giere, R. N. and A. W. Richardson, eds. (1996) *The Origins of Logical Empiricism* (Minneapolis: University of Minnesota Press).

Gillispie, C. G. (2004) *Science and Polity in France: The Revolutionary and Napoleonic Years* (Princeton: Princeton University Press).

Gödel, K. (1930) 'Vortrag über die Vollständigkeit des Funktionenkalküls', in K. Gödel, *Collected Works*, vol. 3 (Oxford: Oxford University Press, 1995), pp. 16–23.

Gödel, K. (1953/9) 'Is Mathematics Syntax of Language?' in K. Gödel, *Collected Works*, vol. 3 (Oxford: Oxford University Press, 1995), pp. 334–63.

Gödel, K. (2003) *Collected Works, vol. 4: Correspondence A-G* (Oxford: Oxford University Press).

Goessler, P. (1951) *Wilhelm Dörpfeld: Ein Leben im Dienst der Antike* (Stuttgart: Kohlhammer).

Goldfarb, W. (1979) 'Logic in the Twenties: The Nature of the Quantifier', *Journal of Symbolic Logic* 44, pp. 351–68.

Goldfarb, W. (1988) 'Poincaré against the Logicists', in W. Aspray and P. Kitcher, eds., *History and Philosophy of Modern Mathematics* (Minneapolis: University of Minnesota Press), pp. 61–81.

Goldfarb, W. (1996) 'The Philosophy of Mathematics in Early Positivism', in R. N. Giere and A. W. Richarson, eds., *Origins of Logical Empiricism* (Minneapolis: University of Minnesota Press), pp. 213–30.

Goldfarb, W. (1997) 'Semantics in Carnap: A Rejoinder to Alberto Coffa', *Philosophical Topics* 25, pp. 51–66.

Goldfarb, W. (2003) 'Introduction' to Gödel's Correspondence with Carnap, in Gödel (2003).

Goldfarb, W. (2005) 'On Gödel's Way In', *Bulletin of Symbolic Logic* 11, pp. 185–93.

Gregory, R. L. (1998) *Eye and Brain: The Psychology of Seeing*, 5th edn (Oxford: Oxford University Press).

Habermas, J. (1968a) *Erkenntnis und Interesse* (Frankfurt am Main: Suhrkamp).

Habermas, J. (1968b) *Technik und Wissenschaft als 'Ideologie'* (Frankfurt am Main: Suhrkamp).

Habermas, J. (1981) *Theorie des Kommunikativen Handelns*, 2 vols. (Frankfurt am Main: Suhrkamp).

Habermas, J. (1985) *Der philosophische Diskurs der Moderne: Zwölf Vorlesungen* (Frankfurt am Main: Suhrkamp).

Habermas, J. (1988) *Nachmetaphysisches Denken: Philosophische Aufsätze* (Frankfurt am Main: Suhrkamp).

Habermas, J. (1995) 'Reconciliation through the Public Use of Reason: Remarks on John Rawls's Political Liberalism', *Journal of Philosophy* 92, pp. 109–31.

Habermas, J. (1996) '"Vernünftig" versus "Wahr" oder die Moral der Weltbilder', in J. Habermas *Die Einbeziehung des Anderen: Studien zur politischen Theorie* (Frankfurt am Main: Suhrkamp), pp. 95–127.

Habermas, J. (1999) *Wahrheit und Rechtfertigung: Philosophische Aufsätze* (Frankfurt am Main: Suhrkamp).

Habermas, J. (2000) 'Nach dreißig Jahren: Bemerkungen zu *Erkenntnis und Interesse*', in S. Müller-Dohm, ed., *Das Interesse der Vernunft: Rückblicke auf das Werk von Jürgen Habermas seit 'Erkenntnis und Interesse'* (Frankfurt am Main: Suhrkamp), pp. 12–20.

Haeckel, E. (1899) *Die Welträtsel* (Leipzig: Kröner), trans. J. McCabe as *The Riddle of the Universe at the Close of the Nineteenth Century* (New York: Harper 1902).

Hahn, H. (1929) 'Empirismus, Mathematik, Logik', repr. in H. Hahn, *Empirismus, Logik, Mathematik* (Frankfurt am M: Suhrkamp), pp. 55–8, trans. H. Kaal as 'Empiricism, Mathematics, and Logic', in B. McGuinness, ed., *Empiricism, Logic, and Mathematics: Philosophical Papers* (Dordrecht: Reidel 1980), pp. 39–42.

Hahn, H., R. Carnap, and O. Neurath (1929) *Wissenschaftliche Weltauffassung: Der Wiener Kreis* (Vienna), repr. in O. Neurath, *Wissenschaftliche Weltauffassung, Sozialismus und logischer Empirismus*, ed. R. Hegselmann (Frankfurt:

Suhrkamp), pp. 81–101; trans. P. Foulkes and M. Neurath as 'Wissenschaftliche Weltauffassung: Der Wiener Kreis', in O. Neurath, *Empiricism and Sociology*, ed. M. Neurath and R. S. Cohen (Dordrecht: Reidel 1973), pp. 299–318.

Hahn, H. *et al.* (1931) 'Diskussion zur Grundlegung der Mathematik', *Erkenntnis* 2, pp. 135–49.

Haller, R. (1993) *Neopositivismus: Eine historische Einführung in die Philosophie des Wiener Kreises* (Darmstadt: Wissenschaftliche Buchgesellschaft).

Hands, W. (2001) (*Reflection*) *without Rules: Economic Methodology and Contemporary Science Theory* (Cambridge: Cambridge University Press).

Hanfling, O. (1996) 'Logical Positivism', in S. Shanker, ed., *Philosophy of Science, Logic, and Mathematics in the Twentieth Century*, Routledge History of Philosophy, vol. 9 (London: Routledge), pp. 193–213.

Hatfield, G. (1990) *The Natural and the Normative: Theories of Spatial Perception from Kant to Helmholtz* (Cambridge, MA: MIT Press).

Hayek, F. von (1952) *The Counter-Revolution of Science: Studies on the Abuse of Reason* (Glencoe, IL: Free Press).

Heijenoort, J. van (1967) 'Logic as Calculus and Logic as Language', *Synthese* 17, pp. 324–30.

Heesch, M. (1999) *Johann Friedrich Herbart zur Einführung* (Hamburg: Junius).

Helmholtz, H. v. (1852) 'Über die Natur der menschlichen Sinnesempfindungen', repr. in H. v. Helmholtz *Wissenschaftliche Abhandlungen*, vol. 2 (Leipzig 1883: Barth), pp. 591–609.

Helmholtz, H. v. (1853) 'Über Goethes naturwissenschaftliche Arbeiten', repr. in H. v. Helmholtz, *Vorträge und Reden*, vol. 1 (Braunschweig 1903: Vieweg), pp. 1–24; translated as 'On Goethe's Scientific Researches' in H. v. Helmholtz, *Science and Culture: Popular and Philosophical Essays*, ed. D. Cahan (Chicago: University of Chicago Press 1995), pp. 1–17.

Helmholtz, H. v. (1855) 'Über das Sehen des Menschen', repr. in H. v. Helmholtz *Vorträge und Reden*, vol. 1 (Braunschweig 1884: Vieweg), pp. 365–96.

Helmholtz, H. v. (1862) 'Über das Verhältnis der Naturwissenschaften zur Gesamtheit der Wissenschaften', repr. in H. v. Helmholtz, *Vorträge und Reden*, vol. 1 (Braunschweig 1903: Vieweg), pp. 117–46; translated as 'On the Relation of Natural Science to Science in General', in H. v. Helmholtz, *Science and Culture: Popular and Philosophical Essays*, ed. D. Cahan (Chicago: University of Chicago Press 1995), pp. 76–95.

Helmholtz, H. v. (1870) 'Über den Ursprung und die Bedeutung der geometrischen Axiome', repr. in H. v. Helmholtz, *Vorträge und Reden*, vol. 2 (Braunschweig 1884: Vieweg), pp. 1–31; translated as 'On the Origin and Significance of Geometrical Axioms', in H. v. Helmholtz, *Science and Culture: Popular and Philosophical Essays*, ed. D. Cahan (Chicago: University of Chicago Press 1995), pp. 226–48.

Helmholtz, H. v. (1878a) 'Die Tatsachen in der Wahrnehmung', repr. in H. v. Helmholtz, *Vorträge und Reden*, vol. 2 (Braunschweig 1884: Vieweg), pp. 217–51; translated as 'The Facts in Perception', in H. v. Helmholtz, *Science and*

Culture: Popular and Philosophical Essays, ed. D. Cahan (Chicago: University of Chicago Press 1995), pp. 342–80.

Helmholtz, H. v. (1878b) 'Über den Ursprung und Sinn der geometrischen Sätze: Antwort gegen Herrn Professor Land', repr. in H. v. Helmholtz, *Wissenschaftliche Abhandlungen*, vol. 2 (Leipzig 1883: Barth), pp. 640–62, translated as 'The Origin and Meaning of Geometrical Axioms (II)', in *Mind* 4 (1878), pp. 212–24.

Helmholtz, H. v. (1884) 'Vorwort' in H. v. Helmholtz, *Vorträge und Reden*, vol. 1 (Braunschweig 1884: Vieweg).

Helmholtz, H. v. (1887) 'Zählen und Messen', repr. in Helmholtz (1921), pp. 70–97.

Helmholtz, H. v. (1892) 'Goethes Vorahnungen kommender naturwissenschaftlicher Ideen', in *Vorträge und Reden*, vol. 2 (Braunschweig 1903: Vieweg), pp. 337–61; translated as 'Goethe's Presentiments of Coming Scientific Ideas', in H. v. Helmholtz, *Science and Culture: Popular and Philosophical Essays*, ed. D. Cahan (Chicago: University of Chicago Press 1995), pp. 393–412.

Helmholtz, H. v. (1896) *Handbuch der physiologischen Optik*, 2nd edn. (Hamburg: Voss).

Helmholtz, H. v. (1921) *Schriften zur Erkenntnistheorie*, ed. P. Hertz and M. Schlick (Berlin: Springer).

Hempel, C. G. (1963) 'Implications of Carnap's Work for the Philosophy of Science', in Schilpp (1963), pp. 685–710.

Hepp, C. (1987) *Avantgarde: Moderne Kunst, Kulturkritik und Reformbewegungen nach der Jahrhundertwende* (Munich: dtv).

Herbart, J. F. (1813) *Lehrbuch zur Einleitung in die Philosophie* (repr. Hamburg: Meiner, 1993).

Hiebert, E. N. (1971) 'The Energetics Controversy and the New Thermodynamics', in D. H. D. Roller, ed., *Perspectives in the History of Science and Technology* (Norman, OK: University of Oklahoma Press), pp. 67–86.

Hilbert, D. (1917) 'Axiomatisches Denken', repr. in D. Hilbert, *Gesammelte Abhandlungen*, vol. 3 (Berlin: Springer, 1935), pp. 146–56.

Hilbert, D. (1924) 'Die Grundlagen der Physik', *Mathematische Annalen* 92, pp. 1–32, repr. in D. Hilbert, *Gesammelte Abhandlungen*, vol. 3 (Berlin: Springer, 1935), pp. 258–89.

Hilbert, D. and W. Ackermann (1928) *Grundzüge der theoretischen Logik* (Berlin: Springer).

Hintikka, J. (1990) 'Quine as a Member of the Tradition of the Universality of Language', in R. Barrett and R. Gibson, eds., *Perspectives on Quine* (Oxford: Blackwell), pp. 159–75.

Hönigswald, R. (1912) 'Substanzbegriff und Funktionsbegriff: Kritische Betrachtungen zu Ernst Cassirers gleichnamigem Werk', *Deutsche Literaturzeitung* 33, cols. 2821–43 and 2885–902.

Hofstedter, R. (1963) *Anti-Intellectualism in American Life* (New York: Knopf).

Horkheimer, M. and T. W. Adorno (1947) *Dialektik der Aufklärung: Philosophische Fragmente* (Amsterdam: Querido) (repr. Frankfurt am Main: Suhrkamp, 1981).

Hübinger, G. (1996a) 'Der Verlag Eugen Diederichs in Jena: Wissenschaftskritik, Lebensreform und völkische Bewegung', *Geschichte und Gesellschaft* 22, pp. 31–45.

Hübinger, G., ed. (1996b) *Versammlungsort moderner Geister: Der Eugen Diederichs Verlag – Aufbruch ins Jahrhundert der Extreme* (Munich: Diederichs).

Husserl, E. (1900) *Logische Untersuchungen, vol. 1: Prolegomena zur reinen Logik* (Tübingen: Niemeyer).

Husserl, E. (1911) 'Philosophie als strenge Wissenschaft', *Logos* 1, pp. 289–341.

Husserl, E. (1913) *Ideen zu einer reinen Phänomenologie und phänomenologischen Philosophie* (The Hague: Nijhoff, 1976).

Husserl, E. (1936) *Die Krisis der europäischen Wissenschaften und die transzendentale Phänomenologie,* (The Hague: Nijhoff, 1954).

Hylton, P. (1990) 'Logic in Russell's Logicism', in D. Bell and N. Cooper, *The Analytic Tradition: Meaning, Thought, and Knowledge* (Oxford: Blackwell), pp. 137–72.

Hylton, P. (1998) 'Analysis and Analytic Philosophy', in A. Biletzki and A. Matar, eds., *The Story of Analytic Philosophy* (London: Routledge), pp. 209–28.

James, W. (1907) *Pragmatism: A New Name for Some Old Ways of Thinking,* in W. James *Pragmatism and Other Writings* (Harmondsworth: Penguin, 2000).

Janich, P., ed. (1984) *Methodische Philosophie: Beiträge zum Begründungsproblem der exakten Wissenschaften in Auseinandersetzung mit Hugo Dingler* (Mannheim: Bibliographisches Institut).

Jeffrey, R. (1994) 'Carnap's Voluntarism', in D. Prawitz, B. Skyrms, and D. Westerståhl, eds., *Logic, Methodology, and Philosophy of Science IX* (Amsterdam: Elsevier), pp. 847–66.

Kaila, E. (1926) *Die Prinzipien der Wahrscheinlichkeitslogik* (Turku: Annales Universitatis Fennicae Aboensis).

Kaila, E. (1930) *Der logische Neupositivismus: Eine kritische Studie* (Turku: Annales Universitatis Fennicae Aboensis); trans. A. and P. Kirschenmann as *Logistic Neopositivism. A Critical Study,* in E. Kaila, *Reality and Experience: Four Philosophical Essays,* ed. R. S. Cohen (Dordrecht: Reidel, 1979), pp. 1–58.

Kant, I. (1783) *Prolegomena zu einer jeden künftigen Metaphysik, die als Wissenschaft wird auftreten können,* ed. K. Vorländer, 5th edn (Hamburg: Meiner, 1913), trans. G. Hatfield as *Prolegomena to any Future Metaphysics That Will be Able to Come Forward as a Science,* in I. Kant *Theoretical Philosophy after 1781,* ed. H. Allison and P. Heath (Cambridge: Cambridge University Press, 2002), pp. 29–170.

Kant, I. (1786) *Metaphysische Anfangsgründe der Naturwissenschaft,* in I. Kant *Schriften zur Naturphilosophie* (Frankfurt am Main: Suhrkamp 1977), trans. M. Friedman as *Metaphysical Foundations of Natural Science,* in I. Kant *Theoretical Philosophy after 1781,* ed. H. Allison and P. Heath (Cambridge: Cambridge University Press, 2002), pp. 171–270.

Kant, I. (1787) *Kritik der reinen Vernunft,* ed. J. Timmermann (Hamburg 1998: Meiner); page references to 2nd ('B') edition according to pagination of

Akademie-Ausgabe, trans. P. Guyer and A. W. Wood as *Critique of Pure Reason* (Cambridge: Cambridge University Press, 1998).

Kant, I. (1796) *Von einem neuerdings erhobenen vornehmen Ton in der Philosophie*, ed. W. Weischedel (Suhrkamp 1958/1977: Frankfurt am Main), vol. 6, pp. 377–97; trans. P. Heath as *On a Recently Prominent Tone of Superiority in Philosophy* in I. Kant, *Theoretical Philosophy after 1781*, ed. H. Allison and P. Heath (Cambridge: Cambridge University Press, 2002), pp. 425–46.

Kaufmann, A. (1940) 'Freude und Bereicherung durch Onkel Wilhelm', in *Wilhelm Dörpfeld* (Berlin: Wilhelm-Dörpfeld-Stiftung), pp. 57–65.

Kaufmann, F. (1930) *Das Unendliche in der Mathematik und seine Ausschaltung: Eine Untersuchung über die Grundlagen der Mathematik* (Vienna: Deuticke).

Kertzer, D. I. and T. Fricke (1997) *Anthropological Demography: Toward a New Synthesis* (Chicago: University of Chicago Press).

Kintsch, W. (1998) *Comprehension: A Paradigm for Cognition* (Cambridge: Cambridge University Press).

Kitcher, P. (1989) 'Explanatory Unification and the Causal Structure of the World', in P. Kitcher and W. C. Salmon, eds., *Scientific Explanation* (Minneapolis: University of Minnesota Press), pp. 410–505.

Klein, C. (2004) 'Carnap on Categorical Concepts', in Awodey and Klein (2004), pp. 291–312.

Köhnke, C. K. (1986) *Entstehung und Aufstieg des Neukantianismus: Die deutsche Universitätsphilosophie zwischen Idealismus und Positivismus* (Frankfurt am Main: Suhrkamp); trans. R. J. Hollingdale as *The Rise of Neo-Kantianism: German Academic Philosophy between Idealism and Positivism* (Cambridge: Cambridge University Press, 1991).

Koenigsberger, L. (1895) *Hermann v. Helmholtz's Untersuchungen über die Grundlagen der Mathematik und Mechanik* (Heidelberg: Hörning).

Koenigsberger, L. (1902–3) *Hermann von Helmholtz*, 3 vols. (vol. 1, 1902; vols. 2 and 3, 1903) (Braunschweig: Vieweg).

Kripke, S. (1979) 'A Puzzle about Belief', in A. Margalit, ed., *Meaning and Use* (Dordrecht: Reidel).

Kronecker (1887) 'Über den Zahlbegriff', reworked and expanded in K. Hensel, ed., *Werke*, vol. 3 (Leipzig: Teubner, 1899), pp. 251–74.

Kuhn, T. S. (1962) *The Structure of Scientific Revolutions* (Chicago: University of Chicago Press).

Kuhn, T. S. (1977) 'Objectivity, Value Judgment, and Theory Choice', in T. S. Kuhn, *The Essential Tension* (Chicago: University of Chicago Press), pp. 320–39.

Kuntze, F. (1912) 'Zum Gedächtnis an Henri Poincaré', *Kant-Studien* 17, pp. 337–48.

Lanier, J. (2006) 'Digital Maoism: The Hazards of the New Online Collectivism', *Edge: The Third Culture*, 30 June 2006 (www.edge.org/3rd_culture/lanier06/lanier06_index.html).

Langton, R. (1999) *Kantian Humility: Our Ignorance of Things in Themselves* (Oxford: Oxford University Press).

Laqueur, W. Z. (1962) *Young Germany: A History of the German Youth Movement* (New York: Basic Books).

Leitgeb, H. (2007) 'A New Analysis of Quasi-Analysis', *Journal of Philosophical Logic*: 36, pp. 181–226.

Leitgeb, H. forthcoming 'New Life for Carnap's Aufbau?'

Lenoir, T. (2006) 'Operationalizing Kant: Manifolds, Models, and Mathematics in Helmholtz's Theory of Perception', in M. Friedman and A. Nordmann, eds., *The Kantian Legacy in Nineteenth-Century Science* (Cambridge, MA: MIT Press), pp. 142–210.

Levi, I. (1980) *The Enterprise of Knowledge* (Cambridge, MA: MIT Press).

Longino, H. (1995) 'Gender, Politics, and the Theoretical Virtues', *Synthese* 104, pp. 383–97.

Lowe, E. J. (2000) *An Introduction to the Philosophy of Mind* (Cambridge: Cambridge University Press).

McDowell, J. (1996) *Mind and World*, 2nd edn, with a new introduction (Cambridge, MA: Harvard University Press).

Mach, E. (1905) *Erkenntnis und Irrtum: Skizzen zur Psychologie der Forschung*, repr. 1991 (Darmstadt: Wissenschaftliche Buchgesellschaft).

Mach, E. (1912) *Die Mechanik in ihrer Entwicklung: Historisch-kritisch dargestellt*, 7th edn. (Darmstadt: Wissenschaftliche Buchgesellschaft, 1988).

Maher, P. forthcoming 'Explication Defended', *Studia Logica*.

Malament, D. (2002) 'A No-Go Theorem about Rotation in Relativity Theory', in D. Malament, ed., *Reading Natural Philosophy: Essays in the History and Philosophy of Science and Mathematics in Honor of Howard Stein* (LaSalle, IL: Open Court), pp. 267–93.

Mann, T. (1918) *Betrachtungen eines Unpolitischen* (Berlin: S. Fischer).

McLarty, C. (1997) 'Poincaré: Mathematics & Logic & Intuition', *Philosophia Mathematica* 5, pp. 97–115.

Marr, D. (1982) *Vision: A Computational Investigation into the Human Representation and Processing of Visual Information* (New York: Freeman).

Martin, R. (1959) *Toward a Systematic Pragmatics* (Amsterdam: North-Holland).

Messer, A. (1924) *Die freideutsche Jugendbewegung: Ihr Verlauf von 1913 bis 1922* (Langensalza: Beyer).

Miles, M. (2006) 'Kant's "Copernican Revolution": Toward Rehabilitation of a Concept and Provision of a Framework for the Interpretation of the *Critique of Pure Reason*', *Kant-Studien* 97, pp. 1–32.

Mises, R. von (1928) *Wahrscheinlichkeit, Statistik und Wahrheit* (Vienna: Springer).

Mises, R. von (1939) *Kleines Lehrbuch des Positivismus: Einführung in die empiristische Wissenschaftsauffassung* (Frankfurt am Main: Suhrkamp, 1990).

Monk, R. (1990) *Wittgenstein: The Duty of Genius* (London: Cape).

Mormann, T. (2000) *Rudolf Carnap* (Munich: Beck).

Mormann, T. (2001) 'Carnaps Philosophie als Möglichkeitswissenschaft', *Zeitschrift für philosophische Forschung* 55, pp. 79–100.

Mormann, T. (2006) 'Werte bei Carnap', *Zeitschrift für philosophische Forschung* 60, pp. 169–89.

Morris, C. W. (1938) *Foundation of the Theory of Signs* (Chicago, University of Chicago Press).

Musil, R. (1912) 'Profil eines Programms', in R. Musil, *Prosa und Stücke, Kleine Prosa, Aphorismen, Autobiographisches, Essays und Reden, Kritik* (Hamburg: Rowohlt, 2000), pp. 1315–19.

Musil, R. (1913a) 'Der mathematische Mensch', repr. in R. Musil, *Prosa und Stücke, Kleine Prosa, Aphorismen, Autobiographisches, Essays und Reden, Kritik* (Hamburg: Rowohlt, 2000), pp. 1004–8.

Musil, R. (1913b) 'Analyse und Synthese', repr. in R. Musil, *Prosa und Stücke, Kleine Prosa, Aphorismen, Autobiographisches, Essays und Reden, Kritik* (Hamburg: Rowohlt, 2000), pp. 1008–9.

Musil, R. (1931) *Der Mann ohne Eigenschaften* (Hamburg: Rowohlt, new edn 1978); trans. S. Wilkins as *The Man without Qualities* (New York: Knopf, 1995).

Natorp, P. (1901a) 'Zu den logischen Grundlagen der neueren Mathematik', *Archiv für systematische Philosophie* 7, pp. 177–209 (Parts I and II), 372–84 (Part III).

Natorp, P. (1901b) 'Zur Frage der logischen Methode', *Kant-Studien* 6, pp. 270–83.

Natorp, P. (1904) *Logik: Grundlegung und logischer Aufbau der Mathematik und mathematische Naturwissenschaft* (Marburg: Elwert).

Natorp, P. (1909) 'Über Philosophie und philosophisches Studium', in P. Natorp, *Philosophie und Pädagogik: Untersuchungen auf ihrem Grenzgebiet* (Marburg: Elwert), pp. 209–96.

Natorp, P. (1910) *Die logischen Grundlagen der exakten Wissenschaften* (Leipzig: Teubner).

Natorp, P. (1912) *Allgemeine Psychologie nach kritischer Methode* (Tübingen: Mohr-Siebeck).

Natorp, P. (1921) *Platos Ideenlehre: Eine Einführung in den Idealismus*, 2nd edn (Hamburg: Meiner).

Neiman, S. (1994) *The Unity of Reason: Rereading Kant* (Oxford: Oxford University Press).

Nelson, K. (1996) *Language in Cognitive Development* (Cambridge: Cambridge University Press).

Nelson, L. (1906) 'Vorwort', *Abhandlungen der Fries'schen Schule*, Neue Folge 1, pp. III–XII.

Netz, R. (1999) *The Shaping of Deduction in Greek Mathematics: A Study in Cognitive History* (Cambridge: Cambridge University Press).

Neurath, O. (1928) 'Rezension: R. Carnap, *Der logische Aufbau der Welt* und *Scheinprobleme in der Philosophie*', *Der Kampf* 21, pp. 624–6.

Neurath, O. (1932) 'Protokollsätze', *Erkenntnis* 3, pp. 204–14.

Neurath, O. (1934) 'Radikaler Physikalismus und "wirkliche Welt"', *Erkenntnis* 4, pp. 346–62.

Newcombe, N. S. and J. Huttenlocher (2000) *Making Space: The Development of Spatial Representation and Reasoning* (Cambridge, MA: MIT Press).

Newton, I. (1687) *Principia Mathematica Philosophiae Naturalis*, trans. A. Motte (repr. Amherst, NY: Prometheus, 1995).

Newton, I. (1717) *Opticks, or a Treatise of the Reflections, Refractions, Inflections and Colours of Light* (repr. New York: Dover, 1952).

Noll, R. (1994) *The Jung Cult: Origins of a Charismatic Movement* (Princeton: Princeton University Press).

Norton, J. (2003) 'Causation as Folk Science', *Philosopher's Imprint*, 3, no. 4.

Norton, J. (forthcoming) 'Do the Causal Principles of Modern Physics Contradict Causal Anti-Fundamentalism?', in P. K. Machamer and G. Wolters, eds., *Causality: Historical and Contemporary* (Pittsburgh: University of Pittsburgh Press).

O'Neill, J. and T. Uebel (2004) 'Horkheimer and Neurath: Restarting a Disrupted Debate', *European Journal of Philosophy* 12, pp. 75–105.

Ostwald, W. (1895) *Die Überwindung des wissenschaftlichen Materialismus* (Leipzig: Veit).

Ostwald, W. (1905) 'Zur Theorie der Wissenschaft', *Annalen der Naturphilosophie* 4, 1–27.

Ostwald, W. (1908) *Grundriß der Naturphilosophie* (Leipzig: Reclam).

Ostwald, W. (1914a) *Auguste Comte: Der Mann und sein Werk* (Leipzig: Unesma).

Ostwald, W. (1914b) 'Vorrede', to *Comte* (1822), pp. VII–XI.

Ostwald, W. (1914c) *Moderne Naturphilosophie: I. Die Ordnungswissenschaften* (Leipzig: Akademische Verlagsgesellschaft).

Paetzold, H. (1995) *Ernst Cassirer – Von Marburg nach New York: Eine philosophische Biographie* (Darmstadt: Wissenschaftliche Buchgesellschaft).

Parrini, P., W. C. Salmon and M. H. Salmon, eds. (2003) *Logical Empiricism: Historical and Contemporary Perspectives* (Pittsburgh: University of Pittsburgh Press).

Pincock, C. (2002) 'Russell's Influence on Carnap's *Aufbau*', *Synthese* 131, pp. 1–37.

Plato, J. von (1994) *Creating Modern Probability: Its Mathematics, Physics and Philosophy in Historical Perspective* (Cambridge: Cambridge University Press).

Planck, M. (1896) 'Gegen die Neuere Energetik', *Annalen der Physik und Chemie* 57, pp. 72–8.

Poincaré, H. (1902) *La Science et l'Hypothèse* (repr. Paris: Flammarion, 1968).

Poincaré, H. (1904) *Wissenschaft und Hypothese* [German translation of Poincaré (1902)], trans. with commentary F. and L. Lindemann (Leipzig: Teubner).

Poincaré, H. (1913) *The Value of Science*, trans. G. B. Halstead (New York: Dover).

Poincaré, H. (1914) *Science and Method*, trans. F. Maitland, with a preface by B. Russell (repr. Bristol: Thoemmes, 1996).

Popper, K. R. (1935) *Logik der Forschung* (Vienna: Springer); trans. K. R. Popper as *The Logic of Scientific Discovery* (London: Hutchinson, 1959).

Popper, K. R. (1963) 'The Demarcation between Science and Metaphysics', in Schilpp (1963), pp. 183–226.

Proops, I. (2001a) 'The New Wittgenstein: A Critique', *European Journal of Philosophy* 9, pp. 375–404.

Proops, I. (2001b) 'Logical Syntax in the *Tractatus*', in R. Gaskin, ed., *Grammar in Early Twentieth-Century Philosophy* (London: Routledge), pp. 163–81.

Putnam, H. (1981) *Reason, Truth, and History* (Cambridge: Cambridge University Press).

Quine, W. V. O. (1936) 'Truth by Convention', repr. in *The Ways of Paradox and other Essays*, rev. and enl. edn (Cambridge, MA: Harvard University Press), pp. 77–106.

Quine, W. V. O. (1951) 'Two Dogmas of Empiricism', repr. in W. V. O. Quine, *From a Logical Point of View* (New York: Harper, 1953), pp. 20–46.

Quine, W. V. O. (1960) *Word and Object* (Cambridge, MA: MIT Press).

Quine, W. V. O. (1963) 'Carnap and Logical Truth', repr. in Quine (1976), pp. 107–32.

Quine, W. V. O. (1969) *Ontological Relativity and Other Essays* (New York: Columbia University Press).

Quine, W. V. O. (1970) *Philosophy of Logic* (Englewood Cliffs, NJ: Prentice-Hall).

Quine, W. V. O. (1974) *The Roots of Reference* (LaSalle, IL: Open Court).

Quine, W. V.O (1976) *The Ways of Paradox and Other Essays*, 2nd edn (Cambridge, MA: Harvard University Press).

Quine, W. V. O. (1978) 'On the Nature of Moral Values', repr. in *Theories and Things* (Cambridge, MA : Harvard University Press, 1981), pp. 55–66.

Quine, W. V. O. (1984) 'Carnap's Positivistic Travail', *Fundamenta Scientiae* 5, pp. 325–33.

Quine, W. V. O. (1987) *Quiddities: An Intermittently Philosophical Dictionary* (Cambridge, MA: Harvard University Press).

Quine, W. V. O. (1990) 'Comment on Hintikka', in R. Barrett and R. Gibson, eds., *Perspectives on Quine* (Oxford: Blackwell), p. 176.

Ram, A. and K. Moorman (1999) *Understanding Language Understanding: Computational Models of Reading* (Cambridge, MA: MIT Press).

Rawls, J. (1995) 'Political Liberalism: Reply to Habermas', *Journal of Philosophy* 92, pp. 132–80.

Rawls, J. (1996) *Political Liberalism*, 2nd edn (New York: Columbia University Press).

Reck, E. (1997) 'Frege's Influence on Wittgenstein: Reversing Metaphysics via the Context Principle', in W. W. Tait, ed., *Early Analytic Philosophy: Frege, Russell, Wittgenstein: Essays in Honor of Leonard Linsky* (LaSalle, IL: Open Court), pp. 123–86.

Reck, E. and S. Awodey (2005) *Frege's Lectures on Logic: Carnap's Jena Notes 1910–1914* (LaSalle, IL: Open Court).

Reichenbach, H. (1913) 'Die Militarisierung der deutschen Jugend', *Die freie Schulgemeinde* 3, pp. 97–110.

Reichenbach, H. (1916) *Der Begriff der Wahrscheinlichkeit für die mathematische Darstellung der Wirklichkeit* (Leipzig: Ambrosius Barth).

Reichenbach, H. (1920) *Relativitätstheorie und Erkenntnis Apriori* (Berlin: Springer).

Reichenbach, H. (1925) *Axiomatik der relativistischen Raum-Zeit-Lehre* (Braunschweig: Vieweg).

Reichenbach, H. (1928) *Philosophie der Raum-Zeit-Lehre* (Berlin: de Gruyter).

Reichenbach, H. (1929) 'Ziele und Wege der physikalischen Erkenntnis', in *Handbuch der Physik, vol. 4: Allgemeine Grundlagen der Physik* (Berlin: Springer), pp. 1–80.

Reichenbach, H. (1930) 'Kausalität und Wahrscheinlichkeit', *Erkenntnis* 1, pp. 158–88.

Reichenbach, H. (1938) *Experience and Prediction: An Analysis of the Foundations and the Structure of Knowledge* (Chicago: University of Chicago Press).

Reichenbach, H. (1951) *The Rise of Scientific Philosophy* (Berkeley and Los Angeles: University of California Press).

Reisch, G. (1991) 'Did Kuhn Kill Logical Empiricism?', *Philosophy of Science* 58, pp. 264–77.

Reisch, G. (2005) *How the Cold War Transformed Philosophy of Science: To the Icy Slopes of Logic* (Cambridge: Cambridge University Press).

Richardson, A. W. (1998) *Carnap's Construction of the World: The Aufbau and the Emergence of Logical Empiricism* (Cambridge: Cambridge University Press).

Richardson, A. W. (2007) 'Carnapian Pragmatism', in R. Creath and M. Friedman, eds., *The Cambridge Companion to Carnap* (Cambridge: Cambridge University Press).

Rickert, H. (1921) *System der Philosophie* (Tübingen: Mohr).

Ricketts, T. (1994) 'Carnap's Principle of Tolerance, Empiricism, and Conventionalism', in P. Clark and B. Hale, eds., *Reading Putnam* (Oxford: Blackwell), pp. 176–200.

Ricketts, T. (1996) 'Pictures, Logic, and the Limits of Sense in Wittgenstein's *Tractatus*', in H. Sluga and D. Stern, eds., *The Cambridge Companion to Wittgenstein* (Cambridge: Cambridge University Press), pp. 59–99.

Ricketts, T. (2004a) 'Languages and Calculi', in G. L. Hardcastle and A. W. Richardson, eds., *Logical Empiricism in North America*, Minnesota Studies in the Philosophy of Science, vol. 18 (Minneapolis: University of Minnesota Press), pp. 257–80.

Ricketts, T. (2004b) 'Frege, Carnap, and Quine: Continuities and Discontinuities', in Awodey and Klein (2004), pp. 181–202.

Riehl, A. (1904) 'Helmholtz in seinem Verhältnis zu Kant', *Kant-Studien* 9, pp. 261–85.

Rohden, G. von (1940) 'Wilhelm Dörpfeld', in *Wilhelm Dörpfeld* (Berlin: Wilhelm-Dörpfeld-Stiftung), pp. 27–30.

Rorty, R. (1967) 'Introduction', in R. Rorty, ed., *The Linguistic Turn: Recent Essays in Philosophical Method* (Chicago: University of Chicago Press).

Rorty, R. (1998) 'Against Unity', *Wilson Quarterly*, pp. 28–38.

Russell, B. (1897) *An Essay on the Foundations of Geometry* (Cambridge: Cambridge University Press) (repr. London: Routledge, 1996).

Russell, B. (1903) *The Principles of Mathematics* (Cambridge: Cambridge University Press).

Russell, B. (1912) *The Problems of Philosophy* (Oxford: Oxford University Press).

Russell, B. (1914a) *Our Knowledge of the External World as a Field for Scientific Method in Philosophy* (LaSalle, IL: Open Court).

Russell, B. (1914b) 'The Relation of Sense-Data to Physics', *Scientia*, repr. in *Mysticism and Logic* (London: Longmans, 1918), pp. 145–79.

Russell, B. (1919) *Introduction to Mathematical Philosophy* (London: Allen and Unwin).

Russell, B. (1922) 'Introduction' to Wittgenstein's *Tractatus*, repr. in L. Wittgenstein, *Logisch-philosophische Abhandlung*, ed. M. McGuinness and J. Schulte (Frankfurt am Main: Suhrkamp, 1998), pp. 258–86.

Salmon, W. (1994) 'Comment: Carnap on Realism', in W. Salmon and G. Wolters, eds., *Logic, Language, and the Structure of Scientific Theories: Proceedings of the Carnap-Reichenbach Centennial, University of Konstanz, 21–24 May 1991* (Pittsburgh: University of Pittsburgh Press), pp. 279–86.

Sanger, L. (2006) 'The New Politics of Knowledge' *Digital Universe Blog*, 31 July 2006 (www.dufoundation.org/blog/?m=200607).

Schilpp, P., ed. (1963) *The Philosophy of Rudolf Carnap* (LaSalle, IL: Open Court).

Schlick, M. (1911) Review of Natorp (1910), *Vierteljahrsschrift für wissenschaftliche Philosophie und Soziologie* 35, pp. 254–60.

Schlick, M. (1918) *Allgemeine Erkenntnislehre* (Berlin: Springer).

Schlotter, S. (2004) *Die Totalität der Kultur: Philosophisches Denken und politisches Handeln bei Bruno Bauch* (Würzburg: Königshausen & Neumann).

Sengoopta, C. (2000) *Otto Weininger: Sex, Science, and Self in Imperial Vienna* (Chicago: University of Chicago Press).

Sher, G. (1999) 'Is There a Place for Philosophy in Quine's Theory?', *Journal of Philosophy* 96, pp. 491–524.

Smith, G. (2001) 'The Newtonian Style in Book II of the *Principia*', in J. Z. Buchwald and I. B. Cohen, eds., *Isaac Newton's Natural Philosophy* (Cambridge, MA: MIT Press), pp. 249–98.

Smith, G. (2002a) 'From the Phenomenon of the Ellipse to an Inverse-Square Force: Why Not?', in D. Malament, ed., *Reading Natural Philosophy: Essays in the History and Philosophy of Science and Mathematics* (LaSalle, IL: Open Court), pp. 31–70.

Smith, G. (2002b) 'The Methodology of the *Principia*', in I. B. Cohen and G. Smith, eds., *The Cambridge Companion to Newton* (Cambridge: Cambridge University Press), pp. 138–73.

Soames, S. (2003) *Philosophical Analysis in the Twentieth Century, Vol. 1: The Dawn of Analysis* (Princeton: Princeton University Press).

Stadler, F. (1997) *Studien zum Wiener Kreis: Ursprung, Entwicklung und Wirkung des logischen Empirismus im Kontext* (Frankfurt am Main: Suhrkamp), trans. Camilla Nielson *et al.* as *The Vienna Circle: Studies in the Origins, Development, and Influence of Logical Empiricism* (Vienna: Springer, 2001).

Staiger, E. (1949) *Goethe*, vol. 1 (Zurich: Atlantis).

Stein, H. (1958) 'An Examination of Some Aspects of Natural Science' diss. University of Chicago.

Stein, H. (1967) 'Newtonian Space-Time', *The Texas Quarterly* 10, pp. 174–200, repr. in R. Palter, ed., *The Annus Mirabilis of Sir Isaac Newton* (Cambridge, MA: MIT Press, 1970), pp. 258–84.

Stein, H. (1988) '*Logos*, Logic, and *Logistiké*: Some Philosophical Remarks on the Nineteenth-Century Transformation of Mathematics', in W. Asprey and P. Kitcher, eds., *History and Philosophy of Modern Mathematics* (Minneapolis: University of Minnesota Press), pp. 238–59.

Stein, H. (1989) 'Yes, but . . . Some Skeptical Remarks on Realism and Anti-Realism', *Dialectica* 43, pp. 47–65.

Stein, H. (1990) 'On Locke, "the Great Huygenius, and the incomparable Mr. Newton"', in P. Bricker and R. I. G. Hughes, eds., *Philosophical Perspectives on Newtonian Science* (Cambridge, MA.: MIT Press), pp. 17–48.

Stein, H. (1992) 'Was Carnap Entirely Wrong, After All?', *Synthese* 93, pp. 275–95.

Stein, H. (1993) 'On Philosophy and Natural Philosophy in the Seventeenth Century', in P. A. French, T. E. Uehling, and H. K. Wettstein, eds., *Midwest Studies in Philosophy XVIII: Philosophy of Science* (Notre Dame, IN: University of Notre Dame Press), pp. 177–201.

Stein, H. (1994) 'Some Reflections on the Structure of Our Knowledge in Physics', in D. Prawitz, B. Skyrms, and D. Westerståhl, eds., *Logic, Methodology, and Philosophy of Science IX* (Amsterdam: Elsevier), pp. 633–55.

Stein, H. (2002) 'Newton's Metaphysics', in I. B. Cohen and G. E. Smith, eds., *The Cambridge Companion to Newton* (Cambridge: Cambridge University Press), pp. 256–307.

Stein, H. (2004) 'The Enterprise of Understanding and the Enterprise of Knowledge', *Synthese* 140, pp. 135–76.

Stich, S. (1983) *From Folk Psychology to Cognitive Science: The Case against Belief* (Cambridge, MA: MIT Press).

Stich, S. (1996) *Deconstructing the Mind* (Oxford: Oxford University Press).

Sterelny, K. (2003) *Thought in a Hostile World: The Evolution of Human Cognition* (Oxford: Blackwell).

Strong, T. B. and F. A. Sposito (1995) 'Habermas's Significant Other', in S. K. White, ed., *The Cambridge Companion to Habermas* (Cambridge: Cambridge University Press), pp. 263–88.

Surowiecki, J. (2004) *The Wisdom of Crowds: Why the Many are Smarter than the Few and How Collective Wisdom Shapes Business, Economies, Societies, and Nations* (New York: Doubleday).

Tait, W. W. (1986) 'Truth and Proof: The Platonism of Mathematics', *Synthese* 69, pp. 341–70.

Tait, W. W. (1997) 'Frege versus Cantor and Dedekind: On the Concept of Number', in W. W. Tait, ed., *Early Analytic Philosophy: Frege, Russell, Wittgenstein, Essays in Honor of Leonard Linsky* (LaSalle, IL: Open Court), pp. 213–48.

Tait, W. W. (2001) 'Beyond the Axioms: The Question of Objectivity in Mathematics', *Philosophia Mathematica* 9, pp. 21–36.

Tappenden, J. (2006) 'The Riemannian Background to Frege's Philosophy', in J. Gray and J. Ferreirós, eds., *The Architecture of Modern Mathematics: Essays in History and Philosophy* (Oxford: Oxford University Press).

Tenorth, H.-E. (2003) 'Schulmänner, Volkslehrer und Unterrichtsbeamte: Friedrich Adolph Wilhelm Diesterweg, Friedrich Wilhelm Dörpfeld,

Friedrich Dittes', in H.-E. Tenorth, ed., *Klassiker der Pädagogik, vol. 1: Von Erasmus bis Helene Lange* (Munich: Beck), pp. 224–45.

Tomasello, M. (1999) *The Cultural Origins of Human Cognition* (Cambridge, MA: Harvard University Press).

Toretti, R. (1978) 'Hugo Dingler's Philosophy of Geometry', *Dialogos* 32, pp. 85–128.

Tyson, K. (1995) *New Foundations for Scientific Social and Behavioral Research: The Heuristic Paradigm* (Boston: Allyn & Bacon).

Uebel, T. E. (1992a) *Overcoming Logical Positivism from Within: The Emergence of Neurath's Naturalism in the Vienna Circle's Protocol Sentence Debate* (Amsterdam: Rodopi).

Uebel, T. E. (1992b) 'Rational Reconstruction as Elucidation? Carnap in the Early Protocol Sentence Debate', *Synthese* 93, pp. 107–40.

Uebel, T. E. (1998) 'Enlightenment and the Vienna Circle's Scientific World-Conception', in A. O. Rorty, ed., *Philosophers on Education; Historical Perspectives* (London: Routledge), pp. 418–38.

Uebel, T. E. (2001) 'Carnap and Neurath in Exile: Can their Disputes Be Resolved?', *International Studies in the Philosophy of Science* 15, pp. 211–20.

Uebel, T. E. (2004) 'Carnap, the Left Vienna Circle, and Neopositivist Antimetaphysics', in Awodey and Klein (2004), pp. 243–74.

Ulbricht, J. H. and M. Werner, (1999) *Romantik, Revolution and Reform: Der Eugen Diederichs Verlag im Epochenkontext 1900–1949* (Göttingen: Wallstein).

Urmson, J. O. (1956) *Philosophical Analysis: Its Development between the Two World Wars* (Oxford: Oxford University Press).

Vaihinger, H. (1922) *Die Philosophie des Als Ob: System der theoretischen, praktischen und religiösen Fiktionen der Menschheit auf Grund eines idealistischen Positivismus*, 8th edn (Leipzig: Meiner).

Verley, X. (2003) *Carnap, le symbolique et la philosophie* (Paris: L'Harmattan).

de Vries, Jan (1976) *The Economy of Europe in an Age of Crisis* (Cambridge: Cambridge University Press).

Vygotsky, L. S. (1978) *Mind in Society: The Development of Higher Psychological Processes* (Cambridge, MA: Harvard University Press).

Waismann, F. (1930) 'Logische Analyse des Wahrscheinlichkeitsbegriffs', *Erkenntnis* 1, pp. 228–48.

Waismann, F., ed. (1967) *Wittgenstein und der Wiener Kreis* (Oxford: Blackwell).

Wang, H. (1987) *Reflections on Kurt Gödel* (Cambridge, MA: MIT Press).

Werner, M. (1996) 'Die Erfindung einer Tradition: Der Verleger Eugen Diederichs als "kultureller Reichsgründer"', in L. Ehrlich and J. John, eds., *Weimar 1930: Politik und Kultur im Vorfeld der NS-Diktatur* (Weimer: Böhlau 1998), pp. 261–74.

Werner, M. (2003) *Moderne in der Provinz: Kulturelle Experimente im Fin de Siècle Jena* (Göttingen: Wallstein).

Wertsch, J. (1985) *Vygotsky and the Social Formation of Mind* (Cambridge, MA: Harvard University Press).

Weyl, H. (1926) *Philosophie der Mathematik und Naturwissenschaft* (Munich: Oldenbourg).

Wilson, C. H. (1984) *England's Apprenticeship, 1603–1763* (London: Longmans).

Wilson, E. O. (1998) 'Resuming the Enlightenment Quest', *Wilson Quarterly* 22, pp. 16–27.

Windelband, W. (1894) 'Geschichte und Naturwissenschaft', repr. in *Präludien: Aufsätze und Reden zur Philosophie und ihrer Geschichte*, 6th edn (Tübingen: Mohr, 1919, pp. 137–60.

Wittgenstein, L. (1922) *Tractatus Logico-Philosophicus* repr. in L. *Wittgenstein Logisch-philosophische Abhandlung*, ed. B. McGuinness and J. Schulte (Frankfurt am Main: Suhrkamp, 1998), pp. 1–178.

Wittgenstein, L. (1980) *Wittgenstein's Lectures, Cambridge 1930–32*, from the notes of John King and Desmond Lee, ed. J. King (Totowa, NJ: Rowman & Littlefield).

Wolin, R. (2004) *The Seduction of Unreason: The Intellectual Romance with Fascism from Nietzsche to Postmodernism* (Princeton: Princeton University Press).

Wolters, G. (2004) 'Styles in Philosophy: The Case of Carnap', in Awodey and Klein (2004), pp. 25–39.

Zabell, S. L. (2005) *Symmetry and its Discontents: Essays on the History of Inductive Probability* (Cambridge: Cambridge University Press).

Index